How the Chicago School Overshot the Mark

HOW THE CHICAGO SCHOOL OVERSHOT THE MARK

The Effect of Conservative Economic Analysis
on U.S. Antitrust

Edited by Robert Pitofsky

OXFORD
UNIVERSITY PRESS
2008

OXFORD
UNIVERSITY PRESS

Oxford University Press, Inc., publishes works that further
Oxford University's objective of excellence
in research, scholarship, and education.

Oxford   New York
Auckland   Cape Town   Dar es Salaam   Hong Kong   Karachi
Kuala Lumpur   Madrid   Melbourne   Mexico City   Nairobi
New Delhi   Shanghai   Taipei   Toronto

With offices in
Argentina   Austria   Brazil   Chile   Czech Republic   France   Greece
Guatemala   Hungary   Italy   Japan   Poland   Portugal   Singapore
South Korea   Switzerland   Thailand   Turkey   Ukraine   Vietnam

Copyright © 2008 by Robert Pitofsky

Published by Oxford University Press, Inc.
198 Madison Avenue, New York, New York 10016

www.oup.com

Oxford is a registered trademark of Oxford University Press

Library of Congress Cataloging-in-Publication Data
How the Chicago School overshot the mark : the effect of conservative economic
analysis on U.S. antitrust / edited by Robert Pitofsky.
Includes bibliographical references and index.
ISBN 978-0-19-537282-3; 978-0-19-533976-5 (pbk.)
1. Antitrust law—Economic aspects—United States. 2. Antitrust law—United States.
3. Competition—United States. 4. Industrial concentration—United States.
I. Pitofsky, Robert.
KF1649.W48 2008
343.73'0721—dc22   2008002505

9 8 7 6 5 4 3 2 1

Printed in the United States of America
on acid-free paper

Contents

Contributors

Jonathan B. Baker is Professor of Law at American University's Washington College of Law, where he teaches courses primarily in the areas of antitrust and economic regulation. From 1995 to 1998, Professor Baker served as the Director of the Bureau of Economics at the Federal Trade Commission. Previously, he worked as a senior economist at the President's Council of Economic Advisers, special assistant to the Deputy Assistant Attorney General for Economics in the Antitrust Division of the Department of Justice, an assistant professor at Dartmouth's Amos Tuck School of Business Administration, as attorney advisor to the Acting Chairman of the Federal Trade Commission, and as an antitrust lawyer in private practice. Professor Baker is a senior consultant with CRA International. He is the co-author of an antitrust casebook, a past editorial chair of Antitrust Law Journal, and a past member of the Council of the American Bar Association's Section of Antitrust Law. Professor Baker has published widely in the fields of antitrust law and policy and empirical industrial organization economics. In 2004 he received American University's Faculty Award for Outstanding Scholarship, Research, and Other Professional Accomplishments, and in 1998 he received the Federal Trade Commission's Award for Distinguished Service. He has a J.D. from Harvard University and a Ph.D. in economics from Stanford University.

Stephen Calkins is Professor of Law and Director of Graduate Studies at the Wayne State University Law School, where he teaches courses and seminars on antitrust and trade regulation, consumer law, and torts. He has taught at the Universities of Michigan, Pennsylvania, and Utrecht (The Netherlands), and has served as Wayne State's interim dean. During 1995–97, Professor Calkins served as general counsel of the Federal Trade Commission, a position to which he was nominated by FTC Chairman Robert Pitofsky. Professor Calkins lectures widely throughout the United States and abroad (most recently in Europe and Australia), has authored many publications on competition, consumer law, policy, and related subjects (including the co-authored 5th edition of the *Antitrust Law and Economics Nutshell*), and is a journal editor. He is a member of the American Law Institute, a fellow of the American Bar Foundation, and a senior fellow of the American Antitrust Institute. He is currently serving his third three-year term on the Council of the American Bar Association Section of Antitrust Law and is a former member of the Council of the ABA Section of Administrative Law and Regulatory Practice. He is also a former chair of the Association of American Law School's Antitrust and Economic Regulation Committee. He holds degrees from Yale (B.A.) and Harvard (J.D.).

Eleanor M. Fox is the Walter J. Derenberg Professor of Trade Regulation at New York University School of Law, where she teaches antitrust, European Union law, international and comparative competition policy, and torts. Her scholarship is in the area of competition, trade, economic development, and global governance. She was a partner and is of counsel at the New York law firm Simpson Thacher & Bartlett. Professor Fox served as a member of the International Competition Policy Advisory Committee to the Attorney General and the Assistant Attorney General for Antitrust of the United States Department of Justice (1997–2000) (President Clinton) and as a commissioner on President Carter's National Commission for the Review of Antitrust Laws and Procedures (1978–79). She has served as chair of the Section of Antitrust and Economic Regulation of the Association of American Law Schools, chair of the New York State Bar Association's Section on Antitrust Law, vice president of the Association of the Bar of the City of New York, and vice chair of the ABA Antitrust Section. Professor Fox is a frequent visitor and lecturer at the Competition Directorate of the European Commission. She has advised numerous younger antitrust jurisdictions, including South Africa, Indonesia, Russia, and Central and Eastern European nations. Her books include *Antitrust Stories* (co-edited with Daniel Crane, Foundation 2007); *Competition Policy and the Transformation of Central Europe* (with J. Fingleton, D. Neven and P. Singleton 1996), *Cases and Materials on U.S. Antitrust in Global Context* (2d ed. Thomson/West 2004) (with Lawrence Sullivan and Rudolph Peritz), and *European Union Law: Cases and Materials* (2d ed. West 2002) (with G. Bermann, R. Goebel, and W. Davey).

Harvey J. Goldschmid is Dwight Professor of Law at Columbia University, as which he has served since 1984, and was assistant professor (1970–71), associate professor (1971–73), and professor of Law (1973–84) at Columbia. He is also senior counsel at the law firm of Weil, Gotshal & Manges. From 2002 to 2005, Professor Goldschmid served as a commissioner of the United States Securities and Exchange Commission, and in 1998–99 he was the SEC's general counsel (chief legal officer). In 1997–98, Professor Goldschmid was a consultant on antitrust policy to the Federal Trade Commission, and in 1995–96 was a member of the FTC's Task Force on High Tech/Innovation Issues. He now serves as chair of the Board of Directors of the Greenwall Foundation, as a public governor of the Financial Industry Regulatory Authority, as a director of the National Center on Philanthropy and the Law, as a director of Transparency International-USA, and on the governing board of the Center for Audit Quality. He is the author of numerous publications on corporate, securities, and antitrust law, and is a co-author, with Robert Pitofsky and Diane P. Wood, of *Cases and Materials on Trade Regulation* (5th ed. 2003 and 2007 Supplement).

Warren S. Grimes is a law professor at Southwestern Law School in Los Angeles. He is co-author (with Lawrence A. Sullivan) of a well-known antitrust treatise: *The Law of Antitrust, An Integrated Handbook* (2d ed. 2006). Professor Grimes is a graduate of the University of Michigan Law School. He worked for the FTC and served as chief counsel of the House Judiciary Committee's Monopolies Subcommittee before turning to full-time teaching in 1988. He has authored numerous articles on antitrust, including a number that address issues involving distribution restraints. His most recent publications include *Illinois Tool Works, Inc. v. Independent Ink, Inc., Requirements Tie-Ins and Intellectual Property* (with Lawrence A. Sullivan), 13 Sw. J. L. & Trade in Americas 335 (2007); *From Schwinn to Sylvania to Where? Historical Roots of Modern Vertical Restraints Policy,* in *Antitrust As History,* D. Crane & E. Fox, eds. 146–170 (2007); *The Future of Distribution Restraints Law: Will the New Learning Take Hold?* Utah L. Rev. 829 (2006).

Herbert Hovenkamp is the Ben V. & Dorothy Willie Professor of Law and History at the University of Iowa, where his principal areas of teaching and scholarship are federal antitrust law and American legal history. He also teaches property law, torts, and IP/Antitrust. He is the surviving author of *Antitrust Law* (Aspen, 18 vols & Supp., 1980–2007, formerly with the late Phillip E. Areeda and the late Donald F. Turner). His other publications include *The Antitrust Enterprise: Principle and Execution* (Harvard Univ. Press, 2006); *IP and Antitrust: An Analysis of Antitrust Principles Applied to Intellectual Property Law* (with Mark Janis and Mark Lemley, Aspen 2002–2007); of a standard one-volume textbook, *Federal Antitrust Policy: the Law of Competition and its Practice* (West Group, 3d ed. 2005); a casebook, *Antitrust Law, Policy and Procedure* (with E. Thomas Sullivan, Lexis Press, 5th ed. 2003); *Enterprise and American Law, 1836–1937* (Harvard Univ. Press, 1991); and some 80 other books and articles. He has also consulted extensively with the federal government, various state attorneys general, and private firms, and is a member of the American Academy of Arts and Sciences.

Thomas E. Kauper is the Henry M. Butzel Professor of Law at the University of Michigan Law School. He is a graduate of the University of Michigan Law School, where he served as editor in chief of the Michigan Law Review. He served as law clerk to Associate Justice Potter Stewart of the Supreme Court of the United States and then practiced law for two years before joining the Michigan faculty. From 1969 through 1971 he served as Deputy Assistant Attorney General in the Office of Legal Counsel, United States Department of Justice. From 1972 through 1976 he was Assistant Attorney General in Charge of the Antitrust Division at the Department of Justice. He has served as both a member of the Council and officer of the Antitrust Section of the American Bar Association. He speaks and writes regularly on a variety of antitrust topics.

John B. Kirkwood is an associate professor at Seattle University School of Law, co-editor of *Research in Law and Economics*, and a member of the Board of Advisors of the American Antitrust Institute. He has edited two books and published numerous articles, including an article on buyer power that was quoted by the Supreme Court and the Ninth Circuit. He has spoken frequently at national conferences on antitrust law and testified at the hearings on predatory pricing held by the Department of Justice and the Federal Trade Commission. After graduating magna cum laude and with Honors of Exceptional Distinction in Economics from Yale, he received a masters degree in public policy from the Kennedy School and a law degree from Harvard, where he was an editor of the CIVIL RIGHTS-CIVIL LIBERTIES LAW REVIEW. Before joining the faculty at Seattle University, he directed two antitrust policy offices and the premerger notification program at the Federal Trade Commission in Washington, D.C., managed antitrust cases and investigations at the FTC's Seattle office, and taught antitrust at both the University of Washington and Seattle University. He received the Outstanding Faculty Award in 2006 and the Dean's Medal in 2007.

Robert H. Lande is the Venable Professor of Law at the University of Baltimore School of Law, and a co-founder and director of the American Antitrust Institute. Before becoming an academic he worked at Jones, Day, Reavis and Pogue and at the Federal Trade Commission. He has authored or co-authored 75 U.S. and 11 foreign legal publications. Seven of his articles have been republished in books or collections of articles. Professor Lande has been quoted in the media hundreds of times about antitrust issues and has appeared on television in the United States, France, the United Kingdom, and China. He has spoken at national events sponsored by many organizations, including the American Bar Association, Association of American Law Schools, National Association of Attorneys General, American Antitrust Institute, American Economic Association and INCECOPI (Peru). He has testified before the U.S. House of Representatives Judiciary Committee, the U.S. Senate Commerce Committee, the Antitrust Modernization Commission, and the federal antitrust enforcement agencies. He has given competition advice to enforcement officials from several foreign nations. He is a past chair of the AALS Antitrust Section and has held many positions in the ABA Antitrust Section. He is an elected member of the American Law Institute and a member of the District of Columbia Bar. He received his J.D. and masters in public policy from Harvard University and his B.A. from Northwestern University.

Marina Lao has been on the faculty of Seton Hall University School of Law since 1994. She received a Fulbright Fellowship to teach U.S. Antitrust Law at the University of Munich's graduate law program in 2007. In addition, she has been a visiting professor at the University of Connecticut School of Law and has lectured on U.S. Corporate Law at the University of International Business and Economics, School of Law, Beijing, China. Professor Lao began her legal career with the U.S. Department of Justice, Antitrust Division, as a trial attorney under the Honors Program in 1980. Before joining the faculty of Seton Hall, she served for two years as a teaching fellow and lecturer in law at Temple University School of Law. Professor Lao has written extensively in the antitrust area and is a frequent speaker at antitrust conferences. She serves on the executive board of the Section on Antitrust Law of the American Association of Law Schools, and is the current chair-elect. She also formerly served on the Antitrust and Trade Regulation Committee, and the Consumer Affairs Committee, of the Association of the Bar of the City of New York.

Robert Pitofsky is Sheehy Professor of Trade Regulation Law at Georgetown University Law Center, and of counsel at Arnold & Porter, Washington, D.C. Professor Pitofsky formerly held positions as Director, Bureau of Consumer Protection, Federal Trade Commission; Commissioner of the Federal Trade Commission; Dean at Georgetown University Law Center; Professor of Law at New York University School of Law, and Visiting Professor of Law, Harvard Law School and Columbia Law School; Chairman of the Federal Trade Commission.

Professor Pitofsky is co-author of *Cases and Materials on Trade Regulation* (with Harvey Goldschmid and Diane Wood, 5th ed. 2003), and author of numerous books and articles on antitrust including *Revitalizing Antitrust in its Second Century* (1991, co-editor); *Antitrust and Intellectual Property, Unresolved Issues at the Heart of the New Economy*, 16 BERKELEY TECH L.J. 535 (2001); *Proposals for Revised U.S. Merger Enforcement in a Global Economy*, 81 GEO. L. REV. 195 (1992); *New Definitions of Relevant Market and the Assault on Antitrust*, 90 Colum. L. Rev. 1805 (1990); *The Political Content of Antitrust*, 127 U. PA. L. REV. 1051 (1979); and *The Sylvania Case: Antitrust Analysis of Non-Price Vertical Restrictions*, 78 COLUM. L. REV. 1 (1978). He has been a member of the Council, Administrative Conference (1980–81); member of the Board of Governors, District of Columbia Bar Association (1981–84); member of the Council, Antitrust Section of the ABA (1986–89); chair, Defense Science Board Task Force on Antitrust Aspects of Defense Industry Downsizing, March 1994; and fellow, American Academy of Arts and Sciences (2000–Present).

Daniel L. Rubinfeld is Robert L. Bridges Professor of Law and Professor of Economics at the University of California, Berkeley. He served from June 1997 through December 1998 as Deputy Assistant Attorney General for Antitrust in the U.S. Department of Justice. Professor Rubinfeld is the author of a variety of articles relating to antitrust and competition policy, law and economics, and public economics, and two textbooks, *Microeconomics* and *Econometric Models and Economic Forecasts*. He has consulted for private parties for a range of public agencies including the Federal Trade Commission, the Antitrust Division of the Department of Justice, and various state attorneys general. In the past he has been a fellow at the National Bureau of Economic Research (NBER), the Center for Advanced Studies in the Behavioral Sciences, and the John Simon Guggenheim Foundation. Professor Rubinfeld teaches courses in law and economics, antitrust, and law and statistics, and is a member of the American Academy of Arts and Sciences and a research fellow at NBER. He is the past president of the American Law and Economics Association.

Steven C. Salop is Professor of Economics and Law at the Georgetown University Law Center, where he has taught since 1981. He is the author of numerous articles on industrial organization economics, antitrust law and policy, and the economic analysis of law. A number of his articles examine a variety of economic and legal issues involving exclusionary conduct and monopolization, involving both section 2 and section 1. These articles take a "post-Chicago" approach to antitrust economics. These articles include *Exclusionary Conduct, Effect on Consumers, and the Flawed Profit-Sacrifice Standard*, 73 Antitrust Law Journal 311 (2006); *Anticompetitive Overbuying by Power Buyers*, 72 ANTITRUST L.J. 669 (2005); *The First Principles Approach to Antitrust, Kodak and Antitrust at the Millennium*, 68 ANTITRUST L.J. 187 (2000); *Equilibrium Vertical Foreclosure*, 80 AM. ECON. REV. 127 (1990) (written with Janusz Ordover and Garth Saloner); *Antitrust Analysis of Exclusionary Rights: Raising Rivals' Costs to Gain Power Over Price*, 96 YALE L.J. 209 (1986) (written with Thomas Krattenmaker); *Raising Rivals' Costs*, 73 AM. ECON. REV. 267 (1983) (written with David Scheffman).

Carl Shapiro is the Transamerica Professor of Business Strategy at the Haas School of Business at the University of California at Berkeley. He also is Director of the Institute of Business and Economic Research, and Professor of Economics in the Economics Department, at UC Berkeley. He earned his Ph.D. in economics at M.I.T. in 1981, taught at Princeton University during the 1980s, and has been at Berkeley since 1990. He has been editor of the Journal of Economic Perspectives and a fellow at the Center for Advanced Study in the Behavioral Sciences, among other honors. Professor Shapiro has published extensively in the areas of industrial organization, competition policy, patents, the economics of innovation, and competitive strategy. His current research interests include antitrust economics, intellectual property and licensing, patent policy, product standards and compatibility, and the economics of networks and interconnection. Professor Shapiro served as Deputy Assistant Attorney General for Economics in the Antitrust Division of the U.S. Department of Justice during 1995–96. He founded the Tilden Group, and is now a senior consultant with CRA International, an economic consulting company. He has consulted extensively for a wide range of private clients as well as for the U.S. Department of Justice and the Federal Trade Commission.

F. M. Scherer is Aetna Professor Emeritus at the John F. Kennedy School of Government, Harvard University. He has also taught at Princeton University, the University of Michigan, Northwestern University, Swarthmore College, Haverford College, the Central European University, and the University of Bayreuth. In 1974–76, he was chief economist at the Federal Trade Commission. His undergraduate degree is from the University of Michigan; he received his M.B.A. and Ph.D. from Harvard University. His research specialties are industrial economics and the economics of technological change, leading inter alia to books *Industrial Market Structure and Economic Performance* (3d ed. with David Ross); *The Economics of Multi-Plant Operation: An International Comparisons Study* (with three co-authors); *International High-Technology Competition*; *Competition Policies for an Integrated World Economy*; *Mergers, Sell-offs, and Economic Efficiency* (with David J. Ravenscraft); *Innovation and Growth: Schumpeterian Perspectives*; *The Weapons Acquisition Process* (two volumes, one with M. J. Peck); *Industry Structure, Strategy, and Public Policy*; *New Perspectives on Economic Growth and Technological Innovation*, and most recently, *Quarter Notes and Bank Notes: The Economics of Music Composition in the 18th and 19th Centuries*. His personal Web page is found at the Kennedy School of Government faculty profiles site.

Richard Schmalensee is the Howard W. Johnson Professor of Economics and Management at the Massachusetts Institute of Technology (MIT). He served as the John C. Head III Dean of the MIT Sloan School of Management from 1998 through 2007 and as deputy dean of MIT Sloan from 1996 through 1998. He was as a member of the President's Council of Economic Advisers from 1989 through 1991. Professor Schmalensee is the author or co-author of 11 books and over 110 articles in professional journals and books, served as co-editor of volumes 1 and 2 of the *Handbook of Industrial Organization*, and serves as editor in chief of COMPETITION POLICY INTERNATIONAL. He has served as a consultant on antitrust matters to the U.S. Federal Trade Commission, the Antitrust Division of the U.S. Department of Justice, and numerous private firms. He is a Director of LECG.

Irwin M. Stelzer is Director of Economic Policy Studies at the Hudson Institute, U.S. columnist for the *Sunday Times* (London), a contributing editor at *The Weekly Standard*, and a visiting fellow at Nuffield College (Oxford). He received his Ph.D. in economics from Cornell University, and his B.A. and M.A. degrees from New York University. He founded and was president of National Economic Research Associates and has been a scholar at the American Enterprise Institute and director of the Energy and Environmental Policy Studies at Harvard University's John F. Kennedy School of Government. His articles have appeared in *The Weekly Standard*, *Commentary*, and learned journals. He is co-author of *The Antitrust Primer* and editor of and contributor to *The Neocon Reader*, published in the United Kingdom and the United States. A collection of his essays has been published by the Institute of Economic Affairs as "Lectures on Regulatory and Competition Policy."

How the Chicago School Overshot the Mark

Introduction: Setting the Stage

Robert Pitofsky

The occasion for this book is a growing concern that antitrust, a system of regulation that for over a century has generally had wide professional and public support, is under attack. The recent trend appears to be toward more limited interpretation of doctrine (especially in the Supreme Court) and less aggressive federal enforcement.

A brief review of the essence of antitrust and the highs and lows of enforcement should help frame the important issues.

For most of our history, a free market and free trade have been central characteristics of the United States economy. These approaches have contributed to the efficient use of resources and the avoidance of predatory behavior by particular firms toward other businesses and consumers. Toward the end of the nineteenth century, however, people began to realize that absolute free market opportunities could be abused by giant corporations, and indirectly by the concentration of economic power, and that some limits on private sector behavior had to be established.

General suspicion of concentrated economic power led to the enactment of the Sherman Act in 1890 and the initiation of antitrust, a set of rules designed to outlaw the worst abuses by players in the private sector of the free market. The principal targets were improper exercise of monopoly power and agreements among rivals to set prices and divide markets. Over time, other forms of behavior that facilitated such abuses—mergers, distribution practices, boycotts—were incorporated into the antitrust system. Eventually basic concepts of a free market, regulated in some aspects by the government, migrated to other sectors of the economy—for example transportation and communication—and eventually to many other countries throughout the world.

Fashions in levels of enforcement have varied, including two time-outs to fight two world wars and a period of serious neglect in the 1920s. But in general, a free market approach protected by antitrust has served the country well—demonstrably better than centralized control that produced unfortunate results in Stalinist Russia, Maoist China, North Korea, and East Germany. In general, the system had wide popular support, even among people who may not have understood its arcane jargon, but knew, almost instinctively, that private interests, unchecked by some government-inspired rules, could serve the interests of corporate officers and shareholders but might abuse consumer welfare.

During the 1920s, most of the 1930s, and during World War II, antitrust often appeared to be a "faded passion."[1] But after World War II things began to change. First, antitrust enforcers, backed by a Congress generally hostile to Big Business, and an unusually liberal and indulgent Supreme Court, introduced the most aggressive enforcement program in the nation's history—before or since. During the 1950s and 1960s, tiny mergers that could not seriously be viewed as challenges to a competitive market were consistently blocked, abbreviated (so-called *per se*) rules were introduced to outlaw behavior that rarely produced anticompetitive or anticonsumer effects, and licensing practices were challenged, which were little more than efforts to engage in aggressive innovation.[2] All of this was accompanied by an almost total disregard for business claims of efficiency.

The excesses of the 1950s and 1960s, almost entirely rejected by liberals and conservatives today, are summarized fairly and thoroughly by Tom Kauper in this volume.

The period of the 1950s and 1960s—often associated with the Warren Court—did not just result in unwise decisions that are almost impossible to defend today; more important, it offered an inviting target for conservative lawyers and scholars, subsidized by generous private sector grants to think tanks and universities, to demonstrate how much damage overenforcement of antitrust could do. Two brilliant academics, Richard Posner and Robert Bork, led a small army of academics in devastating criticism of the output of the Warren Court.

During the same period, a more subtle, and in the long run more influential, trend was developing. Antitrust had been fueled by a general popular mistrust of Big Business and a desire to divide, diffuse, and control economic power for political reasons. But now a band of economists and economically trained lawyers and academics began to challenge that premise. Their approach was to examine business behavior from a purely economic point of view and to exclude from consideration any political or social values—for example, protection of small business for the sake of the social values inherent in smallness—and place their faith in an automatic beneficial free market system. Considerations of noneconomic factors—for example, concern that a wave of mergers among television outlets or book publishers—might have adverse effects on opportunities for free speech were dismissed as vague and therefore irrelevant.

Those concerned about the excesses of the Warren Court and in favor of the ascendance of economics were handed an enormous political boost when President Ronald Reagan announced "government was the problem and not the solution." It is unlikely President Reagan had antitrust in mind, but aggressive antitrust enforcement fell squarely in the crosshairs of that approach, with the result that in the 1980s, antitrust enforcement virtually disappeared. There was a continuation of challenges to cartels and very large mergers during the decade, but virtually all the rest of antitrust—challenges to vertical mergers, boycotts, all distribution practices, price discrimination, and so forth—disappeared. There was, in effect, a return to the period of neglect of the 1920s.

Post-Reagan, there occurred a decade or so—the Clinton years and the first term of President George W. Bush—when there was an effort to find a middle ground between overenforcement of the 1960s and underenforcement of the 1980s, but that came to an end with appointments during President Bush's second term of some agency enforcement officials, lower court judges and, most important, the confirmation of two conservative justices to the Supreme Court, who produced a working majority for the skeptical view that antitrust really did more harm than good.

All of this history brings us to the occasion for this book.

Contributors to this collection of essays are Republicans and Democrats, lawyers and scholars left of center and right of center, one-time enforcers, and private sector representatives. But virtually all share the view that U.S. antitrust enforcement, as a result of conservative economic analysis, is *better* today than it was during the Warren years—more rigorous, more reasonable, more sophisticated in terms of economics. But virtually all also confess to a sense of unease about the direction of antitrust interpretation and enforcement. Specific concerns include current preferences for economic models over facts, the tendency to assume that the free market mechanisms will cure all market imperfections, the belief that only efficiency matters, outright mistakes in matters of doctrine, but most of all, lack of support for rigorous enforcement and willingness of enforcers to approve questionable transactions if there is even a whiff of a defense. Like the indulgent Warren Court of the 1960s, which found the government was right every time, the current Supreme Court majority, often on the basis of what is called "Modern Economic Analysis," finds a way of ensuring that the pro-antitrust position always loses.

Why should we care? Contrary to what some believe, antitrust is not only or primarily a system to ensure that business rivals do not behave unfairly or in a predatory manner toward other businesses. It is rather a "consumer welfare" system of laws. If businesses grow in unfair ways to be too dominant in their sectors of the market, rivals conspire to raise prices or divide markets, use patents and other forms of intellectual property to fence out rivals in unreasonable ways, merge to monopoly or dominant positions, or engage in the scores of other practices that traditionally have been regarded on balance as anticompetitive, and are protected by less than vigorous enforcement, prices will be higher, quality of products lower, and innovation diminished—and consumers will suffer the consequences.

Because extreme interpretations and misinterpretations of conservative economic theory (and constant disregard of facts) have come to dominate antitrust, there is reason to believe that the United States is headed in a profoundly wrong direction. This collection of essays is designed to examine and analyze these issues.

Notes

1. Richard Hofstadter, The Paranoid Style in American Politics 188 (Alfred A. Knopf 1965).
2. The per se rule and the rule of reason are common concepts that arise often in antitrust analysis and therefore in this book. A transaction or type of behavior is illegal per se if experience shows they are almost always anticompetitive and almost never have redeeming virtues. Thus they are declared illegal without an elaborate inquiry into market power, purpose or effect. A leading example is cartel price fixing. Most types of behavior or transactions are examined under a rule of reason. Under that approach, the factfinder examines all the circumstances surrounding a matter including, among many others, market power, barriers to entry, business justifications, and possible less anticompetitive alternatives and strikes a balance as to whether the conduct is pro- or anti-competitive.

1

Conservative Economic Analysis and Its Effects

Introduction

Most of the themes in the opening chapter foreshadow themes in the remainder of the book. It is unanimous that conservative economic analysis—often characterized as "Chicago School Analysis"—demolished some aspects of the antitrust approach of the 1950s and 1960s (Warren Court period) and eventually displaced it with a more rigorous approach. That approach emphasized exclusively economic considerations (to the complete exclusion of other social and political values), uncertainty about whether government regulation (except in the area of hard-core horizontal price-fixing) does more harm than good, and strong reliance on the free market to achieve efficiency, encourage innovation, and serve the ultimate interests of consumers. Authors of papers in this volume agree that in the process of challenging the premises of the Warren Court and earlier scholarship, the Chicago School led the way to a sounder form of regulation of the United States' competitive system.

As virtually all observers note, however, including the most ardent advocates of conservative analysis, there is a growing unease about current antitrust enforcement and the direction it appears to be going: ever more complete reliance on the free market and generous treatment of the private sector.

The various chapters of this book will illustrate why many moderate observers are concerned and will discuss alternative approaches. The opening chapter includes contributions from some of the most eminent people in the antitrust field.

Richard Schmalensee

The first paper, written by Richard Schmalensee, dean of the MIT Business School, is strongly pro-Chicago, describing its victories and even its losses as constructive, because the losses stimulated more rigorous thinking. It revisits the theoretical battles of the 1950s and 1960s and demonstrates how conservative economic analysis called a halt to some questionable initiatives like deconcentration of major industries as a result of "no-fault" monopoly enforcement, preference for small businesses for the sake of their smallness, and disregard of the value of efficiencies in various transactions, even holding efficiencies against the legality of a transaction.[1] We start this book with a paper that is emphatically pro-Chicago because we think it fair to state fully and fairly the view, by a relatively enthusiastic and prominent scholar, that will be challenged in subsequent chapters; but we note that even in Schmalensee's paper, some of the early proposals of the Chicago School are seen as extreme,[2] and while they may have stimulated thought, were wisely not adopted.

Irwin M. Stelzer

Irwin Stelzer characterizes the conservative view as follows: it looks at antitrust as inefficient, contributing unwisely to an excess of government regulation, and unnecessary because market power is transient and only economic analysis (i.e., efficiency) matters.

Stelzer then examines various kinds of anticompetitive behavior, particularly low or "predatory" prices by a dominant firm, from an unusual and perhaps unique point of view. Conservative analysis argues that if there is ease of entry, there is no problem that antitrust needs to address. If the wrongdoer tries to raise prices or curtail output, it will be swamped, so the argument goes, by new entry. Stelzer asks what a venture capitalist would consider before supporting efforts of a smaller challenger to enter a dominant firm's market. If the entrenched dominant incumbent can rely on a variety of coercion and intimidation tactics, as conservatives seem to allow, venture capitalists will often not support the challenger. As a result, the goal of protecting a free market to provide a fair and open opportunity to all comers will not be served. To achieve that goal, the antitrust laws must be vigorously enforced. In Stelzer's view, that is not the state of affairs today.

Thomas E. Kauper

Thomas Kauper, head of antitrust enforcement at the Department of Justice during the Nixon and Ford Administrations, starts his paper where many end—noting a widespread unease, indeed a sense of "something gone wrong"—with today's antitrust enforcement. In particular, he notes a growing sense of too much emphasis on oversimplified and unrealistic economic models and too little emphasis on actual market effects.

In an effort to understand Chicago School influence, Kauper turns the clock back to the 1950s and 1960s and describes the inviting target offered by excessive antitrust enforcement during those decades, citing many Supreme Court decisions ridiculed by almost all today. The Chicago School succeeded in part because of the nature of its opponent. Despite Chicago's undoubted, and generally constructive influence, Kauper notes it has not always achieved its sought-after outcomes. State-engineered exemptions from the federal antitrust laws (the "State Action Doctrine") have grown in a way contrary to a primary reliance on the free market; there is no sign of Chicago influence in the federal legislative arena, and there is a growing concern about Chicago's oversimplified and unrealistic economic models that seem to ignore actual market facts.

F. M. Scherer

F. M. Scherer observes, as do virtually all contributors to this book, that antitrust analysis has moved sharply to the conservative side. He emphasizes the complexity of issues, however. First, he notes that the move toward less enforcement does not reflect just the influence of economists but also of lawyers, enforcement officials, and judges who believe in the precept that government is the problem and not the solution. Second, he observes that conservative approaches avoiding government intervention is not a consistent view of the Chicago School. It has advocated vigorous antitrust enforcement in the area of price-fixing among direct rivals (cartel policy) and occasionally advocated limits on the size of corporations. He notes, however, extreme Chicago views, which in recent years have influenced enforcement, particularly during Republican administrations. Illustrations include declining enforcement efforts with respect to predatory pricing, concentrated (i.e., oligopoly) markets, and mergers. As an example of scholarship that argues that market forces will solve all problems, he cites an article by J. McGee to the effect that with the exception of industries where the state blocks entry "[t]here is the strongest presumption that the existing structure [of industry] is the efficient structure."[3]

In a concluding section, Scherer takes on a specific issue that has been advocated as a result of conservative economic analysis and has achieved substantial support. That view, virtually a consensus in terms of conservative economic analysis, is that government regulation of intellectual property—particularly mandatory licensing of patents as a remedy for wrong-doing—will reduce investments in innovation and, in the long run, injure consumers. That conclusion, Scherer states, is inconsistent with a body of empirical evidence that antitrust enforcement had little adverse impact on investments in innovation.[4]

Daniel L. Rubinfeld

Like Scherer, Daniel Rubinfeld notes the difficulty of defining "conservative economic analysis" and insists that many changes that have occurred in recent decades, both for the better and the worse, are the result of a variety of influences that have had an impact. While he concludes that various schools of economic analysis overall have had a positive impact (including most emphatically conservative economic approaches), he concludes that there are significant areas where the more extreme applications of economic thought "overshot the mark," listing in his final pages examples such as overconcern with "false positives" that lead to underenforcement, the move to generous treatment of all vertical restraints, and the tendency of conservative economics to downplay, in the name of preserving innovation, vigorous enforcement in dynamic high-tech industries.

Thoughts on the Chicago Legacy in U.S. Antitrust

Richard Schmalensee

In preparation for writing this chapter, I reread Robert Bork's *The Antitrust Paradox*,[5] and I thoroughly enjoyed doing so. Not because I agree with everything in it, though there is much with which to agree. And not only because I enjoy Judge Bork's writing, though it is always a pleasure to see a sledgehammer used with such precision. The main reason I enjoyed going through *The Antitrust Paradox* again was nostalgia: I was reminded how much fun it was to teach antitrust policy to economics students in the 1970s. Then-recent decisions and ongoing policy debates provided enough sharp disagreements and economic howlers that it was easy to keep students interested and amused—and even, on good days, outraged. A clearly negative aspect of the conservative economic or, as I prefer, Chicago School, legacy in U.S. antitrust policy is that much of this fun has been taken away.[6]

Nonetheless, I think it is now widely accepted that the Chicago legacy in antitrust has on balance been strongly positive. In this essay I will take a look back at some decisions and issues that were in the antitrust mainstream around 1970 through the lens of *The Antitrust Paradox,* with occasional use of Richard Posner's roughly contemporaneous *Antitrust Law*.[7] My main objective is to review some of the aspects of U.S. antitrust policy that outraged Chicago School lawyers and economists in the early 1970s and some of Chicago's subsequent victories that are now generally accepted as positive changes. I conclude with a few words on some of Chicago's defeats.

This essay is rather more of a hymn of praise than I would have written if I had attempted a finely balanced treatment, but my assignment was to praise Chicago, not to help those who would bury it. I have no doubt that other contributors to this volume will tell other sides of this interesting story well. I consider four broad issues: the objectives of antitrust, policy toward "no-fault" concentration, the treatment of productive efficiency, and the evaluation of nonstandard business conduct.

Economic Welfare

Can anyone who has ever studied antitrust forget Chief Justice Warren's dictum on legislative intent in the 1962 *Brown Shoe* decision?

> But we cannot fail to recognize Congress' desire to promote competition through the protection of viable, small, locally owned businesses. Congress appreciated that occasional higher costs and prices might result from the maintenance of fragmented industries and markets. It resolved these competing considerations in favor of decentralization.[8]

Lawyers and economists of the Chicago School strongly attacked this formulation of the law's objectives, making two main arguments.[9] First, they questioned the Chief Justice's characterization of legislative intent. They argued that it is impossible to find Congressional statements recognizing the existence of tradeoffs between the welfare of small business and that of consumers, let alone instructions that such tradeoffs should be always resolved in favor of small business.

Second, and to me more important, Chicago argued that antitrust could not aspire to the consistency or predictability required of a policy that necessarily functioned primarily by deterrence rather than regulation if it were tasked to pursue two diametrically opposed objectives with no useful guidance as to which was to be more important under what conditions. For instance, the 1966 *Von's Grocery* decision suggests small businesses should be preserved by barring almost all mergers among them,[10] even though such a policy would discourage small business formation by making it harder for entrepreneurs to capture the value they create. If antitrust is to be seriously concerned with the welfare of small businesses, perhaps it should take no notice of mergers between large firms seeking to obtain market power, since the predictable result of such mergers is an increase in price and an easing of competitive pressure faced by smaller rivals.

As of 2007, Chicago has decisively carried the day as regards the objective of antitrust. As Ken Heyer has recently put it,

> Over the past several decades, there has emerged a rough consensus among professional antitrust practitioners…that the "competition" referred to in our antitrust statutes is not to be interpreted simply as

pre-merger rivalry among entities. Rather it is best viewed as a process, the outcome of which is welfare, with welfare—not rivalry—being the object of interest.[11]

There remains a persistent ambiguity as to whether "welfare" refers to the welfare of consumers only or to total welfare: that of consumers plus producers.[12] Classic Chicago texts typically ignore this distinction. While the enforcement agencies seem to have chosen consumer welfare,[13] I believe the economic case for using total welfare is stronger. In any case, while theory shows that the choice can be very important in some situations, my sense is that it is rarely critical in practice.

This victory may be the most important component of the Chicago legacy. This is of course not because economic welfare is the only worthy policy objective, though Chicago School writers sometimes seem to believe this. The stronger argument is that there are plenty of other instruments that can be used at least as efficiently to promote small business, ameliorate income inequality, or pursue other goals that have sometimes been associated with antitrust, while antitrust is particularly well suited to pursue the broad objective of economic welfare or efficiency.

Having only a single objective at least *permits* the consistency and predictability needed to make a deterrence-based policy effective. Moreover, having consumer or total economic welfare as the single objective of antitrust policy gives economic analysis (or, in classical Chicago language, price theory) a significant role in policy debates and the analysis of most particular cases. Before Chicago, economic input into antitrust was based heavily on empirical work, initially industry case studies and then interindustry regressions, in the Chamberlin-Mason-Bain Harvard tradition.[14] As efficiency emerged as an objective, price theory emerged as a more appropriate tool. Because economic analysis is a deductive system, and thus more coherent than a collection of empirical findings, this change enhanced consistency and predictability. Economic theory, informed by relevant evidence, can be used to make informed judgments about the likely effects of particular policies and decisions. And in the broad areas in which precedent does not rule out analysis, competition between economic models necessarily turns on alternative views of the broad public interest, drawing policy away from the service of special interests of various sorts.

I think the thoroughness of the Chicago victory on this fundamental point is at least one important reason why the 1967 *Utah Pie* decision,[15] which was great fun to teach in its day, now seems to have been handed down on another planet. As some may still recall, Utah Pie, a regional producer of frozen fruit pies, cut prices, and its national rivals responded. During the relevant period Utah Pie was the market leader, grew, and was profitable, and the market as a whole expanded. Nonetheless, Utah Pie's *rivals* were found to have injured competition (and thereby violated the Robinson-Patman Act) by responding to its price cuts because at some times they charged lower prices in Utah than in other regional markets. Most observers would now agree with Bork that "[d]efendants were convicted not of injuring competition but, quite simply, of competing."[16] While the Robinson-Patman Act remains on the books,[17] *Utah Pie* has become something of a curious antique.

Deconcentration

In 1959, Carl Kaysen and Donald Turner published an influential book on antitrust policy that proposed "no-fault" deconcentration legislation.[18] The basic idea was that some industries were more concentrated than productive efficiency required and that leading firms in such industries should be broken up to reduce concentration and thereby enhance competition. A similar proposal was made in 1968 by the White House Task Force on Antitrust Policy, chaired by then-dean of the University of Chicago Law School, Phil C. Neal.[19] This proposal was endorsed by 11 of the 13 members of the task force, including the three economist members who hailed from MIT, Vanderbilt, and the State University of New York at Buffalo. Judge Bork was one of the two lonely dissenters. In 1972 and 1973, Senator Philip A. Hart introduced legislation that would have set in motion a broad, economy-wide program of no-fault deconcentration. These bills received serious attention and debate.[20]

All these proposals were made by well-respected individuals, and they were taken quite seriously at the time. The White House Task Force could cite no less a Chicago pillar than George Stigler in support of its analysis.[21] Nonetheless, I think it is fair to say that before the Reagan Administration took office the antitrust mainstream had shifted so significantly that no-fault deconcentration proposals were no longer within it. It is hard to imagine that such proposals will be taken seriously again anytime soon. What happened in the 1970s to cause this change?

I cannot pretend to provide a complete answer in this brief essay, and the causes clearly extend well beyond Chicago. For instance, declining faith in government, itself in part a product of the Vietnam debacle, surely played a major role. The deregulation movement, led to an important extent in the 1970s by now-Justice Stephen Breyer, Senator Ted Kennedy, and Professor Alfred Kahn—hardly a Chicago cabal—favored markets over regulators, a view broadly consistent with Chicago principles.[22] Whatever other causes were at work, during the 1970s, Chicago did contribute directly by significantly weakening two of the intellectual buttresses supporting the deconcentration movement.

The first of these was the belief that there is an economically significant positive, causal relationship between seller concentration and collusive, anticompetitive behavior. This belief was based largely on a few pioneering industry-level cross-section statistical studies using profitability as the dependent variable, since economic theory had (and has) few definite predictions regarding the impact of changes in concentration on behavior or performance. During the 1970s, many more studies of this general sort were performed and critiqued, however, and the empirical support for a strong concentration-profitability relationship diminished.[23] While most studies found a positive correlation, it tended to be relatively weak, and the implied economic effects of changes in concentration tended to be small.

Moreover, Harold Demsetz, a card-carrying member of the Chicago School in residence at UCLA, argued persuasively in the early 1970s that even if there were a strong *correlation* between concentration and profitability, one could infer nothing about *causation*.[24] He advanced an alternative explanation for the observed correlation. Suppose there is no collusion anywhere, but there are economically significant and persistent efficiency differences among sellers in some industries. Then in those industries both concentration and industry-average profitability will be high, as more efficient firms gain large market shares and earn rents on the sources of their differential efficiency. To the extent that this mechanism operates,[25] concentration that arises by internal growth should be applauded as reflecting innovation, which would surely be discouraged by systematic no-fault deconcentration.

If concentration also facilitates collusion, of course, as I think most economists still believe, one might in principle be able to enhance welfare by careful no-fault deconcentration. But in practice the task of balancing increases in competition against reductions in efficiency in particular industries simply could not be performed with any confidence that welfare would be enhanced. But, a belief that concentration does affect behavior under some conditions rationalizes taking changes in concentration seriously in evaluating proposed horizontal mergers.

The Demsetz critique also implicitly attacked a second buttress that supported the deconcentration movement: the notion that intra-industry differences in cost and productive efficiency mainly reflect differences in scale. The extent of economies of scale, particularly in manufacturing, had been a major research focus in the 1950s and 1960s. This work generally took an engineering-economic approach, focused mainly on production, and sought to identify industry-specific minimum efficient scales, beyond which the long-run average cost curve was generally found to be roughly flat. Other sources of intra-industry differences were not much studied, and observed efficiency differences among firms above minimum efficient scale were generally treated as transitory departures from the industry-specific long-run average cost curve. All the no-fault proposals mentioned above allowed deconcentration to be avoided if it could be shown to result in a substantial loss of efficiency, but the emphasis was clearly on scale-determined efficiency. Indeed, the White House Task Force proposal mentioned only "substantial loss of economies of scale" as a potential defense against deconcentration.

The Demsetz critique, in contrast, assumed that productive efficiency differences unrelated to scale were both important and persistent over time. This assumption rested on a broad definition of productive efficiency, one that went well beyond engineering considerations. As Bork put it:

> The relative efficiency of firms is therefore measured by their success in the market. Attention must be focused on this definition of productive efficiency rather than on the wide variety of factors that contribute to it. Economies of scale, specialization of function, ability to obtain capital, management skill—all of these and many more are elements that contribute to the firm's ability to please consumers, but they are causes rather than manifestations of efficiency. Efficiency is at bottom a value concept, not a description of mechanical or engineering operation.[26]

For the definition in the first sentence to correspond to the normal meaning of "efficiency," it must be assumed that rivalry is at least reasonably vigorous. With that assumption, this statement is an elaboration of George Stigler's "survivor principle."[27]

If the sources of firm-specific productive efficiency are in fact diverse and complex, it is hard to imagine how the impact on efficiency of splitting firms in the name of deconcentration could be reliably assessed. It is thus hard to imagine how a systematic deconcentration program could be carried out without risking substantial losses of productive efficiency. And as time has gone on, it has become clearer as an empirical matter that intra-industry profitability differences not easily attributed to scale are important and persistent in at least some industries.[28] Toyota's design and production systems have been studied extensively and intensively over the years, for instance, but firms that were once much larger than Toyota have been unable even to copy them effectively, let alone surpass them. Much effort is devoted in business schools to studying factors that might create such persistent differences in firm performance. While no doubt there are some who lament the passing of the no-fault deconcentration movement, I believe I join most observers in the view that the Chicago victory on this front (won with much help from a variety of allies) was a good thing for both consumers and total economic welfare.

Productive Efficiency

Once one accepts either consumer welfare or total welfare as *the* objective of antitrust policy, productive efficiency, broadly defined as above and including innovation as well as production, logically becomes at least as important a concern as allocative efficiency in most contexts. Thus, Chicago's persistent focus on welfare as *the* objective of antitrust did much more than blunt the no-fault deconcentration movement. It eventually made productive efficiency count as a virtue rather than a vice in most anti-trust decision-making.

This was not a small thing. If interfirm rivalry were the objective of antitrust, rather than economic welfare, making a leading firm more effi-cient would almost always be a bad thing. It might generally benefit con-sumers and increase total welfare, but it would almost always make less efficient rivals less effective. Perhaps the high-water mark of the "efficiency at the top is bad" view is Learned Hand's classic 1946 *Alcoa* decision.[29] After accepting that Alcoa had committed "no moral derelictions after 1912," Judge Hand nonetheless found it to have monopolized because

> It was not inevitable that it should always anticipate increases in the demand for ingot and be prepared to supply them. Nothing compelled it to keep doubling and redoubling its capacity before others entered the field. It insists that it never excluded competitors; but we can think of no more effective exclusion than progressively to embrace each new opportunity as it opened, and to face every newcomer with new capacity already geared into a great organization, having the advan-tage of experience, trade connections, and the elite of personnel.[30]

Had Alcoa not done these things, had it been slow to add capacity and not built a strong, efficient organization—in short, had it been less efficient—its customers and society as a whole would almost certainly have been worse off, but it might have prevailed in court.

By the early 1970s, *Alcoa* was an old case, and there had been no impor-tant subsequent monopolization cases in which the pursuit of efficiency had been similarly condemned. But the notion that it was undesirable to make a leading firm more efficient and thus a more formidable competitor was clearly alive and well in antitrust. In its 1967 *Procter & Gamble* deci-sion, the Supreme Court blocked P&G's acquisition of Clorox, the leading producer of liquid bleach, a product P&G did not produce, in part because the record showed that the post-acquisition Clorox would be more efficient in production, sales, distribution and, especially, advertising.[31] Justice Douglas, writing for the majority, issued a *Brown Shoe*-like dictum:

> Possible economies cannot be used as a defense to illegality. Congress was aware that some mergers which lessen competition may also result in economies, but it struck the balance in favor of protecting competition.[32]

"Competition" here clearly means active rivalry, not, as it generally means now, consumer or total welfare.

The 1968 Department of Justice *Merger Guidelines* reflected this same lack of concern for productive efficiency:

> Unless there are exceptional circumstances, the Department will not accept as a justification for an acquisition normally subject to challenge under its horizontal merger standards the claim that the

merger will produce economies (i.e., improvements in efficiency) because....[33]

Among the reasons given in what followed was the claim that "there usually are severe difficulties in accurately establishing the existence and magnitude of economies claimed in a merger." The *Merger Guidelines* also echoed the *Procter & Gamble* decision directly by expressing concerns about conglomerate mergers "which may enhance the ability of the merged firm to increase product differentiation in the relevant markets"— presumably markets in which differentiating firms' products was an important form of competition.

In sharp contrast, the current DOJ/FTC *Horizontal Merger Guidelines* commit the agencies to give a positive weight to merger-specific gains in productive efficiency by considering "whether cognizable efficiencies likely would be sufficient to reverse the merger's potential to harm consumers in the relevant market, e.g., by preventing price increases in that market."[34]

It is important to note, however, that the treatment of efficiency in the current *Guidelines* represents in part a Chicago defeat. While Chicago authors such as Bork and Posner generally stressed the positive value of productive efficiency, both argued that the assessment of merger-specific economies that Oliver Williamson (in his classic 1968 article) urged be performed in merger analysis, and that the agencies are now committed to performing, simply could not be done reliably.[35] They argued instead for looser standards as regards concentration, based on a presumption that mergers almost always enhance efficiency. The subsequent research on mergers has not been kind to that presumption, however, and I think most observers are now glad that Chicago's victory on the productive efficiency front was less than total.[36]

Inhospitality

Donald Turner is quoted as having said during the 1960s that "I approach territorial and customer restrictions not hospitably in the common law tradition, but inhospitably in the tradition of antitrust law."[37] This "inhospitality tradition" applied more broadly to non-standard or unfamiliar contracting practices—those that did not appear in textbook descriptions of perfectly competitive markets. By establishing economic welfare as the sole objective of antitrust and thus economic theory as a primary engine of analysis, Chicago has effectively destroyed this tradition in academic circles, though the power of precedent has kept it alive in the courts in some contexts.

In an influential early paper, Aaron Director and Edward Levi argued that a monopolist could not use tying to "leverage" monopoly from one market to another, because the firm had only a single monopoly profit available to it.[38] Chicago scholars went beyond this influential "single monopoly profit theorem" to demonstrate how, in theory at least, various practices traditionally accorded inhospitable treatment *could* enhance efficiency. Some commentators in this tradition took the argument one giant step further and contended that these practices should be *per se* legal because they would *always* enhance efficiency or at least never be anticompetitive.[39]

That last step was unjustified as a matter of logic. Moreover, post-Chicago economic analysis, making liberal use of noncooperative game theory, has shown that it is positively wrong. The "single monopoly profit theorem" rests on rather strong assumptions, and some traditionally suspect practices, such as the assumption that tying and exclusive dealing can indeed play an exclusionary role under some—but not all—circumstances.[40]

But, I think it is now accepted by most economists that if a contracting practice, no matter how odd it seems on the surface, is regularly used by firms without market power or hope of obtaining it, that practice plays a procompetitive, efficiency-enhancing role in at least those contexts and thus does not deserve condemnation there. When market power is present, most commentators now seem to think that the rule of reason in some form should generally be employed to analyze nonstandard contracting practices. In terms used in recent EU debates regarding article 82 of the Treaty of Rome, this represents movement from a "form-based" to an "effects-based" mode of analyzing seller conduct.[41] While rule of reason or effects-based analysis is necessarily less predictable than the application of *per se* rules, it seems much more likely to enhance welfare on average than across-the-board condemnation of practices that are demonstrably efficiency-enhancing in some instances.

The remainder of this section briefly reviews and evaluates Chicago's attempts to move policy from "form-based" to "effects-based" analysis of horizontal restraints, vertical mergers, vertical restraints, and tying arrangements.

Horizontal Restraints

In its 1967 *Sealy* decision, the Supreme Court struck down the market-division agreement entered into by a set of mattress manufacturers without inquiring into the effects of that agreement.[42] In the 1972 *Topco* decision, the Court similarly struck down the market division agreement employed in the private label program of an association of supermarket chains even though only about 10 percent of the goods sold by its members bore the Topco name.[43] The *Topco* Court held simply that "...the restraint in this case is a horizontal one, and, therefore, a *per se* violation...."[44]

As Bork argued persuasively, these decisions make no economic sense: "Absent the power to restrict output, the decision to eliminate rivalry can only be made in order to achieve efficiency."[45] And beginning with the

Supreme Court's 1979 *BMI* decision,[46] antitrust policy has retreated significantly from *per se* condemnation of all horizontal restraints. Indeed, the current DOJ/FTC *Antitrust Guidelines for Collaborations Among Competitors* states that "If...participants in an efficiency-enhancing integration of economic activity enter into an agreement that is reasonably related to the integration and reasonably necessary to achieve its pro-competitive benefits, the Agencies analyze the agreement under the rule of reason, even if it is of a type that might otherwise be considered per se illegal."[47] Judge Bork could hardly have wished for more.

Vertical Mergers

In the 1962 *Brown Shoe* decision, Chief Justice Warren asserted that the adverse impact of vertical mergers on competition "results primarily from a foreclosure of a share of the market otherwise open to competitors."[48] He went on to condemn the merger before him because the upstream partner had been found to intend to "force" the downstream partner to take around 1 percent of total U.S. shoe output. This form-based analysis lacks any economic support, particularly when market power is nowhere to be seen.[49] Nonetheless, the 1968 *Merger Guidelines* dutifully followed the Court and asserted that vertical mergers, at least those involving market shares above the single digits, would ordinarily be challenged because they raise entry barriers by "foreclosing equal access" to potential customers and/or suppliers.

In contrast, the current DOJ *Non-Horizontal Merger Guidelines,* originally issued in 1984, mention neither "foreclosure" nor specific critical market shares and instead outline how the Department will analyze whether any particular vertical merger is likely to raise barriers to entry.[50] This is a clear shift in the Chicago direction, from concern about form to concern about effects.

Vertical Restraints

The vertical restraints story is more complex. The courts were long hostile to non-price restraints such as exclusive territories but never quite condemned them *per se*. In the 1967 *Schwinn* decision, however, the Supreme Court flirted with the idea.[51] It found exclusive territories *per se* illegal if the goods in question were sold to retailers but subject to rule of reason treatment if the goods were instead sent on consignment. This distinction obviously makes no economic sense, and during the 1970s making no economic sense became more widely condemned. The Court's 1977 *Sylvania* decision overruled *Schwinn* and made territorial exclusivity subject to rule of reason analysis in general.[52] This is not quite a definitive end to the inhospitality tradition in this area, but it seems pretty close.

In a classic "form-based" decision, resale price maintenance was declared *per se* illegal in the Supreme Court's 1911 *Dr. Miles* decision because it involved agreement on price.[53] Except for the "fair trade" period between the passage of the Miller-Tydings Act of 1937 and its repeal (along with the clearly anticompetitive McGuire Act) in 1975, *Dr. Miles* governed agreements on minimum resale prices for nearly a century. In its 1968 *Albrecht* decision, the Court carried this "form-based" analysis to its logical conclusion, finding that agreements specifying *maximum* resale prices were also per se illegal, even though on their face they benefited consumers.[54]

Beginning in the 1970s, work in industrial organization economics showed that vertical price restraints, like the vertical non-price restraints for which they were substitutes, could be pro-competitive under plausible conditions.[55] Of course it doesn't take much fancy economics to show that agreeing on *maximum* resale prices does not deserve *per se* condemnation under an economic welfare standard, but *Albrecht* was not overruled until 1997.[56] *Dr. Miles* proved more durable, but it was finally overruled by the 2007 *Leegin* decision.[57] While these recent decisions have broad support among economists and reflect the sort of analysis that Chicago did so much to inject into antitrust deliberations, they were not clear victories for Chicago. Vertical price and non-price restraints remain subject to the rule of reason, even though Bork and others had argued that they were always procompetitive and thus should be *per se* legal.[58] And it remains to be seen how rule of reason analysis of these cases will be structured and how permissive it will be.

Tying Arrangements

Here Chicago has mainly won in the seminar room but has made little headway in the courts. Justice Frankfurter's famous 1949 *Standard Stations* dictum that "tying arrangements serve hardly any purpose beyond the suppression of competition" has cast an amazingly long shadow, even though, as Bork noted, "[t]his remarkable assertion has never been supported either theoretically or empirically.... "[59] Ward Bowman showed in 1957 that tying could simply be merely a method of price discrimination in some circumstances, though recent theoretical work has shown that tying can be anticompetitive under other market conditions.[60]

Nonetheless, without any analysis of effects, the Supreme Court's 1969 *Fortner Enterprises* decision, which deservedly makes Judge Bork's short list of truly bad antitrust decisions, managed to construe the granting of credit on favorable terms by a competitively insignificant seller of homes as a potentially dangerous tie-in sale.[61] The Supreme Court's latest venture into this arena, its 1984 *Jefferson Parish* decision, did serve to clarify the immunity of sellers with absolutely no market power, but otherwise the *per se* rule against tying remained intact.[62] Justice Stevens, writing for the majority, simply relied on the age of the relevant precedents: "It is far too late in the history of our antitrust jurisprudence to question the proposition that certain tying arrangements pose an unacceptable risk of stifling competition and are therefore unreasonable *per se*."[63] To an economist, this echoes the medieval preference for Aristotle over experiment based on Aristotle's antiquity. Particularly noteworthy is the Supreme Court's refusal thus far even to follow some lower courts and treat "technological ties" differently than ties based on contract terms alone, thus leaving in perpetual doubt the legality of WordPerfect's incorporation of a spell-checker into its then-dominant word processor.[64]

Summation

I have tried to show that the work of lawyers and economists associated with the Chicago School, particularly in the 1970s, had a strongly positive effect on U.S. antitrust policy by defanging judicial decisions and policy proposals that could have had substantial economic costs. Chicago's major intellectual victories, now widely accepted, include fixing economic welfare as the sole objective of antitrust, rejecting no-fault deconcentration as a plausible policy option, attaching a positive weight to productive efficiency, and recognizing that business practices not engaged in by textbook wheat farmers may nonetheless be efficiency-enhancing. I believe that consumers and overall economic efficiency have benefited substantially from these changes in antitrust policy.

One response to all this praise might be that many of these positive developments were the work of many hands, some of which had never been to Hyde Park. I would agree, though I think it is nonetheless fair to say that the bulk of the leadership, particularly early on, came from the Chicago School. Recall Bork's lonely dissent from the 1968 White House Task Force report.

Another response might be that if the most extreme Chicago proposals had been adopted, particularly those involving *per se* legality, the costs would have been substantial. Thus, one must give appreciable credit for the positive changes in antitrust policy to those who resisted Chicago. Again, I would agree: Chicago has not always prevailed, as I have noted, and some of its 1970s proposals are inconsistent with current economic thinking. For instance, Bork argued that the law "should abandon its concern with such beneficial practices as small horizontal mergers, all vertical and conglomerate mergers, vertical price maintenance and market division, tying arrangements, exclusive dealing and requirements contracts, 'predatory' price cutting, price 'discrimination,' and the like."[65] All of the practices *can* indeed be welfare-enhancing, but Bork seems to have jumped from there to the unjustified conclusion that they are welfare-enhancing under all plausible market conditions. Moreover, as I have noted, that conclusion has been shown to be incorrect by subsequent analysis of many of the practices Bork lists. Similar reasoning seems to have led Richard Posner to assert that "I would like to see the antitrust laws other than Section 1 of the Sherman Act repealed,"[66] which would legalize all horizontal mergers, in addition to the practices listed by Bork.

Yet, I would argue that even extreme Chicago proposals like these, which have failed even to gain much seminar-room acceptance, have also had a positive effect on antitrust policy by forcing those who favor more interventionist policy to provide economic justifications for their views. The resulting debate has had the broad effect of shifting antitrust's intellectual center of gravity from no-fault liability and *per se* illegality to rule of reason, "effects-based" analysis. Pointing out that the emperor has no clothes may raise local sartorial standards either by driving him from the scene or by compelling him to dress, and the Chicago critique of economically unclothed antitrust circa 1970 has done both.

Some Practical Thoughts About Entry

Irwin M. Stelzer

I approach this discussion essay with very considerable trepidation. First, it is daunting to be included with such distinguished antitrust scholars, and to be expected to add anything of value to what they have written. Second, we are here writing about what the conference's organizers have called "Conservative Economic Influence on U.S. Antitrust Policy."

Let me begin by explaining this second worry. I would very much like to discuss the conservative influence on the economics of antitrust policy, since I style myself a conservative economist, the alternative position in fields such as housing, welfare, macroeconomic policy, and other areas having been proven to be rather dismal failures. But when it comes to antitrust policy and other aspects of government supervision of markets, I find myself at odds with my conservative friends and therefore cannot speak for them.

I have always believed that the free market system can be defended in the long run only if it provides fair and open opportunity to all comers, that its principal virtue is its contribution to social mobility, and that anti-competitive practices by dominant firms, and abuses created by the Berle and Means effect—the ability of managers to pursue their own rather than their shareholder-owners' enrichment—are the greatest threat to the cap-italist free market system. The best defense of a system that periodically produces increases in the inequality of income and wealth is that those inequalities are transient because the system by and large maintains fair access to upward movement. All of which means that the antitrust laws must be vigorously enforced, and even perhaps—I am less certain about this, but think it an idea worthy of your consideration—that the risks of what Herbert Hovenkamp calls underdeterrence of anticompetitive acts are greater than the risks of overdeterrence.[67]

Unfortunately, this view is not enthusiastically received by my fellow conservatives. They mainly see government intervention as efficiency-reducing, induced by inefficient whining competitors who just cannot cut it in open competition, at best useless, at worst counterproductive. Besides, the concept of the dominant firm is simply not in their lexicon—to them, all market power is transient (the period of transition is of little concern to them). In addition, attempts to cope with anticompetitive practices by recourse to the antitrust laws more likely to result in overdeterrence rather than in efficiency-increasing, consumer-welfare enhancing, equity-producing solutions.

These colleagues have, of course, been much comforted by the emergence of the Chicago School, and not only for the quite sensible reason that its contribution to economic discourse helped move us away from an excessively rigid concentration on static market structure tests. Conservative economists take added joy from the fact that the Chicago School urges focus solely on the economic goals of antitrust policy, and that it liberates them from the necessity of considering possible social objectives,[68] because (1) they believe they are capable of quantifying such concepts as marginal cost, recoupment possibilities, which competitors are efficient and which are not, and (2) that judges are incapable of dealing with noneconomic concepts such as equity. In one case in which I was involved, a Chicago School devotee was asked about the equity of a certain practice and referred the judge to "his honor's priest." My own view is that the empirical basis for much of what passes for economic testimony should be viewed as considerably less than precise and far from determinative, and that although, as Hovenkamp points out, judges do make mistakes, that does not mean it is good policy to excuse them from attempting to come to grips with all of the aspects of the antitrust laws, including its social goals.

All of this is by way of disclaimer: I do not pretend to speak for conservative economists, most of whom prefer less rather than more enforcement of the antitrust laws, and almost all of whom reject Hovenkamp's suggestion that "The time seems ripe to become more aggressive about structural remedies once again, particularly for repeat offenders."

Now to my first worry: that I am not well qualified to comment on my learned colleagues' papers. Ever since I found that participating in antitrust cases as an expert witness meant forfeiting control of my life's schedule to a cartel of lawyers and judges who arranged schedules to suit their own professional needs, and around such matters of greater importance, such as their fishing trips, vacations, and daughters' weddings, I have not participated in the many cases discussed in the papers presented at this conference. So if I stumble over some obscure footnote, or fail to understand just how to implement some of the exquisitely phrased tests sprinkled through-out these papers, I do apologize.

1. Hovenkamp seems relieved that economic thinking has progressed to the point where decisions no longer condemn as predatory "prices above any measure of cost." I wonder whether that position gives full weight to the fact that an entrenched incumbent, charging monopoly prices, can lower those prices quite a lot without reducing them below some concept of cost—as a signal not only to potential entrants, but to the venture capitalists who increasingly finance these entrants, of what might be in store for them if they challenge the incumbent. It seems to me that we have to balance our understandable fear of preventing the price competition that we hope new entry will produce, against the possibility that such entry will not occur if a dominant firm is allowed to signal its intent to crush any newcomer by offering a small taste of the price wars to come. So I think it is worth con-sidering whether predation is possible (or would the lawyers call this more accurately monopolizing behavior?) when prices are lowered to level well above average *total* cost.

Leave aside the question of the difficulty of determining whether the prices with which an incumbent chooses to confront a newcomer exceed some concept of marginal, or incremental, or average variable cost; assume they do. Assume even that they exceed average total cost. As Peggy Lee once asked in a different connection, "Is that all there is, my friend?"

I think not. An examination of the entire range of competitive practices of the incumbent over time, not each one of those practices in isolation, seems to me to provide a better basis for deciding whether or not we are dealing with predation, or with attempts to raise rivals' costs by depriving them of an opportunity to achieve economies of scales. True, as Hovenkamp argues in chapter 3, there is a "risk of chilling procompetitive behavior," but it is worth discussing whether that risk is, as Hovenkamp characterizes it, "intolerable," and whether it is really the case that "juries are not able to distinguish such strategies with sufficient clarity to avoid condemning procompetitive behavior."

After all, there is always a risk that cases will be wrongly decided, even by judges, much less the much-maligned juries, often accused of being unable to make sense of economists' testimony that is so convoluted that it would, in the words of Tevye in "Fiddler on the Roof," "cross a Rabbi's eyes." There is also the ever-present risk that later scholarship will reveal a decision to have been wrongly decided. The question we have to ask ourselves is whether a wrongly decided case that penalizes procompeti-tive behavior is a greater threat to the free market system than a case that is wrongly decided and allows a potential competitor to be nipped in its incipiency. That surely is a legitimate task for policymakers.

All of which is why the *Brooke* decision's conclusion that "the exclusion-ary effect of prices above a relevant measure of cost . . . is beyond the practical ability of a judicial tribunal to control without courting intolerable risks of chilling legitimate price cutting..." might be worthy of reexamination.[69] Certainly a judicial tribunal that considers itself competent to decide which of the competing measures of cost presented to it by learned economists (and, worse still, by accountants whose concepts of cost are as devoid of economic content as their audits often are of any meaning) is the "relevant measure" and is accurate, is capable of employing all of the evidence unearthed in multimillion dollar discoveries to reach a judgment as to whether a price cut is predatory or not, without being bound by a rigid cost test.

I would suggest that any reevaluation along the lines I have suggested consider the relatively new role of venture capitalists in financing new entrants, especially in the increasingly important high-tech industries to which we look for advances in productivity. These capitalists, the first port of call for a newcomer after he has exhausted his own and his family's resources, are notably hard-headed realists. If they believe that an entrenched incumbent will be allowed to snuff out incipient competition by inducing manufacturers to boycott the new product, or by using technological legerdemain to tie its own competing product to its monopoly product, or by setting a pricing schedule that in effect results in bundling or full-line forcing,[70] venture capitalists will, at the very least, raise the cost of capital to reflect the enhanced risk, and more likely suggest to the newcomer that completion of his doctoral dissertation or a job with the entrenched incumbent is his best option. They must always be satisfied, before opening their wallets, that the incumbent does not have sufficient market power to nip the competition in its incipiency. Potential suppliers cannot be threatened with retaliation if they do business with the newcomer; most distributors cannot be fearful of the consequences of dealing with the new entrant; the dominant incumbent cannot manipulate its multiproduct price schedule so as to make it uneconomic for its customers to divert part of their purchases to a new entrant. Only with the assurance that the law protects their investment from being washed away by such tactics that have nothing to do with the relative merits of the competing products, will venture capitalists write the checks the challenger needs.

They know what some academic analysts do not: experience suggests that dominant firms are willing to have recourse to tactics that are related to their market power, rather than merely to their efficiency. The use of these tactics turns the battle into one in which the firm with greater market power wins, rather than the firm with the best mousetrap. It is those tactics that the antitrust laws, applied both by the enforcement agencies and by private parties, are uniquely equipped to prevent.

I have no doubt that the suggestion that even above-cost price cuts might in some circumstances be found to be anticompetitive flies in the face of what businessmen always claim they need: certainty. I have often suggested that such certainty is easily available: create a long list of competitive practices, and make them *per se* illegal, like price-fixing. That is not the certainty they seek: it is the certainty that when they push the outer limits of competitive behavior, that behavior will be deemed *per se* lawful. The better policy alternative is, I fear, a degree of uncertainty, rather like other aspects of decision-making; for example, the future course of interest rates, exchange rates and the like. Businessmen should be as capable of factoring their lawyers' nuanced advice into their pricing decisions as they are their economists' even less reliable forecasts of the economic variables that make the difference between profit and loss.

2. For some of the same reasons I wonder whether it might not be useful to consider carefully the proposition that a multiproduct firm selling a bundle of products above the incremental cost of producing the bundle should be allowed to price one of those products below the incremental cost of that product, even if it destroys the competitive prospects of a single-product firm. That decision is not one that should be based solely on economic considerations but on a balancing of the desire to maximize some concept of efficiency and consumers' interests in the lowest immediate prices, against the reduction of opportunities to enter a market by a challenging, small competitor, with all of the long-run advantages associated with such freer entry, including not least the possibility that the new single-product entrant, by the very virtue of its specialization, might introduce a hitherto unrealized dynamic into the market.

3. Let me conclude with a point of agreement: that we should resurrect interest in structural solutions. It is increasingly clear that in fashioning remedies we cannot rely on anything requiring ongoing judicial supervision of the practices of a company, especially those specializing in the creation of intellectual property, or involved in industries in which technology is changing rapidly. This is so for two reasons.

First, we do not want to slow the pace of innovation to accommodate the more leisurely one of the judicial process. Experience with Judge Green's supervision of the telecommunications industry is reason enough for caution.

Second, it is not at all certain that the courts can cope with firms understandably reluctant to comply promptly with their orders. This is evidenced by the recent confession of the judge in the Microsoft case that the remedies she had ordered are not working terribly well, or the frustration of the EU competition authorities as they attempt to develop and enforce a behavioral remedy for the anticompetitive tactics deployed by Microsoft. This difficulty with behavioral solutions might mean that relief has to be more radical in the case of high-tech violators of the antitrust laws than in the case of lower-tech ones, with divestiture and structural solutions playing a larger role relative to the prohibition of specific practices.

I should warn you of two things, which in combination you will not find cheering. The first is that the weight of conservative economists is on the side of the anti-antitrusters: they see enforcement of competition policy as government interference in the workings of markets, interference some-where between unnecessary and downright harmful. The second warn-ing is that these economists, based in the think tanks of Washington and elsewhere, are far more influential than the legal and economic scholars housed in the chairs of America's universities. It is no coincidence, as the Left was wont to say, that Justice Scalia spent several years imbibing the intellectual climate of the American Enterprise Institute before unburden-ing himself of *Trinko*.[71]

Conservative Economics and Antitrust: A Variety of Influences

F. M. Scherer

Introduction

Our task, as I interpret it, is to evaluate the influence conservative economics has had on the enforcement and adjudication of antitrust in the United States. I assume it to be proven, without undertaking the arduous task of providing support, that the economic doctrines underlying the corpus of judicially accepted antitrust law have gravitated during the past half century in a more conservative direction.

This statement of the problem immediately demands a deeper level of analysis. Antitrust is accomplished through enforcement, and what gets done depends in significant measure on the laws Congress passes and how the courts, especially the higher courts, interpret statutes whose implications and intent are often not precisely stated. What gets written into the statutes and how the courts interpret the statutes depends in part upon economic analysis, although to be sure, much else is thrown into the stew. If there has been a change in emphasis over time, the cause may lie in the underlying economics. But it is much more probable, in my opinion, that changes are attributable to how antitrust enforcers and the courts read what economics has to say; that is, on which among conflicting propositions they have placed emphasis and which ones they have downplayed. And those choices depend importantly upon the values the decision-makers—typically, lawyers rather than economists—bring to the table. As Paul Samuelson wisely quipped, "Economists should be on tap, not on top."

No one can deny that there are conflicting economic analyses. That, in my opinion, is an unmitigated blessing. Knowledge advances through the juxtaposition of alternative theories and testing against evidence to determine which ones are more nearly correct. "More nearly correct" is as close as I dare come in characterizing what economics can add to the debate, because economic propositions are among the least provable of those addressed in the various sciences. Economists' subject matter is intrinsically complex, characterized by uncertainty, reciprocal expectations puzzles (the analogue of physicists' three-body conundrum), and incommensurable values. Our data are often deficient and our empirical methodologies less than satisfactory (but improving). Accepting that we cannot conclusively separate what is true from what is untrue, the best one can hope for from economics in informing antitrust enforcement and adjudication is that differences in the findings from economic analyses will be made clear, as will the probable reasons why those differences cannot readily be resolved.

If the above premises are anywhere near correct, we should be thankful for the existence of a so-called Chicago School of economics, which is often (incorrectly, I shall argue) associated with conservative economics. One clear characteristic of the Chicago School—not the only one, to be sure—is what I, as a person born and raised in what *Chicago Tribune* publisher Robert R. McCormick called "Chicagoland," identify as the great Chicago "a'giner" tradition. If the conventional wisdom says X is true, one redoubles one's efforts to find the flaws supporting that inference and perhaps also to show that instead Y is true. Epitomizing this attitude was the role of Aaron Director at the University of Chicago.[72] Director encouraged legal and economic scholars at Chicago to investigate critically the facts, assumptions, and theories underlying important antitrust doctrines. Those investigations often identified weaknesses in the foundations and sometimes showed that the emperor had no clothes. That train of scholarly work has been of enormous benefit to all of us.

It should be recognized too that virtually all professional economists plying their trade in the United States are conservatives, in the sense that we believe in free markets and capitalism as instruments of discovery and engines of progress—views we adopt inter alia from Friedrich Hayek[73]— and in markets as relatively efficient allocators of resources. If some of us (not I) once believed in central planning as a superior alternative, we were disabused of that notion by the failure of communism in the Soviet Union and China and the rather more equivocal triumph of capitalism. I believe it was Chicago's George Stigler who once observed that "the study of economics makes a person conservative."

That said, it must be recognized that there are widely varying degrees of conservatism in the economics practiced within the United States (as elsewhere). The differences stem more from fundamental values and assumptions about human behavior and about the desirability of such phenomena as unequal income distribution than from the choice of one analytic or empirical technique over another. It would certainly be a mistake to view Chicago as the citadel of all conservative economics. One could with equal accuracy point to conservative schools with roots at Auburn University (uniquely attached to the pronouncements of Ludwig von Mises), the University of Virginia, George Mason University, the University of Rochester, and Washington University, not to mention minority groups at a host of institutions including my alma mater and employer, Harvard. And for dogmatic differentiation, one would be hard-pressed to match the range of extremes represented by economic think tanks.

I. The Influence of "Chicago" Economics

As I have indicated, the University of Chicago is often singled out as the leading bastion of conservative economics. This, I believe, is wrong for at least two reasons. First, by digging into and exposing flaws in accepted antitrust doctrines, Chicago has focused and sharpened the debate—a virtue that I identify with enlightened liberal scholarship. But second and more tellingly, Chicago economists and antitrust scholars have been far from monolithic in advocating a retrenchment of antitrust enforcement programs. I mention briefly four of the most prominent counterexamples.

(1) While New Deal politicians were backing off from their ill-fated experience with cartelization under the National Recovery Administration, "conservative" Chicago economist Henry Simons proposed in 1936, among various policy redirections:

> Operating companies must be limited in size, under special limitations prescribed for particular industries by the Federal Trade Commission. . . . There would be a breaking down of enormous integrations into more specialized firms, with ownership separation among phases of production which are now largely separate in place and management. For horizontal combinations, the policy would require ownership separation among operating units which are now connected by little more than common advertising and selling organizations.[74]

(2) The most sweeping proposals for deconcentration of concentrated industries made by an official governmental commission came in 1968 from the so-called Neal Report, chaired by University of Chicago Law School dean Phil Caldwell Neal, who had co-taught the School's antitrust law course with Aaron Director.[75]

(3) Richard Posner's 1976 book and related articles recommended much more stringent enforcement of the Sherman Act toward jointly acting oligopolies even in the absence of classical conspiracy evidence.[76]

(4) A powerful demonstration of the welfare distortions that can result from tying arrangements in other than fixed-proportions cases was published by John McGee, who was an associate professor of economics at Chicago between 1957 and 1962.[77]

Other better-known work by McGee gravitated in the opposite direction, diluting the presumptions of antitrust violation through predatory pricing. In his appreciation of Aaron Director's influence, Sam Peltzman asserts that the largest antitrust change attributable to Director was on the question of predatory pricing.[78] Up to the time of McGee's seminal article,[79] the research for which was suggested by Aaron Director, it was generally assumed that the Supreme Court acted correctly in 1911 when it condemned Standard Oil and, in a parallel case, American Tobacco, for achieving and retaining their near-monopoly positions, among other things through predatory pricing. Through his analysis of the *Standard Oil* case facts, McGee challenged this supposition. His work was cited by the Supreme Court in its 1986 dictum that "there is a consensus among commentators that predatory pricing schemes are rarely tried and even more rarely successful."[80]

However, McGee was by no means the only economist writing on predation. Already by the time of the *Matsushita* decision, there was a substantial scholarly literature documenting what should have passed for predation by any reasonable definition and showing the rationality of sharp price-cutting by a dominant firm to discourage new entrants.[81] Since there was a diversity of scholarly views at the time key Supreme Court pronouncements were rendered on predation, the fault for ignoring one side of the scholarship must be attributed to the Court's myopia or (without the obiter dictum) compelling facts, and not to economists' contributions.[82] More recently, a careful analysis has cast doubt on whether McGee's reading of the *Standard Oil* case facts was accurate and brings forward considerable evidence supporting an inference of predation.[83] In a world governed by the canons of scholarship rather than *stare decisis,* one might in some future case expect a renunciation by the Supreme Court of its previous misconceptions.

Reversion from the tough predatory pricing precedents of *Standard Oil,* 1911, also was influenced by Phillip Areeda and Donald Turner through a journal article, in which they almost certainly intended to influence ongoing cases against IBM alleging predation against plug-compatible computer equipment makers.[84] Areeda and Turner, professors at Harvard Law School, can hardly be characterized as Chicagoans. Yet their article has been cited favorably in subsequent predation cases, including *Matsushita* and the Supreme Court decision in *Brooke Group.*[85] The main novelty of *Brooke Group* was the Supreme Court's emphasis that to be predatory, a strategy required a reasonable prospect (or dangerous probability) that early profit sacrifices would later be recouped despite oligopolistic coordination obstacles. In its opinion, the Court considered a broad array

of expert opinions. If there was favoritism, it was not in the economic literature evaluated, but in the weighing of alternative perspectives.[86]

The domain of judicial interpretation most closely associated with
University of Chicago doctrines involves vertical restraints such as
exclusive franchises, exclusive territorial arrangements, and resale price
maintenance. In that area of the law, Sam Peltzman recorded "a partial
victory for the analysis inspired by [Aaron] Director."[87] Two key contributions were Lester Telser's 1960 article on free rider problems and Robert
Bork's argument that, by providing the wherewithal for demand-expand-
ing merchandising efforts, minimum-price restrictions imposed by manufacturers upon their retailers can be welfare-enhancing.[88] There are three
problems with this attribution. First, the sharpest swerve in Supreme Court
interpretations concerning the desirability of vertical restraints came in
a decision that considered a wide spectrum of scholarly views.[89] Telser's
contribution went unmentioned, although the free rider concept entered
indirectly through Justice White's concurring opinion, citing an article
by Richard Posner, other facets of which were relied upon heavily by the
majority.[90] Second, recognition that vertical pricing relationships could
cause welfare losses that might be solved by vertical integration had a much
longer history, dating back at least to the 1830s.[91] And third, the Bork proof
has been shown to be a special case, by no means applicable in all vertical
pricing or resale price maintenance situations.[92]

After Peltzman's declaration of "partial victory," the Supreme Court
returned to the core of the vertical restraints question and, openly abandoning *stare decisis,* overturned the per se presumption against resale price
maintenance embedded for nearly a century in the *Dr. Miles* precedent. Its
decision in *Leegin*[93] moving from per se to rule of reason treatment might be
considered the "et tu, Brute" in adjudication of vertical restraint questions.
Yet one cannot say that the Court's 5–4 decision, with a strong dissent written by Justice Breyer, was one-sided. A broad range of scholarly arguments
was evaluated by both the majority and the minority. Numerous amicus
curiae briefs were filed, including one arguing for certiorari and eventual
rule of reason treatment by 25 economists, only four of whom had graduate
study or faculty appointment ties with the University of Chicago, and ten of
whom were educated in the MIT-Harvard-Yale-Princeton axis.[94] I co-signed
that amicus brief but also, with William S. Comanor, filed a separate amicus
brief on the merits.[95]

Believing that a transition from a *per se* rule was inevitable, Comanor
and I had two main objectives: persuading the Court to take a balanced
view of the merits and demerits of resale price maintenance, and seeking to simplify rule of reason cases by articulating presumptions under
which per se illegality would be retained. We (and other amici) succeeded, I believe, on the first point. Recognizing that both good and
bad effects could exist, the majority stated squarely that "the potential

anticompetitive effects of vertical price restraints must not be ignored or underestimated."[96] On the second point, success was mixed. The majority recognized that "courts would have to be diligent in eliminating...anticompetitive uses from the market"[97] and stating, as Comanor and I urged, that resale price maintenance was most likely to be harmful when it "spreads to cover the bulk of an industry's output." We failed in persuading the Court to adopt quantitative presumptions paralleling those already accepted for merger adjudication. Rather than engaging in such arguably legislative rule-making, the Court suggested that as the lower courts gained experience with such cases, they could "devise rules over time for offering proof, or even presumptions where justified, to make the rule of reason a fair and efficient way to prohibit anticompetitive restraints and to promote procompetitive ones."[98] The burden passes now to the antitrust enforcement agencies and (with more difficulty) private plaintiffs to see that consumers are not seriously injured. One cannot say that *Leegin* left them without powerful Supreme Court obiter dicta on which to stand.

An even more dramatic pro-conservative swing has been evident in the enforcement and adjudication of mergers. How dramatic it has been is suggested by figure 2.1, from various tabulations of the average annual rate of exit through merger from *Fortune* magazine's annual lists of the top 100 U.S. industrial corporations.[99] From the mid-1930s into the late-1970s, exit rates were quite low, but they then soared after 1982. Through the Celler-Kefauver Act of 1950, Congress eliminated previous loopholes in Clayton Act, section 7 with respect to mergers and made clear its intent that the law be enforced vigorously. A series of tough precedents followed, leading Justice Stewart to exclaim in a dissent, "[t]he sole consistency that I can find is that in litigation under Section 7, the Government always wins."[100] A decisive turn toward greater lenience was the 1974 decision in the General Dynamics-United Electric Coal case, which is attributable more to a change in the ideological composition of the Supreme Court than to identifiable intellectual influences. But enforcers' zeal has undoubtedly been dampened to some extent through articles inter alia by Henry Manne[101] and Michael Jensen,[102] leaders of what might be called a Chicago-Rochester axis, stressing the benefits of mergers. A substantial dissenting literature exists on their contributions too. At the enforcement level, the Merger Guidelines of 1982 were shepherded through the antitrust agencies by a Harvard-trained economist, Lawrence J. White, and drew upon Chicago (George Stigler[103]) mainly in choosing the once-mysterious Herfindahl-Hirschman index rather than previously emphasized concentration ratios to measure merger consequences. A significant modification occurred in 1984, when the Merger Guidelines incorporated an efficiency defense whose intellectual basis was a classic 1968 article by Oliver Williamson[104]—not a Chicagoan. However, its implementation has been more Borkian than Williamsonian, emphasizing directly prospective cost-based price reductions to consumers over the freeing of resources to satisfy other consumer wants.[105]

Also noteworthy is the absence of enforcement against jointly acting oligopolies since the *Kellogg* case of the late 1970s and the tetraethyl lead case of 1983.[106] Diverse economic analyses led to government defeats in both of those cases. Kellogg's principal economist was Harvard-trained and -chaired. Game-theoretic considerations not associated with Chicago (and anticipated in my 1980 textbook edition[107]) were influential in the tetraethyl lead case. But the composition of the Federal Trade Commission had become more conservative under the Reagan Administration. And there may have been some backlash from challenges to accepted oligopoly structure—performance doctrine by Chicagoans Yale Brozen[108] and Harold Demsetz.[109] The intellectual dispute was crystallized at the Columbia Law School *New Learning* conference, whose proceedings were published in 1974,[110] which threw the economics profession into a state of doctrinal disarray. That matters were more complex than a simple flow of causation from concentration to high profits was shown through articles resulting from the Federal Trade Commission's Line of Business program, most notably, by David Ravenscraft.[111] Clearly, as a result of such work, what economics taught about oligopoly was perceived by antitrust enforcers as more mixed, and enforcement became less vigorous. But again, the influences here are complex and point to many locales other than the University of Chicago.

II. Other Influences

To the extent that there has been significant backtracking in antitrust precedents and enforcement, I suspect that there are two more important root causes, each of which can be identified with conservatism per se, even if not with conservative scholarship and especially economic scholarship.

For one, a foundational belief among many conservatives—not all, to be sure—is that "government is the problem." This was a belief embodied in Henry Simons's approach to monopolies. He recognized that monopolies existed and that they had harmful effects, but he was reluctant to let government agencies regulate them. Instead, he proposed that they be broken up structurally so that they would act competitively without sustained government intervention. His proposal probably underlay Assistant Attorney General William Baxter's readiness to break AT&T into eight fragments in what for at least a while was the greatest monopolization case of the second half of the twentieth century. If I interpret his position correctly, Baxter saw as AT&T's greatest sin the abuse of regulatory processes in order to suppress entry and preserve its monopoly. Judge Greene agreed in his interim decision, suggesting that the Federal Communications Commission "may realistically be incapable of efficiently regulating a company of AT&T's size, complexity, and power."[112] Where this belief goes too far is when it leads to the appointment to key positions in the federal antitrust enforcement and adjudication hierarchy persons who believe it so passionately that they adopt a "do nothing" approach to their jobs. I believe it went too far during the Reagan Administration, and it has clearly gone too far, not only in antitrust but many other federal agencies, under the Bush II Administration.

An argument rooted more deeply in conservative perspectives on economics is the assertion by John McGee, whom I have singled out previously as a believer in vertical market failure. At least with respect to merger and monopolization policy, McGee has argued that

> Unless we are dealing with industries into which the State blocks entry, industrial reorganization schemes have very much the same results as simply dictating to consumers what and from whom they can buy. In my view, this is both antieconomic and, to use an old-fashioned word, tyrannical. In sum, I conclude that apart from those industries dominated by State controls, there is the strongest presumption that the existing structure is the efficient structure.[113]

Professor McGee may be extreme in this Panglossian diagnosis (roughly, everything that is, is good), but such views in attenuated form have been held by many of the individuals who have led the antitrust agencies under recent Republican administrations and the jurists appointed by those administrations to the higher courts. Antitrust policy has almost surely been affected.

Let me add one point in the same general vein. Those who from firmly held conservative or libertarian principles believe that government is the problem, and/or that free markets are unlikely to go astray for more than brief anomalous periods, tend to be fervent in their beliefs. Those like myself who believe that markets do a pretty good job, but on occasion need a corrective nudge, are inclined to be the kinds of economists President Harry Truman deplored—those who equivocate with, "On the one hand, but on the other hand...." When one has such a complex perception of economic reality, one is unlikely to be fervent. And when there is a clash of views, at least in the currently polarized and showmanship-infatuated United States, fervor tends to trump ambivalence.[114] And that, I believe, more than anything else, explains the ascendance of conservative thinking in antitrust law and economics.

III. Technological Innovation and Patent Antitrust

I turn finally to a matter I have neglected, but that cannot be ignored, because it is far more important than the efficacy of markets in allocating resources and distributing income at any moment in time: the impact of market structure and related institutions on the vigor and pace of technological innovation. A more rapid rate of technological progress can in a relatively short period overwhelm any resource allocation inefficiencies attributable to monopoly, which tend in any event, as shown by Chicagoan Arnold Harberger,[115] to be modest in relation to gross domestic product.[116] The subject is a huge one, and here I must be highly selective.

Joseph A. Schumpeter, a conservative economist teaching at Harvard during the 1930s and 1940s, argued in 1942 that even when markets were monopolized, "creative destruction" would ensure a rapid pace of technological innovation and progress in an advanced capitalistic economy. As I show in a paper written for an American Bar Association compendium, he was partly right.[117] Competition through creative destruction does work, but sometimes it needs a helping hand, among other things, from antitrusters limiting barriers to competitive entry by firms with superior new ideas.

Here I address a narrower but important point. Half a century ago, antitrust enforcement took a generally skeptical view of restrictive patent agreements. Reviewing the findings of the Temporary National Economic Committee, George Stigler (then at the University of Minnesota, not Chicago) found the patent policies of the Hartford-Empire Company to be "an eloquent example of an evil demanding correction" and concluded that "[t]he case for limitation of restrictive [patient] licensing is surely irrefutable."[118] The antitrust case waged against Hartford-Empire provided an important precedent for tough-minded compulsory licensing of patents used to monopolize industries and sustain their monopolization.[119] In the ensuing decade and a half, more than 100 compulsory licensing orders were issued under antitrust proceedings.[120]

Attempting to ascertain how such governmental intervention, and in particular the 1956 decrees that ordered compulsory licensing of all patents held by innovative giants AT&T and IBM, affected investment in research and development, eight colleagues and I at the (conservative) Harvard Business School interviewed and administered mail questionnaires to 91 companies. We found to our surprise that the decrees had little adverse impact on R&D investment, and more generally, that for established corporations, the expectation of patent protection was in most cases unimportant to R&D commitments.[121] This finding has been validated by several more ambitious studies, among others, Taylor and Silberston in the United Kingdom[122] and (in the U.S. context) by Edwin Mansfield[123] and the current president of Yale University, Richard Levin.[124]

Ignoring this literature but echoing the empirically unsupported arguments in a book by a Chicago-affiliated lawyer,[125] Reagan Administration appointees to the Antitrust Division backpedaled significantly, staking out a broad area in which restrictive patent licensing agreements would not be challenged. Underlying the policy reversal was an assumption that

> Efforts to appropriate as much as possible of the surplus—the social value in excess of marginal cost—lying under the demand curve for patented technology do not harm competition. Indeed, the potential for appropriating those rents is *the* engine [emphasis added] that drives the technology market.[126]

The increased rent appropriation was to be accomplished through a variety of practices extending the duration and (e.g., through tying practices as well as restrictive cross-licensing) the scope of patent grants. This premise is quite inconsistent with the large body of empirical evidence on the conditions under which well-established corporations are willing to invest in innovation. And yet it was used, despite the great Chicago tradition of supporting one's findings with empirical evidence, to justify a substantial policy change.

That the change was more than transitory is evidenced in major statements on the intersection between patent and antitrust policy by the two federal antitrust enforcement agencies and the Antitrust Modernization Commission.[127] Both support the changed presumptions stemming from Department of Justice initiatives in the 1980s and endorse a rule of reason approach to cases in which the exercise of patent rights might conflict with antitrust objectives. Recognizing the complexity of the issues, I concur that a rule of reason approach is appropriate. But ignoring the empirical literature on the incentive effects of patent protection, both reports imply that the expectation of patent protection is a *principal* basis for investment in new technology. The DOJ-FTC report, for example, opens by stating that "[i]ntellectual property laws create exclusive rights that provide incentives for innovation... [and] prevent others from appropriating much of the value derived from... inventions or original expressions," and that "intellectual property laws protect the ability to earn a return on the investments necessary to innovate."[128] Beginning with a favorable citation to the 1981 Department of Justice statement quoted above,[129] the Antitrust Modernization Commission asserts that "the courts and the antitrust agencies in recent decades have evidenced a greater appreciation of the importance of intellectual property."[130] It goes on to suggest that "[i]ntellectual property may be critical to future innovation in an industry," and (correctly, in the specifically cited pharmaceutical industry case) that "in innovative industries... intellectual property assets are key."[131] Nowhere to be found in either report is more than peripheral recognition of the substantial empirical evidence demonstrating that in most industries (not all), intellectual property plays a relatively unimportant role as a stimulus to R&D investment. If one believes that the expectation of patent rights is the *principal* inducement to innovation, one will be wrong more often than right in balancing antitrust objectives against intellectual property considerations in rule of reason cases. It is like positioning a 300-pound gorilla on the pro-patent side of the balancing scale when the real-world counterpart is a 35-pound chimpanzee. A correction in the intellectual foundations of U.S. antitrust policy toward intellectual property is clearly needed.

Influence of Conservative Economic Analysis on the Development of the Law of Antitrust

Thomas E. Kauper

Most of us identify the so-called Chicago School[132] with an antitrust policy based on "consumer welfare," a phrase with a number of ambiguities, but that has generally come to mean allocative and productive efficiency.[133] That most of us identify *antitrust* policy with consumer welfare is itself some measure of Chicago's influence. Nothing reflects the influence of an idea so much as the acceptance and use of its language, even if it is not always used in the same way.

An antitrust policy predicating antitrust intervention in the marketplace on injury to consumer welfare in the Chicago sense requires a showing of adverse price and/or output effects with, perhaps, examination of probable offsetting efficiency gains.[134] In this view of the world, the business of antitrust is the prohibition of conduct that injures consumers through increases in allocative inefficiency,[135] conduct that without efficiency justification collectively or individually increases market power. Most of us would find this approach acceptable in some—indeed most—cases, but there is, I believe, an unease that has caused some either to retreat from, or advance beyond, Chicago. There is a sense of something gone wrong, of a dissatisfaction about antitrust based on the notion that consumers' welfare has not always served consumers well. Those who believe consumers have been well-served will give a large measure of credit, as they should, to Chicago.

Those who are not satisfied will put the blame squarely on Chicago. Either way, Chicago's influence is virtually conceded.

Most participating in this book are antitrust professionals. But I invite you for a moment to become consumers and ask whether Chicago's consumer welfare standard, assuming for the moment its strong influence on the law and with the lines of inquiry and modes of analysis based upon it that we use everyday, has served us well as buyers and sellers. Most, I suspect, would answer "yes," but with some caveats. If we are truly honest, some of us would admit to a certain uneasiness about antitrust in its present form, and perhaps a greater uneasiness about its future. This uneasiness underlies the publication of books like this one.

Is this uneasiness justified? Consider a few examples. How many of us bank today at a bank whose identity has changed at least twice in the past five years? In my case, identity changes have been sufficiently rapid that signage has, on occasion, been simply a name painted on canvas that is draped over signs having the previous name. My checks are two banks back. Do these rapid changes benefit me as a consumer? Am I benefited by having had one major airline connecting my home airport to most other destinations (an airline that has managed despite its position in the market to end up in bankruptcy)?[136] My ability to obtain the benefits of competition when I go out to purchase a major household appliance is dependent, I am told, on the further entry into the market by foreign firms that are not yet present on a significant scale.[137] AT&T, reconfigured as a result of government action, seems to have morphed back to its original form.[138] Major cruise lines are down to three.[139] Consumers in Chicago are hardly enthralled when they wake up and find that their beloved Marshall Field's is, heaven forbid, Macy's.[140] Ease of entry, both domestically and now internationally, has become the primary reason for nonintervention. As for me, a veteran of the airline deregulation battle, I hope never to hear the magic story of "contestable markets" again.[141] I am apparently getting too old, harking back to the days when choice meant "NOW." We all understand how in legal and economic terms these outcomes have come about. The explanations generally make sense. But surely we must wonder from time to time about what we have been doing for twenty or more years.

In none of these examples, influenced heavily by the teachings of the Chicago school, is the outcome itself necessarily anticompetitive. I do not mean to suggest that consumers are suffering. Bank mergers may indeed have brought efficiencies, and may have broken down regulatory barriers, to the benefit of consumers (But they have surely enhanced the length of telephone menus.) As a consumer, I may benefit from being at a major airline hub, even though choices may be limited. Entry actually may preserve choice for appliance purchasers. And maybe department stores are not a market. Stops at a dozen other stores in the mall actually may be an adequate substitute.[142] In short, antitrust outcomes in these instances, even if predicated on the views of the Chicago School, may in fact adequately protect consumers against output restrictions and price increases and, moreover, may, by simply keeping antitrust out of the marketplace, promote efficiencies, the achievement of which antitrust in the past directly thwarted. Even if particular outcomes do seem wrong in competitive terms, the basic theoretical structure may not be the cause; errors of fact and judgment do not necessarily impugn the theory being applied, albeit wrongly. Nevertheless, the unease has persisted. Thus, for example, even a judge as conversant with economics as Douglas Ginsburg said in the *Heinz-Beechnut* case that no court had ever permitted a merger to duopoly and pretty much let it go at that.[143] His unease led him to conclude that "enough is enough."

From the beginning, the views of the Chicago School have been severely criticized. The criticisms are familiar. Contrary to the views of Robert Bork[144] and others, the legislative history of the Sherman Act is not consistent with a single-minded focus on efficiency.[145] Chicago's focus on long-run effects fails to account for short-run strategizing conduct.[146] Too much reliance is placed on oversimplified and unrealistic economic models, with too little emphasis on actual market facts.[147] Entry is neither easy nor does entry check market power as Chicago theorists sometimes suggest. Efficiencies cannot be assumed to explain conduct absent some proof that they are or are likely to be real. There is some merit to each of these criticisms, some of which are further developed in this volume.

To the most vocal critics of "Conservative Economic Analysis," the Chicago School is akin to the "Grinch Who Stole Christmas," rejecting tradition and stealing away decades of antitrust development with a kind of single swoop down the mountain. The "Grinch" view assumes that it is the villains of the Chicago School alone who have done us in, taking us away from happier times in the antitrust valley. This kind of criticism has become muted over the years but has not disappeared altogether. The stoutest supporters of the Chicago School accept and indeed applaud Chicago's analysis, again assuming that it is the Chicago School alone that has brought the antitrust revolution of the last three decades. The critics have tended to place too much blame, and the proponents to take too much credit. Change has come, not from a single source, but from many, including Phillip Areeda, Bob Pitofsky, and Herb Hovenkamp, whose views are not always easily pigeonholed, but who have exerted a considerable influence along with those from Chicago.[148] Change has come in the best of legal methods, taking from one source, shaping it in light of another, and so on. If there is a Grinch at all, in other words, it is a collective Grinch, a Chicago-Harvard Grinch and perhaps a good Grinch besides.

With these introductory remarks, let me turn to an assessment of what the influence of the Chicago School has been. We would not be contributing to this book were it not considerable. The impact of the Chicago School began to be felt by the mid-1970s. This timing was not simply coincidental.

The antitrust of the fifties and sixties demanded change, and clearly change was going to be influenced by someone. It was simply waiting for the Grinch to take and never to be returned. Today, antitrust doctrine formulated by the Supreme Court in those days seems a kind of historical curiosity, an anachronism. To those of us involved with antitrust forty years ago, however, those decisions were the reality of antitrust. We had to deal with them every day, often in giving advice to disbelieving clients.

In assessing the influence of the Chicago School, we should start with a brief consideration of the antitrust that was its immediate target, a target that was not hard to hit and, so, a brief reminder of what a few may still view as the golden age of antitrust. Highly interventionist, concerned as much (or more) with the well-being of small entrepreneurs as with efficiency,[149] antitrust doctrine was a reflection of its times. At the end of World War II, the United States was the dominant economic power in the world. The industrial base of most of its rivals had been destroyed or at least severely injured. At home and abroad, U.S. firms were doing well. Employment rates were high. Pent-up demand drove rapidly expanding production. It was easy to ignore concerns over efficiency and to adopt policies focused on protecting and rewarding small enterprises. This highly interventionist antitrust policy was a luxury we could afford.

It was in this setting that the Supreme Court provided a series of decisions that set the stage for the rise of economic analysis in antitrust matters and, in particular, the economic analysis identified in Chicago. I remind you of just a few of these decisions. In *Topco,*[150] the Court's unwillingness to distinguish a joint venture from a cartel led to application of a *per se* rule where it was highly inappropriate. The *Griffith*[151] case with its ambiguously stated leveraging principle has caused difficulty for decades. A series of vertical cases—*Albrecht,*[152] *Simpson,*[153] *Schwinn,*[154] to name but a few—seemed to be based squarely on concerns over what might be called the "rights" of distributors. With these vertical decisions, dealer termination cases became a mainstay of antitrust litigation, continuing education programs were heavily focused on problems of distribution, and antitrust lawyers sent their children to college on distribution counseling fees. These vertical decisions were easy targets, to say the least. Merger decisions reached their high (or low, depending on one's point of view) with the decisions in *Von's Grocery,*[155] where the Court condemned a merger with a combined market share of 7.5 percent, and seemed preoccupied with the number of independents exiting the market (often by selling out to smaller chains). The Court's attitude appeared to be that the way to prevent exit was to close the exit door. Add to all this the Court's handling of the Robinson-Patman Act, making price discrimination among competing firms virtually a *per se* violation.[156] *Utah Pie*[157] came perilously close to doing the same with territorial price discrimination, protecting a local monopolist against the price reductions of new entrants. With the exception of the *Philadelphia Bank*[158] case, none of these decisions reflected what any of us today would characterize as economic analysis or anything even reasonably close to it. Antitrust of the time reflected an almost randomized mix of economic, social, and political values.

These substantive rulings were aided and abetted by a series of procedural rulings. The *Poller*[159] decision frowned on the use of summary judgment in antitrust cases, influencing lower courts for decades. Summary judgments were rarely granted. Proof of damages was made remarkably easy.[160] Coupled with substantive rulings, these and other procedural benefits brought a burgeoning of treble damage cases.

Virtually all of these decisions, so familiar to those of us around in the sixties and seventies, are gone.[161] Even the *Dr. Miles*[162] case—viewed today as establishing the oldest simple rule in all of antitrust, the *per se* rule against vertical price fixing—has now disappeared, even though most nations still adhere to a simple rule of illegality. The antitrust world of today consists largely of concerns over cartels and large horizontal mergers, with perhaps a few dominant firm and tying cases remaining. The *Trinko* case seems to state a preference for regulatory, as opposed to antitrust, solutions to market failures, even in competitive markets.[163] The argument that the antitrust laws other than section 1 of the Sherman Act should be repealed is no longer simply a debating point. We are nearly there already.

The thinking of the Chicago School has played a major role in these developments. Indeed, the emphasis on large mergers and cartels is, in large part, their antitrust policy. The targets were there. And the time was right. By the seventies, U.S. firms were losing their dominance in both foreign and domestic markets. The industrial facilities destroyed during World War II were rebuilt, and foreign competitors were increasingly aggressive. It was the time of the fear of Japan, Inc. There was a general gloom, emanating from the Carter White House on down. The great cry was the need for greater efficiency and less regulation in order to assure continuing U.S. market successes. An antitrust policy based on efficiency concerns fit these concerns almost perfectly. And the election of Ronald Reagan brought appointment of judges who placed heavy emphasis on free market solutions.[164]

Others using a less conceptual, more fact-oriented approach, scholars like Philip Areeda, Don Turner, Bob Pitofsky, and a number of others, were after many of the same targets. After all, decisions like *Utah Pie*,[165] and *Schwinn*[166] were not just criticized but ridiculed by virtually everyone.[167] Not all of this criticism rested on economics. Much of it did not. So in any attempt to measure the influence of conservative economics on the law, the role of others must also be recognized. Having said that, however, in my own view, in the last three decades the voices of Chicago have been the dominant influence in shaping antitrust. Chicago has even shaped the views of others who see themselves as apart from, or "beyond" Chicago, but have, consciously or subconsciously, incorporated much of Chicago's thinking into their own.

Chicagoans writing in the sixties were not immediately embraced. Critics were many and often severe. Some of these critics remain. An occasional small business advocate may still be found. Most of today's critics, however, recognize at least to some degree the influence Chicago has had and build upon it. The respect given Chicago may be grudging, but given the influence it has had, the power of its ideas must be taken as considerable.

How do we measure the influence Chicago has had in the development of antitrust? We could go case by case. Earlier, I referred to a number of Supreme Court decisions of the fifties, sixties, and seventies. None is good law today. Chicago economics can be seen directly or indirectly in virtually every decision overruling or sharply curtailing these earlier outcomes. We can see this influence in an array of Supreme Court and lower court opinions beginning with *Sylvania*[168] and continuing through *Leegin*.[169] In addition to these two, *BMI*,[170] *State Oil v. Khan*,[171] *Business Electronics*,[172] and a number of merger decisions[173] reflect this influence. But these decisions do not accept all of the specific positions advocated by Chicago. For example, vertical non-price and price restrictions may not be illegal *per se* after *Leegin*, but they are not *per se* legal. The highly conceptual Chicago-based argument in *Kodak*[174] was rejected. And all of these decisions are at least equally, if not more, consistent with the Areeda, Turner, Hovenkamp treatise, surely the most influential antitrust treatise of the past two decades.[175] The Court's expansive development of the state action doctrine, often allowing states to create exceptions to the antitrust laws, is surely not consistent with Chicago's strong antipathy to government regulation. *Trinko*'s embrace of a regulatory regime as preferable to the use of antitrust to deal with the conduct at issue in that case is hardly what we would expect from Chicago.[176] No one could claim, then, that Chicago has yet carried the day, and the advancements in economic analysis in the past two decades virtually assure that it will not. Post-Chicago is what it says it is, albeit after giving Chicago credit.

Courts normally do not make ex cathedra pronouncements. They are confined to specific matters before them. It is not likely, therefore, that over any given period of time they would even have the opportunity to deal with more than a small portion of Chicago's specific recommended outcomes. Judges continually change. New ideas will continue to come to the fore. It is hardly surprising, therefore, that we do not find in decided cases anything like a complete acceptance of Chicago's views.

Cataloguing decided cases is, in any event, a poor measure of Chicago's influence. It may indicate that these views have not been fully accepted, but that is hardly a basis for asserting that Chicago has, in the end, failed to exert any dramatic influence any more than a collection of particular cases dealing with discrete functional problems in a manner consistent with Chicago's views would demonstrate the opposite. Chicago's influence is best seen elsewhere.

The law develops in response to a large variety of sources, some formal and some informal. No one could doubt that the law as it has evolved under section 7 owes much of its present shape to the Merger Guidelines,

guidelines that have the clear imprint of the Chicago school.[177] Most of us today, when confronted with merger issues, turn almost instinctively to these guidelines. The treatment of entry as a trump card in the guidelines comes straight from the Chicago bible. (It is the same chapter of that bible that gave us the contestable markets analysis, i.e., the threat of entry will keep prices low, so critical to airline deregulation.) Indeed, the entire deregulation movement, driven by strong suspicion of government regulation and an equally strong faith in entry as the vehicle for keeping market power in check once regulatory regimes were removed, owes much to the Chicago School, as does the perception now virtually taken for granted that antitrust itself is a regulatory regime that imposes substantial costs in the form of false positives and a variety of other ways as well on the economy as a whole.

Chicago's influence is, of course, not confined to U.S. antitrust law. Through academic scholarship, available around the world, and through the voices of scholars and enforcement officials whose views over the years have been shaped in part by Chicago (whether they like to think so or not), those views have had a considerable impact on the shape of antitrust systems all around the globe.[178] Nor is Chicago's influence confined to antitrust. The laws of property, contracts, and torts, to use but a few examples, have all been influenced through the use of economic analysis, a development for which partial credit goes to Chicago, a major player in the earliest stages of the law and economics movement.[179]

Chicagoans have consistently asserted a simple, but remarkably expendable, set of ideas. As I said many years ago in a review of Richard Posner's 1976 volume of antitrust law, based on "a single minded concern with economic efficiency, as he defines it,"[180] Posner proposed a form of analysis and body of doctrine of striking structural symmetry and, in a sense of stark simplicity, a description that I believe is still accurate and goes a long way toward explaining Chicago's influence. I once compared Posner's analysis as akin to a great cathedral, a structure with every stone, every stained glass window, in the right place.[181] Just as one cannot build a cathedral with but some of its supporting stones, judges have had difficulty accepting some, but not all, of the Chicago analysis. Its completeness has been a major part of its appeal. This influence is found not in outcomes, although outcomes are not irrelevant, but in the shaping of thought and the setting of the parameters for debate. In the end, outcomes may not be those asserted by Chicago. But it is difficult today to find academic pieces, court decisions, and commentaries that do not, first, begin by accepting certain basic premises that are central to Chicago thinking, second, use at least some part of Chicago's methodology, and third, deal directly, even if by rejection, of Chicago's results. So while we have not seen total acceptance of the Chicago program, its real influence is found in how we think.

The combination of central assumptions and price theory methodology gave to the Chicago approach a kind of elegant ubiquity, providing either answers or a structure for analysis for virtually every antitrust issue. It provided judges, many of whom actually received Chicago-oriented economics training, an understandable structure that could by used at trial, or in an appellate opinion. Thus, short of a *per se* rule, plaintiffs must prove market power.[182] Defendants would win upon a showing of ease of entry. The framework provided an order to the judicial process that had been sorely lacking. Similarly, over a twenty year period, scholarly work has tended to accept certain core assumptions, and to accept much of the methodology of Chicago.[183]

What key assumptions of Chicago have achieved this kind of broad scale acceptance? First, and most obviously, antitrust is economic policy and is governed by the teachings of economics. Others, of course, take a similar position, but it was Chicago that hammered it home. Other concerns—fairness, the plight of small entrepreneurs, political and social power—become irrelevant in antitrust analysis. This "sole value" approach to antitrust is a given today, but to those of my day, the rejection of these other values was almost revolutionary in and of itself. Second, the sole concern of antitrust is not simply economics, but economic efficiency in both the allocative and productive senses. The shorthanding of this to "consumer welfare" has been a matter of controversy, but the core efficiency proposition is, I believe, today widely accepted. While somewhat less widely accepted, the proposition that competitive harm equates with adverse price and output effects has a wide judicial following. *Per se* rules ought apply only where there is no plausible efficiency justification for the conduct in any significant number of cases. Antitrust interventions should be confined to cases where there is a significant degree of market power. Freedom of entry is itself a virtual trump card. Vertical integration generally results in efficiency. Leveraging generally cannot bring about double monopoly profits. These are simple propositions that are now virtual givens in antitrust, so much so that one might wonder why they are even mentioned. Debate today is over possible exceptions to such basic propositions.[184] We are too far removed in time to realize how dramatic each of these propositions in the development of a rational antitrust policy and perhaps to credit them to anyone. But Chicagoans should be given their due before moving beyond.

Yet as I have noted, even given the general acceptance of many of its key assertions, *outcomes* have not always been in accord with Chicago analysis. This is, I believe, largely because of what is perceived as a disparity between Chicago's model and provable facts, as in *Kodak*,[185] or because Chicago's emphasis on the long term seems to ignore demonstrable competitive damage measured in far shorter time frames. It is one thing to assert that free entry is a trump card. It is quite another to assume that absent one of but a few possible barriers, free entry will, in fact, occur. Entry as a matter of faith can go only so far. The unease to which I referred earlier is often a concern that predicted entry will not occur. To reject antitrust intervention because of a high risk of false positives, when the analysis of those false positives seems to be little more than theoretical explanation, is not satisfying. It is in the move from general theory to particular outcomes that Chicago has been less successful. When firms do not seem to maximize profits as Chicago theory assumes, we are at a loss to know how to respond. Moreover, judges, particularly conservative judges, are both by training and temperament cautious in their approach to legal issues. Thus, while Chicago would posit that certain conduct (e.g., vertical non-price restrictions) should be *per se* legal, a judge usually has no need to make such a pronouncement. And to simply throw a case into the rule of reason is safe, leaving an out in the rare case where basic assumptions prove wrong.

Chicago seems to have had peculiarly little success in dealing with issues relating to the antitrust-regulation interface and antitrust exemptions. One would expect strong opposition from Chicagoans to an expansive state action doctrine, a doctrine that shields the very kind of market power that in their mind is the most pernicious, namely, that created or protected by government. It is in such markets that entry is least likely to occur. Similarly, as a general rule, Chicagoans would prefer that economic regulation be avoided, even if the price is the potential intervention of antitrust (hopefully in a manner consistent with their approach to antitrust). But at least in the Supreme Court the trends have been precisely the opposite. Decisions like *Southern Motor Carriers* and *Omni* have been expansive, shielding a variety of anticompetitive state regimes from antitrust scrutiny.[186] This, of course, is an example of conflict between two very broad sets of principles: the free market consumer welfare approach to antitrust, on the one hand, and the high value placed in recent years on principles of federalism, on the other. There are cases, in other words, where antitrust is trumped by some other policy. The *Noerr* doctrine[187] has likewise been enlarged over the years to the point where, for example, litigation can be used to harass a rival with virtual impunity.[188] Yet Robert Bork, for one, cautioned about the damage that misuse of government processes by a competitor can inflict and urged the use of antitrust as a corrective to such misuse.[189] And where the traditional Chicago view would prefer a free market rather than a regulatory solution unless there is little choice otherwise, the Court in *Trinko* moved in precisely the opposite direction. The regulatory regime was clearly relevant in the case, but it was embraced with a warmth that was surprising, while at the same time antitrust was described as a system with "sometimes considerable disadvantages," with high costs in the form of false positives about which the Court seemed quite prepared to speculate.[190] I doubt that a real Chicagoan would have treated the regulatory regime with such enthusiasm.

These cases—state action, *Noerr*, the antitrust regulatory interface— bring antitrust directly into conflict with other social and political values. Chicago's influence in these areas has been limited. The neat, clean, and systematic Chicago approach to antitrust has fared poorly in the muddy waters of federalism and First Amendment values. Nor has it had a significant effect in the legislative arena where antitrust policy is at issue (except, perhaps, during debates over varying deregulation efforts). Chicagoans, for example deplore the Robinson-Patman Act (as do most of us). Proposals to modify or repeal the Act have been made repeatedly.[191] Yet arguments that consumer welfare is ill-served by that Act have fallen on deaf ears in the halls of Congress. Proponents of repeal of Robinson-Patman have encountered the political reality that a powerful set of economic interests values wants policies other than "consumer welfare." I think we may see an even more graphic example coming. Although the *per se* rule against vertical price fixing had existed for 96 years without direct congressional rejection, and the Court in 1977 itself recognized that Congress intended that a *per se* rule be applied; the Supreme Court in *Leegin* overruled *Dr. Miles,* subjecting all vertical price fixing cases to the rule of reason,[192] a result not fully in accord with Chicago, but one they surely would applaud. Legislation to overturn *Leegin* and return to the *per se* rule of *Dr. Miles* is likely to be introduced in the Congress, where there is surely a significant possibility it will pass.

This is not a particularly bold prediction. The Supreme Court in *Sylvania* after all virtually predicted the same thing when it recognized Congress's intent in repealing the Miller-Tydings and McGuire amendments.[193] But if this prediction fails, most of our states are likely to preserve the *per se* rule as a matter of state law giving us what may be the worst of all worlds, a lack of uniformity throughout the country.

Chicago analysis has fared less well in the political and legislative arenas than in court and at the enforcement agencies. It has far greater appeal to antitrust professionals than to the public at large. Chicagoans have traditionally urged that antitrust be confined to economic efficiency concerns in part because a more multivalued approach improperly would require courts to make political decisions, a perversion of their role. But when antitrust is at issue in more obviously political arenas, there has been little sentiment to confine antitrust to efficiency effects. The public at large seems more in accord with antitrust of the sixties than that of today, a fact that often is reflected in congressional hearings and poses significant difficulty in bringing legislative, administrative, and judicial outcomes into a unified whole.

Conclusion

It seems highly unlikely that antitrust would look as it does today without the influence of the Chicago School. Neither the courts nor the Congress has accepted all of the outcomes that would follow from rigorous application of Chicago analysis. But without regard to specific outcomes, Chicago provided the most significant building block in the reshaping of antitrust from the mid-seventies until the present time. Schools of thought have come and gone in the antitrust world. But Chicago has been more significant and dominating in the development of the law than any of the rest. This is partially because Chicago did not simply build on what had gone on before. It virtually destroyed existing doctrine and, in a sense, built upon its ashes. Today analysis almost always begins with Chicago. Chicago must get much of the credit (and much of the blame) for antitrust as it exists today. Its influence has been generally positive, focusing attention on economic analysis, recognizing the costs of a body of antitrust rules gone astray and providing a rigorous analysis that has eliminated many of the inefficiencies imposed by prior antitrust regimes.

Yet there is a dissatisfaction with Chicago analysis. The structure is rigid, the assumptions, most of which are generally accepted, cannot cover all the cases that Chicago would have us cover. The Chicago School is in a sense too perfect, too comprehensive, to always be in accord with reality. And some of us wonder whether, bound as we are to the rigors of Chicago's intellectual analysis, antitrust is missing the forest for the trees. Do we honestly believe that American Airlines' conduct in Dallas, inviting Braniff to engage in price fixing, was not anticompetitive? Are we satisfied with performance of our banks when they have gone through three or four mutations in a decade? I, for one, am uneasy, both over past outcomes and over antitrust's future. There simply may not be much left. And that, of course, is exactly as at least some Chicagoans would have it.

On the Foundations of Antitrust Law and Economics

Daniel L. Rubinfeld

Introduction

There has been considerable debate about two related but distinct questions. First, to what extent has "conservative economics" influenced developments in the law? Second, to what extent, if any, has the influence of conservative economics influenced the public and private enforcement of the antitrust laws? I will comment briefly on the latter, but my energy will be focused on the former.

There is no clear understanding in the economics profession as to what defines conservative economics, and indeed no one individual whose perspective would necessarily be seen as inherently conservative. However, for purposes of this commentary I will presume that conservative economics is built on the following: (1) a substantial faith in the workings of the market; (2) a lack of confidence in the ability of government to successfully intervene to remedy perceived market failures; and, (3) a belief that the antitrust laws should emphasize economic efficiency (for some this means an emphasis on the welfare of producers as well as consumers), and not the interests of particular subgroups of the population (e.g., small businesses). For many, but not all, who support this perspective, aggressive intervention in cases involving price-fixing and market allocation is warranted, whereas vertical non-price restraints (e.g., exclusionary relationships with dealers) are seen as likely to be procompetitive, and attempts to target monopolizing behavior are likely to fail.

In the comments that follow, I suggest that while the influence of industrial organization economics has grown substantially over time, it would be overly simplistic to characterize that influence as having been driven solely by a group of conservative antitrust legal and/or economic scholars. I explain further that differences among antitrust economists are as likely due to the fact economists hold a range of views as to the meaning of economic efficiency, and they differ significantly in their beliefs as to the likely efficacy of government intervention. In section I, I begin with an overview of the history of antitrust policy.[194] In the process I explain how important precedents in the law have followed, albeit with a substantial lag, important developments in the economics of industrial organization that serve as important underpinnings of the law. In section II, I explain why and how economists' views of antitrust policy differ, and I make it clear how and why conservative economics has overshot the mark to some degree.

To summarize my views briefly: the influence of conservative economics has been substantial, and to a large extent positive. The state of knowledge with respect to the economic analysis of antitrust is much further along today than it was two or three decades ago. Nevertheless, conservative economics has overshot the mark in a number of ways. It has worried more about false positives (bringing the wrong case) than false negatives (failing to bring the right case). It has been too quick to dispense with troubling vertical issues (both price and non-price restraints). And, it has fostered a tendency to downplay enforcement in dynamic technological industries in which innovation issues play a significant role.

I. The Evolution of Antitrust Policy

As an empirically oriented antitrust law and economics scholar, I find it useful on occasion to think of antitrust enforcement from an empirical time-series perspective. Thinking in this vein, it is fruitful to distinguish phenomena such as private and public antitrust enforcement, that is (1) seasonal (e.g., an increase in mergers just prior to Christmas—with the hope that the enforcement agencies would prefer to enjoy the holiday season rather than investigate a merger); (2) driven by the political business cycle (e.g., whether the sitting president is a Republican or Democrat), and (3) is affected by long-run structural changes in the economy and/or in economic thinking.

Seasonable enforcement patterns appear to be apolitical—they occur in both Republican and Democratic administrations. Take merger policy as an example. Wherever the line that a particular enforcement authority is perceived to have drawn between anticompetitive actions and actions that are not anticompetitive (or not enforceable), merger parties are likely to take into account the effect of the timing of their arrangement on the likelihood of success. The role that Chicago School conservative economics has played in driving the enforcement political cycle is one that has been hotly debated and is covered in the Baker and Shapiro article in this volume (see chapter 6). Consequently, I will leave it to others to engage in that discussion. In this commentary, I focus solely on longer-run structural changes in antitrust perspectives by the courts and by the enforcement agencies.

My sense of history is that the development of the economics of industrial organization has had a substantial affect on antitrust law and antitrust enforcement, but with a substantial lag of at least one decade and perhaps as much as two. Looking back historically, some might recall the normative analysis of the 1950s and the 1960s—a period in which the government agencies were aggressively interventionist. Economists emphasized that antitrust analyses should begin with a specification of the structure of the industry (monopoly, oligopoly, competitive market, etc.). Given a particular structure, the analysis would then move to an evaluation of the conduct of the firms in the industry, and the implications of that conduct for the economy as a whole (hence the characterization of the paradigm as "structure-conduct-performance").

The early influence of industrial organization economics was clearly not conservative, having been driven by the work of Joe Bain and others. At the core of Bain's relatively interventionist philosophy was the view that barriers to entry are often high and can be manipulated by dominant incumbent firms, and that supracompetitive monopolistic pricing is relatively prevalent. The influence of this structure-conduct-performance approach to antitrust was felt in a host of court decisions, many of which stand today.

In this early part of this era, industrial organization economists tended to see firms as shaped by their technology. As a result, practices that changed the boundaries of the firm (e.g., joint ventures) were often seen as suspect. Because the government was viewed as benign, antitrust enforcers tended to look at mergers and acquisitions with a highly critical eye. While some opinions[195] are viewed favorably by most analysts today, others that did not appear to seriously evaluate the tradeoffs between efficiencies and the potential for anticompetitive harm or put too much weight on the need to preserve small business are not.[196]

Again, consistent with past economic learning, the government has tended to take a hard look at practices of firms competing in differentiated product oligopolies. Interestingly, the possibility that exclusive dealing might be procompetitive was not given serious consideration during the 1950s and 1960s. Moreover, the economic analysis of price discrimination was not fully developed at this time. It is not surprising, therefore, that antitrust enforcers failed to appreciate the potential benefits of differential treatment (or, as some would see it, discriminatory practices) in their enforcement of the Robinson-Patman Act ,which spells out specific conditions under which price discrimination is illegal, as well as potential cost and competitive response defenses to the presumption of illegality. Views about such practices are widely different today. I attribute this not to the influence of conservative economics, but to the substantial economic learning (in the past two decades) with respect to the behavior of firms in differentiated products markets.

The late-1960s and 1970s marked a period of substantial analysis in antitrust, motivated by structural considerations. Here, the tension between conservative economics and others was in evidence. The empirical literature on profit rates and industry structure initially showed a weak positive correlation, suggesting that high concentration was likely to be the source of anticompetitive firm behavior.[197] However, this interpretation was hotly debated by Demsetz—clearly a Chicago School protégé—among others.[198] Demsetz argued that concentration was a consequence of economies of scale and the growth of more efficient firms, and that the empirical work just cited suffered from confusion about causality. Absent more detailed analyses, one could not distinguish the possibility that high concentration led to higher prices and profitability, from the alternative possibility that high profits were the result of economies of scale, which was associated with lower costs, larger firms, and more concentrated industries. If concentrated markets led to higher industry profits, these profits were the consequence and not the cause of the superior efficiency of large firms and consistent with competitive behavior. Today, our knowledge has progressed—we view the early studies as flawed, since they omitted variables that account for research and development, advertising, and economies of scale. However, contrary to the views of Demsetz, most observers believe that there is a positive correlation between market share and profitability, representing the effects of market power in some cases, and economic efficiency in others.

All of the assumptions that underlie the tradition of the 1950s and 1960s were criticized in the 1970s, led in part by the influence of the Chicago School.[199] Those views, which relied heavily on new learning in industrial organization economics, were seen by many (but not necessarily all) to include the following beliefs: (1) Efficiencies associated with economies of scale and scope are of primary importance; (2) Most markets are competitive, including many in which relatively few firms are competing; (3) Monopoly power is not likely to be durable, since supra-competitive profits will induce entry; (4) Barriers to entry (excepting those that are government created) are likely to be less significant than previously thought; (5) Monopoly leveraging (e.g., conditioning the purchase of one "tying product" on the purchase of another "tied product") is not a sensible strategy, since there is a "single monopoly rent," i.e., the monopoly profits generated through the sale of the tying product will be such that there are no additional profits to be enjoyed through a tying strategy; and (6) Antitrust enforcement is only appropriate if there is a substantial likelihood that it will increase social welfare.

It is not surprising, given the views of the 1970s, that many contractual practices that had been seen as anticompetitive were often seen as serving legitimate economics purposes. The Court's decision to strike down a *per se* rule limiting exclusive distribution arrangements offers a reasonable characterization of the sentiment of the Supreme Court at that time.[200] Indeed, if the Chicago School view had prevailed, such a range of vertical non-price restraints would have been deemed to be per se legal.

One might be tempted to conclude that the influence of the Chicago School has continued in unabated form to the present, with recent decisions being credited as driven entirely by those under the influence of the Chicago views just outlined.[201] From my perspective, such a characterization would be improper. It is noteworthy that many non-Chicago economists supported the move to a rule of reason based on a combination of theoretical argument and empirical evidence. Furthermore, as Einer Elhauge has recently sketched out in some detail, recent Court decisions were influenced by a wide range of scholars, many with no ties to the Chicago School.[202] The reality is that there were significant improvements in our understanding of industrial organization economics from the 1970s through the 1990s, which focused on strategic behavior rather than market structure. This new post-Chicago School perspective should be given substantial credit for its influence on courts and on the competition authorities.

The post-Chicago School approach uses game theory to examine the ways in which established firms behave strategically in relation to actual and potential rivals. The distinction between credible and noncredible threats, absent from the Chicago School literature, became important in the assessment of the ability of established firms to exclude competitors and in the evaluation of exclusionary conduct and its implications for social welfare.[203] Among other things, these theories illuminated a broader scope for predatory pricing and predatory behavior. Non-price competitive strategies that raise rivals' costs[204] are now thought by many to be quite prevalent. Indeed, a number of models of the dynamic strategic behavior of firms highlight the ability and opportunity for firms with substantial market power to engage in coordinated actions and to profit from conduct that excludes rivals.[205]

The implications of the analyses of strategic behavior continue to be hotly debated by antitrust economists and attorneys. Whatever one's particular view about these issues, however, it would be overly simplistic to view current debates as solely involving the "Chicago School" on one side and the "post-Chicago School" on the other. Consider the following two examples. First, Franklin Fisher offers a highly critical view of the power of the game-theoretic strategic models,[206] while Carl Shapiro is more supportive.[207] Neither is in any way tied to the Chicago School. Second, Ronald Coase, an important Chicago School participant, explained that nonmarket organizations could provide a viable alternative means of organizing market activities.[208] Oliver Williamson, on the other hand, has shown from a non-Chicago transactions cost perspective that contractual restraints can improve incentives for beneficial investments in human and physical assets.[209]

In the past twenty or thirty years, rapid changes in technology have altered the nature of competition in many markets. While earlier debates centered on the supply side and economies of scale, in many dynamic high technology industries, the demand side gets most of the attention. Demand rather than supply can be the source of substantial consumer benefits as well as significant market power. As a result, debate has centered on the importance of demand-side economies of scale arising from network effects (which are present when the individuals' demand for products increase as more and more consumers are seen to utilize the products—the success of Microsoft Word is a prime example), and on the implications of scale for firms' incentives to innovate.

Because network industries such as those relating to computer software and hardware are often characterized by large sunk costs and low marginal costs, it is likely that successful firms will come to dominate markets and to persist in that dominance for a substantial period of time. While there is no assurance that a single standard will arise in network industries, it is often the case that users will move toward comparable products. The associated efficiencies have been emphasized by many with a conservative economics perspective, while others have raised the concern that the resulting increase in concentration might lead firms to adopt price and non-price policies that exclude competition, reduce, innovation, and raise prices to supracompetitive levels.[210]

Today, a more balanced normative approach to antitrust would take into account the broad set of efficiencies associated with various organizational forms and contractual relations, as well as the possibilities for anticompetitive strategic behavior in markets with or without dominant firms. It would also be open to the possibility of early intervention in dynamic industries in which innovation plays an important role.

II. Why Economists Differ

As we move through the first decade of the new millennium, we continue to see a variety of economists' perspectives on antitrust law and its enforcement. In this section, I briefly highlight a few of the key differences among economists. First, there remain differences as to whether economic efficiency should be the sole norm in antitrust or whether efficiency should be balanced against other norms such as consumer welfare and/or the promotion of small business. One interesting debate surrounding norms arises with respect to daily newspaper joint ventures and acquisitions. Allen Grunes and Maurice Stuckey, both writing at the time as attorneys in the antitrust division, argue that editorial diversity is an important and distinct norm that should be highly valued in newspaper transactions.[211] The parties to transactions typically argue that editorial diversity should not be part of a Clayton Act, section 7 analysis.

Second, there remain differences in economists' views of the ability of courts to sort out complex legal and economic questions and the ability of the antitrust authorities to successful undertake and complete investigations accurately and in a timely manner. This is particularly the case when investigations involve dynamic network industries. One such surrounds the Antitrust Division's case, *U.S. v. Microsoft*.[212] Fisher and Rubinfeld support active intervention in this case, in part because of the significance of innovation in computer software.[213] Evans and Schmalensee argue against the case, claiming in part that intervention is unnecessary in a world of dynamic Schumpeterian competition.[214]

Third, there remain differences as to the importance of economic theory and empirical regularities—some economists place more weight on the former and some on the latter. The *Leegin* case described previously (moving vertical minimum price-fixing from *per se* to *rule of reason*) offers a prime example. A number of economists who support the decision believe as a matter of economic theory that the incentive to engage in free riding is so powerful that even a rule of reason approach to vertical minimum price-fixing goes too far (they would support per se legality). However, many economists who oppose the decision believe that there is substantial empirical evidence supporting the anticompetitive use of vertical price restrictions.

Fourth, differences remain as to the ability to the authorities and the courts to successful enforce the antitrust laws in complex cases. For those that support a reduced enforcement effort, cases are that brought by the agencies and lost in the courts are seen as evidence of overenforcement. For those who more aggressively support enforcement, a primary concern lies with the failure to bring cases against firms that are violating the antitrust laws.

My own reading of recent developments is that while conservative economics has added much to our understanding of antitrust law and economics, it has to some extent overshot the mark. As I noted earlier, I am troubled that the concern about false positives (bringing inappropriate cases) has tended to trump worries about false negatives (failing to bring appropriate cases). Losing cases or cases that are seen as inappropriate often come under visible attack, whereas one has to listen carefully to hear about cases that should be been pursued that were not. Furthermore, the move to dispense with difficult vertical issues (price and non-price restraints) may be too forceful. While many economists see great value in the use of rule of reason in the evaluation of vertical restraints, it is important to acknowledge that some restraints may on balance be anticompetitive. Per se legality is not where antitrust should be located. Finally, conservative economics has fostered a tendency to downplay enforcement in dynamic technological industries in which innovation issues play a significant role.

The economics of innovation is no doubt quite difficult, and our empirical knowledge is limited. However, innovation is too important for antitrust to use the limits of our knowledge as an excuse for failing to take action in appropriate cases.

Conclusion

If one were to take a poll of economists as to their positions on the issues I have just raised, I have no doubt that one would find a wide range of responses and a substantially less-than-perfect correlation between those responses and the association of surveyed individuals to the Chicago School. Recent decisions by the Supreme Court notwithstanding, the long-run evolution of the antitrust laws and antitrust enforcement is heavily driven (with a lag) by antitrust economics. That is not to say, however, that politics does not matter. One's views as to the likely success of particular types of antitrust enforcement may well differ over the political business cycle.

Notes

1. Two prominent examples are *Brown Shoe Co.* v. *United States,* 370 U.S. 294 (1962) and *United States* v. *Vons Grocery Co.,* 384 U.S. 270 (1966).

2. *See* Richard Schmalensee: *Thoughts on the Chicago Legacy in Antitrust, infra* Chapter 1 at 21–22.

3. J. McGee, *Commentary, in* INDUSTRIAL CONCENTRATION: THE NEW LEARNING, 104 (H. Goldschmid, H. M. Mann, & J. F. Weston, eds. Boston: Little-Brown, 1974).

4. F. M. Scherer, et al., PATENTS AND THE CORPORATION, 2d. ed., privately published (Boston 1959).

5. Robert H. Bork, THE ANTITRUST PARADOX: A POLICY AT WAR WITH ITSELF (Basic Books 1978). As its preface makes clear, most of the work on this book was done in the late 1960s and early 1970s.

6. Despite the usage of "conservative" in recent U.S. political discourse, it seems to me an inappropriate label for those seeking fundamental change, and the Chicago School did seek fundamental change in antitrust policy. Moreover, because of recent U.S. political discourse, "Chicago" carries much less emotional baggage than "conservative." On the Chicago School generally, *see* Edmund W. Kitch, *The Fire of Truth: A Remembrance of Law and Economics at Chicago: 1932–70,* 26 J. L. & ECON. 163 (1983).

7. Richard A. Posner, ANTITRUST LAW (Chicago: University of Chicago Press, 1976).

8. *Brown Shoe Co. v. United States,* 370 U.S. 294, 344 (1962).

9. *See, e.g.,* Bork, *supra* note 5, chs. 2 and 3, and Posner, *supra* note 7, ch. 2.

10. *United States v. Von's Grocery Co.,* 384 U.S. 270 (1966).

11. Ken Heyer, *Welfare Standards and Merger Analsysis: Why Not the Best?*, 2 COMP. POL. INTL. 29 (2006).

12. *Compare* Ken Heyer, *Id., with* Joseph Farrell and Michael L. Katz, *The Economics of Welfare Standards in Antitrust*, 2 COMP. POL. INTL. 3 (2006). For an interesting recent discussion, *see* Dennis W. Carlton, *Does Antitrust Need to be Modernized?*, 21 J. ECON. PERSPECTIVES 155 (2007).

13. *See* Richard Schmalensee, *Sunk Costs and Antitrust Barriers to Entry*, 94 AMER. ECON. REV. PAP. & PROC. 471 (2004).

14. *See* Richard Posner, *The Chicago School of Antitrust Analysis*, 127 U. PA. L. REV. 925 (1979).

15. *Utah Pie Co. v. Continental Baking Co.*, 386 U.S. 685 (1967).

16. Bork, *supra* note 6, at 387.

17. The Antitrust Modernization Commission has recently called for its repeal. *See* Antitrust Modernization Commission, *Report and Recommendations*, Washington, D.C.: April 2007.

18. Carl Kaysen & Donald F. Turner, ANTITRUST POLICY (Cambridge: Harvard University Press, 1959), at 265–272.

19. *Report, Comments, and Separate Statements,* reprinted in 2 ANTITRUST L. & ECON. REV. 11 (Winter 1968–69). Dean Neal's affiliation makes it clear that "Chicago" is an imperfect label.

20. S. 3832, 92nd Congress, 2nd Session (1972) and S. 1167, 93rd Congress, 1st Session (1973). For discussion, *see* INDUSTRIAL CONCENTRATION: THE NEW LEARNING (H. Goldschmid, H. M. Mann, & J. F. Weston, eds.; Boston: Little-Brown, 1974).

21. The citation was to George J. Stigler, *A Theory of Oligopoly*, 72 J. POLIT. ECON. 44 (1964).

22. *See, e.g.,* Kitch, *supra* note 6.

23. For a survey of this literature, *see* Richard Schmalensee, *Inter-Industry Studies of Structure and Performance, in* HANDBOOK OF INDUSTRIAL ORGANIZATION, VOL. 2 951 (R. Schmalensee & R. D. Willig, eds.; Amsterdam: North-Holland, 1989).

24. Harold Demsetz, *Industry Structure, Market Rivalry, and Public Policy,* 16 J. L. & ECON. 1 (1973), and *Two Systems of Belief about Monopoly, in* Goldschmidt, Mann, & Weston, eds., *supra* note 21.

25. This turns out not to be easy to assess; *see* Richard Schmalensee, *Intra-Industry Profitability Differences in U.S. Manufacturing: 1953–1983,* 37 J. IND. ECON. 337 (1989).

26. Bork, *supra* note 5, at 105.

27. George J. Stigler, *The Economies of Scale,* 1 J. L. ECON. 54 (1958).

28. For an excellent overview, see Nancy Beaulieu, Robert Gibbons, and Rebecca Henderson, *Microeconomic Evidence of Persistent Performance Differences among Seemingly Similar Enterprises,* working paper, MIT Sloan School of Management, April 2007.

29. *United States v. Aluminum Co. of America,* 148 F.2d 416 (2d Cir. 1945).

30. *Id.* at 431.

31. *Federal Trade Commission v. Procter & Gamble Co.,* 386 U.S. 568 (1967). The merger was also condemned on that grounds that it would have removed P&G as a potential entrant into the liquid bleach market. It may

be worth noting that in the subsequent 40 years, P&G has not entered that market.

32. *Id.* at 580.

33. 1 CCH Trade Reg. Rep. ¶ 4430 (1968).

34. Section 4, p. 31, as revised April 8, 1997.

35. *Compare* Oliver E. Williamson, *Economies as an Antitrust Defense: The Welfare Trade-off,* 58 AMER. ECON. REV. 18 (1968), *with* Bork, *supra* note 6, at 124–9 and Posner, *supra* note 8, at 112–3.

36. An influential study was David J. Ravenscraft & Frederic M. Scherer, MERGERS, SELL-OFFS, AND ECONOMIC EFFICIENCY (Washington: Brookings, 1987).

37. The source usually cited for this quotation is Stanley Robinson, NEW YORK STATE BAR ASSOCIATION, ANTITRUST SYMPOSIUM, 1968, 29.

38. Aaron Director and Edward H. Levi, *Law and the Future: Trade Regulation,* 51 Nw. U. L. REV. 281 (1956).

39. *See, e.g.,* Bork, *supra* note 5, ch. 21.

40. *See, e.g.,* Antonio Cucinotta et al., eds., POST-CHICAGO DEVELOPMENTS IN ANTITRUST LAW (Edward Elgar 2003).

41. *See* Jordi Gual et al., *An Economic Approach to Article 82,* 2 COMP. POL. INTL. 111 (2006).

42. *United States v. Sealy, Inc.,* 388 U.S. 350 (1967).

43. *United States v. Topco Associates, Inc.,* 405 U.S. 596 (1972).

44. *Id.* at 608.

45. Bork, *supra* note 5, at 278.

46. *Broadcast Music, Inc. v. Columbia Broadcasting System, Inc.,* 441 U.S. 1 (1979).

47. Washington, D.C., April 2000, section 3.2

48. *Brown Shoe,* 370 U.S. at 328–29.

49. This sort of "foreclosure" does reduce the demand for the output of other manufacturers—while also reducing the supply with which they compete by an exactly equal amount. For more problems with "foreclosure" theory, see Bork, *supra* note 5, at 211–14.

50. The Non-Horizontal Merger Guidelines were initially issued as part of *U.S. Department of Justice Merger Guidelines, June 14, 1984.* The Non-Horizontal Merger Guidelines are available online at http://www.usdoj.gov/atr/public/guidelines/2614.htm.

51. *United States v. Arnold Schwinn & Co.,* 388 U.S. 365.

52. *Continental T.V., Inc. v. GTE Sylvania, Inc.,* 433 U.S. 36 (1977).

53. *Dr. Miles Medical Co. v. John D. Park & Sons Co.,* 220 U.S. 373 (1911).

54. *Albrecht v. Herald Co.,* 390 U.S. 145 (1968).

55. For a recent summary by a broad collection of economists, *see* Brief of Amici Curiae Economists in Support of Petitioner, *Leegin Creative Leather Products, Inc. v. PSKS, Inc.,* (S. Ct. 2007) (No. 06–480).

56. *State Oil v. Khan,* 527 U.S. 3 (1997).

57. *Leegin Creative Leather Products, Inc. v. PSKS, Inc.,* 127 S.Ct. 2705 (June 28, 2007).

58. *See* Bork, *supra* note 5, at 406.

59. *Standard Oil of California and Standard Stations, Inc. v. United States,* 337 U.S. 293, 305 (1949); Bork, *supra* note 6, at 367.

60. Ward S. Bowman, Jr., *Tying Arrangements and the Leverage Problem*, 67 YALE L.J. 19 (1957). On recent theoretical work, see Dennis W. Carlton & Michael Waldman, *The Strategic Use of Tying to Preserve and Create Market Power in Evolving Industries*, 33 RAND J. ECON. 194 (2002).

61. *Fortner Enterprises v. United States Steel Corp.*, 394 U.S. 495 (1969); Bork, *supra* note 6, at 210.

62. *Jefferson Parish Hospital District No. 2 v. Hyde*, 466 U.S. 2 (1984)

63. *Id.* at 14.

64. *See, e.g.*, David S. Evans & Richard Schmalensee, *Some Aspects of Antitrust Analysis in Dynamically Competitive Industries, in* INNOVATION POLICY AND THE ECONOMY, VOL. 2 (A. Jaffee, J. Lerner, & S. Stern, eds.; Cambridge: MIT Press, 2002) 1, 28–31, and the references there cited.

65. Bork, *supra* note 5, at 406.

66. Posner, *supra* note 7, at 212. On the other hand, Posner did propose to use section 1 to prosecute tacit collusion. *Id.* at 71.

67. *See* Herbert Hovenkamp, THE HARVARD AND CHICAGO SCHOOLS AND THE DOMINANT FIRM, *infra* chapter 3.

68. The best statement of this position is in Robert H. Bork, THE ANTITRUST PARADOX: A POLICY AT WAR WITH ITSELF (New York: The Free Press, 1993).

69. *See Brooke Group v. Brown & Williamson Tobacco*, 509 U.S. 209 (1993).

70. John Vickers, "Abuse of Market Power," 20, notes that a dominant firm can raise rivals' costs—unduly deny scale economies to rivals—by offering price reductions that are "*conditional* on the buyer not dealing with rivals."

71. For a discussion of the anti-antitrust attitude expressed in *Trinko*, see Harvey Goldschmid, *Comment on Herbert Hovenkamp and the Dominant Firm: The Chicago School Has Made Us Too Cautious About False Positives and the Use of Section 2 of the Sherman Act, infra* Chapter 3.

72. On Director's influence, *see* Stephen Stigler, *Aaron Director Remembered*, and Sam Peltzman, *Aaron Director's Influence on Antitrust Policy*, 48 J. L. & ECON. 307–330 (October 2005). In the preface to his book, THE ANTITRUST PARADOX, ix (Basic Books: 1978), Robert Bork acknowledges the decisive role Director played in Bork's education and says that Director "has long seemed to me, as he has to many others, the seminal thinker in antitrust economics and industrial organization." Director was in residence at the University of Chicago from 1947 to 1965.

73. *See* Friedrich A. Hayek, THE ROAD TO SERFDOM (University of Chicago Press: 1944).

74. Henry C. Simons, *The Requisites of Free Competition*, 26 AM. ECON. REV.103–4 (supplement), March 1936. *See also* his ECONOMIC POLICY FOR A FREE SOCIETY, 52–9 (University of Chicago Press: 1948).

75. Report of the White House Task Force on Antitrust Policy, July 5, 1968. The text of the task force's proposed legislation is reproduced in INDUSTRIAL CONCENTRATION: THE NEW LEARNING, 449–456 (Harvey J. Goldschmid, H. Michael Mann, & J. Fred Weston, eds., Boston: Little Brown: 1974). A commentary by Dean Neal appears in the same volume at 377–383.

76. Richard A. Posner, ANTITRUST POLICY (University of Chicago Press: 1976), Chapter 4. *See also* Posner, *Oligopoly and the Antitrust Laws: A Suggested Approach*, 21 STANFORD L. REV.1562–1606 (June 1969).

77. John S. McGee, *Compound Pricing,* 25 Econ. Inquiry 315–339 (April 1987).

78. Peltzman, *supra* note 69 at 325.

79. John McGee, *Predatory Price Cutting: The Standard Oil (N.J.) Case,* 1 J. L. & Econ.137–169 (October 1958). *See also* McGee, *Predatory Pricing Revisited,* 23 J. L. & Econ. 289–330 (October 1980); and Lester G. Telser (another Chicagoan), *Cutthroat Competition and the Long Purse,* 9 J. L. & Econ. 259–277 (October 1966).

80. *Matushita Electric Industrial Corp. Ltd. et al. v. Zenith Radio Corp. et al.,* 475 U.S. 574, 589 (1986). The Court cites McGee and also Robert Bork, *supra* note 69. Bork in turn at the page of his book cited by the Court gives pride of place to McGee.

81. *See* the literature review in my text, F. M. Scherer, Industrial Market Structure and Economic Performance, 2d ed., 336–340 (Chicago: Rand McNally, 1980); David Kreps & Robert Wilson, *Reputation and Imperfect Information,* 27 J. Econ. Theory 253–279 (August 1982); and Paul Milgrom & John Roberts (not the Supreme Court Chief Justice), *Predation, Reputation, and Entry Deterrence,* 27 J. Econ.Theory 280–312 (August 1982).

82. The facts in *Matsushita* were indeed compelling. I was present at oral arguments before the Supreme Court. Although such inferences are often wrong, I believed a majority would rule for Matsushita when I heard Justice Thurgood Marshall ask counsel for Zenith, "And how was the consumer affected by the protracted low prices?" Shortly thereafter I invited a leading spear-carrier from each side of the case to present their arguments before my seminar on Japanese industrial policy (jointly taught with MITI official Ryozo Hayashi). The pro-Matsushita spokesperson clearly carried the day.

83. James A. Dalton & Louis Esposito, *Predatory Price Cutting and Standard Oil: A Re-Examination of the Trial Record,* 22 Res. L & Econ. 155–205 (2007).

84. Phillip Areeda & Donald Turner, *Predatory Pricing and Related Practices under Section 2 of the Sherman Act,* 88 Harv. L. Rev. 697–733 (February 1975). The article was cited in a subsequent IBM appeal, *California Computer Products Inc. v. International Business Machines,* 613 F.2d 727, 743 (1979). But in the same section, the appellate court cited numerous other articles disputing the Areeda-Turner theses.

85. *Brooke Group Ltd. v. Brown & Williamson Tobacco Corp.,* 509 U.S. 209, 224 (1993).

86. Citing my textbook, *supra* note 78, to support the proposition that predation to discipline price-cutting rivals is difficult, the Court failed to note one documented probable instance of such behavior.

87. Peltzman, *supra* note 69 at 325.

88. Lester G. Telser, *Why Should Manufacturers Want Fair Trade?,* 3 J. L. & Econ. 86–105 (October 1960); and Robert H. Bork, *A Reply to Professors Gould and Yamey,* 76 Yale L. J., 731 (March 1967); Bork, *Resale Price Maintenance and Consumer Welfare,* 77 Yale L. J. 950–960 (April 1968); and The Antitrust Paradox, *supra* note 68 at 295–296.

89. *Continental T.V., Inc., et al. v. GTE Sylvania, Inc.,* 433 U.S. 36, 48, 53, 54 (1977). Justice Rehnquist, who added weight to a new conservative

majority on the Court, abstained. Citing "a leading critic of vertical restraints," the Court disagreed with William S. Comanor's argument that product differentiation efforts reduce interbrand competition more than they convey socially valuable information. *Id.* at 56; *see Vertical Territorial and Customer Restrictions: White Motor and Its Aftermath,* 81 HARV. L. REV. 1419–1438 (May 1968). This is an issue that engaged (and continues to engage) scholars over a much broader ideological spectrum.

90. Richard Posner, *Antitrust Policy and the Supreme Court: An Analysis of Restricted Distribution, Horizontal Merger and Potential Competition Decisions,* 75 COLUM. L. REV. 282–293 (1975). Following the decision, Posner applauded it in *The Rule of Reason and the Economic Approach: Reflections on the* Sylvania *Decision,* 45 U. CHI. L. REV. 1–20 (Autumn 1977).

91. *See, e.g.,* Charles Ellet Jr., AN ESSAY ON THE LAWS OF TRADE IN REFERENCE TO THE WORKS OF INTERNAL IMPROVEMENT IN THE UNITED STATES (Richmond, VA: Bernard: 1839; Reprinted by Augustus Kelley, 1966). Ellet's insight can also be found in Alexander Hamilton's *Federalist Paper* No. 22. *See also* Joseph Spengler (not a Chicagoan), *Vertical Integration and Antitrust Policy,* 58 J. POL. ECON. 347–352 (August 1950).

92. *See* F. M. Scherer & David Ross, INDUSTRIAL MARKET STRUCTURE AND ECONOMIC PERFORMANCE, 3d ed., 542–548 (Houghton-Mifflin: 1990). For a parallel proof, *see* William S. Comanor, *Vertical Price Fixing and Market Restrictions and the New Antitrust Policy,* 98 HARV. L. REV. 990–998 (March 1985).

93. *Leegin Creative Leather Products Inc. v. PSKS Inc.,* 127 S.Ct. 2705 (2007). Subsequent citations are to the slip opinion.

94. Brief of Amici Curiae Economists in Support of Petitioner, case no. 06–480 (November 3, 2006). Most of the signatories filed a later brief squarely on the merits.

95. Brief for William S. Comanor and Frederic M. Scherer as Amici Curiae Supporting Neither Party, Case no. 06–480 (undated).

96. Slip opinion section IIIB, 14.

97. Slip opinion at 17.

98. Slip opinion at 10.

99. The sources are described in F. M. Scherer, *A New Retrospective on Mergers,* 28 REV. INDUS. ORG. 328–29 (June 2006).

100. *U.S. v. Von's Grocery Co. et al.,* 384 U.S. 270, 301 (1966).

101. Henry G. Manne, *Mergers and the Market for Corporate Control,* 73 J. POL. ECON. 110–120 (April 1965). Manne's J.D. decree was from the University of Chicago in 1952.

102. *See, e.g.,* Michael Jensen, *Takeovers: Their Causes and Consequences,* 2 J. ECON. PERSP. 21–48 (Winter 1988). Jensen's Ph.D. was from the University of Chicago.

103. *A Theory of Oligopoly,* 72 J. POL. ECON. 55–59 (February 1964).

104. *Economies as an Antitrust Defense: The Welfare Tradeoffs,* 58 AM. ECON. REV. 18–36 (March 1968).

105. For what is probably the initial joining of this issue in a litigated case, *see* my *Affidavit on Efficiency Defenses in U.S. v. Archer-Daniels-Midland Co. et al.* (May 1987), *in* F. M. Scherer, COMPETITION POLICY, DOMESTIC AND INTERNATIONAL, 259–269 (Edward Elgar: 2000). The district

court decided the case on other grounds and took no position on how an efficiency defense should be tried.

106. *In the matter of Kellogg et al.,* 99 F.T.C. 8, 16, 289 (1982); *In the matter of Ethyl Corp. et al.,* 101 F.T.C. 425 (1983).

107. *Supra* note 78 at 163–164.

108. *Concentration and Structural and Market Disequilibria,* 16 ANTITRUST BULL. 244–248 (Summer 1971).

109. *Industry Structure, Market Rivalry, and Public Policy,* 16 J. L. & ECON. (April 1973); and *Two Systems of Belief About Monopoly,* in Goldschmid, ed., *supra* note 72, at 175–181.

110. Goldschmid, ed., *supra* note 72.

111. *Structure-Profit Relationships at the Line of Business and Industry Level,* 65 REV. ECON. & STAT. 22–31 (February 1983). Ravenscraft might be called a Chicagoan; he grew up in Peoria and received his Ph.D. from Northwestern University.

112. *U.S. v. American Telephone and Telegraph Co. et al.,* 524 F. Supp. 1336, 1359. Judge Greene quoted at 1362 Robert Bork's suggestion that "Predation by abuse of governmental procedures ... presents an increasingly dangerous threat to competition ... [with] almost limitless possibilities." Bork, *supra* note 69, at 347.

113. *Commentary, in* Goldschmid et al., eds., *supra* note 72, at 104.

114. Or the ambivalent are cited only for inferences consistent with conservative values and ignored on other points.

115. Arnold C. Harberger, *Monopoly and Resource Allocation,* 44 AM. ECON. REV. 77–87 (May 1954).

116. For a quantitative illustration, *see* Scherer & Ross, *supra* note 89, at 31.

117. F. M. Scherer, *Technological Innovation and Monopolization,* forthcoming *in* ISSUES IN COMPETITION L. & POL'Y, W. D. Collins, ed. The article analyzes "great" monopolization cases in seven major industries.

118. George J. Stigler, *The Extent and Bases of Monopoly,* 32 AM. ECON. REV. supplement, 14 (June 1942).

119. *U.S. v. Hartford-Empire Co. et al.,* 46 F. Supp. 541 (1942), 323 U.S. 386 (1944), 324 U.S. 570 (1944).

120. Marcus A. Hollabaugh & Robert Wright, *Compulsory Licensing Under Antitrust Judgments,* staff report, Subcommittee on Patents, Trademarks, and Copyrights, Senate Committee on the Judiciary, 2–5 (1960).

121. F. M. Scherer et al., PATENTS AND THE CORPORATION, 2d ed., privately published (Boston: 1959).

122. C. T. Taylor & Z. A. Silberston, THE ECONOMIC IMPACT OF THE PATENT SYSTEM (Cambridge University Press 1973). Taylor and Silberston estimated from extensive interviews that R&D expenditures in the United Kingdom would be reduced on average by 8 percent if no patent protection were available. For pharmaceuticals, however, the reduction would be 64 percent.

123. *Patents and Innovation: An Empirical Study,* 173 MGMT. SCI. 173–181 (1986). Mansfield's estimated percentage shortfalls are similar to those found by Taylor and Silberston.

124. R. C. Levin, Alvin Klevorick, Richard R. Nelson, & Sidney Winter, *Appropriating the Returns from Industrial Research and Development,* BROOKINGS PAPERS ON ECONOMIC ACTIVITY, 783–820 (1987: Microeconomics).

125. Ward Bowman, PATENT AND ANTITRUST LAW: A LEGAL AND ECONOMIC APPRAISAL (University of Chicago Press 1973), especially at 64 and 254–55.

126. Remarks by Abbott P. Lipsky Jr. before the American Bar Association November 5, 1981, reproduced in CCH TRADE REGULATION REPORTER para. 13, 129.

127. U.S. Department of Justice and Federal Trade Commission, ANTITRUST ENFORCEMENT AND INTELLECTUAL PROPERTY RIGHTS: PROMOTING INNOVATION AND COMPETITION (April 2007); Antitrust Modernization Commission, REPORT (2007).

128. ANTITRUST ENFORCEMENT AND INTELLECTUAL PROPERTY RIGHTS, at 1, 2. *supra* note 128.

129. *Supra* note 128.

130. Antitrust Modernization Commission, 38–40. *supra* note 128.

131. *Id.*

132. Those in the Chicago School begin with the premise that the sole goal of antitrust is the achievement of economic efficiency, and then apply price theory as the vehicle for determining efficiency effects. Entry is generally thought easy and monopoly is therefore most likely self-correcting. Efficiencies are more common than thought by others. Chicagoans are basically noninterventionist, more likely to fear harmful efficiency effects from the application of the antitrust laws. Most vertical restraints should be lawful. Antitrust therefore should focus primarily on cartels, large horizontal mergers and the erosion of market power created or protected by government. The classic statements of these views are Robert H. Bork, THE ANTITRUST PARADOX: A POLICY AT WAR WITH ITSELF (1978); Richard A. Posner, ANTITRUST LAW (1976; 2d ed. 2001); Richard A. Posner, *The Chicago School of Antitrust Analysis,* 127 U. PA. L. REV. 925 (1979).

133. For a discussion of the meaning of "consumer welfare," *see* UNITED STATES MODERNIZATION COMMISSION, REPORT AND RECOMMENDATIONS 26, n.22 (2007).

134. *See, e.g., Schor v. Abbott Laboratories,* 457 F.3d 608, 611 (7th Cir. 2006) ("if a manufacturer cannot make itself better off by injuring consumers through lower output and higher prices, there is no role for antitrust law to play").

135. Allocative inefficiency occurs when the exercise of monopoly power results in a restriction of the output that would be produced in a competitive market. The result is that fewer resources being utilized in the market than would be allocated to the same market under competitive conditions. This is suboptimal, an inefficient result.

136. Northwest Airlines has over time controlled 64 of the 86 gates, and almost 78 percent of all flights, at Detroit Metro Airport. *See Spirit Airlines, Inc. v. Northwest Airlines, Inc.,* 431 F.3d 917 (6th Cir. 2005) (summary judgment in favor of Northwest on claim of predatory pricing targeting low cost carrier reversed). *Cf. United States v. AMR Corp.,* 335 F.3d 1109 (10th Cir. 2003) (rejecting similar claims by low cost airline).

137. *See* U.S. DEPARTMENT OF JUSTICE ANTITRUST DIVISION, STATEMENT ON THE CLOSING OF ITS INVESTIGATION OF WHIRLPOOL'S ACQUISITION OF MAYTAG, 7 CCH TRADE REG.REP. ¶ 50, 209 (2006).

138. Broken up by a government consent decree in 1980, AT&T was purchased by SBC, originally Southwestern Bell (one of the Bell operating companies that resulted from the decree, and had previously acquired Pacific Telesis and Ameritech, two of the other regional "baby Bells"). Following its acquisition of AT&T, SBC changed its corporate name to AT&T Inc. AT&T Inc. has since acquired Bell South, another of the baby Bell operating companies, and with that acquisition acquired control of Cingular Wireless and Yellow Pages, Inc.

139. *See* Royal Caribbean Cruises, Ltd./P & O Princess Cruises p/c and Carnival Corporation/P & O Princess Cruises, CCH TRADE REG. REP. ¶ 15,100, 2001–2005 TRANSFER BINDER (FTC 2002) (Statement re closing of investigation of two major cruise line mergers).

140. *See* Federated/May, CCH TRADE REG. REP. ¶ 15,790, 2001–2005 TRANSFER BINDER (FTC 2005) (letter closing investigation of acquisition by Federated Department Stores of May Department Stores). Shortly after the consummation of the transaction the venerated Marshall Field's stores were changed to Macy's.

141. The contestable market theory asserts that even where there is a single monopoly incumbent in the market, if entry and exit are costless or virtually so, the threat of entry can prevent restricted output and monopoly prices. *See generally* William J. Baumol, J. C. Panzer, & Robert D. Willig, CONTESTABLE MARKET THEORY OF INDUSTRY STRUCTURE (1982). The theory was used throughout the analysis of airline deregulation to explain away fears of air carriers that might be the sole carriers in particular markets.

142. In rejecting a market definition of department stores in Federated/May, *supra* note 137, the Commission stressed that department stores today are in malls, and that consumers can buy virtually everything sold in a department store in other stores within the mall.

143. *FTC v. H.J. Heinz Co.,* 246 F.3d 708 (D.C. Cir. 2001) (granting FTC interim relief).

144. Robert H. Bork, THE ANTITRUST PARADOX 50–71 (1978) ("...conventional indicia of legislative intent overwhelmingly support the conclusions that the antitrust laws should be interpreted as designed for the sole purpose of forwarding consumer welfare").

145. *See, e.g.,* Richard Hofstadter, *What Happened to the Antitrust Movement, in* THE PARANOID STYLE IN AMERICAN POLITICS AND OTHER ESSAYS 205–211 (1965); Herbert Hovenkamp, *Antitrust Policy After Chicago,* 84 MICH. L. REV. 213, 249 (1985) ("The legislative histories of the various antitrust laws fail to exhibit anything resembling a dominant concern for economic efficiency."); Robert H. Lande, *Wealth Transfers as the Original and Primary Concern of Antitrust: The Efficiency Interpretation Challenged,* 34 HASTINGS L.J. 65 (1982); Robert Pitofsky, *The Political Content of Antitrust,* 127 U. PA. L. REV. 1051, 1051–1066 (1979).

146. *See* Herbert Hovenkamp, *supra* note 142, at 260–284.

147. *Id.* at 255–260.

148. As we shall see, actual *outcomes* in cases decided over the past twenty-five years have probably been more consistent with what Herbert Hovenkamp in this volume has characterized as the "chastised Harvard School" identified with Professors Areeda and Hovenkamp and, in my view, with Robert Pitofsky as well. The views of this "chastised" school are most clearly set forth in Herbert Hovenkamp, The Antitrust Enterprise: Principle and Execution (2005). The views of this school have now been characterized as "Chicago lite," accepting much of the structure of Chicago analysis but "more skeptical over the predictive power of theoretic models in litigation." Daniel A. Crane, *Antitrust Modesty,* 105 Mich. L. Rev. 1193, 1194 (2007).

149. *See* Thomas E. Kauper, *The Antitrust Revolution and Small Business: On "The Turnpike to Efficiencyville," in* Law and Class in America 120 (P. Carrington & T. Jones eds., 2006); Thomas E. Kauper, *The "Warren Court" and the Antitrust Laws: Of Economics, Populism and Cynicism,* 67 Mich. L. Rev. 325, 331–334 (1968).

150. *United States v. Topco Associates,* 405 U.S. 596 (1972).

151. *United States v. Griffith,* 334 U.S. 100 (1948).

152. *Albrecht v. The Herald Co.,* 390 U.S. 145 (1968).

153. *Simpson v. Union Oil Co.,* 377 U.S. 13 (1964).

154. *United States v. Arnold, Schwinn & Co.,* 388 U.S. 365 (1967).

155. *United States v. Von's Grocery Co.,* 384 U.S. 270 (1966).

156. *Federal Trade Commission v. Morton Salt Co.,* 334 U.S. 37 (1948).

157. *Utah Pie Co. v. Continental Baking Co.,* 386 U.S. 685 (1967).

158. *United States v. Philadelphia National Bank,* 374 U.S. 321 (1963).

159. *Poller v. Columbia Broadcasting System,* 368 U.S. 464 (1962).

160. *See Bigelow v. RKO Radio Pictures,* 327 U.S. 251 (1946).

161. Three of the decisions referred to in the text have been expressly overruled. *See Continental T.V., Inc. v. GTE Sylvania Inc.,* 433 U.S. 36 (1971) (overruling *Schwinn*); *State Oil v. Khan,* 522 U.S. 3 (1997) (overruling *Albrecht*); *Leegin Creative Leather Products, Inc. v. PSKS, Inc.,* 127 S.Ct. 2705 (2007) (overruling *Dr. Miles*). *Utah Pie* was virtually dismissed out of hand in *Brooke v. Brown & Williamson Tobacco,* 509 U.S. 209 (1993). In the minds of many, *Topco* was implicitly overruled in *Broadcast Music, Inc. v. Columbia Broadcasting System, Inc.,* 441 U.S. 1 (1979). *See* discussion in *Rothery Storage & Van Co. v. Atlas Van Lines, Inc.,* 792 F.2d 210, 229 (D.C. Cir. 1986). The leveraging principle of *Griffith* has been substantially modified in cases like *Alaska Airlines, Inc. v. United Airlines, Inc.,* 948 F.2d 536 (9th Cir. 1991), an outcome the Supreme Court seemed to approve in *Verizon Communications Inc. v. Law Offices of Curtis V. Trinko, LLP,* 540 U.S. 398, 415 n.4 (2004). In view of the development of the law generally and of lower court analysis in modern merger cases, *Von's Grocery* would clearly not be followed today. *See Hospital Corporation of America v. FTC,* 807 F.2d 1381, 1386 (7th Cir. 1986). The presumption of competitive injury created in *Morton Salt* appears to have been substantially modified in *Volvo Trucks North America, Inc. v. Reeder-Simco GMC, Inc.,* 546 U.S. 164 (2006). And the basic hostility to the use of summary judgment in antitrust case

was substantially weakened in *Matsushita Elec. Indus. Co. v. Zenith Radio Corp.*, 475 U.S. 574 (1986).

162. As noted, *Dr. Miles* was overruled in *Leegin*, 127 S.Ct. 2705.

163. *Verizon Communications Inc. v. Law Offices of Curtis V. Trinko, LLP, supra* note 30, at 412–416.

164. Among these appointments were three prominent Chicagoans— Robert Bork, Frank Easterbrook and Richard Posner—who were in turn able to use their judicial opinions to further influence antitrust policy.

165. *Utah Pie*, 386 U.S. 685.

166. *Arnold, Schwinn & Co.*, 388 U.S. 365.

167. The classic stinging critique of *Utah Pie* is Ward Bowman, *Restraint of Trade by the Supreme Court: The Utah Pie Case*, 77 YALE L.J. 70 (1967). The opinion of the Court in the *Continental T.V., Inc. v. GTE Sylvania Inc., supra* note 30 at 48, n.13, recites much of the criticism from a broad range of commentators attacking the decision in *Schwinn. See also* Thomas E. Kauper, *The "Warren Court" and the Antitrust Laws: Of Economics, Populism and Cynicism, supra* note 146, at 340–341.

168. The emphasis in *Sylvania* on potential efficiencies and the structural analysis relying on price theory is straight from the Chicago playbook, although the Court did not conclude that vertical non-price restrictions are per se legal.

169. *Leegin*, 127 S.Ct. 2705. The efficiency explanations used by the Court in rejecting the traditional *per se* rule against vertical price fixing are drawn directly from Bork and Posner, as well as from Herbert Hovenkamp, THE ANTITRUST ENTERPRISE 186 (2005).

170. *Broadcast Music*, 441 U.S. 1. The analysis of blanket licensing in this case closely tracks the ancillary restraint analysis set forth by Judge Taft in *United States v. Addyston Pipe & Steel Co.*, 85 F. 271 (6th Cir. 1898), *aff'd*, 175 U.S. 211 (1899), a decision characterized by Robert Bork as "one of the greatest, if not the greatest, opinion in the history of law." Robert H. Bork, THE ANTITRUST PARADOX 26 (1978).

171. *State Oil v. Khan*, 522 U.S. 3. The Court's analysis of maximum resale price maintenance was very heavily influenced by the opinion in the court below, an opinion written by Judge Richard Posner.

172. *Business Electronics Corp. v. Sharp Electronics Corp.*, 485 U.S. 717 (1988). The Court in *Business Electronics* justified the *per se* rule against vertical price fixing primarily on the ground that the practice could be used to facilitate a cartel, thus moving away from the simple vertical effects Chicagoans find benign to horizontal effects that are of concern to Chicagoans. *See* Richard A. Posner, ANTITRUST LAW 172 (2d ed. 2001). This concern is expressed, albeit minimalized, in *Leegin*.

173. The influence of the Chicago School on antitrust policy with respect to mergers in large part is the result of the utilization by the courts and enforcement agencies of the merger guidelines, initially guidelines of the Department of Justice and now guidelines of the Federal Trade Commission as well. U.S. DEPT. OF JUSTICE & FTC, HORIZONTAL MERGER GUIDELINES, as amended, http.11www.usdoj.gov/atr/public/guidelines/hmg.pdf. The current guidelines are simply a modest revision of the guidelines issued in 1982, when the principal draftsman and person primarily responsible for

their content was William Baxter, the Assistant Attorney General in charge of the Antitrust Division and a true Chicagoan.

174. *Eastman Kodak Co. v. Image Technical Servs.*, 504 U.S. 451 (1992) (rejecting argument, based on Chicago economic model, that a manufacturer could not have had monopoly power in a market for servicing its machines when its machines were sold in a competitive market).

175. Published beginning in 1978 as Philip Areeda & Donald F. Turner, ANTITRUST LAW, the multivolume treatise has been through a number of revisions with several revisers. Herbert Hovenkamp is the principal reviser, and the work is increasingly his. Most volumes today list Areeda and Hovenkamp as co-authors. It is a rare appellate court antitrust opinion that does not cite to something in the treatise. Daniel Crane, in *Antitrust Modesty, supra* note 145, at 1193 puts it this way: "As custodian of the treatise, Hovenkamp speaks with oracle-like authority on antitrust matters." The publication of Herbert Hovenkamp, THE ANTITRUST ENTERPRISE: PRINCIPLE AND EXECUTION (2005) will further extend the influence of what Hovenkamp has called the "chastised" Harvard school.

176. *Verizon Communications Inc. v. Law Offices of Curtis V. Trinko, LLP,* 540 U.S. at 412.

177. *See supra* note 170.

178. In the small world in which we live, antitrust enforcers and judges abroad tend to be quite familiar with U.S. antitrust law developments of the last three decades. As the Chicago school has affected U.S. legal developments, those following U.S. law are also affected. For a good example, see EUROPEAN COMMISSION, GREEN PAPER ON VERTICAL RESTRAINTS IN EC COMPETITION POLICY ¶ 54 (1997). The Green Paper also illustrates the fact that antitrust analysis often begins with the Chicago position, even if some reason is ultimately given for coming to different conclusions.

179. *See, e.g.,* Harold Dermsetz, *Toward a Theory of Property Rights,* 57 AM. ECON. REV. 347 (Pap & Proc. 1967). An early influential work on the consideration of externalities in the development of property rights. More broadly, the work of Richard Posner has extended to, and had an influence upon, a number of fields. *See* Richard A. Posner, ECONOMIC ANALYSIS OF LAW (7th ed. 2007). The Chicago analysis initially developed in antitrust was in a sense a precursor of much of what we think of today as the whole law and economics movement.

180. Thomas E. Kauper, *Review of Richard A. Posner, Antitrust Law: An Economic Perspective,* 75 MICH. L. REV. 768, 771 (1977).

181. *Id.* I further noted that while such cathedrals are a great human achievement, they also have a sense of unreality about them, that "they do not seem to speak to the world in which most of us live and work."

182. Except where adverse effect is directly proven, as in *National Collegiate Athletic Association v. Board of Regents of University of Oklahoma,* 468 U.S. 85 (1984), it is now simply given that plaintiffs in section 1 rule of reason cases must establish that defendant has (or had) market power. *See, e.g., Republic Tobacco Co. v. North Atlantic Trading Co., Inc.,* 381 F.3d 717 (7th Cir. 2004); *K.M.B. Warehouse Distributors, Inc.,* 61 F.3d 123 (2d Cir. 1995).

183. One recent commentator puts it this way (defining the "new" Harvard school):

> It accepts the essential theoretic insights of the Chicago School but acts cautiously in applying them to real cases because of skepticism over the predictive power of theoretic models in litigation. Hovenkamp readily admits that the main differences between the new Harvard and Chicago schools "lies in details."
>
> Daniel A. Crane, *supra* note 145, at 1194.

184. *See* Andrew I. Gavil, William E. Kovacic, & Jonathan B. Baker, ANTITRUST LAW IN PERSPECTIVE CASES, CONCEPTS AND PROBLEMS IN COMPETITION POLICY 68 (2002) ("Post-Chicago commentators generally propose qualifying rather than supplanting Chicago views...both schools rely on formal arguments from microeconomics and the post-Chicago school does not propose to demonstrate the logical fallacies of the Chicago school."). *Eastman Kodak,* 504 U.S. 451, is a good illustration of starting with a Chicago model and examining exceptions and reasons why the teaching of the model does not apply.

185. *Eastman Kodak,* 504 U.S. 451.

186. In *Southern Motor Carriers Rate Conference v. United States,* 471 U.S. 48 (1985), the Court rejected the implication in *Cantor v. Detroit Edison Co.,* 428 U.S. 579 (1976) that in order to assert protection from the federal antitrust laws for conduct taken in accord with state law the conduct at issue would need to have been *compelled* by the state; it is sufficient that it be authorized by the state. In *Columbia v. Omni Outdoor Advertising, Inc.,* 499 U.S. 365 (1991), the Court further expanded the state action immunity by rejecting a conspiracy exemption, declining to examine whether there were faults in the authorization process as a matter of state law and denying that the immunity would be lost even if officials were bribed. But in *Ticor Title Ins.Co. v. FTC,* 504 U.S. 621 (1992), the Court curtailed the immunity by requiring evidence that the state took active steps to supervise the allegedly immune conduct. The Chicago view here is somewhat ambivalent, as Chicagoans have also tended to be strong believers in permitting the states, in the name of federalism, some latitude to impose regulatory regimes within their authority. *See, e.g.,* Bork, *supra* note 167 at 350.

187. *Eastern Railroads Presidents Conference v. Noerr Motor Freight, Inc.,* 365 U.S. 127 (1961) creates a broad immunity from antitrust liability for petitioning government bodies to take action that are on their face anticompetitive. Litigation is generally within the protection of *Noerr.*

188. *See Professional Real Estate Investors, Inc. v. Columbia Pictures Industries, Inc.,* 508 U.S. 49 (1993) (imposing very high standards that must be met in order to remove the *Noerr* immunity from litigation targeted at rivals).

189. Bork, *supra* note 167 at 347–364 (entire chapter entitled "Predation Through Government Process," with particular emphasis on misuse of litigation).

190. *Trinko,* 540 U.S. at 414.

191. As far back as 1955, the Act was criticized in U.S. DEPARTMENT OF JUSTICE, REPORT OF THE ATTORNEY GENERAL'S NATIONAL COMMITTEE TO STUDY THE

Antitrust Laws 132 (1955). The Neal Report urged a major overhaul. Philip C. Neal, et al., *Report of the White House Task Force on Antitrust Policy,* reprinted in 2 Antitrust L. & Econ. Rev. 11, 41 (1968–69). Repeal was suggested in U.S. Department of Justice, Report On the Robinson-Patman Act 260 (1977). The latest to tilt at this windmill is the Antitrust Modernization Commission. *See* U.S. Antitrust Modernization Commission, Report and Recommendations 317 (2007).

192. *Leegin,* 127 S.Ct. 2705 (2007).

193. *Continental T.V., Inc. v. GTE Sylvania, Inc.,* 433 U.S. 36, 51, n.18 (1977).

194. For a more complete discussion, *see* Daniel Rubinfeld, *Antitrust Policy, in* International Encyclopedia of the Social and Behavioral Sciences (2001), *available at* www.iesbs.com.

195. *United States v. Aluminum Co of America,* 377 U.S. 271 (1964)

196. *See, e.g., United States v. Von's Grocery Co.,* 384 U.S. 270 (1966).

197. *See, e.g.,* Leonard Weiss, *The Concentration-Profits Relationship and Antitrust Law, in* H. Goldschmid , H. M. Mann, & J. F. Weston (eds.), Industrial Concentration: The New Learning, 184–232 (Little Brown, Boston: 1974).

198. H. Demsetz, *Two Systems of Belief About Monopoly, in* Goldschmid, Mann, Weston (eds.) Industrial Concentration: The New Learning, 164–183 (Little Brown, Boston: 1974).

199. *See, e.g.,* Richard Posner, *The Chicago School of Antitrust Analysis,* 127 U. PA. L. Rev. 925 (1979); Frank Easterbrook, *The Limits of Antitrust,* 63 Tex. L. Rev. 1 (1984).

200. *GTE Sylvania, Inc., v. Continental TV, Inc.,* 433 U.S. 36 (1977).

201. *See, e.g., Leegin Creative Leather Products v. TSKS, Inc.,* 127 S. Ct. 2705 (2007) (overturning a prior decision making vertical minimum price fixing or "resale price maintenance" per se illegal).

202. Einer Elhauge, *Harvard Not Chicago: Which Antitrust School Drives Recent Supreme Court Decisions?,* 3 Competition Pol'y Int'l., No. 2, Autumn, (2007) forthcoming.

203. Avanash Dixit, *A Model of Duopoly Suggesting a Theory of Entry Barriers,* 10 Bell J. Econ. 20 (1979).

204. Thomas G. Krattenmaker & Steven C. Salop, *Anticompetitive Exclusion: Raising Rivals' Costs to Achieve Power over Price,* 96 Yale L.J. 209 (Dec. 1986); Janusz A. Ordover, Garth Saloner, & Steven C. Salop, *Equilibrium Vertical Foreclosure,* 80 Am. Econ. Rev. 127 (1990).

205. David M. Kreps & Robert Wilson, *Reputation and Imperfect Information,* 27 J. Econ.Theory 253 (1982); Paul Milgrom & John Roberts, *Predation, Reputation and Entry Deterrence,* 27 J. Econ.Theory 280 (1982).

206. Franklin M. Fisher, *Games Economists Play: A Noncooperative View,* 20 Rand J. Econ. 113 (1989).

207. Carl Shapiro, *The Theory of Business Strategy,* 20 Rand J. Econ. 125 (1989).

208. Ronald Coase, *The Nature of the Firm,* 4 Economica 380 (1937).

209. Oliver Williamson, The Economic Institutions of Capitalism (Free Press, New York: 1985).

210. Daniel Rubinfeld, *Antitrust Enforcement in Dynamic Network Industries,* Antitrust Bull., Fall-Winter, 859–882 (1998).

211. Allen Grunes & Maurice E. Stuckey, *Antitrust and the Marketplace of Ideas,* 69 ANTITRUST L.J., No. 1, 249–302 (2001).

212. *U.S. v. Microsoft,* 253 F.3d 34 (D.C. Cir. 2001).

213. Franklin M. Fisher & Daniel L. Rubinfeld, *United States v. Microsoft: An Economic Analysis,* 1–44, in Evans, Fisher, Rubinfeld, & Schmalensee, DID MICROSOFT HARM CONSUMERS? TWO OPPOSING VIEWS, AEI-Brookings Joint Center for Regulatory Studies (2000).

214. Evans and Schmalensee, *Be Nice to Your Rivals: How the Government Is Selling an Antitrust Case without Consumer Harm in* United States v. Microsoft," 45–86, *in* Evans, Fisher, Rubinfeld, & Schmalensee, DID MICROSOFT HARM CONSUMERS? TWO OPPOSING VIEWS, AEI-Brookings Joint Center for Regulatory Studies (2000).

Bibliography

Bain, Joseph. *Industrial Organization.* New York: Wiley, 1968.

Coase, Ronald. "The Nature of the Firm," 4 *Economica* (1937): 380–405.

Demsetz, H. "Two systems of belief about monopoly," in Goldschmid H., Mann H. M., Weston, J. F. (eds.) *Industrial Concentration: The New Learning.* Boston: Little Brown, 1974, 164–83.

Dixit, Avanash. "A Model of Duopoly Suggesting a Theory of Entry Barriers," 10 *Bell Journal of Economics* (1979): 20–32.

Easterbrook, Frank. "The Limits of Antitrust," 63 *Texas Law Review* (1984): 1–40.

Elhauge, Einer. "Harvard Not Chicago: Which Antitrust School Drives Recent Supreme Court Decisions?" 3 *Competition Policy International,* No. 2, Autumn 2007, forthcoming.

David Evans and Richard Schmalensee. "Be Nice to Your Rivals: How the Government Is Selling an Antitrust Case without Consumer Harm in *United States v. Microsoft,*" in Evans, Fisher, Rubinfeld, and Schmalensee, *Did Microsoft Harm Consumers? Two Opposing Views,* AEI-Brookings Joint Center for Regulatory Studies, 2000, 45–86.

Fisher, Franklin M. "Games Economists Play: A Noncooperative View," 20 *Rand Journal of Economics* (1989): 113–124.

Fisher, Franklin M. and Daniel L. Rubinfeld. "United States v. Microsoft: An Economic Analysis" (with Franklin M. Fisher), in Evans, Fisher, Rubinfeld, and Schmalensee, *Did Microsoft Harm Consumers? Two Opposing Views,* AEI-Brookings Joint Center for Regulatory Studies, 2000, 1–44.

Grunes, Allen and Maurice E. Stuckey. "Antitrust and the Marketplace of Ideas," 69 *Antitrust Law Journal* No. 1 (2001): 249–302.

Kauper, Thomas. "Influence of Conservative Economic Analysis on the Development of the Law of Antitrust," in this volume.

Kreps, David M. and Robert Wilson. "Reputation and Imperfect Information." 27 *Journal of Economic Theory* (1982): 253–279.

Milgrom, Paul and John Roberts. "Predation, Reputation and Entry Deterrence." 27 *Journal of Economic Theory* (1982): 280–312.

Posner, Richard."The Chicago School of Antitrust Analysis" 127 *University of Pennsylvania Law Review* (1979): 925–948.

Rubinfeld, Daniel. "Antitrust Enforcement in Dynamic Network Industries." *The Antitrust Bulletin* Fall-Winter (1998): 859–882.

———. "Antitrust Policy." *International Encyclopedia of the Social and Behavioral Sciences* (2001), www.iesbs.com.

Ordover, Janusz A., Garth Saloner, and Steven C. Salop. "Equilibrium Vertical Foreclosure." 80 *American Economic Review* (1990):127–142.

Schmalensee, Richard. "Thoughts on the Chicago Legacy in Antitrust," in this volume.

Shapiro, Carl. "The Theory of Business Strategy." 20 *Rand Journal of Economics* (1989): 125–137.

Weiss, Leonard. "The Concentration-Profits Relationship and Antitrust Law," in Goldschmid H., Mann H. M., Weston J. F., eds., *Industrial Concentration: The New Learning.* Boston: Little Brown, 1974, 184–232.

Williamson, Oliver. *The Economic Institutions of Capitalism.* New York: Free Press, 1985.

Cases

GTE Sylvania, Inc., v. Continental TV, Inc., 433 U.S. 36 (1977).

Leegin Creative Leather Products v. PSKS, Inc., 127 S. Ct. 2705 (2007).

U.S. v. Arnold, Schwinn & Co., 388 U.S. 365 (1907).

U.S. v. Von's Grocery Co., 384 U.S. 270 (1966).

2

Is Efficiency All That Counts?

Introduction

In most matters of policy, where you end up depends on where you start. Almost all conservative economic advocates believe that competition policy should focus primarily, and probably exclusively, on efficiency, which they believe will lead to consumer welfare. As a result, economic considerations and enhanced efficiency, and no other social or political value, should be taken into account. Conservatives have sold that view remarkably well to private sector lawyers, most academics, and many judges—partly on grounds (clearly wrong) that when the Sherman Act was passed that was the will of Congress. The next two papers, written by John Kirkwood and Robert Lande, and by Eleanor Fox, challenge those premises.

Fox first defines various concepts of efficiency and then demonstrates how conservative economic approaches, spelled out in the following section by Kirkwood-Lande, have led to wrong results in several important cases. Kirkwood and Lande take on directly the major precept of Chicago School antitrust policy—the claim that the sole objective of antitrust policy was to achieve industrial efficiency when the Sherman Act was enacted. They argue (and demonstrate) that a careful review of legislative history and of recent case law including recent Supreme Court opinions shows that the Chicago School is just wrong. They proceed to argue that the original and more sensible goal of antitrust enforcement should be to protect consumers and enhance their welfare.

The Efficiency Paradox

Eleanor M. Fox

Introduction

In 1978 Robert Bork wrote his influential book, *The Antitrust Paradox*. The paradox was that antitrust was meant to unleash competition but, Bork argued, it actually restrained competition. It did so by favoring small business and the underdog. His antidote was to reconstitute antitrust in the service of efficiency.

Thirty years later a chorus of conservative and libertarian policy makers and specialist technicians proclaim the new litany: Antitrust is for efficiency. The perspective has shifted from the notion that antitrust is for competition[1] to the notion that antitrust is for efficiency. Many influential supporters of antitrust as efficiency, including jurists, presume that what business does is efficient and what government (antitrust enforcement) does is usually inefficient. Consequently, today, we face the Efficiency Paradox: Modern antitrust (I assume arguendo) is meant to help us reach efficiency. However, by trusting dominant firm strategies[2] and leading firm collaborations[3] to produce efficiency, modern U.S. antitrust protects monopoly and oligopoly, suppresses innovative challenges, and stifles efficiency.

To set the stage, this essay asks first, what is efficiency? Second, it asks: Can antitrust law produce efficiency, and how does it try to do so? It observes that one way antitrust pursues efficiency is by choosing a proxy; notably, either trust in the dynamic of the competition process or trust in (even) the dominant firm. Third, by case examples, it shows the effect of conservative economics in choosing as the proxy trust in the dominant firm. It argues that this phenomenon has produced the Efficiency Paradox: In the name of efficiency, conservative theories of antitrust cut off the most promising paths to efficiency. Fourth, the essay suggests that we can eliminate the Efficiency Paradox by readjusting the pendulum to give more regard to the incentives of mavericks and challengers and less regard to the freedom and autonomy of dominant firms.

I. Mapping Efficiency

Efficiency is often categorized as allocative, productive, or dynamic. Allocative efficiency refers to the allocation of resources to their most valued uses, in view of the choices buyers make given their ability and willingness to pay at least cost for goods and services.

Productive efficiency refers to a firm's production and distribution at the lowest feasible cost. Given the cost of inputs and the quality desired of outputs, a firm is productively efficient when it produces and distributes a good or service at the lowest cost possible.

Innovative or dynamic efficiency refers to the efficiency benefits achieved through research, development, and innovation, including the diffusion of technology to produce new products and processes. It includes firms' production of knowledge (of what to make and how to make it), and cross-fertilization among firms to enhance the body of knowledge, all leading to improvements in the state of art.[4]

Dynamic efficiency gains can easily swamp static efficiency gains; that is, they can swamp the gains that result from pushing price closer to costs.[5]

Efficiency is sometimes assessed in terms of total welfare. For example, will a particular merger or course of conduct cause the sum of consumer plus producer surplus to shrink?[6] Sometimes it is assessed in terms of consumer welfare. For example, will the merger or conduct cause *consumer* surplus to shrink. Even jurisdictions that define antitrust as a consumer welfare prescription (rather than a total welfare prescription) seldom focus only on whether consumer surplus will shrink. They also—at least sometimes—value consumer choice, both in terms of the variety of goods and services and the autonomy of consumers to choose.[7] Moreover, they value producer incentives to invest and to innovate, which will normally inure to consumer benefit.[8]

In large economies such as the United States, conduct and transactions seldom lessen consumer welfare without also lessening total welfare, so the distinction between consumer and total welfare is often moot. The distinction is most likely to be material in merger analysis, and even then it is usually insignificant because merger parties usually cannot prove that their merger is likely to produce net efficiencies that could not otherwise be achieved.[9]

Efficiency also applies to the form and formulation of rules and standards in view of administrative capabilities—the ease or difficulty of applying the law.[10] As applied to conduct that is almost always harmful and almost never beneficial, a rule of per se illegally or quick look (and quick condemnation) is efficient. It saves enforcement resources, gives business greater certainty, and more effectively deters inefficient conduct. If the category is well-drawn, the bright-line rule will not be inefficient in the sense of condemning procompetitive and efficient conduct; but if it is overbroad—a problem produced by the growing per se category in the 1960s, per se illegality will handicap efficiency.

II. How to Achieve Efficiency

How to achieve efficiency is a complex question. In a market society, many factors and arrangements drive toward efficiency, in all of its senses. Eliminating unnecessary regulation produces substantial efficiency gains. A robust corporate take-over market often spurs firms to achieve more productive and dynamic efficiency.[11] Intellectual property protection can spur innovation—although too much protection can create perverse counterincentives, frustrating innovative moves by outsiders. Antitrust *policy,* such as policy to dismantle antidumping duties on low-priced imports, can significantly unleash efficient firm behavior.

It is easy to see how antitrust policy can increase efficiency; but what can antitrust *law* do?

Antitrust *law* does not necessarily *produce* efficiency because it is proscriptive, not prescriptive.[12] It can preserve an environment in which firms have the incentive to behave rivalrously and in which upstarts have a clear and open path to wage their challenges. This process or open-market perspective helps to preserve the incentives that produce productive, dynamic, and market efficiency. Since 1980, U.S. courts have retreated from the tradition of protecting the competition process (rivalry) and the openness of markets. They have shifted to a different inquiry: Will the *outcome* of a particular merger or conduct be inefficient by inducing the aggregate of all producers to reduce the total amount of goods they produce (i.e., will it lower market output)? If so, the merger or conduct is probably illegal, at least unless firm efficiencies outweigh consumer loss or, ex ante, the conduct was an attempt to serve consumers and the market. If not, the merger or conduct is legal. I discuss both perspectives below. I argue that the outcome paradigm is a crabbed perspective that was intended to and does minimize antitrust law. I argue that limiting antitrust to condemning inefficient outcomes and embroidering the analysis with conservative Chicago School economic presumptions (markets are robust; antitrust enforcement normally harms the market) shrinks antitrust law to its smallest possible scope and in doing so harms efficiency in the sense of undermining rivalry and forestalling dynamic change, and as a result makes us economically worse off.[13]

A. The View of Antitrust That It Should and Does Prohibit Only Conduct and Transactions That Will Probably Produce Inefficient Outcomes

By this view, antitrust guards against certain limited ("anticompetitive") interferences with market efficiency by firm conduct or transactions.

What are these interferences? (1) Dominant firms' strategies that make no business sense[14] except to put costs on rivals or block them from access to needed inputs or markets and that thereby confer on the dominant firm more power to increase price and lessen output are anticompetitive and inefficient;[15] (2) Mergers that take competitors off the market under circumstances that will probably lessen output across the whole market, raise prices, and entail no offsetting cost-savings are also anticompetitive and inefficient.[16] Permutations can extend the category of anticompetitive interferences,[17] but not by much.

Apart from competitor price-fixing and other hard-core cartels, very little private action interferes with both competition and market efficiency.[18] Moreover, if one presumes (as does conservative economics) that markets are efficient, *the market unencumbered by antitrust* produces efficiency.[19] Accordingly, antitrust should largely "stay out of the way." This is akin to the argument of the late-nineteenth-century Social Darwinists such as William Graham Sumner "who had nothing but contempt for the antitrust movement which was merely trying to place artificial obstacles in the way of natural evolution."[20]

B. The View of Antitrust That It Should Also Preserve the Competitive Structure (Rivalry) and Openness of the Market

Supporters of this "process" view also want an efficient economy that produces what people want and need and that fosters innovation and growth of robust firms. They, too, know that we cannot engineer efficiency. But they believe that we can enhance efficiency and economic welfare (and other goals as well) by maintaining an *environment* congenial to mavericks and upstarts;[21] an environment that induces firms to be rivalrous, to seek new ways to reduce their own costs, and to vie to meet buyers' wants.[22] A task of antitrust is to prevent this dynamic process from being undermined. Therefore, preserving access by outsiders, preserving contestability of markets, and, at high levels of concentration, valuing diversity, are seen as mechanisms of efficiency. Preventing inefficient outcomes is also an objective, but safeguarding the process is the first-line protector against bad outcomes.

This second perspective was embodied in the U.S. antitrust law for nearly a century, albeit without consciousness that the law was fulfilling an

efficiency goal. Indeed, in earlier times, the Supreme Court preferred competition (rivalry among sufficient numbers) to the lower costs of dominant
firms, if a trade-off had to be made.[23] By the late 1970s, the Court reckoned
with the law's overbreadth (it was trading off more firm efficiency for more
rivalry) and eventually redefined competition of the sort the law should
preserve to be harmonious with efficiency. But, in the 1980s and 1990s and
in the new century, a conservative Court[24] swung the pendulum from one
inefficient position (too much antitrust because it disregarded incentives
and efficiencies of dominant firms) to another (too little antitrust because it
disregards incentives and efficiencies of firms without power).

This swing of the pendulum was possible because efficiency and how
to reach it are complex concepts. There is no one thing called "efficiency."
Conduct, transactions, and markets have efficiency and inefficiency properties at the same time, and the relative dimensions of each property are
affected by assumptions regarding how well markets work. How one applies
a goal of efficiency, therefore, depends on what one values and stresses, as
well as hunches as to what will produce the most efficiency—in all of its
senses.

III. Conservative Economics

While the Supreme Court today purports to apply the antitrust laws in the
name of efficiency,[25] in fact it can be demonstrated that efficiency is not the
guide to the resolution of the Supreme Court cases,[26] which, in contemporary United States, are almost invariably decided for defendants.

In this section I take examples from four cases of the United States
Supreme Court, and one case from the European Union. I ask: Did efficiency
drive or determine this outcome? If not efficiency, what did?

A. The United States

I look at four United States Supreme Court cases: *Brooke Group,*[27] *California
Dental Association,*[28] *Trinko,*[29] and *Leegin.*[30]

1. Brooke Group

In *Brooke Group,*[31] Liggett pioneered a generic (unbranded) cigarette, which
threatened to make great inroads into the market shares of the branded cigarette oligopoly. Brown & Williamson (B&W), the smallest member of the
oligopoly, fearing that generics would cannibalize its market share, introduced a no-frills fighting brand cigarette and a strategy of below-cost pricing. It expressed willingness to lose $48.7 million to discipline Liggett; it
did lose almost $15 million by below-average variable-cost pricing over
an 18-month period, and it won the war by forcing Liggett to raise its

own prices, closing the lion's share of the price gap between branded and unbranded cigarettes and stemming the challenge of generics. B&W's strategy was successful; it killed the generic segment of the market, just as it had set out to do.

The Supreme Court was called upon to adopt and apply a rule or standard that would govern predatory pricing. It was properly concerned about formulating a rule that would chill sustainable low pricing, but it was not particularly concerned by the prospect that an overly pro-defendant rule might cause the demise of new products that would threaten the established oligopoly. The Court announced, as it had done before,[32] and contrary to fact: "there is consensus among commentators that predatory pricing schemes are rarely tried, and even more rarely successful…."[33] The Court concluded that there was a need for a noninterventionist rule in price predation cases, and it formulated such a rule. It found that B&W had not violated the law because, the Court thought, B&W was unlikely to recoup its losses by raising prices in the future, and if that was the case the below-cost strategy not only benefited consumers in stage 1 (the low price) but threatened no harm to consumers in stage 2 (postpredation). The Court overturned the jury verdict for the maverick plaintiff. The *Brooke Group* rule—requiring below-cost pricing and probable recoupment by monopoly pricing—is the U.S. rule on price predation.

The Court's presumption about the rarity of predatory pricing that works to exploit consumers was based on "theory" only, as adumbrated by conservative economists.[34] Scholarship establishes,[35] to the contrary, that selective price predation is a recurring phenomenon; it is used effectively to eliminate young rivals and to deter potential entry into noncompetitive markets.[36] Recoupment (the payback) can come in many forms, including preserving the predator's market power that would otherwise have been lost—as in *Brooke Group* itself.

Is the rule announced in *Brooke Group* efficient? It certainly has efficiency aspects, although the Court was overly bold in ignoring B&W's own estimation that its predation would be worth it, and in ignoring the reality that B&W's predation had killed off the challenge to the tobacco oligopoly from generic cigarettes. Would a ruling for Liggett have been efficient? It, too, would have had clear efficiency properties. A plaintiff's victory along lines argued by its Supreme Court advocate Phillip Areeda[37] would have encouraged competitive challenges to entrenched oligopolies. What broke the tie in this dramatic contest (in which Robert Bork argued for the defendant while Phillip Areeda argued for the plaintiff)? Conservative economics, which consistently privileged theory over facts.

2. California Dental Association

The California Dental Association was a professional association composed of most of the dentists in California.[38] The dentists agreed to bylaws that greatly restricted themselves from advertising their dental services. For example, the dentists agreed that they could not advertise simply: "10% discount for students," "reasonable prices," or "gentle care." The Federal Trade Commission examined the bylaws. It found the restrictions on price advertising illegal per se, and it found the restrictions on quality and other advertising illegal after a quick (but still significant) look at the details of the market. The appellate court substantially affirmed the FTC's decision. The Supreme Court reversed. Whereas the FTC had deemed the dentists' rules harmful to consumers, who might, for example, want to locate a low-priced dentist, the Supreme Court took a different tack. First, The Supreme Court defined "anticompetitive" more narrowly—and statically—than the FTC had done. The advertising restrictions could be anticompetitive, the Court said, only if they caused California dentists to reduce the quantity of dental services provided in California.[39] (This is the outcome perspective described above.) Indeed, the Court ruminated, the dentists' bylaw restrictions might be procompetitive. They may have been used by the profession to prevent deceptive advertising. If they did prevent deception, the bylaws would give people more trust in dentists, and the increased trust might lead to an *increase* in demand and supply of dental services.

Was *California Dental* an efficient decision? Or were the dentists' bylaws inefficient by suppressing information consumers wanted and chilling price discounting?[40] Both the FTC and the Association had efficiency arguments. What broke the tie and induced the Court to hold that the FTC had to prove output limitation? Conservative economics, combined with a conservative—but widely held—view that professionals try to operate in the public interest and should be given wide range to regulate themselves.[41]

3. Trinko

AT&T, the old Ma Bell, was broken into one long distance telephone service company and seven regional "Baby Bells," which were at the time legal monopolies.[42] Bell Atlantic was a baby bell. It was the incumbent telecom service provider in the Northeast. Among other things, it inherited the local loop, access to which all local service providers need. When technological developments made competition in the local markets feasible, Congress passed the 1996 Telecoms Act, inviting multiple service providers into the formerly monopolized regional and local markets, and it required the incumbents to give the entrants full and nondiscriminatory access to the elements of the local loop on a cost-plus-reasonable-profit basis.

Bell Atlantic was not happy about the new competition and the cost-plus cap and it decided to impair its new competitors' access to the local loop as a means to forestall their rivalry and prevent its customers from being siphoned off by the rivals. The discriminated-against rivals complained to the Federal Communications Commission. The FCC found that

Bell Atlantic had violated the 1996 Act and ordered remedies. A customer of one of the buffeted rivals sued Bell Atlantic in antitrust, claiming that the conduct of Bell Atlantic was also an antitrust violation.[43] Bell Atlantic moved to dismiss the complaint, and the issue—was there an antitrust remedy for Bell Atlantic's defaults—eventually went to the Supreme Court.

The Supreme Court ruled that the complaint had to be dismissed; the plaintiffs could not get to trial. The Court characterized Bell Atlantic's strategy as a simple refusal to deal. It then asked: Did Bell Atlantic's conduct come within the general principle that a seller—even a monopolist—has the right to refuse to deal; or did its conduct fall within a "narrow exception" from that rule? So framing the question was nine-tenths of a defendant's victory. (The Court might have asked: Is the monopolist's use of its power over a needed input to prevent its competitors from competing on the merits for the monopolist's customers a violation of the Sherman Act?) The Court declared that freedom to deal is a first principle of monopoly law; that compelling a firm to share what it owns and may well have created is (1) a very serious infringement of the right to property and is likely to chill a firm's innovation, and (2) is likely to drive competitors into cartels. Note that Bell Atlantic inherited the local loop, it did not invent it; and that cartelization was not a possible scenario in the case; the competitors needed the input to compete, not cartelize. Stressing that duties to deal are exceptional, the Court suggested that such duties should be ruled out in the absence of a prior voluntary course of dealing followed by a refusal to continue dealing in order to get higher monopoly profits in the future;[44] or possibly, a duty to deal might be found in the case of denial of access to an essential facility where *no* access was being provided and no regulatory agency had a right to order access.

In the course of so deciding, Justice Scalia, writing for the Court, said that monopoly power is "good" because monopoly pricing "attracts 'business acumen' in the first place; it induces risk taking that produces innovation and economic growth."[45] The Justice called on courts to avoid false positives (erroneously condemning procompetitive conduct), and, separately to find no antitrust violation where effective relief would require considerable court or agency supervision.

Was *Trinko* efficient? The principles it recites certainly had efficiency properties—for duties to share what one has created may induce less investment to create. A judgment more sympathetic to the abused rivals and more concerned by Bell Atlantic's perverse incentive to degrade the rivals' access to the essential input over which it had sole control would also have had efficiency properties.

But what appears to have motivated Justice Scalia's remarkable and unprecedented formulation of pro-dominant-firm antitrust law principles in *Trinko*?[46] Conservative economics.

4. Leegin

Leegin designed and produced belts under the brand name Brighton.[47] It decided to sell only to select retail stores and to maintain one price, hoping not to "confuse" consumers with constant sales. It established a policy of not selling to retailers who sold Brighton products below its suggested prices. Kay's Closet (PSKS), a women's apparel store in Lewisville, Texas, pledged to adhere to Leegin's new policy but later marked down its Brighton line by 20 percent in order to compete with nearby retailers. Leegin demanded that PSKS stop discounting, PSKS refused, Leegin cut it off, and PSKS sued, invoking the nearly century-old precedent that resale price maintenance is illegal per se (Dr. Miles).[48] PSKS won a jury verdict that, as trebled, amounted to nearly $4 million. The case made its way to the Supreme Court, which confronted the question: Should resale price maintenance agreements remain illegal per se? The Court held no, reversing Dr. Miles by a vote of five to four.

The Court, by Justice Kennedy, said that per se rules are a disfavored category and are reserved for types of conduct that have manifestly anticompetitive effects; conduct that would always or almost always tend to restrict competition and decrease output. RPM does not fit this category. It can encourage retailers to invest in services and promotion by eliminating free riders, who would let other resellers provide the service and then undercut their prices; and it may give consumers more options to chose among low-price, low-service brands and high-price, high-service brands. It can encourage market entry of new firms that may choose to use RPM to induce investment and establish a reputation. The Court acknowledged that RPM can have anticompetitive effects, but, it said, these can be identified in rule of reason inquiry.

The Court rejected the argument that per se rules can properly serve a function of administrative convenience. It worried that per se rules in general might increase the total cost of the antitrust system by prohibiting procompetitive conduct, and increase litigation costs by promoting frivolous lawsuits.

Justice Breyer, dissenting, had a different view. He was reluctant to overturn the century-old Dr. Miles's rule without any evidence showing that it had produced harmful effects on consumers; and there was no such evidence in the record. He cited a study showing that prices rose 19 percent to 27 percent when RPM was allowed. "The law assumes that ... a marketplace, free of private restrictions, will tend to bring about the lower prices, better products, and more efficient production processes that consumers typically desire," he said.[49] Sometimes the probable anticompetitive consequences of a practice are so serious and the potential justifications are so few or so difficult to prove that a per se rule is justified, and these characteristics might justify the per se prohibition of RPM. As Breyer noted, the Court majority assumed that free riding that chills provision of services consumers find useful is a significant problem. Breyer refused to accept this assumption. He cited respected economists who are skeptical that harmful free riding actually occurs. Moreover, he said, relegating RPM cases to a rule of reason category can make consumer-harming RPM cases too difficult to prove, and may tempt producers and dealers to adopt anticompetitive RPM that will go untouched by the law.

Did *Leegin* have efficiency properties? Yes. RPM can be used to enhance interbrand competition. But is it so used? And should we treat sympathetically a practice that always raises prices, as Breyer asked? Breyer wanted evidence.

Did efficiency drive the outcome in *Leegin?* No; it was conservative economics-based theory rather than fact.

Virtually every other contemporary U.S. Supreme Court antitrust case but one[50] reflects the same ambiguities regarding efficiency. The majority opinions in all of these cases have applied some combination of the narrow output paradigm and a heavy thumb on the scale in favor of the autonomy of the dominant or leading firms.

B. The European Union

The European Union values openness, access, rivalry, and the competitive structure of markets as mechanisms to produce economic welfare, competitiveness, innovation, and market integration.[51] The *Microsoft* case illustrates this perspective, which is an alternative to the outcome/output paradigm.[52]

In this section I concentrate on one of the two sets of conduct condemned by the European Commission and court as violating the abuse of dominance prohibition of the EC Treaty of Rome:[53] Microsoft's strategic withholding of information necessary for its rivals' workgroup server software to interoperate with Microsoft's operating system and other software.

Microsoft supplies more than 95 percent of personal computer operating systems (OSs). It has a "superdominant" position on this market, given its near monopoly and the constant reinforcement of its power as a result of network effects.

Novell and Sun Microsystems pioneered workgroup server software. Workgroup servers are computer servers for relatively small business establishments that deliver common file and print services and administration services to the group network. To do their job, workgroup servers must interoperate with Microsoft's PC operating system.

Before Microsoft developed its own workgroup server software, Microsoft gave full interoperability information to the providers of workgroup server software. But it developed its own competing product and then withheld information, handicapping the competitors and causing them to underperform merely because they could no longer "speak" clearly to the operating system. The question before the European Court was whether

Microsoft's refusal to provide the necessary information constituted an abuse of a dominant position within Article 82(b) of the Treaty of Rome, which prohibits dominant firms from abusing their dominance and in particular "limiting production, markets or technical development to the prejudice of consumers."

The European Union, like the United States, generally allows firms, even dominant firms, to refuse to deal, since freedom of firms to choose their customers is normally good for the market and good for consumers. However, EU law—more than U.S. law—has crafted duties to deal. These duties are tightly circumscribed when they entail licensing intellectual property.

In the European *Microsoft* case, as noted, the European Commission charged Microsoft with withholding necessary interoperability information. Somewhat belatedly, Microsoft asserted that disclosing the information would entail disclosing intellectual property. The Commission disputed the claim that the protocols for which it sought disclosure were protected by intellectual property. It pointed out that Microsoft's assertion of IP rights was an afterthought, and it argued that it was a pretext. Nonetheless, on Microsoft's appeal from an adverse Commission decision to the European Court of First Instance, the Commission decided to frame its case under the demanding standards designed for refusal to license intellectual property.

The European Court upheld the Commission and found that Microsoft had indeed violated article 82. In doing so, the Court took a process-and-access approach to consumer welfare and efficiency.

The Court cited "the public interest in maintaining effective competition on the market...."[54] It found that the Commission had established that the rivals' products were innovative; that Microsoft, by strategic withholding of protocols, had killed off specific innovations by the rivals that consumers liked;[55] that users rated the rivals' workgroup server software more highly than they rated Microsoft's on all qualities (e.g., reliability, availability, security) except interoperability; and that Microsoft's "manifest and increasing lead over its competitors [was explainable]...not so much by the merits of its products as by its interoperability advantage."[56]

The Court endorsed the Commission's findings that "the refusal at issue had limited technical development to the prejudice of consumers," and its judgment that "Microsoft's arguments regarding its incentives to innovate did not outweigh" the exceptional circumstances that gave rise to the duty to disclose.[57]

Microsoft found no shelter in arguments (so well tailored to the ears of conservatively economic U.S. jurists)[58] that it had "made significant investments in designing its protocols and the commercial success which its products have achieved represents the just reward";[59] that disclosure of its protocols would undermine its incentive to invent;[60] and that an obligation to share the fruits of its investment with others would mean less investment in R&D.[61]

Was the European Court's decision efficient? It has significant efficiency properties. Computer users benefit from interoperability and from rivalry on the merits to supply the best applications. And they profit from rivals' enhanced incentives to innovate better products.

Would a decision for Microsoft have had efficiency properties? Yes. A firm's exclusive right to its system and particularly to its intellectual property conduces to productive efficiency and to innovation by the dominant firm.

Did "efficiency" decide the case? No. What made the difference? A perspective that applies nonconservative economics.

IV. The Future of "Efficiency" in Antitrust: Solving the Efficiency Paradox

For nearly 100 years, U.S. antitrust law stood against power. U.S. antitrust law was for competition, not centrally for efficiency, although efficiency was an expected by-product. The contemporary antitrust community posits that antitrust law is for efficiency and that the efficiency goal should drive the outcome of antitrust cases and limit the scope of antitrust.

In this chapter, I have assumed that antitrust law is for efficiency. I have demonstrated that efficiency is a multifaceted concept; that efficiency does not and usually cannot determine the outcome of cases;[62] and that enforcers and judges know little about how to "reach" efficiency.

I have shown that contemporary U.S. cases are commonly (although not always) determined by a conservative perspective that has created the Efficiency Paradox. The Efficiency Paradox is that, in the name of efficiency, economically conservative U.S. antitrust law protects inefficient conduct by dominant and leading firms and thus protects inefficiency. Antitrust enforcers and jurists can topple the Efficiency Paradox. They can do so by recognizing that the output/outcome paradigm is just one means to identify anticompetitive conduct and transactions; by appreciating that conservative economic presumptions are commonly misaligned with the reality of markets; and by adjusting the pendulum to put more trust in open markets and dynamic rivalry and less trust in the autonomy of dominant firms.

The Chicago School's Foundation Is Flawed:
Antitrust Protects Consumers, Not Efficiency

John B. Kirkwood and Robert H. Lande

One of the foundations of Chicago School antitrust policy is that the only permissible objective of antitrust law is to enhance economic efficiency.[63] The centrality of this lodestar to the Chicago School was explained eloquently by then-Professor Robert Bork:

> Antitrust policy cannot be made rational until we are able to give a firm answer to one question: What is the point of the law—what are its goals? Everything else follows from the answer we give.... Only when the issue of goals has been settled is it possible to frame a coherent body of substantive rules.[64]

Bork not only supplied the question; he also was the original supplier of its answer. He performed a "strict constructionist" analysis of the antitrust laws' legislative history in a famous and often-cited 1966 law review article.[65] Bork appeared to demonstrate how the legislative history of the Sherman Act established that when Congress debated and passed this law it had only one concern: increased economic efficiency.[66] As part of this analysis he made an apparently convincing argument that, if the legislative debates were analyzed closely, the then-common "populist" views of antitrust, including the belief that the antitrust laws were passed to further a variety of social and political goals, such as combating the political power of big business, or assisting small businesses, were not a concern of Congress.[67] The efficiency conclusion is now Chicago School gospel. Indeed, Judge Richard Posner recently asserted that virtually everyone now agrees that the antitrust laws have a single objective—maximizing economic efficiency.[68]

The purpose of this chapter is to demonstrate that the Chicago School is wrong, as to both congressional intent and to recent case law. The primary goal of antitrust actually is to prevent "unfair" transfers of wealth from purchasers to firms with market power. We submit that the antitrust laws on the books today best can be explained as a congressional declaration that the property right we term "consumers' surplus"[69] belongs to consumers,[70] not to cartels or to no one. The antitrust laws were enacted primarily to award this relatively amorphous property right to consumers, and to prevent cartels and monopolies from taking it. Another way to express this is to note that the primary goal of the antitrust laws can be expressed in consumer protection terms[71]: these laws better define consumers' property rights and protect them from being stolen by firms with market power.[72]

This chapter first will demonstrate that the wealth transfer concern is the primary reason for the passage of the antitrust laws and is a far more plausible explanation than the efficiency goal. Its next section will analyze the treatment of these issues in recent antitrust cases. It will show how these cases can be best explained in terms of a concern with wealth transfers, as opposed to a concern with efficiency. For these reasons, we conclude that the foundation of the Chicago School is flawed, and that the correct path of antitrust policy should not be determined by the view that increasing efficiency is more important than protecting consumers.

I. The Legislative History

Judge Bork argued that the original framers of the Sherman Act had a single intent: to enhance economic efficiency. He argued that "the whole task of antitrust can be summed up as the effort to improve allocative efficiency without impairing productive efficiency so greatly as to produce either no gain or a net loss in consumer welfare."[73] Bork explicitly rejected distributive issues as a possible area of congressional concern: "[I]t seems clear the income distribution effects of economic activity should be completely excluded from the determination of the antitrust legality of the activity."[74]

Bork pointed to dozens of statements revealing an overriding congressional concern that cartels and certain other business forms would acquire the power to artificially raise prices and restrict output.[75] Bork presented many statements of concern by Senator Sherman[76] and other legislators[77] that some of the trusts and other businesses of the period had enough power to raise prices. Bork summarized this portion of the debates succinctly: "[t]he touchstone of illegality is raising prices to consumers. There were no exceptions."[78] Since we know of no serious disagreement that this indeed was the preoccupation of the debates, we will not discuss it further. Bork then used modern economic analysis to explain how monopoly power

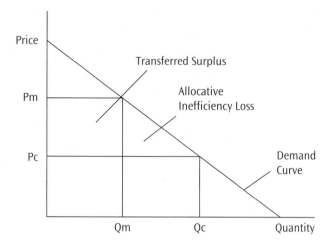

leading to higher prices for consumers can produce the form of economic inefficiency we today term allocative inefficiency.[79]

Bork reasoned that since we now know that the "only" harm to "consumer welfare" from higher prices is allocative inefficiency, congressional displeasure with market power can fairly be equated with a concern about allocative inefficiency. He then presented a smaller, although still significant, number of quotations that showed a congressional desire to preserve and enhance corporate productive efficiency.[80] On the basis of this evidence, Bork concluded that the antitrust laws embody only a concern for "consumer welfare," which he equated with the "maximization of wealth or consumer want satisfaction"[81] and the aggregate economic efficiency of our economy.[82]

The key question, however, is precisely why Congress objected when the trusts, cartels, and monopolies raised prices to consumers. As the diagram illustrates, these higher prices cause two direct types of economic effects: the transfer of surplus from consumers to cartels and monopolists, and allocative inefficiency. Which one was Congress's concern? Or were both a concern?

Bork's efficiency conclusion cannot reasonably account for many important statements from the Sherman Act's legislative history.[83] For example, Senator Sherman termed the higher prices "extortion"[84] and "extorted wealth."[85] One congressman referred to the overcharges as "robbery,"[86] and a complaint was made that the trusts "without rendering the slightest equivalent" have "stolen untold millions from the people."[87] Another congressman complained that the beef trust "robs the farmer on the one hand and the consumer on the other."[88] Another declared that the trusts were "impoverishing" the people through "robbery."[89] Senator Hoar declared that monopolistic pricing was "a transaction the direct purpose of which is to extort from the community...wealth which ought to be generally diffused over the whole community."[90] Another senator complained: "They aggregate to themselves great enormous wealth by extortion...."[91]

Do terms like "stealing," "robbery," "extortion," and "stolen wealth" sound like allocative inefficiency? Is it not much more likely that Congress in effect awarded the property right we today call "consumers' surplus" to consumers, and under the antitrust laws, the taking of consumers' surplus by cartels constitutes theft?[92]

To further contrast the efficiency and wealth transfer goals, consider why stealing is illegal. Why does society make it illegal for people to reach their hands into other peoples' wallets and take their money?

Stealing is inefficient. There is no doubt that if it were legal to steal, this would lead to inefficiency.[93] But, do we condemn stealing because of its inefficiency effects? Is not the real reason we condemn stealing because it constitutes an "unfair" taking of property without consent and without compensation? Stealing is an unfair transfer of wealth, and this is the reason why stealing money out of someone's wallet is—and should be—illegal.

Moreover, even though Congress's main complaint about trusts— that they were perceived to raise prices to purchasers—cannot equate to a concern with allocative inefficiency, could Congress primarily have been concerned with corporate productive efficiency? Did Congress pass the Sherman Act primarily to help corporations save costs and otherwise increase corporate productive efficiency?

While it is true the Congresses that enacted the antitrust laws did appreciate corporate efficiency,[94] they nevertheless passed the antitrust laws that in so many ways attacked these highly efficient organizations.[95] If all they had wanted to do was to encourage that form of industrial organization that was then the most productively efficient, they would have praised the trusts, not condemned them in the legislative debates and enacted a law that condemned many of their activities. Congress must have been concerned with other goals. This leaves the wealth transfer explanation as being most consistent with the evidence.

II. The Case Law

In recent years, the case law has largely adopted the view that the ultimate goal of the antitrust laws is to protect consumers, not increase efficiency. While most decisions do not address the issue, those that do almost always indicate that the fundamental objective of antitrust is to improve the welfare of consumers. When courts use the term "consumer welfare," moreover, they do not appear to be referring to economic efficiency. Judges rarely describe the goal of antitrust as enhancing efficiency and, more important, they *never* say that conduct that harms consumers in the relevant market is justified if it increases the efficiency of the economy. While it is possible that courts are using "consumer welfare" as Bork did, recent opinions provide little evidence of that. Instead, most judges seem to believe that the aim of antitrust is to prevent conduct that deprives consumers of the benefits of competition and transfers their wealth to firms with market power.[96]

In section A, we provide an overview of the case law by explaining why most courts, even when they use the ambiguous term "consumer welfare," likely believe that the preeminent objective of the antitrust laws is to protect consumers, not enhance efficiency. Then we examine the cases themselves. In section B, we focus on recent Supreme Court and appellate court decisions that illuminate the ultimate purpose of the antitrust laws. In section C, we look at the area where the courts have most often faced a conflict between protecting consumers and enhancing efficiency—merger cases.

A. "Consumer Welfare" and the Welfare of Consumers

The term "consumer welfare" is ambiguous because it could refer either to the welfare of consumers in the relevant market or to economic efficiency. This ambiguity arose because Bork equated "consumer welfare" with the efficiency of the economy,[97] and the Supreme Court quoted Bork when it declared that the legislative history of the Sherman Act suggests it is a "consumer welfare prescription."[98] As a result, when courts use "consumer welfare" today, they could be invoking Bork's concept, not the literal meaning of the term, and thus could be indicating that what they really care about is total welfare, not the welfare of consumers. For four reasons, however, we doubt this is so.[99]

First, some decisions clearly take the position that the ultimate objective of antitrust law is to benefit consumers, not increase efficiency. As we will see, in *Brooke Group*,[100] the Supreme Court equated "consumer welfare" with the welfare of consumers, not with total welfare, and accorded primacy to the former.

Second, while most opinions are less clear, they appear to support a consumer-oriented view of antitrust law because they focus on consumer impact rather than efficiency. In assessing the conduct at issue, they expressly examine its effect on things that matter to consumers—such as price, quality, or choice—but they rarely examine its effect on total welfare.

Third, in recent years, very few decisions state that any aspect of efficiency is a goal of the antitrust laws and those that do refer only to allocative efficiency. If these courts had been following Bork, they would have mentioned productive efficiency as well.[101] Moreover, the decisions that identify allocative efficiency as a goal always treat it as a correlate of consumer impact, not an independent value.[102]

Fourth, and most important, whenever the courts have addressed an actual or potential conflict between consumer well-being and efficiency, consumer interests have always prevailed. As section C illustrates, no recent decision has taken the position that an improvement in economic efficiency trumps an adverse impact on consumers.

B. Decisions Illuminating the Ultimate Objective

In contrast to Bork and Posner, antitrust decisions today rarely describe the ultimate goal of the antitrust laws as increasing efficiency. In recent years, however, many decisions have indicated that the purpose of the antitrust laws is to protect consumers or enhance consumer welfare.[103]

1. Supreme Court

In *Brooke Group,* the Court identified the "traditional concern" of the antitrust laws as "consumer welfare and price competition."[104] The Court equated consumer welfare, moreover, not with economic efficiency but with the benefits received by consumers in the relevant market. In analyzing whether unsuccessful predatory pricing should be illegal, the Court noted that below-cost pricing could sometimes cause allocative inefficiency. It declared, however, that unsuccessful predatory pricing "produces lower aggregate prices in the market, and consumer welfare is enhanced."[105] In measuring consumer welfare by the level of prices in the market rather than by allocative efficiency, the Court signaled that the ultimate aim of antitrust law is to enhance the well-being of consumers in the relevant market, not maximize economic efficiency or minimize inefficiency.[106] Thus, the Court noted that unsuccessful predation is "in general a boon to consumers."[107]

In *Weyerhaeuser,*[108] a more recent case challenging predatory bidding rather than predatory pricing, the Court repeatedly compared the effects of the two practices on consumers. In total, the *Weyerhaeuser* opinion contains 12 references to consumer impact (e.g., "consumer welfare,"[109] "lower prices to consumers,"[110] "consumer harm,"[111] "effect on consumer prices"[112]). The opinion contains no references to economic efficiency. Although the Court ultimately adopted a test for predatory bidding that depends on the practice's effect on suppliers, not consumers, that is consistent with the legislative history's concern with the transfer of wealth from innocent parties (buyers or sellers) to firms with market power. Like the Congress that passed the Sherman Act, therefore, *Weyerhaeuser* focused on harm to these market participants, not to the efficiency of the economy.

In *Leegin,*[113] the Court stated that the rule of reason "distinguishes between restraints with anticompetitive effect that are harmful to the consumer and restraints stimulating competition that are in the consumer's best interest."[114] In articulating a one-to-one correspondence between effects of competition and effects on consumers, the Court indicated that the lodestar of antitrust analysis is impact on consumers. Elsewhere, the Court did state that the *per se* rule against resale price maintenance could cause manufacturers to engage in "inefficient" practices,[115] and it suggested that vertical price fixing was frequently "efficient."[116] On the whole, however, the Court stressed the welfare of consumers. It repeatedly referred to matters of concern to consumers such as price levels, product quality, and options.[117] It never mentioned "total welfare" or "total surplus," even in explaining why inefficient vertical practices were undesirable. On the contrary, the Court said that inefficient practices harmed "consumer welfare" because they forced consumers to pay higher prices.[118]

2. Appellate Courts

This same focus on the well-being of consumers rather than economic efficiency is evident in recent appellate opinions. For example, the Seventh Circuit stated: "The principal purpose of the antitrust laws is to prevent overcharges to consumers."[119] The Sixth Circuit quoted a trial court's statement that "the very purpose of antitrust law is to ensure that the benefits of competition flow to purchasers of goods affected by the violation."[120] Writing for the D.C. Circuit, Judge Ginsburg characterized a court deciding an antitrust case as a "court of consumer welfare,"[121] and his opinion suggests he meant the welfare of consumers, not economic efficiency. When he summarized the FTC's methodology for evaluating horizontal restraints, first announced in *Mass. Board of Optometry*,[122] and explained why it was acceptable, he referred to impact on consumers eight times but never mentioned economic efficiency.[123] Most important, when he described what a defendant must show under the Commission's methodology to justify a restraint, he did not use the metric of economic efficiency. He did not say that a restraint would be justified if it enhances productive efficiency more than it reduces allocative efficiency, or if it increases producers' surplus more than it diminishes consumers' surplus. Instead, a defendant must show that "the restraint in fact does not harm *consumers* or has 'procompetitive virtues' that outweigh its burden upon *consumers*."[124]

Many other appellate decisions have also indicated that the ultimate test of whether a practice violates the antitrust laws is its impact on consumers. In *Microsoft*,[125] the D.C. Circuit declared, "to be condemned as exclusionary, a monopolist's act must have an 'anticompetitive effect.' That is, it must harm the competitive process and thereby harm consumers."[126] Both the Eleventh Circuit and the Fourth Circuit have quoted this statement.[127] The Tenth Circuit stated, "to be judged anticompetitive, the [conduct] must actually or potentially harm consumers."[128] Writing for the Seventh Circuit, Judge Easterbrook echoed the thesis of this article when he declared: "Calling the selection of components for one's product a 'tie-in' does not help to uncover practices that restrict output, drive up prices, and transfer wealth from consumers to producers."[129]

C. Merger Cases: Increased Efficiency Never Excuses Harm to Consumers

In merger cases, courts have frequently faced an actual or potential conflict between economic efficiency and the welfare of consumers.[130] If a merger is likely to generate both cost savings and greater market power, the increase in productive efficiency could easily outweigh the loss in allocative efficiency, causing a net gain in overall efficiency, even though consumers in the relevant market are hurt because they have to pay higher prices.[131] No U.S. court, however, has ever allowed a merger that was likely to increase prices in the relevant market (or otherwise diminish consumer choice) because it would enhance economic efficiency. To the contrary, the courts have uniformly insisted that merging parties cannot establish an efficiencies defense unless they show both that the merger would generate significant cost savings and that enough of those savings would be passed on to consumers that consumers would benefit from (or at least not be hurt by) the merger.

In *Heinz*,[132] for example, the D.C. Circuit stated that a "defendant who seeks to overcome a presumption that a proposed acquisition would substantially lessen competition must demonstrate that the intended acquisition would result in significant economies and that these economies ultimately would benefit competition and, hence, consumers."[133] In *Swedish Match*,[134] Judge Hogan held that the defendants' efficiency evidence was insufficient to overcome the presumption of illegality because the defendants had not shown what proportion of their cost savings they would pass on and "how that will defeat the likely price increases in this market."[135] Both of these decisions stand for the proposition that "an acquisition that lowers costs may still be unlawful 'if it results in an increased likelihood of higher prices.' "[136] Other cases concur,[137] and there is no decision to the contrary. The merger cases to date, therefore, have uniformly applied a consumer impact standard, rather than a total welfare standard, to the evaluation of claimed efficiencies.[138]

In some of these cases, moreover, this position was not simply dictum. The court found actual merger-specific efficiencies but disregarded some or all of them because they were unlikely to benefit consumers. In *Staples*,[139] for example, the defendants asserted that the challenged transaction would produce a variety of efficiencies, including better prices from vendors and reduced distribution costs.[140] Although Judge Hogan identified numerous problems with this defense, he did not conclude that the merger would generate no significant cost savings. To the contrary, he stated that "the Court believes that there would be some efficiencies realized by the merger." [141] He ruled that these savings did not excuse the transaction, however, because most of them would not be passed on,[142] and thus consumers in the relevant markets would likely pay higher rather than lower prices after the merger.[143]

Conclusion

The normative foundation of Chicago School antitrust policy is flawed. Both the legislative history of the antitrust laws and recent case law indicate that the fundamental goal of antitrust enforcement is not increasing economic efficiency. It is protecting consumers in the relevant market from practices that deprive them of the benefits of competition and transfer their wealth to firms with market power.

Notes

1. U.S. antitrust law was adopted to contain private power; to give free and fair access to market actors without power; and to try to assure "that consumers get to determine who wins the competitive race." See Irwin Stelzer, "Coping with Market Power in the Modern Era," White Paper, Hudson Institute (Spring 2007), 12, available at www.hudson.org/files/publications/StelzerWhitePaperMarch07.pdf; Eleanor M. Fox, The Modernization of Antitrust—A New Equilibrium, 66 Cornell L. Rev. 1140 (1981).

2. *See Verizon Communications Inc. v. Law Offices of Curtis V. Trinko, LLP,* 540 U.S. 398 (2004).

3. *See Texaco v. Dagher,* 547 U.S. 1 (2006).

4. *See* Wolfgang Kerber & Nicole J. Sam, *Competition as a Test of Hypotheses: Simulation of Knowledge-generating Market Processes,* 4 J. Artificial Societies & Soc. Simulation n0.3, http://www.soc.surrey.ac.uk/JASSS/4/3/2.html (2001).

5. *See* Joseph F. Brodley, *The Economic Goals of Antitrust: Efficiency, Consumer Welfare, and Technological Progress,* 62 N.Y.U. L. Rev. 1020 (1987); F. M. Scherer, *Antitrust, Efficiency, and Progress,* 62 N.Y.U. L. Rev. 998 (1987).

6. Losses to producers squeezed out of business by exclusionary practices are typically disregarded, whether they are squeezed out by competition itself or by anticompetitive conduct.

7. *See FTC v. Indiana Federation of Dentists,* 476 U.S. 444 (1986). *See also* Thomas B. Leary, *The Significance of Variety in Antitrust Analysis,* 68 Antitrust L.J. 1007 (2001); Neil W. Averitt & Robert H. Lande, *Using the "Consumer Choice" Approach to Antitrust Law,* 74 Antitrust L.J. 175 (2007).

8. *See Trinko,* 540 U.S. 398; *United States v. Microsoft Corp.,* 253 F.3d 34, 49–50, 65 (D.C. Cir. 2001), *cert. denied,* 534 U.S. 952 (2001).

9. *See, e.g., United States v. Oracle Corp.* (Oracle/PeopleSoft), 331 F. Supp. 2d 1098 (N.D. Cal. 2004).

10. *See FTC v. Superior Court Trial Lawyers Ass'n,* 493 U.S. 411 (1990); *Leegin Creative Leather Products, Inc. v. PSKS, Inc.,* 127 S. Ct. 2705 (2007), Justice Breyer dissenting.

11. Even so, particular takeovers are often inefficient. They can increase firms' costs by creating cultural incompatibilities and decreasing flexibility and adaptability. A notorious example is Time Warner/ AOL. *See* Rob Walker, *Creating Synergy Out of Thin Air,* N.Y. Times, July 28, 2002, C13.

12. In rare cases, antitrust law can be prescriptive. It can impose duties to open markets, as opposed to mandates not to close them by anticompetitive acts. Affirmative duties are disfavored in the United States. *See Trinko,* 540 U.S. 398; *see* Makin Delrahim, "Forcing Firms to Share the Sandbox: Compulsory Licensing of Intellectual Property Rights and Antitrust," paper presented at the British Institute of International and Comparative Law, London, England, May 10, 2004, available at http://www.usdoj.gov/ atr/public/speeches/203627.htm.

13. *See* Stelzer, *supra* note 1 at 14.

14. "No business sense" is one of several tests commonly suggested today as the screen and the standard for anticompetitive conduct by dominant firms. It is similar to the test suggested by Judge Bork, when he said in *Rothery Storage & Van Co. v. Atlas Van Lines, Inc.,* 792 F.2d 210 (D.C. Cir. 1986): if the conduct or agreement is not designed "to restrict industry output, then [it] must be designed to make the conduct of their business more effective." *Id.* at 221. Other proposed tests include whether the dominant firm sacrificed profits at stage one to make monopoly profits at stage two, and whether defendant's conduct would destroy an equally efficient competitor. Balancing anticompetitive harms against procompetitive (efficiency) benefits would yield more enforcement, but is disfavored by the current enforcers.

15. *See Schor v. Abbott Labs.,* 457 F.3d 608 (7th Cir. 2006), *cert. denied,* 127 S. Ct. 1257 (2007), Easterbrook, J.: "And if a manufacturer cannot make itself better off by injuring consumers through lower output and higher prices, there is no role for antitrust law to play." *Id.* at 612.

16. Again, this formulation produces the narrowest scope of illegality. It is possible, but less likely, that vertical or potential-competition mergers will have this proscribed effect.

17. *See,* for critical role of presumptions, Andrew J. Gavil, *Exclusionary Distribution Strategies by Dominant Firms: Striking a Better Balance,* 72 ANTITRUST L.J. 3 (2004).

18. This paper is about antitrust law other than cartel law for the following reasons: The strong law against hard-core cartels (meaning: price, output, or market division agreements among competitors that are designed only to get rid of the competition among the parties and have no credible claim of being, for example, a synergistic joint venture) has been a staple of antitrust enforcement for a hundred years and is supported by all perspectives on antitrust. Liberals or pluralists support the law because cartels exploit their customers or suppliers and because they paradigmatically offend the principle of market governance by competition, not powerful firms. Libertarians or conservatives might support the law because cartels are inefficient and output limiting; and, since cartelists have no excuse that they are responding to and serving the market, the costs of error from the prohibition are virtually nonexistent. In the matter of cartels, liberals and

libertarians meet. The law is supported by economics and socio-political concerns. Only industrial policy advocates are likely to take exception.

19. Note that the outcome perspective requires that private action, to be caught by the law, must (probably) decrease output. This means that most tying and other uses of leverage by dominant firms, even if unjustified, will not be caught by antitrust. Leveraging is "only" a *use* of power, not an *increase* of power. *See Trinko,* 540 U.S. 398, at n. 4. For the contrasting EU approach to distortion of competition, *see Microsoft Corp v. Commission,* Case T-201/04, Sept. 17, 2007.

20. Hans B. Thorelli, THE FEDERAL ANTITRUST POLICY: ORIGINATION OF AN AMERICAN TRADITION 566 (1955). Note that Sumner's argument was not that markets would always work well but that, however they worked, no law could stop them. As for the professional economists, "insofar as is known," Congress considered one antitrust bill after another without calling on their advice. The legislators of the time distrusted experts. However, if Congress had sought the advice of the economists, it could not have expected support for the Sherman Act. *Id.* at 120–21.

21. Irwin Stelzer argues that process and access are all the more important in high tech industries, "'lest high-tech' be converted to 'my-tech' by dominant firms" and powerful incumbents slow down or exclude "incursions of technologically superior challengers." Stelzer, *supra* note 1 at 11, 14.

As to the importance of mavericks, *see* Jonathan B. Baker, *Mavericks, Mergers, and Exclusion: Proving Coordinated Competitive Effects Under the Antitrust Laws,* 77 N.Y.U. L. REV. 135 (2002).

22. The process may be regarded as iterative. It provides a learning and feedback mechanism. Firms observe, learn, compete, innovate, and adjust. *See* Kerber, *supra* note 4. *See,* for a description of antitrust rules and standards based on a process/open market approach, E. Fox, *Abuse of Dominance and Monopolization: How to Protect Competition without Protecting Competitors, in* Claus-Dieter Ehlermann & Isabela Atanasiu, eds., EUROPEAN COMPETITION LAW ANNUAL: WHAT IS AN ABUSE OF A DOMINANT POSITION? (Hart, 2006).

23. *See Brown Shoe Co. v. United States,* 370 U.S. 294 (1962).

24. *See* Jeffrey Rosen, *Majority of One: Stevens at the Supreme Court,* N.Y. Times Mag., Sept. 23, 2007, 50.

25. This is not the precise language of the Court, but is readily inferred from the majority opinions. *See, e.g., Leegin,* 127 S. Ct. 2705.

26. *See* Thomas B. Leary, *The Inevitability of Uncertainty,* 3 COMPETITION LAW INT'L 27 (2007) (Journal of Antitrust Committee of International Bar Ass'n): Although the Chicago revolution substituted a "single lodestar"— economic welfare of consumers—for diffuse populist objectives, "this did not mean that cases would necessarily be easier to decide or to handicap. Quite the contrary." *Id.* at 28.

27. *Brooke Group Ltd. v. Brown & Williamson Tobacco Corp.,* 509 U.S. 209 (1993).

28. *California Dental Ass'n v. FTC,* 526 U.S. 756 (1999).

29. *Supra* note 2.

30. *Supra* note 11.

31. *Supra* note 26.

32. *Matsushita Elec. Indus. Co. v. Zenith Radio Corp.* (Japanese Electronics), 475 U.S. 574 (1986).

33. 509 U.S. at 226.

34. *See, e.g.,* John McGee, *Predatory Pricing Revisited,* 23 J. L. & ECON. 289, 292–94 (1980).

35. *See, e.g.,* Joseph F. Brodley, *Predatory Pricing: Strategic Theory and Legal Policy,* 88 GEORGETOWN L.J. 2239 (2000).

36. Nonetheless, in a subsequent case charging predatory buying (*Weyerhaeuser*) in which the dominant defendant overbought saw logs at inflated prices to eliminate its rivals from the market and did eliminate them, the Court reaffirmed its dictum in *Brooke Group.* It said that price predation almost never happens. The Court declared that predatory buying is the mirror image of predatory selling and that enjoining the high buying price (the first leg of buyer predation) was just as harmful to consumers as enjoining a low selling price, and that therefore the tough standards of proof for predatory selling should apply equally to predatory buying. *Weyerhaeuser Company v. Ross-Simmons Hardwood Lumber Co.,* 127 S.Ct. 1069 (2007).

37. A ruling for plaintiff could have been based on the loss of consumer welfare in the particular case, as argued by Liggett's appellate lawyer Phillip Areeda.

38. *Supra* note 27.

39. 526 U.S. at 776–77.

40. *See* Justice Breyer, concurring and dissenting: "[W]hy should I have to spell out the obvious? To restrain truthful advertising about lower prices is likely to restrict competition in respect to price—'the central nervous system of the economy.'" 526 U.S. at 781, 784.

41. I stress conservative and not conservative/libertarian. Skepticism regarding professional self-regulation and state professional regulation is one point at which liberal and libertarian philosophies meet. Both FTC Chairman Michael Pertschuk (appointed by President Jimmy Carter) and FTC Chairman Timothy Muris (appointed by President George W. Bush) brought or supported proceedings against doctors and dentists and restrictive eye glass regulations.

42. *Supra* note 2.

43. The rival was AT&T. AT&T had already settled its regulatory and antitrust claim against Verizon.

44. This is the Court's rendition of the "*Aspen* exception."

45. 540 U.S. at 407.

46. I distinguish formulation of the antitrust principles from the outcome of the case. The case was a regulated industries case and, under an unusually procompetitive regulatory statute, the Federal Communications Commission had already taken action against the anticompetitive conduct.

47. *Supra* note 11.

48. *Dr. Miles Medical Co. v. John D. Park & Sons Co.,* 220 U.S. 373 (1911); *overruled, Leegin,* 127 S. Ct. 2705.

49. *Leegin,* 127 S. Ct. 2705.

50. *State Oil Co. v. Khan,* 522 U.S. 3 (1997) (an antitrust rule of law preventing maximum resale price agreements per se is clearly inefficient).

51. *See* Annual Reports on Competition Policy of the European Commission; e.g., Reports of 2005, 2006.

52. The irony is that the openness/process perspective is sympathetic to the legislative origins of the U.S. antitrust laws, and the outcome/output perspective—which is in the ascendancy in the United States—is not. Nonetheless, there are a number of examples of U.S. courts' taking an openness/process approach. One notable example is *Microsoft, supra* note 8. The court valued market access for competitors, free from unjustified restraints. The government had not proved that Microsoft's abuses cut back the output of computer software. Nonetheless, the court *assumed* harm to competition from Microsoft's "bad acts" that foreclosed competitors from certain efficient channels, combined with Microsoft's failure to assert a good business justification. See Eleanor M. Fox, *What is Harm to Competition?—Exclusionary Practices and Anticompetitive Effect,* 70 ANTITRUST L.J. 371 (2002).

53. Treaty of Rome establishing the European Community, as last amended at Nice, Official Journal C 325, Dec. 24, 2002.

54. *Microsoft Corp. v. Commission,* Case T-201/04, Court of First Instance, para. 691., Sept. 17, 2007, available at http://curia.europa.eu.

55. *Id.* at para. 654.

56. *Id.* at para. 407.

57. *Id.* at paras. 708, 709. The Court endorsed the Commission findings that Microsoft "did not sufficiently establish that [the required disclosure] would have a significant negative impact on its incentives to innovate." Para. 697.

58. *See, e.g., Trinko, supra* note 2.

59. *Microsoft Corp. v. Commission,* para. 666.

60. *Id.* at para. 266.

61. *Id.* at para. 670.

62. An efficiency standard can, however, weed out cases in which a plaintiff's victory would protect inefficient competitors at the expense of consumers. So, too, does a refined understanding of what is harm to competition. *See* Fox, WHAT IS HARM TO COMPETITION, *supra* note 52.

63. Much of this paper's legislative history and some of its analysis was taken from Robert H. Lande, *Wealth Transfers as the Original and Primary Concern of Antitrust: The Efficiency Interpretation Challenged,* 34 HASTINGS L.J. 65 (1982) [hereinafter *Wealth Transfers*]. Many of the cases in this paper were collected and originally analyzed in John B. Kirkwood, *Consumers, Economics, and Antitrust, in* 21 RES. L. & ECON., ANTITRUST LAW AND ECONOMICS 1 (John B. Kirkwood ed., 2004). This paper is an abbreviated version of a much longer paper the authors are preparing. *See* John B. Kirkwood & Robert H. Lande, "The Fundamental Goal of Antitrust Law: Protecting Consumers, Not Increasing Efficiency" (unpublished draft, 2007).

64. Robert H. Bork, THE ANTITRUST PARADOX: A POLICY AT WAR WITH ITSELF 50 (1978).

65. Robert H. Bork, *Legislative Intent and the Policy of the Sherman Act,* 9 J. L. & ECON. 7 (1966).

66. *Id.*

67. *Id.*

68. Richard A. Posner, Antitrust Law *ix* (2d ed. 2001).

69. "Consumers' surplus" is the difference between what something is worth to consumers and the price they pay for it. *See* Luís M. B. Cabral, Introduction to Industrial Organization 16 (2000).

70. We use the term "consumers" to include all individual or business purchasers of products and services, regardless whether they are the ultimate end users.

71. This article will only address the price and quantity effects of situations of antitrust concern, and accordingly will only contrast the efficiency and wealth transfer approaches. Sometimes, however, consumer welfare cannot adequately be protected by antitrust enforcement that only considers price and closely related areas like cost and quantity. The "consumer choice" approach is another, more complex way to articulate the goals of the antitrust laws in those situations when non-price issues are at stake. "Consumer choice" is an emerging paradigm that also is completely economic in nature. It does incorporate the wealth transfer effects of market power. It also differs from the efficiency model in that it gives greater weight to short term non-price choices having to do with quality or variety, and also to long term innovation effects. *See* Neil W. Averitt & Robert H. Lande, *Using The "Consumer Choice" Approach to Antitrust Law,* 74 Antitrust L.J. 175 (2007).

72. The old pre-Chicago, social/political rationale for antitrust is dead and buried. It should not be resurrected. There might, however, be a sharply limited but distinctive way antitrust can and should protect small businesses. Antitrust policy should take small business welfare into account so long as this does not cause consumers to pay supracompetitive prices. For example, the legislative history indicates that Congress intended to protect sellers from buyers' cartels. *See infra* note 26 and accompanying text. For a discussion of buyers' cartels and other situations where antitrust intervention can protect seller welfare but not harm consumers, *see* John B. Kirkwood & Robert H. Lande, "The Fundamental Goal of Antitrust Law: Protecting Consumers, Not Increasing Efficiency" (unpublished draft, 2007).

73. Bork, *supra* note 64, at 91.

74. *Id.* at 111.

75. Bork, *supra* note 65, *passim.*

76. *See* 21 Cong. Rec. 2457 (1890)(statement of Senator Sherman that trusts tend to "advance the price to the consumer"); 21 Cong. Rec. 2460 (1890) (statement of Senator Sherman that it is sometimes contended that trusts reduced prices to the consumer, "but that all experience shows that this saving of cost goes to the pockets of the producer"); 21 Cong. Rec. 2462 (1890) (statement of Senator Sherman asking Congress to protect the public from trusts that "increase the price of articles").

77. *See, e.g.,* 21 Cong. Rec. 2558 (1890) (statement of Senator Pugh that trusts effectively "[destroy] competition in production and thereby [increase] prices to consumers").

78. Bork, *supra* note 65, at 16.

79. To raise prices, a monopoly or cartel reduces output from the competitive level. The goods no longer sold are worth more to would-be purchasers

than they would have cost society to produce. This foregone production is a pure social loss and constitutes the "allocative inefficiency" of monopoly or cartel pricing. For example, suppose that widgets cost $1.00 in a competitive market (their cost of production plus a competitive profit). Suppose a monopolist would sell them for $2.00. A potential purchaser that would have been willing to pay up to $1.50 will not purchase at the $2.00 level. Since a competitive market would have sold the widgets for less than they were worth to this potential purchaser, the monopolist's reduced production has decreased the consumer's satisfaction without producing any countervailing social benefits. This loss is termed "allocative inefficiency." For an extended discussion and formal proof that monopoly pricing creates allocative inefficiency, *see* Edwin Mansfield, MICROECONOMICS: THEORY AND APPLICATIONS 277–292 (4th ed. 1982).

80. Bork, *supra* note 65, at 26–31.

81. *Id.* at 7.

82. Bork, *supra* note 64, at 91.

83. For similar wealth transfer oriented statements from the legislative history of the Clayton Act, *see Wealth Transfers, supra* note 63, at 128; for similar statements from the legislative history of the Celler-Kefauver Act, *see Wealth Transfers, supra* note 63, at 135–36; for similar statements from the legislative history of the Federal Trade Commission Act, see *Wealth Transfers, supra* note 63, at 112–14.

84. 21 CONG. REC. 2461 (1890) (quoting Senator Sherman).

85. 21 CONG. REC. 2461 (1890) (quoting Senator Sherman).

86. 21 CONG REC. 2614 (1890) (statement of Congressman Coke).

87. 21 CONG. REC. 4101 (1890) (statement of Representative Heard).

88. 21 CONG. REC. 4098 (1890) (statement of Congressman Taylor).

89. 21 CONG. REC. 4103 (1890) (statement of Representative Fithian, who was reading, with apparent approval, a letter from a constituent).

90. 21 CONG. REC. 2728 (1890) (statement of Senator Hoar).

91. 21 CONG. REC. (1768) (statement of Senator George).

92. Congress wanted to protect all those who purchased products and services; it made no distinction between wealthy and poor consumers, or between business and individual consumers. Nor did Congress seem concerned whether purchasers absorbed the overcharges or passed them on. While Congress frequently referred to "consumers," it did not appear to care only about ultimate consumers. In other words, any direct purchaser should be deemed a "consumer" for antitrust purposes, regardless what they decided to do with their purchase. Otherwise every price rise by a cartel, etc. would have to be examined to determine whether it affected ultimate consumers, or whether instead it had been absorbed by intermediaries. This can be a very difficult undertaking. Many of the complexities that would arise if antitrust were only concerned with the welfare of ultimate consumers are analyzed in Gregory J. Werden, *Monopsony and the Sherman Act: Consumer Welfare in a New Light,* at 24–30 (Mar. 23, 2007), *available at* http://ssrn.com/abstract=975992.

93. For example, if it were legal to take other peoples' property, their incentives to work hard would likely be diminished.

94. See Bork, *supra* note 65, at 26–31.

95. The Standard Oil trust, for example, was never attacked for being inefficient. *See, e.g.,* Ida M. Tarbell, *The History of the Standard Oil Company,* McClure's Magazine, 1902–1904. *See generally* Ron Chernow, Titan: The Life of John D. Rockefeller, Sr. (1998). Nor did the government ever assert that Standard Oil violated the Sherman Act by being inefficient. For an excellent and thorough analysis of the Standard Oil case, *see* James May, *The Story of Standard Oil Co. v. United States, in* Antitrust Stories 7 (Eleanor M. Fox & Daniel A. Crane, eds., 2007).

96. There are only two exceptions to the preeminent status of consumers in antitrust law. The first is the Robinson-Patman Act, whose principal purpose is not to promote competition (and thus benefit consumers) but in certain circumstances to protect small business from competition. *See, e.g.,* John B. Kirkwood, *Buyer Power and Exclusionary Conduct: Should Brooke Group Set the Standards for Buyer-Induced Price Discrimination and Predatory Bidding?,* 72 Antitrust L.J. 625, 632–35 (2005). The second exception arises in the relatively few cases that involve anticompetitive behavior by buyers. In these cases, the courts usually aim to protect suppliers from exploitation, not consumers. *See, e.g., Telecor Commc'ns, Inc. v. Southwestern Bell Tel. Co.,* 305 F.3d 1124, 1133–34 (10th Cir. 2002), *cert. denied,* 538 U.S. 1031 (2003) ("The Supreme Court's treatment of monopsony cases strongly suggests that suppliers...are protected by antitrust laws even when the anti-competitive activity does not harm end-users.") We will not address these exceptions in this chapter. They are limited in scope, and neither supports the Chicago School view that the paramount objective of antitrust law is economic efficiency.

97. *See supra* note 81–82 and accompanying text.

98. *Reiter v. Sonotone Corp.,* 442 U.S. 330, 343 (1979) (citing Bork, *supra* note 65, at 66). In *Reiter,* the Court did not actually endorse Bork's definition of consumer welfare. It never addressed whether the term referred to economic efficiency rather than the welfare of consumers.

99. *Accord,* Daniel J. Gifford & Robert T. Kudrle, *Rhetoric and Reality in the Merger Standards of the United States, Canada, and the European Union,* 72 Antitrust L.J. 423, 432–33 (2005) ("...the U.S. courts do not appear to be employing [consumer welfare] in the total-surplus sense that Bork formally attributed to it. That is, the U.S. courts use the phrase, but they appear to be following an antitrust policy predicted on the maximization of consumer surplus rather than total surplus.")

100. *Brooke Group Ltd. v. Brown & Williamson Tobacco Corp.,* 509 U.S. 209 (1993).

101. *See* Bork, *supra* note 65, at 91.

102. *See, e.g., Rebel Oil Co. v. Atlantic Richfield Co.,* 51 F.3d 1421, 1433 (9th Cir. 1995): "An act is deemed anticompetitive under the Sherman Act 'only when it harms *both* allocative efficiency *and* raises the prices of goods above competitive levels or diminishes their quality.' " (Emphasis added.)

103. To be sure, it is even more common for courts to say that the purpose of the antitrust laws is to promote competition or the competitive process. *See* Kirkwood, *supra* note 63, at 30–31. Since the courts almost never define competition or the competitive process, however, these formulations do not provide a concrete guide for determining whether or not the antitrust

laws have been violated. In the last 15 years—the scope of our survey—many courts have remedied that problem by declaring that the purpose of the antitrust laws is to protect consumers.

104. 509 U.S. at 221.

105. *Id.* at 224.

106. *Accord,* Aaron S. Edlin, *Stopping Above-Cost Predatory Pricing,* 111 YALE L.J. 941, 947 n. 24 (2002). (*Brooke Group* elevated consumer interests over efficiency because the Court argued that "prices below cost are not problematic from an antitrust perspective, even though they are allocatively inefficient, because such prices increase consumer welfare.")

107. 509 U.S. at 224.

108. *Weyerhaeuser,* 127 S.Ct. 1069.

109. *Id.* at 1077 (quoting *Brooke Group,* 509 U.S. at 224).

110. *Id.* at 1077.

111. *Id.* at 1078.

112. *Id.*

113. *Leegin,* 127 S. Ct. 2705.

114. *Id.* at 2713.

115. *Id.* at 2716.

116. *Id.* at 2717.

117. *See, e.g., id.* at 2715 ("Resale price maintenance also has the potential to give consumers more options.")

118. *Id.* at 2722–23.

119. *Kochert v. Greater Lafayette Health Servs.,* 463 F.3d 710, 715 (7th Cir. 2006) (quoting *Premier Elec. Constr. Co. v. Nat'l Elec. Contractors Ass'n, Inc.,* 814 F.2d 358, 368 (7th Cir. 1987) (Easterbrook, J.)).

120. *Louisiana Wholesale Drug Co. v. Hoechst Marion Roussel, Inc.* (*In re* Cardizem CD Antitrust Litig.), 332 F.3d 896, 904 (6th Cir. 2003).

121. *PolyGram Holding, Inc. v. FTC,* 416 F.3d 29, 37 (D.C. Cir. 2005).

122. *In re* Mass. Bd. of Registration of Optometry, 110 F.T.C. 549 (1988).

123. *See* 416 F.3d at 35–37.

124. *Id.* at 36 (emphasis added).

125. *United States v. Microsoft Corp.,* 253 F.3d 34 (D.C. Cir. 2001).

126. *Id.* at 58 (emphasis omitted).

127. *See Spanish Broadcasting Sys. of Fla., Inc. v. Clear Channel Commc'ns, Inc.,* 376 F.3d 1065, 1071 (11th Cir. 2004); *Dickson v. Microsoft Corp.,* 309 F.3d 193, 206 (4th Cir. 2002).

128. *SCFC ILC, Inc. v. Visa USA, Inc.,* 36 F.3d 958, 965 (10th Cir. 1994).

129. *Digital Equip. Corp. v. Uniq Digital Techs.,* 73 F.3d 756, 761 (7th Cir. 1996). Other courts have stated that the ultimate test is whether the conduct enhances or reduces "consumer welfare." In *Rebel Oil,* for example, the Ninth Circuit declared: "Of course, conduct that eliminates rivals reduces competition. But reduction of competition does not invoke the Sherman Act until it harms consumer welfare." 51 F.3d at 1433. For the reasons described in section A, these decisions were likely referring to the welfare of consumers, not total welfare.

130. The same conflict could arise in other types of cases. *See* Jonathan A. Baker, *Competition Policy as a Political Bargain,* 73 ANTITRUST L.J. 483, 517–18 (2006). To our knowledge, however, no recent decision in any area

of antitrust law has permitted a practice likely to harm consumers on the ground that it would increase efficiency.

131. *See* Oliver E. Williamson, *Economies as an Antitrust Defense: The Welfare Tradeoffs,* 58 AM. ECON. REV. 18 (1968). For an analysis of this conflict that examines whether prices to purchasers are likely to increase, see Alan A. Fisher, Frederick Johnson & Robert H. Lande, *Price Effects of Horizontal Mergers,* 77 CALIF. L. REV. 777 (1989).

132. *FTC v. H.J. Heinz Co.,* 246 F.3d 708 (D.C. Cir. 2001).

133. *Id.* at 720 (quoting *FTC v. Univ. Health, Inc.,* 938 F.2d 1206, 1223 (11th Cir. 1991)).

134. *FTC v. Swedish Match,* 131 F. Supp. 2d 151 (D.D.C. 2000).

135. *Id.* at 172.

136. *Dr. Pepper/Seven-Up Cos. v. FTC,* 798 F. Supp. 762, 777 (D.D.C. 1992), *rev'd on other grounds,* 991 F.2d 859 (D.C Cir. 1993) (quoting FTC letter refusing to approve the acquisition).

137. *See, e.g., FTC v. Arch Coal, Inc.,* 329 F. Supp. 2d 109, 153 (D.D.C. 2004) (in assessing efficiencies, what is relevant are "the potential benefits to consumers from cost reductions and increased competition"); *U.S. v. Franklin Elec. Co. Inc.,* 130 F. Supp. 2d 1025, 1035 (W.D. Wis. 2000) ("Defendants have not made the necessary showing that efficiencies would result *and* that they would lead to benefits for consumers in the relevant market") (Emphasis in original).

138. In contrast, Canada allowed the merger of Superior Propane and ICG Propane, even though it would harm consumers, because it would produce a substantial increase in total welfare. *See Comm'r of Competition v. Superior Propane, Inc.* [2003] 3 F.C. 529.

139. *FTC v. Staples, Inc.,* 970 F. Supp. 1066 (D.D.C. 1997).

140. *See id.* at 1089–90.

141. *Id.* at 1092.

142. *Id.* at 1090.

143. *Id.* at 1091. Likewise, in *Dr. Pepper/Seven-Up* the district court found that the acquisition was likely to yield significant efficiencies. *See* 798 F. Supp. at 777. These cost reductions did not save the acquisition, though, because there was considerable evidence that the acquisition would increase prices in the relevant market. *Id.*

3

Chicago School and
Dominant Firm Behavior

Introduction

From the enactment of the Sherman Act in 1890, unjustifiable acts of monopolization or attempts to monopolize have been explicitly declared illegal by statute[1] and in judicial decisions.[2] One of the most remarkable developments in recent years is hostility to section 2 enforcement by conservative scholars and in language in judicial decisions. For example, in *Verizon Communications* v. *Law Office of Curtis V. Trinko*,[3] in an opinion most people think rightly dismissed a monopolization claim, Justice Scalia commented that "[t]he opportunity to charge monopoly prices—at least for a short period—is what attracts 'business acumen' in the first place; it induces risk taking that produces innovation and economic growth"[4]—an unusually benign view of monopoly power. At a later point in the opinion, he associated refusals to deal by monopolists with "false positives" (i.e., false condemnations) because they chill procompetitive effects. Singling out monopoly enforcement as examples of false positives is curious in light of the fact that, before *Trinko,* the government or private plaintiffs for decades had won virtually every monopoly challenge in the Supreme Court. Herbert Hovenkamp and Harvey Goldschmid examine these developments in this chapter.

Hovenkamp introduces his essay with a wide-ranging comparison of "Chicago School" analysis with the earlier and more liberal "Harvard School" approaches, concluding that each had major influences in various areas of antitrust. He argues in terms of influence that the balance in the *case law* rather than the *scholarship* is in favor of the Harvard School. If the more conservative approach has had an influence, it is in "chastening" and thereby moderating Harvard School preference for vigorous enforcement.

Hovenkamp next turns to the question whether there can be a "general theory" of monopolization, an obsessive recent concern of conservative antitrust officials. He concludes that all proposed tests, while often containing useful insights in specific areas of law, fall short of the goal of a successful "general theory" because they fail to address particular undesirable forms of exclusion and are often underdeterrent. He offers instead an elaboration of tests already in the law, noting that the tests appear in his own treatise.

Finally, Hovenkamp explores two problem areas most controversial in courts today: (1) misuse of government processes, particularly in the form of fraud on the Patent Office; and (2) exclusionary discounting or discounts designed to drive out of the market, or discipline, rivals. While noting that present interpretations occasionally are underdeterrent, his balanced review also notes the danger that aggressive enforcement in these areas may deter procompetitive conduct.

Goldschmid finds commentary in recent Supreme Court cases (especially *Trinko*)[5] and the absence in recent years of serious enforcement of section 2 much more troubling. With respect to Justice Scalia's extensive comments in the *Trinko* decision about the value of aggressive behavior leading to monopoly power, which Goldschmid acknowledges has some merit, he notes the total absence in the Scalia opinion of any concern with the anticonsumer side of monopoly power—"excessive prices, misallocation of resources, and loss of dynamic efficiency." That style of passive acceptance follows from one of the basic canons of conservative economic analysis—the theory that if a monopolist tries to take advantage of its market position, new entry and market corrections will automatically appear and make section 2 law enforcement largely unnecessary.

Goldschmid advocates a balancing test, citing language in *Aspen Ski* and *Microsoft* as a more sensible approach to dominant firm behavior than the rigid passive approach to enforcement, based on general Chicago School scholarship.

With respect to recent cases, Goldschmid notes that a benign attitude toward unreasonable behavior by a monopolist throws into doubt the unanimous opinion of the District of Columbia Court of Appeals finding that Microsoft had violated section 2.[6] As evidence that scholars concerned about enforcement do not agree on everything, however, the two professors sharply disagree on whether the *Kodak* case—the last antitrust case won by a plaintiff in the Supreme Court—was rightly decided.

The Harvard and Chicago Schools and the Dominant Firm

Herbert Hovenkamp

Introduction: The Harvard and Chicago Schools

The Chicago School has produced many significant contributions to the antitrust literature of the last half century. Thanks in part to Chicago School efforts, today we have an antitrust policy that is more rigorously economic, less concerned with protecting noneconomic values that are impossible to identify and weigh, and more confident that markets will correct themselves without government intervention.[7] This Chicago School revolution came at the expense of the Harvard "structural" school, which flourished from the 1930s through the 1950s. That school rested on a fairly rigid theory of Cournot oligopoly, exaggerated notions about barriers and impediments to entry, and a belief that certain types of anticompetitive conduct were more-or-less inevitable given a particular market structure.[8] As a result, the best course for antitrust was to go after the structure, and the conduct would take care of itself. The chastised Harvard School that emerged in the late 1970s in the writings of Phillip E. Areeda and a converted Donald F. Turner were much less ambitious about the goals of antitrust, much more concerned with conduct as such, and significantly more skeptical about the benefits of aggressive judicial intervention.[9]

This story of a victorious Chicago School and a humbled and disciplined Harvard School is incomplete, however. The antitrust case law reveals something quite different. On most of the important issues, this chastised Harvard School has captured antitrust decision making in the courts, and largely in the enforcement agencies.[10] For example, the Chicago position on predatory pricing is largely that predatory pricing is an irrational activity, and those claiming it should be summarily dismissed.[11] Somewhat more moderate Chicago School members, such as Richard A. Posner, argued that the test should be pricing below long-run marginal cost with intent to harm a rival.[12] By contrast, the Harvard literature, beginning with Areeda and Turner's article in 1975, argued that the law of predatory pricing consists of two elements: first, proof that prices were below a given measure of cost, namely short-run marginal cost or average variable cost; and second, that at the time of the predation decision the defendant faced a sufficient prospect of recoupment.[13] In its important *Brooke Group* decision the Supreme Court cited Chicago School as well as Harvard School scholarship,[14] but the test for predation that they adopted was completely taken from a page of the Harvard School: in order to show unlawful predatory pricing a plaintiff had to show recoupment plus prices lower than some measure of cost.[15] The Supreme Court's 2007 *Weyerhaeuser* decision reiterated these requirements.[16]

Perhaps a lingering difference between the Chicago and Harvard approaches to predatory pricing lies in the Chicago preference to consider "recoupment" first and the Harvard preference to look at price-cost relationships. But the fact is that under the Harvard approach, both are essential to a predatory pricing claim. Further, which one is more "fundamental," or best examined first, is heavily driven by facts. In cases of easy entry or numerous rivals who can expand output, lack of recoupment is easy to measure and should lead to a quick dismissal.[17] But other cases, including *Brooke Group* itself, require fairly strong assumptions about oligopoly behavior in order to assess the likelihood of recoupment. That case refused to condemn prices significantly below cost in a market (cigarettes) with no recent entry and a long history of lockstep oligopoly pricing, after observing that even a relatively well-disciplined oligopoly has occasional relapses.

The same thing is true about price-cost relations. In some cases, measuring price-cost relations is extraordinarily difficult, particularly if the defendant produces multiple products with common costs. In other cases measurement is easy, as when prices are clearly above any measure of cost, or when they are below even the direct cost of inputs. In sum, whether recoupment or price-cost relationships is the "bedrock" doctrine in a predatory pricing case depends entirely on the circumstances.

The same thing has largely been true in unilateral refusal-to-deal cases, where the Chicago School generally argued for per se legality and the Harvard School took a more nuanced approach, looking at the nature of the facility or input for which dealing is claimed and the impact of the refusal on competition. In its *Aspen* decision, the Supreme Court adopted a standard for unilateral refusals to deal that was more hostile than either the Chicago or Harvard Schools advocated.[18] In *Trinko,* however, the Supreme Court completely ignored the Chicago School literature but relied numerous times on Harvard School literature in placing stringent limitations on refusal to deal doctrine.[19]

In antitrust policy toward vertical restraints, the strong Chicago position was that they should be lawful per se.[20] Today it seems fairly clear that these stronger views jumped too quickly from the Chicago theory that free riding was an important explanation for vertical restraints[21] to the conclusion that it was virtually the only explanation. The Harvard position has been more nuanced, finding substantial risk that powerful dealers could use resale price maintenance ("RPM") to create a price umbrella for themselves.[22] In 1997 in *State Oil,* the Supreme Court adopted the rule of reason rather than per se legality for maximum RPM, and in *Leegin* in 2007, a divided Supreme Court overruled the nearly century-old *Dr. Miles* decision and did the same thing for minimum RPM.[23] No one advocated the Chicago School "per se legal" position. Justice Kennedy, speaking for the majority, applied a rule of reason but recognized that RPM could impose competitive harm. Justice Breyer, speaking for four dissenters, believed it was too late in the day to abandon the *per se* rule.

In tying and exclusive dealing law, the scope of liability has narrowed considerably over the last 20 years. The Chicago School became famous for its critique of tying law exploding the "leverage" theory and finding little basis for condemning either tying or exclusive dealing.[24] The Harvard School has been more reserved, seeing potential for harm if the market structure is monopolistic or conducive to monopoly.[25] One completely justified development, driven entirely by Harvard School ideology, is the increased use of section 2 of the Sherman Act for exclusionary contracting, sanctioned in both *Microsoft* and *Dentsply.*[26] Anticompetitive tying and exclusive dealing are always best analyzed as "unilateral" practices, because the downstream party is either unwilling or else is agreeing to exclusivity only in exchange for something else.[27] Further, the market share requirements for anticompetitive exclusive dealing or tying are generally significant and make the practices more suitable for evaluation under section 2. Recent case law in tying and exclusive dealing has been driven mainly by Harvard approaches.[28]

In sum, notwithstanding Chicago School efforts to write "foreclosure" out of the list of worthwhile antitrust concerns, the case law continues to recognize a concept of market foreclosure that has been a mainstay of Harvard School antitrust policy since Joe Bain's writings on entry barriers in the 1950s, although it has been considerably disciplined in subsequent years.

On remedies, at least some members of the Chicago School have advocated severe limitations on antitrust enforcement, including the virtual elimination of competitor suits,[29] and significant changes in the way that antitrust measures damages, including measuring of damages in accordance with optimal deterrence rather than plaintiffs' losses, and the at least selective abolition of treble damages.[30] By contrast, the Harvard position has tried to develop a more coherent and economically defensible model for private remedies that preserves more of the traditional doctrine and is more faithful to the statutory language. Thus, the Harvard School developed the concept of "antitrust injury" to ensure that the rationale for private remedies corresponds with the rationale for applying the antitrust laws in the first place.[31] Along with this, it developed much more severe rules for plaintiff standing. By and large the courts have followed the Harvard School approach, refusing to abolish competitor lawsuits but placing more stringent limitations on them.

One significant place where the Supreme Court has adopted Chicago rather than Harvard reasoning is the indirect purchaser rule, which awards the full trebled overcharge to direct purchasers and no damages at all to indirect purchasers. The Supreme Court's opinion in *Illinois Brick* largely followed the Landes-Posner approach.[32] The Harvard approach, which is more consistent with both standard rules of damages measurement and the language of section 4 of the Clayton Act, is that direct purchasing intermediaries should recover lost profits, while end users should recover the overcharge.[33] For direct purchasing intermediaries who pass the monopolized product on down the distribution chain, the overcharge is not even a rough approximation of the injury they sustain.[34] Rather, their injury comes mainly from lost volume. Indeed, the indirect purchaser rule often assigns the full damage action to actors who are not injured by the monopoly price at all, or who would simply be unable to prove any injury if relegated to traditional principles of damages measurement.

In sum, antitrust law as produced by the courts today comes much closer to representing the ideas of a somewhat chastised Harvard School than of any traditional version of the Chicago School. Of course, at least some members of the Chicago School have moved to the left just as Harvard has moved to the right.[35] But the question for today is whether the law making of section 2 has moved far enough. Perhaps this Harvard School influence is nothing more than a stop along the way to a much more hard-core set of Chicago positions in which the courts conclude that practices such as predatory pricing, unilateral refusals to deal, or vertical restraints are simply not worth the expense of litigating them and should be dismissed summarily. If that is the case, then it could be said that section 2 law continues to produce too many false positives and needs even further discipline from its high point in the 1940s and 1950s, when the courts condemned such things as the construction of bigger plants[36] or a lessor's price discrimination[37] as monopolistic.

I believe the Supreme Court and the circuit courts are generally about where they should be in defining '2 standards. This statement needs to be qualified in two ways. First, there are a few areas, elaborated below, where the decisions seem to be systematically overdeterrent or underdeterrent.

Secondly, courts continue to make errors, and they always will. But an error is not necessarily a sign of something fundamentally wrong with antitrust doctrine. For example, the Ninth Circuit's test in the *Kodak v. Image Tech.* case for unilateral refusals to deal, including refusal to license patents and copyrights, is almost certainly wrong, largely because the court either misread or ignored existing law.[38] Likewise, the Sixth Circuit's *Conwood* decision improperly confused tort law with antitrust and improperly admitted a damages study that should never have seen the light of day.[39] And the Third Circuit *LePage's* decision condemned package discounts on a woefully inadequate analysis of cost-price relationships or power to exclude an equally efficient rival.[40]

But none of these decisions tells us very much about the state of section 2 law. The Federal Circuit promptly took issue with the Ninth Circuit's *Kodak* decision and the great weight of scholarly authority rests with the Federal Circuit.[41] Indeed, the Ninth Circuit's 1997 *Kodak* decision is about the only victory that plaintiffs can claim in the wake of the Supreme Court's 1992 decision denying summary judgment in the same case.[42] *Conwood* is probably best described as a case where the court was overwhelmed with the record of tortious conduct, so much that they neglected to require proof that the conduct made any kind of contribution at all to monopoly power and failed to follow *Daubert* standards for expert testimony with sufficient rigor. *LePage's* almost certainly overreached with respect to a practice (package discounts) that was poorly understood and for which more rigorous tests were inadequately developed.[43]

Power and Conduct: Is There a General Theory of Monopolization?

Power

The law of section 2 consists of two parts: the identification of monopoly power and proof of unlawful exclusionary practices. A brief word about power seems appropriate. The concern for both false positives and false negatives also relates to improperly identified monopoly power.

Here the bleakest spot in the Rehnquist Court is undoubtedly its 1992 *Kodak* decision, which permitted courts to define product markets narrowly for buyers who were "locked in" to aftermarket purchases by virtue of their previous purchase of some piece of complex durable equipment.[44] But as noted above, *Kodak* has acquired very little traction in the lower courts.

On the other side, the so-called *"Cellophane"* Fallacy" is still with us and continues to produce false negatives in analysis of single-firm market power.[45] Briefly, assessing single-firm power by observing cross-elasticity of demand at current market prices overlooks the fact that the firm may already be charging monopoly prices. This means that conventional market delineation techniques may systematically understate the market power of dominant firms.[46]

Exclusionary Conduct: The Problematic Quest for a Single Test

The recent literature on section 2 has been preoccupied to the point of obsession with the formulation of a single test for exclusionary conduct. Some have advocated a "sacrifice" test—namely, that anticompetitive exclusion consists in a willingness to sacrifice short-run revenues for the future benefits of high prices in a market from which rivals have been excluded. Others have advocated a "no economic sense" test that condemns conduct under section 2 only if the conduct makes no economic sense unless it is understood as a mechanism for excluding rivals in order to earn monopoly profits down the road. Still others believe conduct should be condemned under section 2 only if it is capable of excluding an equally efficient rival. Yet others would condemn conduct that unreasonably raises rivals' costs. Finally, some believe that no single test captures the entire range of practices that we might wish to condemn as unlawfully exclusionary.

"Sacrifice" and "No Economic Sense"

Together, the "sacrifice" and "no economic sense" tests for unlawful exclusionary behavior offer the narrowest grounds for condemning conduct as monopolistic. Taken literally, they avoid balancing because *any* reasonable prospect of net gain to the monopolist that does not come from injury to competition exonerates the defendant. Thus, these tests avoid the definitional and measurement complexities that can serve to make tests based on net welfare unworkable, at least in close cases.

The *Aspen* decision condemned conduct when the defendant "was not motivated by efficiency concerns and...was willing to sacrifice short-run benefits and consumer goodwill in exchange for a perceived long-run impact on its smaller rival."[47] So-called sacrifice tests for exclusionary conduct look at the defendant's willingness to sacrifice short-term revenues or profits in exchange for larger revenues anticipated to materialize later when a monopoly has been created or the dominant firm's position strengthened. The rationale of the sacrifice test is that conduct that seems rational (profit maximizing or loss minimizing) without regard to the creation or preservation of monopoly has a fully legitimate explanation. Since no firm should be regarded as a trustee for either its rivals' or consumers' welfare, such conduct cannot be condemned without running a severe risk of chilling competitive behavior.

The best example of such a test in the case law is the recoupment test for predatory pricing given in the *Brooke Group* case, although it appeared in lower court opinions and the academic literature much earlier.[48] The sacrifice test is also useful in unilateral refusal-to-deal cases to the extent that, if we are to have law condemning refusals to deal at all, we must have a mechanism for identifying the very small subset of refusals that should be condemned. In *Trinko,* the government relied on a sacrifice theory in arguing that the alleged refusal to deal did not satisfy any Sherman Act standard of illegality.[49]

One particular problem with sacrifice tests is that most substantial investments involve a short term "sacrifice" of dollars in anticipation of increased revenue at some future point. The automobile manufacturer that constructs a new plant is certainly in such a position. It spends money on the plant during a lengthy period of planning and construction, hoping to realize higher profits several years down the road after the plant goes into production. To be sure, the profitability of the new plant need not "depend on" harmful effects on a rival, but in a concentrated market it is certainly likely to have such effects. Further, the new plant might not succeed unless rivals are forced to reduce their own output. Nevertheless, building a new plant under such circumstances is almost always procompetitive.

Likewise, product innovations are always costly to the defendant, and their success may very well depend on their ability to exclude rivals from the market, but neither of these factors is or should be decisive in subsequent antitrust litigation. All innovation is costly, and many successful innovations succeed only because consumers substitute away from rivals' older versions and toward the innovator's version. In sum, the sacrifice test does not adequately distinguish anticompetitive "sacrifice" from procompetitive "investment."

The sacrifice test also seems to work poorly in areas of section 2 law unrelated to predatory pricing or refusal to deal. Some exclusionary practices, such as exclusive dealing or tying, exclude immediately and are likely to be profitable to the dominant firm from the onset of the practice, so neither short-term sacrifice nor subsequent recoupment is necessary to make the practice profitable. Other practices, such as improper infringement suits, are often costly to the defendant in the short-run whether or not they are anticompetitive. Indeed, the improper patent infringement suit is likely to be most costly to the dominant firm when the infringement defendant has the resources to defend it and may not be particularly costly when the infringement defendants are nascent firms who are easily excluded from the market.

The "no economic sense" test, which is similar to the sacrifice test in some respects, would refuse to condemn exclusionary single firm conduct "unless it would make no economic sense for the defendant but for its tendency to eliminate or lessen competition."[50] The "no economic sense" test offers a good deal of insight into the question of when aggressive actions by a single firm go too far, but it can lead to erroneous results unless complicating qualifications are added.

Not all monopolizing conduct that we might wish to condemn is "irrational" in the sense that the only explanation that makes it seem profitable is destruction or discipline of rivals. Indeed, monopolizing conduct is not necessarily extremely costly to the defendant. For example, supplying false information or failing to disclose important information to a government

official or standard-setting organization need not cost any more than supplying truthful information, but it can create monopoly under appropriate circumstances.[51] Indeed, the provision of false information may be less
costly than provision of truthful information, for false information is easier
and cheaper to manufacture. Further, the provision of such information
to a government official might be profitable (i.e., "make sense") whether it
destroys a rival or merely if it results in increased output to the defendant.
For example, the firm that acquires a patent by making false statements to
the patent examiner and then brings infringement actions against rivals
might be dominant and bent on protecting that position.[52] But it might also
be one of many firms in a product differentiated market, seeking to do no
more than protect its sales from a close substitute.

Conduct Capable of Excluding Equally Efficient Rival

Judge Posner's proposed definition of exclusionary conduct would require
the plaintiff to show

> that the defendant has monopoly power and...that the challenged
> practice is likely in the circumstances to exclude from the defen-
> dant's market an equally or more efficient competitor. The defendant
> can rebut by proving that although it is a monopolist and the chal-
> lenged practice exclusionary, the practice is, on balance, efficient.[53]

This definition has enjoyed some recognition in the case law. For example, in condemning the targeted package discounts at issue in *LePage's*,
the Third Circuit observed that "even an equally efficient rival may find
it impossible to compensate for lost discounts on products that it does not
produce."[54] The "equally efficient rival" test has also found acceptance in
predatory pricing cases, particularly in discussions of how to identify a
price as predatory. The reasoning is that a firm should not be penalized for
having lower costs than its rivals and pricing accordingly. As a result, a
price is predatory only if it is reasonably calculated to exclude a rival who
is at least as efficient as the defendant.[55] Judge Posner's own examples in
defense of his definition of exclusionary conduct pertain to pricing. He
writes that it would be absurd to require the firm to hold a price umbrella
over less

> efficient entrants....[P]ractices that will exclude only less efficient
> firms, such as the monopolist's dropping his price nearer to (but not
> below) his cost, are not actionable, because we want to encourage
> efficiency.[56]

Clearly we do not want low-cost firms to hold their prices above their
costs merely to suffer a rival to become established in the market.

The equally efficient rival definition of exclusionary conduct can be
underdeterrent in situations where the rival that is most likely to emerge

is less efficient than the dominant firm. Consider the filing of fraudulent or otherwise improper IP infringement claims.[57] The value of infringement actions as entry deterrence devices is greatest when the parties have an unequal ability to bear litigation costs. This will typically be before or soon after the new entrant has begun production. The filing of a fraudulent patent infringement suit, unlike setting one's price at or a little above marginal cost, is a socially useless practice. But the strategy might very well not be effective against an equally efficient rival, who could presumably defend and win the infringement claim. In this case Judge Posner's definition of exclusionary conduct seems unreasonably lenient and even perverse. It exonerates the defendant in precisely those circumstances when the conduct is most likely to be unreasonably exclusionary.

Raising Rivals' Costs (RRC)

Several anticompetitive actions by dominant firms are best explained as efforts to deny rivals market access by increasing their costs. Such strategies may succeed in situations where more aggressive ones involving the complete destruction of rivals might not. Once rivals' costs have been increased, the dominant firm can raise its own price or increase its market share at their expense.[58]

The real value of RRC theories is not to create a new set of unlawful exclusionary practices, but rather to show that certain practices that have traditionally been subjected to antitrust scrutiny can be anticompetitive even though they do not literally involve the destruction of rivals. Situations in which rivals stay in the market but their costs increase may be more likely to occur and exist in a wider variety than those in which rivals are destroyed. Further, cost-raising strategies might be less detectable and less likely to invite prosecution. Indeed, a strategy of raising rivals' costs need not injure a rival severely at all if the dominant firm increases its own prices to permit smaller firms a price hike that compensates them for their cost increase. As a result, RRC operates as a kind of substitute for the older antitrust theories of anticompetitive exclusion that required the complete foreclosure or destruction of rivals, and accordingly provoked competitive responses. Many cases brought under both sections 1 and 2 of the Sherman Act have acknowledged the theory.[59]

Of course, the law has never required complete market exclusion as a prerequisite to suit. Indeed, some successful section 2 plaintiffs have both grown their market shares and earned high profits even through the period that the exclusionary practices were occurring.[60]

In sum, RRC is a useful but also incomplete definition of exclusionary practices. Further, many practices that raise rivals' cost, such as innovation that either deprives rivals of revenue or forces them to innovate in return, are also welfare enhancing. As a result, "raising rivals' costs" can never operate as a *complete* test for exclusionary conduct.[61] One must always add an adverb such as "unreasonably," but that invariably requires some kind of balancing or trade-off.

No Single Test

Each of the previously discussed tests is useful for assessing some types of exclusionary conduct but much less so for others. Given the current state of the law my own preference is the "test" proposed in the *Antitrust Law* treatise that monopolistic conduct consists of acts that

> (1) are reasonably capable of creating, enlarging or prolonging monopoly power by impairing the opportunities of rivals; and (2) that either (2a) do not benefit consumers at all, or (2b) are unnecessary for the particular consumer benefits that the acts produce, or (2c) produce harms disproportionate to the resulting benefits.[62]

To this should be added that the practice must be reasonably susceptible to judicial control, which means that the court must be able to identify the conduct as anticompetitive and either fashion a penalty producing the correct amount of deterrence or an equitable remedy likely to improve competition. This concern is driven by a proposition that is central to both the Chicago and Harvard positions: administrability is key. More complex rules are not helpful if they cannot be effectively applied.

This formulation given above is not so much a test as a series of premises. Clause (1) of the test ensures that the conduct is both exclusionary and "substantial," in the sense that it is reasonably capable of creating or prolonging monopoly. Clause (2a) deals with the easiest case for identifying anticompetitive exclusion; namely where no consumer benefit whatsoever can be shown. Clause (2b) deals with situations where a less restrictive alternative might produce equivalent benefits, and (2c) deals with the small number of situations thought to require some kind of balancing of harms and gains. Beyond this formulation, courts must still develop specific tests for specific types of conduct, such as the recoupment/price-cost test for predatory pricing, or the "no economic sense" test for unilateral refusals to deal.

Problem Areas

Monopolization law's conceptual and administrative problems will probably never be solved, given the open-ended nature of section 2's "monopolizing" language. A few problem areas seem worth noting.

One area of widespread agreement is that misuse of government process can create monopolies. Patent and other IP exclusions have been particularly problematic and arguably have produced a fair amount of *under*deterrence. For example, ever since the Supreme Court's *Walker Process* decision in 1965, the use of improper or overly broad patent claims to maintain or create monopoly has been a significant source of antitrust litigation.[63] *Walker Process* itself spoke very generally of infringement actions based on patents that were obtained by "fraud." Today the law has become much more technical and stylized. Many claims continue to involve enforcement actions based on patents that were acquired by inequitable conduct before the Patent and Trademark Office (PTO). Not every instance of inequitable conduct renders a patent unenforceable. Federal Circuit law on the question considers enforceability by addressing two issues. One is the nature of the misconduct and the intent behind it; the other is "materiality," or the likelihood that the patent examiner would have disapproved the patent (or a patent claim) had the misconduct not occurred. In general, the more aggressive the misconduct, the smaller the showing of materiality need be to make a patent unenforceable, and vice versa.

Another set of cases involve IP rights where there is not necessarily a claim of misconduct in the acquisition of the right, but rather where the infringement action itself was improperly brought. In a patent case this could be because the patentee had good reason to know that the infringement defendant's technology was not infringing (not covered by a particular patent claim) or that it had a valid license; or where the patent was unenforceable for some other postapplication reason.[64] The Supreme Court addressed one variation of this issue in its *Professional Real Estate* case where the IP claim was under the copyright laws rather than a patent, and the infringement defendant's claim was that the plaintiff had filed its action based on an improper interpretation of a question of law.[65]

Walker Process actions in the Federal Circuit have been frustrated by that court's reluctance to adopt a more objective test for the type of inequitable conduct needed to trigger *Walker Process* liability. For example, in the *Dippin' Dots* case, the infringement plaintiff's patent was rendered unenforceable by some 800 retail sales that occurred more than a year before the initial patent application was filed.[66] The Patent Act's on-sale bar prevents patenting of a product that was sold more than a year prior to the filing of the initial patent application.[67] In this case, the patentee neglected to disclose this information in its application, and the patentee's declaration contained a sworn statement that no such sales had occurred. Further, the information, if disclosed, would certainly have barred patentability.

However, the court also held that the degree of inequitable conduct necessary to invalidate the patent was not as great as the degree needed to support an antitrust claim. In this case, the only evidence of the patentee's anticompetitive intent was the fact that it had made the 800 sales over a one-week period and then later swore to the PTO that the sales had not occurred. Of course, it subsequently also filed a patent infringement suit against those offending one or more of the claims made in the patent. The Federal Circuit held that while this omission clearly qualified as inequitable conduct, it fell short of fraud in the *Walker Process* sense, which requires a stronger showing of both intent and materiality.[68] In order to support a *Walker Process* antitrust case "there must be evidence of intent separable from the simple fact of the omission."[69] The court observed,

> It might be argued that because the omitted reference was so impor-
> tant to patentability, DDI [the patentee] must have known of its impor-
> tance and must have made a conscious decision not to disclose it. That
> argument has some force, but to take it too far would be to allow the
> high materiality of the omission to be balanced against a lesser show-
> ing of deceptive intent by the patentee. Weighing intent and materi-
> ality together is appropriate when assessing whether the patentee's
> prosecution conduct was inequitable. However, when *Walker Process*
> claimants wield that conduct as a "sword" to obtain antitrust dam-
> ages rather than as a mere "shield" against enforcement of the patent,
> they must prove deceptive intent independently.[70]

This approach re-creates some of the same horrors of pre-*Matsushita* antitrust litigation under standards reluctant to grant summary judgment, except in reverse. It requires a discovery trip through the patentee's docu-ments for evidence of anticompetitive "intent" other than that manifested in the patent application itself. Further, it makes the infringement defen-dant's antitrust counterclaim dependent on the vagaries of the patentee's document retention policy or other efforts to suppress incriminating infor-mation, often attending preapplication activities that occurred many years prior to the litigation. For example, in *Dippin' Dots,* the sales found to inval-idate the patent occurred in 1987. The subsequent patent infringement suit was filed in April of 2000, some thirteen years later.[71]

Another problem area is the law of strategic pricing, including various sorts of discounting policies. Both the "recoupment" test and the AVC test for predatory pricing are imperfect and underdeterrent. The "recoupment" test as developed in *Brooke Group* denigrated the value of disciplinary actions within oligopoly. The degree of competitiveness in concentrated industries varies widely and in some the value of disciplinary pricing can be quite high to market leaders and harmful to consumers. Cigarettes, with a long history of lock-step pricing, is very likely such an industry.

The AVC test basically identifies short-run marginal cost as the proper baseline for measuring predation, and the Areeda-Turner variation rec-ognizes prices above average variable cost as a virtual safe harbor for predation claims. It is generally acknowledged that the AVC test can be underdeterrent, particularly in circumstances where fixed costs are high, which is most often the case in markets that are structurally susceptible to monopolization.[72]

Discounting practices have been particularly problematic in recent years. The law seems to be in roughly the same position that the law of predatory pricing was in the seventies and eighties. The early formula-tions focused heavily on intent, and cost tests played a secondary role, to the point that some decisions were willing to condemn predation on prices above any measure of cost.

Single-product and "aggregated" multiproduct discounts can pose different issues.[73] Some single-product discount challenges have been to so-called "market share" discounts, which reward purchasers for purchasing a specified percentage of their needs from the defendant. These discounts differ from and are less harmful to competition than exclusive dealing in several respects. First, because the specified percentage is less than 100 percent, they foreclose less than exclusive dealing imposed by a seller with the same market share. Second, and most significantly, the penalty for falling below the minimum percentage is loss of the discount, which means that the buyer can evade the contract at any time simply by paying the seller the higher price. Third, and most significantly, an equally efficient firm can match a fully discounted price that is above the defendant's costs.[74]

The most common argument for condemning above-cost market share discounts is that they may serve to raise rivals' costs by depriving them of sufficient sales to attain economies of scale equivalent to those enjoyed by the defendant. Here, the same set of considerations would appear to apply as the courts have applied in predatory pricing cases such as *Brooke Group.* First, one might be able to envision circumstances in which above- cost single-product discounts can be used to reduce rivals' scale economies, and welfare might be reduced in the process. But second, one doubts that the courts can administer '2 claims under such a theory without creating an intolerable risk of chilling procompetitive behavior, a result that could be far more socially costly.[75] Manifestly, the law of predatory pricing does not rest on the premise that anticompetitive, above-cost pricing strategies are implausible. In fact, such theories are quite numerous and varied.[76] Rather, the law rests on the observation that article III courts and, in particular, juries, are not able to distinguish such strategies with sufficient clarity to avoid condemning procompetitive behavior.

The situation of aggregated multiproduct discounts is even more complex because an equally efficient firm making only one product or a subset of products in a bundle may not be able to match an aggregated discount. Assume that the defendant is the only firm in the market making products A and B. Rivals make one but not the other. If the defendant ties a discount to combined purchases of A and B, an equally efficient rival making only B might be able to match the discounted B price but not the foregone discount on A that results from the buyers' failure to take the requisite amount of both A and B.

Whether such discounting practices should be condemned at above-cost prices and, if so, when, raises a number of interesting questions that have been explored quite thoroughly in the literature although less so in the case law. *First,* if at least one significant rival also makes both A and B, then the strategy should not be condemned simply because the plaintiff, who makes only one of the products, cannot match the discount. *Second,* the discount will not exclude an equally efficient single-product rival unless when the full discount is attributed to the product upon which exclusion

is claimed the price of that product falls below cost. Or to state this differently: one needs to ask whether the incremental price of the two products
when they are bundled is enough to cover the incremental cost of producing the bundle. Both the Harvard and Chicago School positions currently
require a cost-based test, which can provide both relative administrative
simplicity and avoid the kind of overdeterrence that is certain to result
from non-cost-based tests that invariably look at the defendant's intent. As
the Ninth Circuit noted in its *Cascade Health* decision, the attribution test
is something of a compromise, requiring less than a showing that the entire
package is priced at below cost, but more than impossible-to-administer
formulations that avoid costs altogether or require fairly precise measurement of such things as economies of scale, which has always eluded fact
finders.[77]

Third, even bundling that does not satisfy this incremental cost test is
usually procompetitive; indeed, it may be an important avenue by which
oligopolies are destabilized. For example, the truck dealer in a concentrated
market may be reluctant to cut the nominal price for fear of retaliation; however, it may throw in an air conditioner that costs $1000 for an incremental
price of $300. A firm that sells only truck air conditioners but not the trucks
themselves may be excluded by such a practice, but if the price of the truck-
plus-air-conditioner exceeds its costs it is hard to justify a rule that protects
the air conditioner firm by limiting competition in the truck market.

Finally, a very brief note on remedies. The efficacy of section 2 law
depends on the success of remedies in making the market more competitive. Decades of aggressiveness in use of structural remedies[78] has given way
to a preference for conduct remedies. Which remedy has the comparative
advantage depends on the circumstances. In a case such as *Dentsply,* where
the defendant preserved its dominant position by means of a set of exclusive
dealing practices, an injunction against the variants of such practices may
be all that is needed. But too often nonstructural remedies amount to little
more than price regulation, which rarely satisfies the goals of antitrust.[79] By
contrast, in a case such as *Microsoft* where the behavior is multifaceted and
the defendant has repeatedly been condemned,[80] a carefully tailored structural remedy is probably necessary, including but perhaps not limited to
forced sharing of IP rights. The time seems ripe to become more aggressive
about structural remedies once again, particularly for repeat offenders.

Comment on Herbert Hovenkamp and the Dominant Firm: The Chicago School Has Made Us Too Cautious About False Positives and the Use of Section 2 of the Sherman Act

Harvey J. Goldschmid

From the earliest days of the nation, a concern has existed about centralized economic power and the dominant firm. But in the post–Civil War period, as historian Richard Hofstadter put it, "bigness had come with such a rush that its momentum seemed irresistible. No one knew when or how it could be stopped."[81] Enacted in 1890, section 2 of the Sherman Act was intended to be the nation's answer to wrongful conduct by dominant firms.

Over the years, section 2 has been applied with rigor, with hesitancy, and now, Hovenkamp believes, the "Supreme Court and the circuit courts are generally about where they should be in defining §2 standards." Hovenkamp's essay is highly sophisticated, analytically powerful, and generally wise, but, even taking account of the "qualifications" he states, I believe he is too sanguine about current law and the dominant firm. Indeed, whether the current permissiveness is attributed to the Chicago School, or a combination of the Chicago School and, in Hovenkamp's words, a "chastised Harvard School," the bottom line is law that is overly cautious about use of section 2 and overly concerned about so-called false positives.

Traditional Concerns About Dominance and the Sensible Evolution of Section 2 Law

To understand the views just expressed, step back with me to 1945 and Learned Hand's classic *Alcoa* opinion.[82] Judge Hand described three basic evils associated with monopoly power or dominance. First, the dominant firm would have excessive power over price. Second, excessive price would invariably lead to misallocation of resources; in modern terminology, it would reduce allocative efficiency and create deadweight loss. Finally, there would likely be a loss of dynamic efficiency. As Learned Hand explained in wonderfully colorful language: "possession of unchallenged economic power deadens initiative...depresses energy;...immunity from competition is a narcotic and rivalry is a stimulant."

The problem with *Alcoa,* and cases that followed it, was not this policy approach. The problem was that *Alcoa* took too narrow a view of what conduct was permissible by a dominant firm. Learned Hand required that a dominant could only survive an antitrust claim if it had monopoly power "thrust upon" it. To avoid a finding of "abuse," it had be a "passive beneficiary" and could not, for example, "double and redouble its capacity" in an expanding market.

This *Alcoa* approach was taken to its extreme, in 1964, by one of our strongest federal trial judges, Charles Wyzanski, who concluded there should be a "rebuttable presumption" of a Sherman Act violation (i.e., of improper section 2 conduct) anytime dominance is found. The presumption, Wyzanski expected, would be rebutted only in the rarest of instances.[83]

The Learned Hand and Wyzanski tests seemed to demand that dominant firms behave passively and inefficiently in order to avoid section 2 liability. Obviously, the tests, if applied broadly, would lead to wholly unhealthy economic consequences.

In 1966, the Supreme Court rejected the idea of a "rebuttable presumption" and defined the offense of monopolization in words that continue to set the framework for section 2 analysis today:

> The offense of monopoly under § 2 of the Sherman Act has two elements: (1) the possession of monopoly power in the relevant market and (2) the willful acquisition or maintenance of that power as distinguished from growth or development as a consequence of a superior product, business acumen, or historic accident.[84]

In *Aspen Skiing,* in 1985, the Supreme Court established a sensible modern framework for evaluating permissible and impermissible conduct by a test that I would summarize as requiring "unreasonable exclusionary conduct" before a violation could be found.[85] Investment in research, innovation, and other dynamic competitive activities were all acceptable; only activity that unreasonably harmed competitors—without adequate business justification—could be an abuse.

Recent Reasons for Concern

To this point, I would be as optimistic as Hovenkamp about the development of section 2 law. Recent years, however, have not been kind to section

2. The Supreme Court's most important recent statement came in 2004 in *Verizon Communications v. Law Office of Curtis V. Trinko*.[86] Although I believe *Trinko* was correctly decided, dictum in the opinion—written by Justice Scalia—seriously undermines the traditional policy underpinnings of section 2.[87]

Justice Scalia, wearing rose-colored glasses, asserts that the "mere possession of monopoly power, and the concomitant charging of monopoly prices, is not only not unlawful; it is an important element of the free-market system. The opportunity to charge monopoly prices... is what attracts 'business acumen' in the first place." Scalia is correct that charging monopoly prices would be lawful under the *Grinnell* test so long as unreasonably exclusionary or predatory conduct is not found. Moreover, the prospect of monopoly profits could certainly spur the efforts of rational business executives. But monopoly power and profits exact large costs. Nowhere in Scalia's opinion is there an expression of concern about the traditional evils of dominance or monopoly power—excessive price, misallocation of resources, and loss of dynamic efficiency. Indeed, Scalia suggests that dominance is benign or beneficial because it "induces risk taking that produces innovation and economic growth."

Scalia and others in the Chicago School would argue that concern about the "traditional evils" of monopoly power resulted in the *Alcoa* test requiring harmful passivity. I agree that *Alcoa*'s conduct test was too restrictive, but the *Grinnell* and *Aspen Skiing* formulations—and the focus on unreasonably exclusionary conduct—provided the necessary corrective. Under these formulations, there is plenty of room for efficient, dynamic, innovative conduct.

The Chicago School would argue that new entry and self-correcting markets would alleviate the evils of dominance. They would also question the capacity of our federal courts to handle complex dominance issues. As Scalia put it in *Trinko:* "The cost of false positives [i.e., the condemnation of benign or procompetitive conduct] counsels against undue expansion of §2 liability." [88]

But the current calls for caution and permissiveness unnecessarily endanger potentially dynamic markets and free market competition. I would make the following five points in response to Scalia and the Chicago School.

Trinko Took Too Narrow a View of When Sharing Should Be Required and Too Broad a View of When "Refusal-to-Deal" Threats Should Be Tolerated

Scalia asserted that we must be "very cautious" about "forced sharing" and emphasized that the Supreme Court has never recognized the "essential facilities" doctrine. He explained that "the Sherman Act 'does not restrict the long recognized right [quoting *Colgate*]... [of a seller] freely to exercise his own independent discretion as to parties with whom he will deal.' "[89]

When to require sharing by a dominant firm is a genuinely difficult issue. But Scalia's language suggests that key recent lower court section 2 cases like *Dentsply*,[90] *Microsoft*,[91] and *Kodak*[92] were wrongly decided. In *Dentsply*, the defendant company, a dominant firm, was arguably using the dispensation Scalia provides in *Trinko* to "freely exercise its...independent judgment" and to deal with whom it wished. Dentsply used this dispensation to impose an anticompetitive exclusive dealing plan. The Third Circuit found a violation of section 2. No agreement is required for a section 2 violation. Why not easily condemn the dominant manufacturer that uses a refusal-to-deal threat to significantly inhibit or retard the distribution of products made by its small competitors? Indeed, given the "evils" of monopoly power, why not condemn with rigor significant entry blocking or expansion retarding exclusive dealing—in a dominance context—as did the D.C. Circuit in *Microsoft* and the Third Circuit in *Dentsply*?

Similarly, it seems to me that the Ninth Circuit was correct in condemning Kodak's use of monopoly power in the parts market (for its photocopiers and micrographic equipment) in order to harm or destroy independent service organizations ("ISOs") by refusing to sell parts to them. Hovenkamp cites *Kodak* (where the unilateral refusal to deal included the refusal to license parts that were patented) as a case that was "almost certainly wrong" because the court's conduct test "either misread or ignored existing law."[93] But assume that the Ninth Circuit's and Supreme Court's[94] market definition, of "locked-in" consumers in aftermarkets for parts and services, was correct. Why should dominant Kodak—with monopoly power in parts—be permitted to refuse to deal with competitor ISOs in the service market?

Admittedly some caution is necessary in this difficult area. The Supreme Court went too far in its 1992 *Kodak* opinion when it said,

> It is true that as a general matter a firm can refuse to deal with its competitors. But such a right is not absolute; it exists only if there are legitimate competitive reasons for the refusal.[95]

This statement is overly restrictive. It could unfairly and unwisely do great harm to a dominant firm. What if a dominant firm has, for example, discovered, developed, and patented a new blockbuster drug, must it share the blockbuster drug with a potential competitor? Can it reject the competitor's demand that it share only if it has "legitimate competitive reasons" for doing so? Would a wish to avoid competition be a "legitimate competitive reason"? If not, what kind of disincentives would such a rule create for research and development, innovation, and invention?

But in the Ninth Circuit, Kodak acknowledged that it supplied parts to buyers who were doing repairs themselves. There appeared to be no realistic quality control justification for Kodak's refusal to deal with IPOs. Without a plausible business justification, was not Kodak's refusal to deal an unreasonable exclusionary activity?[96] In my view, sharing may be forced under section 2 when a dominant firm misuses its monopoly power by, for example, creating the exclusive dealing blockages found in *Dentsply* or by leveraging, without business justification, its power in one market to dominate another as in *Kodak*. In addition, sharing should be forced when (1) a dominant firm controls an "essential facility" that cannot reasonably be duplicated by a present or potential competitor; (2) it is practical for the dominant firm to share the facility; and (3) on balance, forcing the sharing of the facility (which, of course, can be compensated) must be both (a) fair and (b) not counterproductive in terms of efficiency incentives.[97]

Under this formulation, it would be easiest to require the sharing of a unique natural resource or a leased municipal stadium, where the dominant firm had invested relatively little and could be adequately compensated. It would be much harder to order the sharing of a patented pharmaceutical, which had been developed at considerable cost and over a period of many years. Of course, this formulation relies on reasoned, balanced decision-making by our federal courts; it would create some uncertainty. But the formulation would only be used after monopoly power is found, and factors (1)–(3) above would not create an easy road for claimants to travel in litigation.

Concern About False Positives Have Lulled Federal Enforcement Agencies into Unwarranted Complacency

In our modern economy, with the enormous role played by intellectual property ("IP"), there may be a need for even greater concern about the dominant firm. Because of copyrights, patents, "network effects," and similar factors, there is at least a tendency for IP markets to drift toward single-firm dominance.

Of course, IP markets are often dynamic and subject to continuous change, but, with enhanced products, companies like Microsoft and Intel have remained dominant for substantial periods of time. I suspect that *Trinko*'s dictum and general Chicago School scholarship have lulled antitrust enforcement agencies and our lower courts into a false sense of complacency about dominant firms. Almost nothing is happening at the Antitrust Division, at the FTC, or in the courts in the section 2 area.

Predatory Pricing Doctrine Has Been Negatively Affected By the Chicago School

As Hovenkamp explained, for many in the Chicago School "predatory pricing is an irrational activity" and predatory pricing cases "should be summarily dismissed." The more moderate Harvard School has largely prevailed in this area, but, in response to both schools, recent scholarship has pointed to the many rational reasons for single-firm predation.[98] In a market with entry barriers, predation to prevent entry, or to discipline competitors, may be perfectly rational. Predatory pricing in a concentrated market by an oligopolistic group may be difficult, but dominant firm predation can be easily accomplished and economically sensible. Indeed, in a dominant firm context, I would interpret *Brooke Group*[99] and *Weyerhauser*[100] to mean that where recoupment (including the rewards stemming from the disciplining of rivals) is probable, a presumption should exist that any price below average total cost is predatory. In this area, skepticism about feasibility and naiveté have led to law that is much too permissive.

Excessive Concern About False Positives Has Led to Unproductive Attempts to Formulate a Single, Narrow Test for Defining Impermissible Conduct By Dominant Firms

Hovenkamp handles this area—and critiques various quite imperfect formulations—with grace and wisdom. Chicago School scholars, for example, have advocated a "no economic sense" test. But if Kodak had economically insignificant reasons for refusing to deal—along with a principal aim of driving competitive IPOs out of business—should the company have been permitted to do so?

Judge Richard Posner has simply suggested that a company with monopoly power should be "free to compete like everyone else."[101] But ask yourself whether on this issue Scalia was not correct when he opined in *Kodak* that a firm with monopoly power should be "examined through a special [presumably more rigorous] lens."[102] Should, for example, exclusive dealing contracts by a dominant firm be looked at the same way as similar agreements by a firm with just 5 percent of a market?

The search for certainty and a single, very narrow monopoly conduct test will undoubtedly continue. But, given my concern about the "evils" of monopoly power, I can live easily with the flexibility provided by the *Grinnell* and *Aspen Skiing* tests, which I have summarized as prohibiting "unreasonably exclusionary conduct."

Agreement

Finally, I agree completely with Hovenkamp that in this critically important area the "time seems ripe to become more aggressive about structural remedies" under section 2.

Notes

1. Sherman Act, section 2, 26 Stat 209 (1890).
2. *Standard Oil Co. of New Jersey* v. *United States,* 221 U.S. 1 (1911).
3. 540 U.S. 398 (2004).
4. Id. at 407.
5. *Trinko,* 540 U.S. 398.
6. *United States v. Microsoft Corp.,* 253 F.3d 34 (D.C. Cir. 2001).

7. A few of the more important writings include Richard A. Posner, ANTITRUST LAW (1976; 2d ed. 2001); Frank H. Easterbrook, *Ignorance and Antitrust, in* ANTITRUST, INNOVATION, AND COMPETITIVENESS 119 (T. Jorde & D. Teece, eds., 1992); Frank H. Easterbrook, *The Limits of Antitrust,* 63 TEX. L. REV. 1, 2 (1984); Richard A. Posner, *The Chicago School of Antitrust Analysis,* 127 U. PA. L. REV. 925 (1979); Robert H. Bork, THE ANTITRUST PARADOX: A POLICY AT WAR WITH ITSELF (1978).

8. On the Harvard School, *see* Herbert Hovenkamp, THE ANTITRUST ENTERPRISE: PRINCIPLE AND EXECUTION 35–38 (2006). *See also* James W. Meehan, Jr. & Robert J. Larner, *The Structural School, Its Critics, and its Progeny: An Assessment, in* ECONOMICS AND ANTITRUST POLICY (Robert J. Larner & James W. Meehan, Jr., eds. 1989), 182.

9. *See* Hovenkamp, ANTITRUST ENTERPRISE, *supra* note 8, at 37; Herbert Hovenkamp, *The Rationalization of Antitrust,* 116 HARV. L. REV. 917 (2003).

10. *See also* William Kovacic, *The Intellectual DNA of Modern U.S. Competition Law for Dominant Firm Conduct: The Chicago/Harvard Double Helix,* 2007 COL. BUS. L. REV. 1 (2007); William H. Page, *Areeda, Chicago, and Antitrust Injury: Economic Efficiency and Legal Process,* 41 ANTITRUST BULL. 909 (1996).

11. *See, e.g.,* Frank H. Easterbrook, *Predatory Strategies and Counterstrategies,* 48 U. CHI. L. REV. 263 (1981). Only a little less strident is Bork, ANTITRUST PARADOX, *supra* note 7, at 144–55.

12. *See* Richard A. Posner, ANTITRUST LAW 189 (1976); and in the second edition, at 215 (repeating the suggestion, but with qualifications). For critiques, *see* 3 Phillip E. Areeda & Herbert Hovenkamp, ANTITRUST LAW &741e2 (2d ed. 2002); Oliver E. Williamson, *Predatory Pricing: A Strategic and Welfare Analysis,* 87 YALE L.J. 284, 322 n.88 (1977). *But see* Richard Posner, *The Chicago School of Antitrust Analysis,* 127 U. PA. L. REV. 925, 941 (1979) (somewhat ambiguously modifying earlier position). Most recently, Posner has modified his position much more significantly, perhaps moving left of the Areeda-Turner test. *See* Richard A. Posner, ANTITRUST LAW (2d ed. 2001) at 217–223 (describing Areeda-Turner test as "toothless"); *but see id.* at 215 (seeing value in a marginal cost test).

13. Phillip E. Areeda & Donald F. Turner, *Predatory Pricing and Related Practices Under Section 2 of the Sherman Act,* 88 HARV. L. REV. 697, 698 (1975): "...the classically-feared case of predation has been the deliberate sacrifice of present revenues for the purpose of driving rivals out of the market and then recouping the losses through higher profits earned in the absence of competition." *See also* the first edition of the *Antitrust Law* treatise: 3 Phillip E. Areeda & Donald F. Turner, ANTITRUST LAW ¶711b at 151 (1978) (similar); *see also* 3 ANTITRUST LAW, Ch. 7C-2 (structural issues and recoupment); 7C-3 (price-cost relationships).

14. *See Brooke Group Ltd. v. Brown & Williamson Tobacco Corp.,* 509 U.S. 209, 233 (U.S. 1993) (citing Bork, *Paradox, supra* note 7); *id.* at 224 (citing Posner, ANTITRUST LAW, *supra* note 7); *id.* at 233 (citing Easterbrook, *Limits of Antitrust, supra* note 7).

15. *Passim* (citing *Antitrust Law* 13 times).

16. *Weyerhaeuser Co. v. Ross-Simmons Hardwood Lumber Co., Inc,* 127 S.Ct. 1069 (2007).

17. *See, e.g., A.A. Poultry Farms v. Rose Acre Farms,* 881 F.2d 1396, 1401 (7th Cir.1989), cert. denied, 494 U.S. 1019 (1990) (looking first at recoupment in competitively structured market with low entry barriers).

18. *Aspen Skiing Co. v. Aspen Highlands Skiing Corp.,* 472 U.S. 585 (1985); *see* 3A Antitrust Law ¶772 (2d ed. 2002).

19. *Verizon Communications, Inc. v. Law Offices of Curtis V. Trinko, LLP,* 540 U.S. 398, 411, 415 (2004). *See also* Spencer Weber Waller, *Microsoft and Trinko: A Tale of Two Courts,* 2006 Utah L. Rev. 741, 915–16 (2006) (emphasizing role of Harvard School in *Trinko* decision); Kovacic, *Intellectual DNA, supra* note 10 (arguing, inter alia, that then-Judge Breyer's distinctly Harvard School approach in *Town of Concord v. Boston Edison Co.,* 915 F.2d 17 (1st Cir. 1990), is the guiding force behind *Trinko*).

20. Richard A. Posner, *The Next Step in the Antitrust Treatment of Restricted Distribution: Per Se Legality,* 48 U. Chi. L. Rev. 6, 9 (1981); Robert H. Bork, *The Rule of Reason and the Per Se Concept: Price Fixing and Market Division II,* 75 Yale L.J. 373 (1966); Frank H. Easterbrook, *Vertical Arrangements and the Rule of Reason,* 53 Antitrust L.J. 135 (1984) (recognizing only vertical arrangements used to facilitate horizontal collusion as worthy of condemnation).

21. *See, e.g.,* Lester Telser, *Why Should Manufacturers Want Fair Trade?,* 3 J. L. & Econ. 86 (1960); Bork, *Rule of Reason, supra* note 20; Richard A. Posner, *The Rule of Reason and the Economic Approach: Reflections on The* Sylvania *Decision,* 45 U. Chi. L. Rev. 1 (1977).

22. *See* 8 Phillip E. Areeda & Herbert Hovenkamp ¶1604 (2d ed. 2004).

23. *State Oil v. Khan,* 522 U.S. 3 (1997); *Leegin Creative Leather Prods., Inc. v. PSKS, Inc.,* 127 S.Ct. 2705 (2007), overruling *Dr. Miles Medical Co. v. John D. Park & Sons Co.,* 220 U.S. 373 (1911). *See* 8 Phillip E. Areeda & Herbert Hovenkamp, Antitrust Law ¶1620 (2d ed. 2004).

24. *See, e.g.,* Bork, Antitrust Paradox, *supra* note 7, at 299–309 (exclusive dealing); 365–381 (tying).

25. *See* 9 Phillip E. Areeda & Herbert Hovenkamp, Antitrust Law ¶¶ 1704, 1705, 1709, 1710 (2d ed. 2004)

26. *See United States v. Microsoft Corp.,* 253 F.3d 34, 66–67 (D.C. Cir. 2001), cert. denied, 534 U.S. 952 (2001) (condemning Microsoft's "commingling" of platform and browser code under Section 2 as a form of tying); *United States v. Dentsply Int'l., Inc.,* 399 F.3d 181, 191 (3d Cir. 2005), *cert. denied,* 126 S.Ct. 1023 (2006) (condemning exclusive dealing under '2).

27. Of course many *pro*competitive uses of tying and exclusive dealing are bilateral, in that both parties stand to gain from the exclusivity itself. *See, e.g., Jefferson Parish Hosp. Dist. No. 2 v. Hyde,* 466 U.S. 2. 6 & n. 3 (1984), in which the defendant hospital and the Roux firm with which it had an exclusive dealing contract promised exclusivity to each other.

28. *See, e.g., Illinois Tool Works, Inc. v. Independent Ink, Inc.,* 547 U.S. 28 (2006) (abolishing presumption of market power for patented tying products and calling per se rule into question); *Jefferson Parish,* 466 U.S. 2 (refusing to reject *per se* rule but imposing serious market power requirement); *Dentsply,* 399 F.3d 181 (condemning exclusive dealing by dominant firm under section 2; citing only *Antitrust Law* treatise); *Microsoft,*

253 F.3d 34 (condemning "commingling" of platform and browser code under section 2 but remanding '1 tying claim).

29. *See, e.g.,* Easterbrook, *Predatory Strategies, supra* note 11; Frank H. Easterbrook, *Treble What?,* 55 ANTITRUST L.J. 95, 101 (1986).

30. *See, e.g.,* William M. Landes, *Optimal Sanctions for Antitrust Violations,* 50 U. CHI. L. REV. 652 (1983).

31. *See* Phillip E. Areeda, Comment, *Antitrust Violations Without Damage Recoveries,* 89 HARV. L. REV. 1127 (1976). The doctrine was adopted by the Supreme Court in *Brunswick Corp. v. Pueblo Bowl-O-Mat, Inc.,* 429 U.S. 477 (1977). *See* Kovacic, *Intellectual DNA, supra* note 10 (TAN 198–200) (describing influence of Areeda article on Supreme Court).

32. *Illinois Brick v. Illinois,* 431 U.S. 720 (1977) (citing Richard A. Posner, ANTITRUST CASES, ECONOMIC NOTES, AND OTHER MATERIALS 147–149 (1974)). *See* William Landes & Richard A. Posner, *Should Indirect Purchasers Have Standing to Sue Under the Antitrust Laws? An Economic Analysis of the Rule of Illinois Brick,* 46 U. CHI. L. REV. 602 (1979); William Landes & Richard A. Posner, *The Economics of Passing On: A Reply to Harris and Sullivan,* 128 U. PA. L. REV. 1274, 1275–1276 (1980).

33. *See* 3 Phillip E. Areeda & Herbert Hovenkamp, ANTITRUST LAW ¶346k (3d ed. 2007). Areeda's and Turner's original position is stated at 3 ANTITRUST LAW ¶337e, at 191–194 (1978). Justice Brennan's dissent (joined by Justices Marshall and Blackmun) relied on Areeda. *See* 431 U.S. at 761: ("But if the broad language of §4 means anything, surely it must render the defendant liable to those within the defendant's chain of distribution. It would indeed be "paradoxical to deny recover to the ultimate consumer while permitting the middlemen a windfall recovery.") (Quoting Phillip E. Areeda, ANTITRUST ANALYSIS: PROBLEMS, TEXT, CASES 75 (2d ed. 1974)). The Antitrust Modernization Commission includes among its recommendations one that the indirect purchaser rule be abolished and that state law and federal antitrust cases be consolidated for the allocation of damages.

34. *See* 2A Phillip E. Areeda, Herbert Hovenkamp, Roger D. Blair, & Christine Piette, ANTITRUST LAW ¶395 (3d ed. 2007) (in press).

35. *See, e.g.,* Judge Posner's position on the law of predatory pricing, discussed *supra* note 12. *See also* Spencer Weber Waller, *Book Review of The Antitrust Enterprise* 2 (2006), http://www.luc.edu/law/academics/special/center/antitrust/antitrust_enterprise.pdf (book review, complaining that position reflected is too close to the Chicago School position); Randal C. Picker, *Review of Hovenkamp, The Antitrust Enterprise: Principle and Execution,* 2 COMPETITION POL'Y INT'L 183 (2006) (similar).

36. *See, e.g., United States v. Aluminum Co. of America,* 148 F.2d 416, 431 (2d Cir.1945).

37. *See, e.g., United States v. United Shoe Machinery Corp.,* 110 F.Supp. 295, 340, 341 (D.Mass.1953), *aff'd* per curiam, 347 U.S. 521 (1954).

38. *Eastman Kodak Co. v. Image Technical Services, Inc.,* 125 F.3d 1195 (9th Cir. 1997), *cert. denied,* 523 U.S. 1094 (1998).

39. *Conwood Co. v. United States Tobacco Co.,* 290 F.3d 768 (6th Cir. 2002), *cert. denied,* 537 U.S. 1148 (2003); *see* Hovenkamp, *Antitrust Enterprise, supra* note 8, at 175–180.

40. *LePage's Inc. v. 3M,* 324 F.3d 141 (3d Cir. 2003) (en banc), *cert. denied,* 542 U.S. 953 (2004).

41. *ISO Antitrust Litigation,* 203 F.3d 1322, 1325–1326 (Fed. Cir. 2000), *cert. denied,* 531 U.S. 1143 (2001).

42. Herbert Hovenkamp, *Post-Chicago Antitrust: A Review and Critique,* 2001 COLUM. BUS. L. REV. 257 (2001).

43. On this point, *see* Areeda & Hovenkamp, ANTITRUST LAW ¶749 (2007 Supp.).

44. *Eastman Kodak Co. v. Image Technical Services, Inc.,* 504 U.S. 451 (1992); *see* 10 Phillip E. Areeda & Herbert Hovenkamp, ANTITRUST LAW ¶1740 (2d ed. 2004).

45. For some fairly pessimistic conclusions by a prominent economist temporarily employed by the Antitrust Division, *see* Dennis W. Carlton, *Market Definition: Use and Abuse,* COMPETITION POL'Y INT'L (2007) (forthcoming).

46. A recent possible example is *HDC Medical, Inc. v. Minntech Corp.,* 474 F.3d 543 (8th Cir. 2007) (single-use and multiple-use dialyzers, which cost more, were in same relevant market because they performed the same function, at least where the plaintiff offered no evidence other than the price difference itself for placing them in separate markets; case can be read narrowly for proposition that plaintiff simply did not carry its burden of showing that the degree of substitutability was insufficient to hold the alleged monopolist's product to cost). *See also Cable Holdings of Ga. v. Home Video, Inc.,* 825 F.2d 1559, 1563 (11th Cir. 1987); *United States v. Syufy Enters.,* 712 F. Supp. 1386 (N.D. Cal. 1989), *aff'd,* 903 F.2d 659, 665 & n.9 (9th Cir. 1990) (all movies: theatrical first- or subsequent-run, video rentals, and cable television); *America Online, Inc. v. GreatDeals.Net,* 49 F.Supp.2d 851 (E.D.Va. 1999) (suggesting that relevant market is not limited to advertising on e-mail, but includes the "World Wide Web, direct mail, billboards, television, newspapers, radio, and leaflets, to name a few"). On the problem, *see* 2B Phillip E. Areeda & Herbert Hovenkamp, ANTITRUST LAW ¶539 (3d ed. 2007); Lawrence J. White, *Market Definition in Monopolization Cases: A Paradigm is Missing* (2005), *in* ISSUES IN COMPETITION LAW AND POLICY (Wayne D. Collins, ed., 2006) (forthcoming); Gregory J. Werden, *Market Delineation under the Merger Guidelines: Monopoly Cases and Alternative Approaches,* 16 REV. IND. ORG. 211 (2000). *See also* Thomas G. Krattenmaker, Robert H. Lande, & Steven Salop, *Monopoly Power and Market Power in Antitrust Law,* 76 GEO. L. J. 241 (1987).

47. *Aspen Skiing,* 472 U.S. at 610–611.

48. *Brooke Group,* 509 U.S. 209; *A. A. Poultry Farms,* 881 F.2d at 1400–1401 (advocating recoupment test). *See* Phillip E. Areeda & Donald F. Turner, *Predatory Pricing and Related Practices Under Section 2 of the Sherman Act,* 88 HARV. L. REV. 697, 698 (1975): (" . . . the classically-feared case of predation has been the *deliberate sacrifice of present revenues* for the purpose of driving rivals out of the market and then recouping the losses through higher profits earned in the absence of competition.") (Emphasis added.) *See also* the first edition of ANTITRUST LAW, ¶711b at 151 (1978) (similar); Richard A. Posner, ANTITRUST LAW: AN ECONOMIC PERSPECTIVE 184 (1976) (similar).

49. *See* Brief for the United States and the Federal Trade Commission as Amici Curiae Supporting Petitioner, 2003 WL 21269559, at *16–17, *Verizon Communications, Inc. v. Law Offices of Curtis V. Trinko,* 540 U.S. 398 (2004) ("... conduct is exclusionary where it involves a sacrifice of short-term profits or goodwill that makes sense only insofar as it helps the defendant maintain or obtain monopoly power."); and *id.* at *19–20 ("If such a refusal involves a sacrifice of profits or business advantage that makes economic sense only because it eliminates or lessens competition, it is exclusionary and potentially unlawful.").

50. Brief for the United States and Federal Trade Commission as Amici Curiae Supporting Petitioner at 15, *Verizon Communications, Inc. v. Law Offices of Curtis V. Trinko, LLP,* 540 U.S. 398 (2004). *See* Gregory Werden, *The "No Economic Sense" Test for Exclusionary Conduct,* 31 J. Corp. L. 293 (2006); A. Douglas Melamed, *Exclusive Dealing Agreements and Other Exclusionary Conduct—are There Unifying Principles,* 73 Antitrust L.J. 375 (2006).

51. *See, e.g., Walker Process Equipment, Inc. v. Food Mach. & Chem. Corp.,* 382 U.S. 172 (1965) (maintaining infringement suit on patent obtained by fraud); *Rambus, Inc.,* 2006 WL 2330117 (FTC, Aug. 2, 2006) (allegedly providing false information to private standard setting organization with the result that organization unknowingly adopts standards protected by defendant's IP rights). *See also Netflix, Inc. v. Blockbuster, Inc.,* 2006 WL 2458717 (slip copy) (N.D.Cal. Aug 22, 2006) (NO. C06–02361 WHA) (refusing to dismiss *Walker Process* style counterclaim against Netflix on business method patent, based on Netflix's alleged failure to disclose prior art in patent application).

52. *E.g., Walker Process, id.*

53. Richard A. Posner, Antitrust Law 194–195 (2d ed. 2001).

54. *LePage's,* 324 F.3d at 155.

55. *See, e.g., Barry Wright Corp. v. ITT Grinnell Corp.,* 724 F.2d 227, 232 (1st Cir. 1983) (noting that an "avoidable" or "incremental" cost test for predatory pricing is irrational because it would be less costly for the defendant to halt production; and moreover, "equally efficient competitors cannot permanently match this low price and stay in business"). *See also MCI Commc'n. Corp. v. AT&T,* 708 F.2d 1081, 1113 (7th Cir.), cert. denied, 464 U.S. 891 (1983) (similar, predatory pricing); *Borden, Inc. v. FTC,* 674 F.2d 498, 515 (6th Cir. 1982), *vacated* on other grounds, 461 U.S. 940 (1983) (same, predatory pricing); *Ortho Diagnostic Systems, Inc. v. Abbott Laboratories,* 920 F.Supp. 455, 466–467 (S.D.N.Y. 1996) ("below-cost pricing, unlike pricing at or above that level, carries with it the threat that the party so engaged will drive equally efficient competitors out of business, thus setting the stage for recoupment at the expense of consumers").

56. Posner, Antitrust Law, note 12 at 196.

57. *See* 3 Antitrust Law ¶706 (2d ed. 2002).

58. *See* Thomas Krattenmaker & Steven Salop, *Anticompetitive Exclusion: Raising Rivals' Costs to Achieve Power Over Price,* 96 Yale L.J. 209 (1986); Steven C. Salop & David T. Scheffman, *Raising Rivals' Costs,* 73 Am. Econ. Rev. 267 (1983). *See also* Herbert Hovenkamp, *Post-Chicago Antitrust: A Review and Critique,* 2001 Colum. Bus. L. Rev. 257.

A particularly interventionist RRC test is proposed in Einer Elhauge, *Defining Better Monopolization Standards,* 56 STAN. L. REV. 253 (2003), which queries "whether the alleged exclusionary conduct succeeds in furthering monopoly power (1) only if the monopolist has improved its own efficiency or (2) by impairing rival efficiency whether or not it enhances monopolist efficiency." The second part of this test would condemn a firm for using practices that lowered its own costs if, in the process, they denied scale economies to a rival. *See, e.g.,* Elhauge, *id.* at 324 (arguing that even if economies of scale are very substantial, above a 50 percent market share, the firm cannot use exclusive contracts to increase its output into a lower cost range but must simply set its price). The Elhauge test would also condemn a firm who used a practice that increased its sales beyond the point that its scale economies topped out, if in so doing it denied scale economies to a rival. *See id.* at 324 (illustration of firm whose tie, exclusive deal, or other agreement requires customers to purchase 70 percent of the market from it, even though its economies of scale top out at 40 percent). Even assuming such tests were desirable, they seem to make unrealistic demands on tribunals to measure relevant scale economies. *See* 2B ANTITRUST LAW ¶408 (3d ed. 2007).

59. *See, e.g., Microsoft,* 253 F.3d at 70 (defendant's exclusionary contracts relegated rival Netscape to higher cost distribution channels); *Dentsply,* 399 F.3d at 191 (similar; defendant's exclusive dealing arrangements relegated rivals to inferior distribution alternatives); *JTC Petroleum Co. v. Piasa Motor Fuels, Inc.,* 190 F.3d 775, 778–779 (7th Cir.1999) (members of cartel may have paid off suppliers to charge cartel rivals significantly higher prices, thus creating a price umbrella under which the cartel could operate); *Brand Name Prescription Drugs Antitrust Litigation,* 123 F.3d 599, 614 (7th Cir. 1997), *cert. denied,* 522 U.S. 1123 (1998) (similar); *Forsyth v. Humana, Inc.,* 114 F.3d 1467, 1478 (9th Cir. 1997), *aff'd* on nonantitrust grounds, 525 U.S. 299 (1999) (health care provider's policy of shifting indigent patients to rivals could have effect of raising their costs); *Multistate Legal Studies, Inc. v. Harcourt Brace Jovanovich Legal and Professional Publications, Inc.,* 63 F.3d 1540, 1553 (10th Cir.1995) (dominant firm's practice of scheduling its own full slate of classes so as to conflict with rivals' specialized classes could have had effect of raising the rival's cost of distributing its own product); *Premier Elec. Const. Co. v. National Elec. Contractors Ass'n, Inc.,* 814 F.2d 358 (7th 1987) (alleged agreement between union and contractors' association under which union would obtain fee from all employers without whom it had collective bargaining agreements, whether or not they were association members, to be paid to the association, probably intended to raise the costs of non-member contractors). *Cf. Ball Memorial Hosp., Inc. v. Mutual Hosp. Ins., Inc.,* 784 F.2d 1325, 1340 (7th Cir. 1986) (rejecting RRC claim that Blue Cross forced hospitals to submit lower bids for taking care of BC patients, with result that it had to impose higher charges on non-BC patients).

60. *See, e.g., Conwood Co. v. United States Tobacco Co.,* 290 F.3d 768, 784 (6th Cir. 2002), cert. denied, 537 U.S. 1148 (2003). The plaintiff claimed that its market share would have grown even faster and that it would have earned even more profits but for the exclusionary conduct.

61. This is apparently the source of Judge Posner's objection. *See* Posner, ANTITRUST LAW note 12 at 196, referring to RRC as "not a happy formula" because one way of raising rivals; costs is to be more efficient than the rival, thus denying it scale economies.

62. *See* 3 ANTITRUST LAW ¶651 (2d ed. 2002).

63. *Walker Process Equipment v. Food Machinery & Chemical Corp.*, 382 U.S. 172 (1965). *See* 3 Phillip E. Areeda & Herbert Hovenkamp, ANTITRUST LAW ¶706 (2d ed. 2002).

64. *See, e.g., United States v. Besser Mfg. Co.*, 96 F.Supp. 304, 312 (E.D.Mich. 1951), *aff'd* 343 U.S. 444 (1952) (infringement action where patentee had no basis for believing that defendant's technology infringed the patent); *Moore USA, Inc. v. Standard Register Co.*, 139 F. Supp. 2d 348 W.D.N.Y. 2001) (refusing to dismiss Sherman '2 counterclaim allegation that patentee filed infringement claim while knowing that counterclaimant's product did not infringe because it did not incorporate an essential ingredient); *International Technologies Consultants v. Pilkington PLC*, 137 F.3d 1382 (9th Cir. 1998) (infringement suit based on expired patents a possible antitrust violation).

65. *Professional Real Estate Investors v. Columbia Pictures Indus.*, 508 U.S. 49 (1993) (purely legal question whether charging money to play a movie video in a hotel room constituted a "performance," and thus an infringement of the copyright, where Circuit Courts had split on the issue; no antitrust violation).

66. *Dippin' Dots, Inc. v. Mosey*, 476 F.3d 1337 (Fed. Cir. 2007).

67. 35 U.S.C. § 102(b).

68. *Dippin' Dots*, 476 F.3d at 1346 (relying on *Nobelpharma AB v. Implant Innovations, Inc.*, 141 F.3d 1059, 1068–1069 (Fed.Cir.1998)).

69. *Id.* at 1347 ("The difference in breadth between inequitable conduct and *Walker Process* fraud admits the possibility of a close case whose facts reach the level of inequitable conduct, but not of fraud before the PTO. This is such a case.").

70. *Id.* at 1348 (internal citations omitted). The Federal Circuit was following dicta from the Supreme Court suggesting that an inquiry into actual subjective intent is necessary. *See Professional Real Estate Investors, Inc. v. Columbia Pictures Indus., Inc.*, 508 U.S. 49, 60 (1993) (("Only if challenged litigation is objectively meritless may a court examine the litigant's subjective motivation. Under this second part of our definition of sham, the court should focus on whether the baseless lawsuit conceals "an attempt to interfere directly with the business relationships of a competitor. . . . ") (Citations omitted.)

71. *See In re Dippin' Dots Patent Litigation*, 249 F.Supp.2d 1346 (N.D.Ga. 2003) (docket entry).

72. *See* 3 ANTITRUST LAW *supra* note 33 at ¶¶735–737.

73. This discussion largely ignores defenses, which are significant and almost certainly explain the great majority of situations in which discounting occurs. *See* 11 Herbert Hovenkamp, ANTITRUST LAW ¶¶1810–1814 (2d ed. 2005).

74. *See, e.g., Concord Boat Corp. v. Brunswick Corp.*, 207 F.3d 1039 (8th Cir.), *cert. denied*, 531 U.S. 979 (2000) (refusing to condemn above cost

market share discounts by dominant firm because equally efficient rival could steal the sales at any time).

75. *See Brooke Group,* 509 U.S. at 223:

> As a general rule, the exclusionary effect of prices above a relevant measure of cost either reflects the lower cost structure of the alleged predator, and so represents competition on the merits, or is beyond the practical ability of a judicial tribunal to control without courting intolerable risks of chilling legitimate price-cutting...." To hold that the antitrust laws protect competitors from the loss of profits due to such price competition would, in effect, render illegal any decision by a firm to cut prices in order to increase market share. The antitrust laws require no such perverse result." Quoting *Cargill, Inc. v. Monfort of Colorado, Inc.,* 479 U.S. 104, 116 (1986).

76. For examples, *see* Jean Tirole, THE THEORY OF INDUSTRIAL ORGANIZATION 367–374 (1992); Frederic M. Scherer & David Ross, INDUSTRIAL MARKET STRUCTURE AND ECONOMIC PERFORMANCE 356–366, 405–6 (3d ed. 1990); Joe S. Bain, INDUSTRIAL ORGANIZATION 269–276 (2d ed. 1968).

77. *See Cascade Health Solutions v. PeaceHealth,* 2007 WL 2473229 (9th Cir. Sept. 4, 2007). The Ninth Circuit relied on the ANTITRUST LAW treatise (Supp., para. 749) in adopting a version of this test. It rejected tests that would condemn prices that were above any measure of cost, such as the Third Circuit's *LePage's* test; but it also rejected tests that would require a showing that the price of the entire bundle was below a measure of the defendant's costs.

78. *See, e.g., Standard Oil Co. v. United States,* 221 U.S. 1 (1911) (ordering dissolution of Standard Oil into 34 companies). *See also United States v. United Shoe Machinery Corp.,* 110 F. Supp. 295 (D. Mass. 1953), *aff'd* per curiam, 347 U.S. 521 (1954); and the eventual dissolution decree in 391 U.S. 244 (1968). These decisions as well as some others are discussed in William E. Kovacic, *Designing Antitrust Remedies for Dominant Firm Misconduct,* 31 CONN. L. REV. 1285 (1999).

79. *See, e.g., Eastman Kodak Co. v. Image Technical Services,* 125 F.3d 1195 (9th Cir. 1997), *cert. denied,* 523 U.S. 1094 (1998). *Cf. In re Rambus, Inc.,* #9302, 2007 WL 431524 (FTC, Feb. 5, 2007) (ordering licensing at specified RAND royalty).

80. *Microsoft,* 253 F.3d at 66–67 (condemning Microsoft's numerous practices directed mainly at Netscape and Sun Microsystems); Proposed Final Judgment and Competitive Impact Statement; *United States of America v. Microsoft Corp.,* 59 Fed. Reg. 42,845 (Dep't Justice Aug. 19, 1994) (consent decree in earlier litigation challenging "per processor" licensing practice directed mainly at IBM's OS/2 operating system); *see also United States v. Microsoft Corp.,* 56 F.3d 1448 (D.C. Cir. 1995) (upholding decree).

81. Richard Hofstadter, *What Happened to the Antitrust Movement?, in* THE PARANOID STYLE IN AMERICAN POLITICS AND OTHER ESSAYS 193–94 (1965).

82. *United States v. Aluminum Co. of America,* 148 F.2d 416 (2d Cir. 1945).

83. *United States v. Grinnell Corp.,* 236 F. Supp. 244, 247–48 (D.R.I. 1964).

84. *United States v. Grinnell Corp.,* 384 U.S. 563 (1966).

85. *Aspen Skiing Co. v. Aspen Highlands Skiing Corp.*, 472 U.S. 585 (1985).

86. 540 U.S. 398 (2004).

87. The Supreme Court unanimously reversed the Second Circuit, but three Justices (Stevens, Souter, and Thomas) did not join Justice Scalia's opinion; they would have rejected plaintiff's standing and would not have decided "the merits of the §2 claim."

88. 540 U.S. at 414.

89. *United States v. Colgate & Co.*, 250 U.S. 300, 307 (1919).

90. *United States v. Dentsply International, Inc.*, 399 F.3d 181 (3d Cir. 2005).

91. *United States v. Microsoft Corp.*, 253 F.3d 34 (D.C. Cir. 2001).

92. *Image Technical Services, Inc. v. Eastman Kodak Co.*, 125 F.3d 1195 (9th Cir. 1997).

93. Herbert Hovenkamp, *The Harvard and Chicago Schools and the Dominant Firm, supra.*

94. *Eastman Kodak Co. v. Image Technical Services, Inc.*, 504 U.S. 451 (1992).

95. *Id.*

96. It is true, as Hovenkamp indicates, that the "Federal Circuit promptly took issue with the Ninth Circuit's *Kodak* decision," but one can legitimately ask whether decisions of the Federal Circuit, with that circuit's focus on patent and intellectual property issues, have not tilted the playing field heavily against key section 2 values.

97. *See* Pitofsky, Patterson, & Hooks, *The Essential Facilities Doctrine Under U.S. Antitrust Law,* 70 ANTITRUST L.J. 443 (2002).

98. *See* R. Pitofsky, H. Goldschmid, & D. Wood, CASES AND MATERIALS ON TRADE REGULATION, 869–71 (5th ed. 2003).

99. *Brooke Group v. Brown & Williamson Tobacco,* 509 U.S. 209 (1993).

100. *Weyerhaeuser Co. v. Ross-Simmons Hardwood Lumber Co.,* 127 S.Ct. 1069 (2007).

101. *Olympia Equipment Leasing Co. v. Western Union Telegraph,* 797 F. 2d 370, 375–76 (7th Cir. 1986).

102. 504 U.S. at 488 (Scalia dissenting).

4

Can Vertical Arrangements
Injure Consumer Welfare?

Introduction

In terms of practical effect, the Chicago School's most pronounced impact on U.S. antitrust law has been to move vertical integration and vertical distribution arrangements virtually out of the range of antitrust enforcement. Thus, vertical mergers and joint ventures, tie-in sales, exclusive dealing contracts, predatory pricing, and minimum price- fixing have almost never been challenged in recent years by federal or state enforcement authorities. The *per se* rule against tie-in sales has never been explicitly eliminated but is certainly on its last legs. The high point in this cleaning out of enforcement against verticals was reached in 2007 when a five-four majority of the Supreme Court declared that the nearly 100-year-old antitrust *per se* rule—vertical agreements between manufacturers and dealers that the dealers not sell at less than a minimum price—was no longer good law. While rule of reason cases are still possible, many have noted that winning a complicated antitrust case on a rule of reason theory is so difficult and expensive that private plaintiffs often do not try.

Theories that have paved the way not just for permissive enforcement but for virtually no enforcement derive principally from Chicago School theory. It was Robert Bork who led the way with comments to the effect that vertical arrangements can hardly ever limit output and thereby injure consumers, and therefore the decision to eliminate that kind of rivalry can only be made in order to enhance efficiency.[1]

In this chapter, Steven Salop and Stephen Calkins take issue with Chicago School thinking at the most basic levels, rejecting the ideas that vertical arrangements rarely if ever can harm consumers, exclusionary vertical conduct is either benign or procompetitive, and that predatory pricing (pricing below some appropriate level of cost) "is rarely attempted and even more rarely succeeds."[2]

Economic Analysis of Exclusionary Vertical Conduct: Where Chicago Has Overshot the Mark

Steven C. Salop

Introduction

Few antitrust issues are less contentious than the analysis of exclusionary vertical conduct and anticompetitive allegations of leverage and foreclosure. These concepts arise in the context of both section 1 and section 2 because they can occur in a wide variety of conduct—tying, exclusive dealing, vertical mergers, refusals to deal, and so on. The Chicago School revolution really began with its analysis of exclusionary vertical restraints and there has been continued controversy ever since.

The Chicago School argument is that the antitrust concepts of anticompetitive foreclosure and anticompetitive leverage are empty and illogical and do not hold up to economic analysis. As for exclusives, the associated argument is that competition for exclusive relationships benefits consumers, just as do other forms of competition. In short, exclusionary vertical conduct is either benign or procompetitive. Thus, the law regarding exclusionary vertical conduct should be very permissive or even per se legal. Judge Posner has suggested the use of a very permissive legal standard, the equally efficient entrant standard, which flows from the *Brooke Group* standard for predatory pricing.

In this chapter, I do not review the case law on this set of issues. Instead, I examine the economic foundations of the controversy as a way to inform the debate. In my view, the strong economic foundations claimed by Chicago School commentators like Robert Bork do not hold up to economic analysis. The concepts of anticompetitive foreclosure and leverage are not empty and illogical. Competition for exclusives is not a panacea for all vertical exclusion claims. Nor is the predatory pricing paradigm the appropriate framework for analyzing exclusionary vertical conduct. Instead, a more refined analysis must be applied. This analysis implies that the better legal approach would be the rule of reason with its focus on consumer harm, not a proxy rule like the equally efficient entrant standard.

This chapter is organized as follows: In section I, I begin by elucidating two general paradigms for exclusionary conduct—predatory pricing and raising rivals' costs. I explain how these paradigms differ and why the predatory pricing paradigm is inappropriate as the foundation for analysis of exclusionary vertical conduct. In section II, I analyze claims of anticompetitive leverage and the criticisms levied against these claims. In particular, I analyze the now-venerable single-monopoly-profit theory and show the limits of its applicability. In sections III and IV, I follow this same basic approach to claims of anticompetitive foreclosure and the view that competition for exclusives can resolve all concerns about vertical exclusion. In section V, I return to the issue of the two paradigms for exclusionary vertical conduct and show the fundamental economic flaw in the equally efficient entrant standard.

I. Fundamental Differences Between Predatory Pricing and Raising Rivals' Costs Theories of Anticompetitive Exclusion

Economic and legal analyses of exclusionary conduct suggest two distinct paradigms of exclusionary conduct by dominant firms—predatory pricing and raising rivals' costs. Some of the controversy over the best legal standard arises because commentators or courts have one or the other paradigm in mind. Many conservative commentators tend to view predatory pricing as the paradigm of all exclusionary conduct. Because of the view that predatory pricing is rarely attempted and even more rarely succeeds,[3] the use of this paradigm leads to an overly permissive view of exclusionary conduct and an overly skeptical view of allegations of anticompetitive exclusionary conduct that does not fit properly into the predatory pricing paradigm. In contrast, the raising rivals' costs ("RRC") paradigm explains how exclusionary vertical conduct raises more significant competitive concerns and suggests a different rule of reason standard to govern such allegations.

The paradigmatic predatory pricing theory involves reducing price with the purpose and effect of causing rivals to exit from the market, generally by winning a war of attrition, and thereby allowing the predator to profit by raising price to the monopoly level.[4] In *Brooke Group,* the U.S. Supreme Court set out a two-part liability standard for predatory pricing that involves (1) evaluating whether the conduct involves below-cost pricing and (2) evaluating the likelihood of recoupment.[5] This standard might be applied to all exclusionary conduct. A court could first evaluate whether the defendant's price exceeds its cost. If it does, then the conduct would not be condemned. If the price falls short of the cost, then the court would evaluate whether the defendant likely would be able to recoup its losses by exercising durable market power in the future.

Raising rivals' costs is another—*and distinct*—paradigmatic type of exclusionary conduct.[6] RRC generally involves conduct to raise the costs of competitors with the purpose and effect of causing them to raise their prices or reduce their output, thereby allowing the excluding firm to profit by setting a supracompetitive price.[7] Analysis consistent with the RRC paradigm is commonly applied to exclusivity arrangements that have the effect of raising rivals' distribution costs.

It is important to draw this distinction because RRC conduct is more likely to harm consumers than is traditional deep-pocket predatory pricing. Therefore, the law of exclusionary conduct should reflect a greater concern about RRC conduct than it does toward predatory pricing. It should be more worried about false negatives and less worried about false positives from RRC conduct, relative to predatory pricing.

RRC conduct is more likely to harm consumers than is traditional deep-pocket predatory pricing for several reasons. First, unlike predatory pricing, or at least the paradigmatic view of predatory pricing, successful RRC does not require a risky investment or associated profit sacrifice during an initial predatory period that may only be recouped at some later point in the future. Instead, recoupment often occurs simultaneously with the RRC conduct. Second, unlike predatory pricing, successful RRC does not require the exit of rivals, or even the permanent reduction in competitors' production capacity. If the marginal costs of established competitors are raised, those rivals will have the incentive to raise their prices and reduce their output, even if they remain viable. Third, unlike paradigmatic predatory pricing, RRC is not necessarily more costly in the short run to the defendant than to its victims. For example, a threat may not be very costly to the perpetrator but could substantially raise the target firm's costs. This clearly could occur with respect to exclusionary vertical conduct.[8] Fourth, unlike predatory pricing, successful RRC does not always involve a short-term consumer benefit that must be balanced against longer-term consumer harm, if any harm occurs during the recoupment period.[9] The consumer harm often would occur immediately. Finally, RRC has an analogue to naked price fixing. "Naked RRC" would refer to exclusionary conduct that lacks valid efficiency benefits, for example, when the defendant's claims are pretextual, noncognizable.[10] RRC also may involve non-naked exclusion, but where the potential benefits are insignificant. In predatory pricing, in contrast, there is an inherent consumer efficiency benefit that must be taken into account—the low prices during the predatory period. Exclusionary vertical conduct can be characterized as RRC conduct. Therefore, the RRC paradigm is relevant to the analysis of these restraints.

Because predatory pricing and RRC are so different, there is no reason to think that they should be governed by the same standards for antitrust liability. For the reasons just stated, RRC conduct raises greater concerns than deeppocket predatory pricing. RRC conduct is more likely to be attempted and more likely to succeed. Therefore, antitrust law should apply tighter liability standards to the conduct of defendants accused of RRC conduct than predatory pricing. The liability standards should exhibit relatively more concern about false negatives and relatively less concern about false positives.[11] This has direct application to the law governing exclusionary vertical conduct.

RRC is generally associated with the post-Chicago approach to antitrust. However, it is important to recognize that this approach has its roots in the economic analysis of Chicago School commentators. Aaron Director and Edward Levi, the founders of the Chicago School approach, recognized the potential anticompetitive effects of exclusive dealing in *Standard Fashions*.[12] Gordon Tullock and Richard Posner recognized that monopoly profits could be converted into deadweight loss from wasteful rent-seeking activities that use the profits to erect entry barriers.[13] In the *Antitrust Paradox*, Robert Bork stressed the anticompetitive effects of cutting off competitors' access to the most efficient distribution system.[14] Thus, when conservative jurists equate predatory pricing and RRC, or treat RRC theories as outside the mainstream, they are deviating from the learning that originated with the Chicago School.

II. Integration, Anticompetitive Leverage, and the Single-Monopoly-Profit Theory

Antitrust opponents of vertical integration and tying claimed that integration (either by merger or through tying) can permit the monopolist in one product to leverage his monopoly to achieve a *second* monopoly in another (downstream or tied product) market.[15] The monopolist allegedly can carry out this leverage strategy by refusing to sell the input to its competitors in the other market or by charging a high price for its monopoly product. Thus, these commentators concluded that vertical merger and tying policy should be restrictive in order to prevent this leverage.

Chicago School critics of this restrictive view of integration (both vertical integration and tying) argued that such leverage would not occur.[16] In the vertical integration context, it was argued that an upstream (input market) monopolist would have no motive to integrate in order to discriminate against rivals, because integration is not necessary to capture monopoly profits.[17] Instead, a standalone (unintegrated) upstream monopolist can capture all of the monopoly profits simply by pricing the input that it sells to the downstream firms at the monopoly level. Applied to tying, the argument is that a monopolist in the tying product can capture all the monopoly profits by pricing the tying product at the monopoly level, while permitting competition in the tied product market.

Simply stated, the Chicago School critics argue that there is a "single" monopoly profit that can be extracted by the monopolist only once. It is not possible profitably to leverage this power by vertical integration or tying into a "second monopoly" in a second market.[18] In light of this single-monopoly-profit (SMP) theory, it then could be further claimed that vertical integration *must* be motivated by efficiency concerns—because there can be no anticompetitive motive.

If tying and vertical integration cannot permit the exercise of additional market power, that raises the question of why firms would choose to tie or vertically integrate. There is a ready answer to this question—to achieve procompetitive efficiency benefits. There are several sources of efficiencies, many of which have been recognized in the case law. These include achieving lower costs or superior product design, and eliminating inefficient product usage that accompanies prices in excess of marginal costs, eliminating double marginalization. Integration and tying also can be used to disguise price discounts. Thus, taken together, the SMP theory and the procompetitive rationales suggest that vertical integration and tying have procompetitive benefits and lack anticompetitive risks.

However, this economic analysis of tying and vertical integration is too simple and, therefore, its policy implications are too optimistic. Tying and vertical integration can be used to achieve and maintain market power.[19] The SMP theory is only true under limited economic circumstances. Its validity requires a number of restrictive assumptions. Therefore, uncritical acceptance of the SMP theory leads to an overly permissive view of tying and vertical integration and an overly skeptical view of antitrust theories premised on leverage or foreclosure. Exclusionary conduct can harm consumers under unexceptional circumstances and should be analyzed under the rule of reason.

As a matter of formal economic theory, the SMP theory is valid under a certain combination of market conditions that are not very general: (1) the monopolist has a durable and unregulated monopoly in the one product; (2) the products are consumed in fixed proportions; (3) all consumers have identical preferences; and (4) there are no efficiencies of integration.

When at least one of these conditions fails to occur, then there is economic motive for tying or vertical integration. For some of these conditions, the integration may have procompetitive tendencies, while for others the tendencies may be anticompetitive. In the real world, integration can have aspects of both. This analysis suggests that such conduct should not be per se legal. Instead, it should be evaluated under the rule of reason in order to separate out procompetitive from anticompetitive use of the conduct.

The circumstances under which such integration can be anticompetitive can be classified as follows. For ease of exposition, I will frame the analysis in the context of tying.

A. Monopolizing the Sale of the Tied Product to Consumers Who Purchase Only the Tied Product

The single-monopoly-profit theory argues that the monopolist can extract all the monopoly profits from the purchasers of the tied product by raising the price of the tying product and permitting competition in the tied product market. Suppose, however, that some consumers do not buy the tying product and only buy the tied product. Those consumers would continue to benefit from tied-market competition. In contrast, if the monopolist engages in tying and drives out of the market all the independent producers of the tied product, then it would be in the position to exercise market power or even to monopolize the tying product. This anticompetitive theory requires an assumption that the tied-product market involves sufficient economies of scale that there would be an insufficient number of viable firms to maintain intense competition, if those firms were restricted to selling solely to consumers who purchased only the tied product market.[20] Or, the number of competitors could fall to the point where tacit coordination is dangerously likely to succeed.

This example can be applied to a hypothetical case based on personal computer operating systems and media players. Suppose that a firm has a monopoly in operating systems for personal computers. Suppose that this monopolist in personal computer operating systems currently is only a small player in operating systems for wireless phones. Suppose further that there is a type of application software, say a media player, that can be used in both personal computers and wireless phones. The SMP theory would suggest that the PC operating system monopolist would have no anticompetitive incentive to tie its media player with its PC operating system software. It could simply extract all the monopoly profits in personal computers by raising the price of the operating system.

But, note that this rent extraction would not affect the purchasers of wireless phones. The competition among media players would benefit the purchasers of wireless phones, who are not subject to the firm's operating system monopoly. However, suppose that the firm tied its media player to its personal computer operating system. In this situation, the media player software competitors would not be able to sell into this segment of the market. If the market for media player software for wireless phones is relatively small, then competition for media players for wireless phones might not be able to survive simply on those sales. In that case, the PC operating system monopolist would be able to monopolize the standalone market for media players used for wireless phones. This is truly a second monopoly.[21]

B. Maintaining the Monopoly in the Tying Product

The single-monopoly-profit theory assumes that the firm has a durable protected monopoly in the tying product market. However, suppose that this is not the case. In this situation, tying can be a way to maintain the tying product monopoly. Absent tying, firms that produce the tied product could use that entry as a foothold for entering the tying product market and thereby break down the monopoly. The firm can use tying to foreclose this opportunity. By tying, the monopolist forces entrants to enter both markets simultaneously. This simultaneous entry at two levels may involve higher barriers to entry than simply entering the tying product market after becoming established in the tied-product market.[22]

The operating system hypothetical example discussed above can be extended to explain a variant of this two-level entry argument. Suppose that the PC monopolist engages in tying of the media player and succeeds in monopolizing the media player as well. In this situation, entrants into PC operating systems would be forced to produce media player software too. In principle, this could raise barriers to entry into operating systems.

These two examples also can be combined in the context of a dynamic analysis over time to produce another variant. Once the PC operating system monopolist gains a monopoly in media players, perhaps it could gain a monopoly in operating systems for wireless phones by tying its wireless phone operating system software to its monopolistically supplied media player software. It might implement this plan by making the software incompatible with rival operating systems or withholding information needed to make the software compatible. Tying thus can be used over time to create a linked set of monopolies.

C. Facilitating Tacit Coordination in the Sale of the Tying or Tied Product

The analysis so far has mainly been framed in terms of achieving or maintaining a monopoly, either in the tied-product or tying-product market. However, the same basic economic forces could apply to a situation where the firm's market power in the tying- product market falls short of a full monopoly. Tying can be used to make the markets more concentrated and entry less easy. In that way, other firms may survive but tacit coordination could be facilitated by the tying.

D. Evading Regulation of the Tying Product

Tying can also be used to evade the effects of price regulation of the tying product. By tying, the regulated firm can collect the monopoly profits in an unregulated tied-product market. For example, returning to the fixed proportions example of the SMP theory above, suppose that the tying product is regulated but the tied product is unregulated. Suppose that the price of the tying product is held down below the monopoly level by regulation. The monopolist could evade this regulation by raising the price of its tied product and requiring consumers to purchase the two products together.[23] This exception to the SMP theory has been well recognized.[24] However, the recent Supreme Court opinions in *Discon* and *Trinko* may have removed evasion of regulation from the purview of the Sherman Act, placing monitoring and enforcement of this concern solely in the hands of the regulatory agencies.[25]

III. Vertical Integration and Anticompetitive Foreclosure

Conservative commentators also have criticized the concept of anticompetitive foreclosure in the older cases like *Brown Shoe*. Bork suggested that the foreclosure alleged to occur from vertical mergers was nothing more than a remixing of supplier-customer relationships. As he cleverly put it, competition would be better served if the FTC had held an industry social mixer instead of bringing an antitrust action to enjoin a vertical merger.[26] Those cases did not explain how foreclosure would lead to market power.

However, uncritical acceptance of this critique of foreclosure leads to an overly permissive view of vertical mergers and other exclusionary vertical conduct and restraints, and an overly skeptical view of antitrust allegations based on anticompetitive foreclosure concerns. Modern economic analysis has drawn the logical linkage between foreclosure and market power. In particular, vertical mergers can lead to real foreclosure that creates market power in either the upstream or downstream market under certain identifiable circumstances.[27]

A vertical merger can lead to market power in the downstream market. Suppose that after the merger, the upstream division of the integrated firm refuses to deal with or raises the input price charged to unintegrated downstream competitors. Suppose that these unintegrated competitors lack equally cost-effective alternative sources of the input. Or, suppose that they only have one or two other alternative suppliers, and that those suppliers realize that the behavior of the now-integrated firm increases their market power over the unintegrated firms. In these circumstances, the merged firm may have the incentive to raise prices or refuse to deal, and that conduct will raise the cost of their integrated rivals. If there is insufficient remaining competition in the downstream market among integrated firms or other unintegrated firms that have cost-effective alternative sources of supply, then the downstream price may increase, leading to consumer injury.

Judge Posner's opinion in *JTC Petroleum* suggested a variant of this foreclosure analysis. In that case, Posner analyzed the case of a downstream cartel that prevents disruptive competition by a maverick by agreeing with input suppliers to refuse to deal with the maverick.[28] The downstream cartel members compensate the input suppliers by paying a supracompetitive price for the inputs they bought, thereby sharing the cartel profits with those suppliers. Thus, the input suppliers enforce the downstream cartel. In this example, there is no actual vertical integration. Instead, there is anticompetitive "integration by contract."

A vertical merger also can lead to market power in the upstream market. Suppose that after the merger, the downstream division of the integrated firm were to refuse to purchase from unintegrated input suppliers and instead began to purchase all of its input needs from the upstream division. If the downstream division of the integrated firm represented a large share of the market, withholding its purchases might drive one or more upstream competitors to exit from the market or be forced into a higher cost niche position. Either way, that might give the upstream division of the integrated firm the power and incentive to raise the prices it charges its other competitors.[29]

Leverage theories of tying discussed above also may be applied to foreclosure analysis. For example, suppose that there were a purely vertical merger of an upstream monopolist and a downstream monopolist. (In terms of complementary products, the analogy would be a merger among the monopolistic producers of two complementary products, for example, hot dogs and hot dog buns.) That merger could be procompetitive by giving the two firms the incentive to reduce their prices. This is the well-known efficiency benefit of "eliminating double-marginalization." Before the merger, a price decrease by one of the firms to a level slightly below the monopoly price would decrease its own profits slightly. At the same time, it would increase the demand for the product and the profits of the other firm. The joint profits of the two firms would rise, but in the premerger world that opportunity would not be taken unilaterally. After the vertical merger, this mutual benefit of lower prices would be taken into account and would lead to the incentive to reduce prices of both products.

However, this vertical merger also could be anticompetitive by reducing or eliminating the potential for entry. Before the merger, each firm would have the incentive to cooperate with firms who were trying to enter the market of the other firm. Competition in the other market would lead to lower prices in that market and, therefore, higher demand and profits for the complementary product. Indeed, each firm might be a potential entrant into the market of the other firm. In contrast, this incentive to facilitate independent entry would disappear. As a result, entrants would need to enter both markets simultaneously. This requirement of two-level entry may raise barriers to entry and lead to higher prices, even after taking the elimination of double marginalization benefit into account.

IV. Competition for Exclusives

It has been argued in a number of recent influential antitrust cases that competition for exclusives can prevent anticompetitive harm. Confidence in the constraining power of competition for exclusives has led a number of U.S. courts to take a very permissive approach to exclusives with a short contractual duration.[30]

However, in my view, the real competitive constraints created by competition for exclusives should not be overestimated when there is a dominant firm or the market is highly concentrated. This process differs from competition in the sale of goods and services in a number of significant ways that can limit its benefits to consumers. To begin with, when a firm pays a supplier, distributor, or customer to deal exclusively with it, it is not simply paying to obtain an additional supply source, or channel of distribution, or customer for itself. It also is paying for the right to exclude rivals from that supply source or channel of distribution or customer. In fact, exclusion may be the sole or primary function of the exclusivity.[31]

This is not to say that exclusives are always anticompetitive. Exclusives can eliminate free riding, improve coordination, or create other efficiency benefits. However, efficiency benefits are not inherent in exclusives. Exclusives instead might reduce competition by destroying rivals' efficient access to key inputs, make experimentation more difficult, and raise switching costs. Stated most simply, the firm may be purchasing market power as well as a channel of distribution, source of supply, or additional customer.

There are a number of other reasons to be skeptical of the consumer protection provided by competition for exclusives. First, in some situations, there may not be real competition for the exclusives. An incumbent firm may obtain long-term exclusives before there is another competitor on the horizon. By the time the entrant is poised to enter, the key input suppliers may be tied up in long-term exclusive contracts. For the reasons discussed later on, one cannot count on the suppliers to make decisions that adequately protect the interests of consumers in these circumstances.

Second, even where competition for exclusives does occur, it may not take place on a level playing field. The exclusives tend to be worth more to a dominant incumbent than undoing the exclusive is worth to an equally efficient entrant. This is because the entrant can earn only the (more competitive) duopoly return, whereas a dominant incumbent may earn the monopoly return if entry is deterred or significantly constrained. For example, suppose that the incumbent could earn $200 if it gets the exclusive and so is able to maintain its monopoly. If the entrant gets distribution and breaks the monopoly, suppose that the entrant and incumbent each would earn $70, for a total of $140. Because competition transfers wealth from producers to consumers, the total profits fall from competition (e.g., from $200 to $140). In this case, the entrant would be willing to bid up only to $70 to obtain distribution, an amount equal to its profits from entry. In contrast, the incumbent would be willing to bid up to $130 for an exclusive that prevents the entry, an amount equal to the reduction in its profits from competition. The incumbent thus would win the bidding against an equally efficient entrant and maintain its monopoly. The monopolist would continue to charge the monopoly price for its output, harming consumers. The only difference is that now the distributors would obtain a share of the monopoly profits.

This result does not depend on unusual conditions. We assumed that the entrant was equally efficient. The monopoly result occurs whenever and because aggregate market profits fall from competition. This is a very general condition when the entrant is equally efficient. This example also shows why competition for exclusives cannot be assumed to reach the efficient outcome.

This is not a "deep-pocket" argument about the incumbent having more wealth or better access to the capital market. The incumbent's bidding advantage comes from the fact that it has already sunk the costs of entry, together with the fact that monopoly profits exceed the profits in the more competitive postentry market. Entry barriers are raised because the entrant's need to outbid the incumbent artificially raises its costs of entry. The bidding disadvantage faced by the entrant is "artificial" in the sense that the exclusivity does not have real and direct efficiency benefits in the example, but instead has the sole effect of raising barriers to entry.

Third, exclusives increase switching costs and eliminate the ability of suppliers or consumers to experiment by devoting only a portion of their business to the entrant. This in turn raises their risk of switching. For the entrant, this decreases the likelihood that entry will succeed. This increased difficulty of coordination and the resulting barriers to entry and expansion are reinforced if the exclusive contracts are long-term and have "staggered" expiration dates.[32] These factors extend the period before the entrant can achieve viability. They also reinforce the consumers' or suppliers' expectations that the entry will not succeed, which will in turn make them less willing to take the risk of forgoing the exclusive in order to remain available to the entrant. As a result, they will require larger inducements to switch to the entrant, thus raising entry costs still further.

This analysis of experimentation and switching costs suggests another reason why the entrant may face a bidding disadvantage. The retailers may not find the entrant's product adequate as its only offering, whereas the incumbent's product may be sufficient. In this situation, the entrant does not desire (nor could it practically obtain) an exclusive. Instead, it wants only to maintain nonexclusivity. In some situations, the distributor might be able to substitute a number of independent brands for the incumbent. But, in a bidding situation, these independent firms would face coordination problems in bidding against the dominant incumbent.

Fourth, even if exclusives are terminable at will or embedded in short-term contracts, they still erect a difficult coordination problem for an entrant. This increases the risk that the entrant will be unable to get enough distributors or enough customers to rapidly achieve minimum viable scale and maintain adequate investment incentives. Bidding still does not take place on a level playing field. It may be difficult for an entrant (or entrants collectively) to convince enough suppliers or consumers to switch at the same time. As a result, the exclusives also can lead retailers to expect entry to fail, raising the fees the entrant must offer.

This is not to say that competition for exclusives has no constraining effects at all. It can constrain the attempt to maintain a monopoly to some extent. This is because the need to purchase exclusives also is costly to the incumbent firm. This cost of buying exclusives can act as somewhat of a deterrent. However, the constraint is limited and does not eliminate competitive concerns. Nor would short duration exclusives legitimately provide the basis for an exemption from antitrust scrutiny. Even with short duration exclusives, the entrant(s) will face certain coordination problems. The more important question is whether the exclusives create real procompetitive efficiency benefits and whether those benefits will be passed on to consumers in a competitive output market. This is only likely when exclusives are divided up among several viable competing firms in the output market.

This last point raises the question of why a retailer or consumers ever would cooperate by agreeing to an exclusive that might allow a dominant firm to achieve market power. However, this result can occur because an individual distributor or consumer ignores the effect of its decision on others. As a result, the dominant firm can compensate the retailer or consumer for its own harm and still earn money from the incremental power gained with respect to others. In addition, if a retailer or consumer believes that the entrant likely will fail because others are granting exclusives, then it would not require significant compensation to grant exclusivity as well. Both these reasons flow from the same point: *competition is a public good.*

Thus, simply because entrants and smaller competitors have the theoretical potential to outbid a monopolist for distribution or shelf space should not be treated as sufficient defense in an antitrust case. The theoretical ability to compete for exclusives may not be a practical ability, and the competition may not take place on a level playing field or in a way that consumer welfare and efficiency will be protected. Similarly, exclusive dealing should not be per se legal.

V. Excluding Less Efficient Competitors: The Equally Efficient Entrant Standard

The analysis of exclusionary conduct and competition for exclusives is related to the question of whether antitrust should apply an equally efficient entrant ("EEE") standard, usually tied to conservative analysis, in antitrust exclusion cases other than predatory pricing. That is, are entrants and other competitors that are less efficient than the excluding firm deserving of the protection of the antitrust laws?

The use of an EEE standard often is motivated by a concern with administrability. That is, a rationale for the use of the *Brooke Group* below-cost pricing prong for predatory pricing is that this price level is the only one that is practically administrable by antitrust courts. This is a controversial issue and deserving of further analysis. But, for the purposes of this paper, the proper rules for predatory pricing are beyond the scope of the analysis. Instead, the analysis here will focus on the question of whether the EEE standard is appropriate for vertical RRC exclusion cases. In my view, it is not.[33]

The predatory pricing paradigm and its price-cost comparison motivates the EEE standard. It is argued that if the dominant firm is pricing above its costs, then an equally efficient competitor would not be forced to exit from the market. In this sense, the below-cost pricing standard for predatory pricing is said to protect equally efficient competitors from being excluded from the market. This prong of the antitrust standard in principle could be mechanically applied to all exclusionary conduct, including RRC conduct. For example, Judge Posner has suggested applying this standard to all exclusionary conduct, not just predatory pricing. Under the equally efficient competitor standard, the plaintiff would need to prove that the conduct "is likely in the circumstances to exclude from the defendant's market an equally or more efficient competitor."[34]

The equally efficient entrant standard is a very permissive standard with respect to exclusionary vertical conduct, even *naked* RRC behavior. For example, suppose that exclusionary conduct would only be condemned if it would cause the exit or deter the entry of an equally efficient firm. That is, the conduct would only be condemned if it leads the dominant firm to set a price below its costs—a price that could not be profitably matched by equally efficient competitors.

For example, under this standard, payments to input suppliers to induce them to refuse to deal with rivals would be allowed unless the payments were so large that the defendant's overall profits turned negative. This would be true even if the sole purpose of the payments were to raise the costs and marginalize competitors. As shown in the competition for exclusives numerical example, the winning bid for the monopolist would place the entrant at a loss if it wins, but it would not place the monopolist at a loss if it wins.[35]

Similarly, burning down a rival's factory would not violate the antitrust laws as long as the arsonist's fee was modest and the predator charged such a high output price that its price remained above its costs. Conduct that was used to *maintain* an existing monopoly would be treated more permissively than conduct used to *achieve* dominance because the defendant's initial price would be at the more highly profitable monopoly level.

The fundamental flaw in applying the EEE standard to RRC conduct is that the unencumbered (potential) entry of less efficient competitors often raises consumer welfare and efficiency. For example, consider the simplest example of limit pricing by a monopolist that has obtained its monopoly legitimately with superior skill, foresight, and industry. Suppose that this monopolist has variable costs of $20, and initially charges the unconstrained monopoly price of $50, because the monopolist faces no threat of entry.[36]

Now suppose that there is a new entry threat by a *less efficient firm,* for example, a firm with variable costs of $40. Facing this threat, the monopolist would have the incentive to reduce its price to the "limit price" of $39 in order to deter the entry into the monopolized market. This limit pricing conduct clearly benefits consumers. Even though the potential entrant does not produce any output itself, it serves as a *perceived potential entrant* and constrains the monopolist's price by waiting in the wings. Its potential for entry reduces price, increases market output, and raises both consumer welfare and total economic welfare.

Suppose instead that the monopolist engages in naked RRC conduct that raises the entrant's costs above the unconstrained monopoly price of $50. For example, suppose that it raises the entrant's costs by $12 to a cost of $52. As a result, the entrant would no longer have the ability to constrain the monopolist from charging the monopoly price of $50. Consumers would be harmed by this RRC conduct, and total economic welfare would fall too.

But, no antitrust liability would attach to this RRC conduct under the EEE standard. This is because a $12 cost increase would not deter an equally efficient potential entrant (i.e., an entrant with costs of $20). If the monopolist were to maintain its price at the $50 monopoly price, such an equally efficient entrant would still be able to enter successfully even if its costs increased from $20 to $32.

The fact that the EEE standard fails to catch and deter this obvious type of anticompetitive conduct demonstrates the fundamental flaw in the standard. The idea that a perceived potential entrant can constrain the pricing of a monopolist is a central idea in the analysis of entry barriers, potential competition and market power. If the EEE standard fails in this simple RRC example, then it obviously also would be deficient for other, more complex non-price exclusionary conduct.[37]

This analysis also means that using the EEE standard would underdeter anticompetitive conduct. A better antitrust standard would be one that found liability when the following two prongs both are satisfied: (1) when the defendant's conduct significantly raises the costs of competitors—even less efficient competitors—for example, when the competitors do not have access to cost-effective alternatives; and (2) when, as a result, the exclusionary conduct permits the defendant to achieve or maintain monopoly power.[38] Of course, if the conduct leads to consumer and efficiency benefits as well as these harms, then the net effect on consumers must also be evaluated. This type of analysis can be carried out in the context of a rule of reason analysis that does not include an EEE prong.

A policy of adopting a standard that finds liability for conduct that harms consumers by raising the costs of competitors, whether or not they are equally efficient, is not one that is at odds with the view of all Chicago School commentators. As discussed earlier, Robert Bork explicitly took the position that eliminating competitors' access to the most efficient distribution pattern could be viewed as anticompetitive. That section of the

Antitrust Paradox has been cited with approval in *Aspen Ski*.[39] And, a similar formulation was used in *Microsoft*.[40]

Conclusion

In light of this analysis, it is clear that the strong economic foundations—and economic implications—claimed by Chicago School commentators like Robert Bork do not hold up to careful economic analysis. The concepts of anticompetitive foreclosure and anticompetitive leverage are not empty and illogical. Competition for exclusives is not a panacea for all vertical exclusion claims. Nor is the predatory pricing paradigm the appropriate framework for analyzing and judging exclusionary vertical conduct. Instead, a more refined analysis must be applied. This analysis implies that the better legal standard would be the rule of reason with its focus on consumer harm, not a proxy rule like the equally efficient entrant standard.

Wrong Turns in Exclusive Dealing Law

Stephen Calkins

Exclusive dealing law has come a long way. Unfortunately, it has not always come the right way.

Robert Bork's influential *Antitrust Paradox,* published in 1978, had a simple prescription for exclusive dealing: it should be *per se* lawful: "[T]here is every reason to believe that exclusive dealing and requirements contracts have no purpose or effect other than the creation of efficiency."[41] Bork's argument was straightforward:

> A seller who wants exclusivity must give the buyer something for it. If he gives a lower price, the reason must be that the seller expects the arrangement to create efficiencies that justify the lower price. If he were to give the lower price simply to harm his rivals, he would be engaging in deliberate predation by price cutting, and that...would be foolish and self-defeating behavior on his part."[42] Bork was especially dismissive of what he considered short-term contracts (two years) entered into by numerous outlets, writing that "as barriers to entry these contacts had about the solidity of a sieve and the tensile strength of wet tissue paper."[43]

We now know that Bork was wrong.[44] Where there is only a single buyer (or perhaps only a couple), that buyer can look out for its long-run interests and prevent a seller from using contractual clauses to exclude competition on reasons other than efficiency. But where buyers are more plentiful, collective action problems[45] (perhaps abetted by the antitrust law's hostility to horizontal agreements[46]) prevent them from doing so. Post-Chicago economists have identified with sophistication a series of ways that exclusive dealing can harm competition.

Unfortunately, it took time for courts to understand the error. In the meantime, exclusive dealing came to be seen as an especially favored practice. Ironically, the fundamental issue of how to respond to uncertainty about likely effect was identified in the Supreme Court's original exclusive dealing cases. As is discussed below, the Court initially resolved doubts in favor of enforcement but then backed away from this approach. The lower courts reacted by going to the other extreme, making exclusive dealing almost automatically lawful as recommended by Bork. In *United States v. Microsoft Corp.*[47] and *United States v. Dentsply International, Inc.*,[48] two courts of appeal, responding to new understandings, have supplied a check on this tendency. This article tells this story and then offers suggestions for future application.

I. Setting the Stage: The Supreme Court

As is so often true, the basic issues have been with us since the beginning. In particular, they were illuminated with remarkable clarity in *Standard Oil Co. v. United States (Standard Stations).*[49] *Standard Stations,* which built upon the Court's early *Standard Fashion* decision,[50] is the source of the "quantitative substantiality" test for evaluating exclusive dealing—the test that soon came to be handled in the treatises as the test *not* followed.[51] Yet even though it set out the test less followed, *Standard Stations* highlighted issues that are at the heart of exclusive dealing debates to this day.

At issue in *Standard Stations* were the exclusive supply agreements long employed by the major petroleum firms and independent service stations carrying their products (sometimes just gasoline, sometimes more).[52] A majority of the contracts "were effective from year to year."[53] Standard Oil had exclusive supply contracts with "16% of the retail gasoline outlets" in the relevant geographic area. It accounted for 23 percent of the gasoline sold in that area—6.8 percent through company-owned stations and 6.7 percent through exclusive contracts with independent dealers.

As too often happens in antitrust, the wrong issue was litigated: the government, invoking the stringent language of Clayton Act, section 3, sought to condemn the agreements as per se illegal. (Section 3 makes it illegal to sell or lease products on the condition that the buyer or lessor shall not carry competing products "where the effect of such...condition...may be to substantially lessen competition or tend to create a monopoly in any line of commerce."[54]) The district court would not agree: "[t]o the contrary,... exclusiveness of outlet is not, in itself, illegal. It becomes illegal only if it result [sic] in a substantial lessening of competition...."[55] But while the court held that "the potential or actual effect of the agreements is important in determining unreasonableness of restraint under the Sherman

Act and substantiality of restraint or tendency to create monopoly under
the Clayton Act," it also held that the substantiality of the restraint or tendency to create a monopoly "is established by (a) the market foreclosed,—
here represented by the controlled units,—and (b) the volume of controlled
business, totalling here in value $68,000,000."[56]

Petitioners complained that the government had utterly failed to prove
its case. Justice Jackson, who dissented with Chief Justice Vinson and
Justice Burton, argued that the government had not established that "the
actual or the probable effect of the accused arrangement is to substantially
lessen competition."[57] Although he regretted "that the Clayton Act submits
such economic issues to judicial determination" (because "the judicial process is not well adapted to exploration of such...questions"[58]), he read the
Clayton Act as requiring such an attempt. The court below did not engage
in such an exercise, so Justice Jackson would have remanded the case—but,
failing that and absent hard evidence, he presumed that the challenged contracts were important to what we know today as interbrand competition.[59]

The majority was surprisingly appreciative of the procompetitive potential of the kind of requirements contracts at issue before the Court. Unlike
tying, wrote the Court,

> [r]equirements contracts...may well be of economic advantage to
> buyers as well as to sellers, and thus indirectly of advantage to the
> consuming public. In the case of the buyer, they may assure supply,
> afford protection against rises in price, enable long-term planning on
> the basis of known costs, and obviate the expense and risk of stor-
> age in the quantity necessary for a commodity having a fluctuating
> demand. From the seller's point of view, requirements contracts may
> make possible the substantial reduction of selling expenses, give pro-
> tection against price fluctuations, and—of particular advantage to
> a newcomer to the field to whom it is important to know what capi-
> tal expenditures are justified—offer the possibility of a predictable
> market. They may be useful, moreover, to a seller trying to establish a
> foothold against the counterattacks of entrenched competitors.[60]

Were one to require proof at trial of actual anticompetitive effects,
suggested the Court, one could look at "evidence that competition has
flourished despite use of the contracts," the reasonableness under the
circumstances of the length of the contracts, whether the defendant is "a
struggling newcomer or an established competitor," or "[p]erhaps most
important,...the defendant's degree of market control."[61]

Having illuminated that approach, the Court shied away from it.
"[S]erious difficulties would attend the attempt to apply these tests,"[62] it worried. At this early point in time it thus invoked the theme long associated
with Professor Areeda[63]—that antitrust standards must be administrable
by generalist judges and an imperfect court system.[64] So what if Standard
Oil could show that the contracts had not increased its influence over the
market? Perhaps that influence would have declined but for the contracts.

So what if the major oil firms' market shares had remained steady? Perhaps the exclusivity clauses had kept out new entry. Intriguingly, the Court noted that if exclusive contracts were outlawed, Standard Oil might just vertically integrate[65] or, perhaps, encourage independent stations to submit particularly large orders—but, rather than being a reason to allow the exclusive contracts, this just showed that "there can be no conclusive proof that the use of requirements contracts has actually reduced competition below the level which it would otherwise have reached or maintained."[66] The court continued:

> to demand that bare inference be supported by evidence as to what would have happened but for the adoption of the practice...or to require firm prediction of an increase of competition as a probable result of ordering the abandonment of the practice, would be a standard of proof, if not virtually impossible to meet, at least most ill-suited for ascertainment by courts.[67]

In the end, the Court found refuge in what it perceived to be the will of Congress in making Clayton Act, section 3 stricter than Sherman Act, section 1, finding that "Congress has authoritatively determined that those practices are detrimental where their effect may be to lessen competition."[68] Congress declared that "requirements contracts are to be prohibited wherever their effect 'may be' to substantially lessen competition."[69] (Note the emphasis on "may," in contrast to Justice Jackson's "probable.") The majority wrote that "[t]o interpret that section as requiring proof that competition has actually diminished would make its very explicitness a means of conferring immunity upon the practices which it singles out."[70] Given a very hard choice between what it saw as a rule of per se legality and a rule that condemned exclusive contracts based on "quantitative substantiality,"[71] the Court concluded that the language of section 3 required the latter.

Having reached that conclusion in *Standard Stations,* the Court backed away from it in *Tampa Electric Co. v. Nashville Coal Co.*[72] After reciting the *Standard Stations* test, the Court just continued on, apparently without worrying about any inconsistency:

> To determine substantiality in a given case, it is necessary to weigh the probable effect of the contract on the relevant area of effective competition, taking into account the relative strength of the parties, the proportionate volume of commerce involved in relation to the total volume of commerce in the relevant market area, and the probable immediate and future effects which pre-emption of that share of the market might have on effective competition therein.[73]

The Court's application of this test—later to be known as the "qualitative substantiality" test[74]—was made easier by the plaintiff's failure to prove any significant foreclosure once errors in market definition were corrected. The Court deemphasized section 3's "may" language, writing that a contract is unlawful only if it has a "tendency to work a substantial—not remote—lessening of competition in the relevant competitive market."[75] Beyond that, the Court quoted *Standard Stations*'s recognition that require-ments contracts can be beneficial, and then distinguished factual situations that had proven troubling—where the seller has a "dominant position," or where these contracts are "an industry-wide practice." The twenty-year length of the contract was found appropriate in the context of electric utilities.

No mention was made of the *Standard Stations* suggestion that requiring proof of actual competitive effect would be unworkable and result effec-tively in per se legality.

The most recent exclusive dealing opinion by the Supreme Court is the remarkably influential four-Justice concurrence in *Jefferson Parish Hospital District No. 2 v. Hyde*.[76] Justice O'Connor explained how courts are to address exclusive dealing:

> In determining whether an exclusive-dealing contract is unreason-able, the proper focus is on the structure of the market for the prod-ucts or services in question—the number of sellers and buyers in the market, the volume of their business, and the ease with which buyers and sellers can redirect their purchases or sales to others. Exclusive dealing is an unreasonable restraint on trade only when a significant fraction of buyers or sellers are frozen out of a market by the exclu-sive deal. *Standard Oil Co. of California v. United States,* 337 U.S. 293 (1949). When the sellers of services are numerous and mobile, and the number of buyers is large, exclusive-dealing arrangements of narrow scope pose no threat of adverse economic consequences. To the con-trary, they may be substantially procompetitive by ensuring stable markets and encouraging long-term, mutually advantageous business relationships.[77]

Justice O'Connor wrote that without any detailed analysis one could "readily conclude" that the arrangement would not lessen competition:

> At issue here is an exclusive-dealing arrangement between a firm of four anesthesiologists and one relatively small hospital....A firm of four anesthesiologists represents only a very small fraction of the total number of anesthesiologists whose services are available for hire by other hospitals, and East Jefferson [that small hospital] is one among numerous hospitals buying such services."[78]

Since that small hospital had a 30 percent market share,[79] however, some courts have looked to that share as the new threshold for possible illegality.[80]

II. Developments in the Lower Courts

The ABA Antitrust Section has supplied a convenient way to track changes in antitrust doctrine by publishing a treatise, *Antitrust Law Developments,* in 1975, and then updating it in 1984, 1992, 1997, 2002, and 2007.[81] A survey of a few of these volumes provides a handy template measuring the evolution of antitrust law.

Even in 1975, exclusive dealing—which was accorded only three pages of attention—was recognized as offering both procompetitive and anticompetitive effects:

> Exclusive dealing arrangements have traditionally been treated somewhat more leniently than tying arrangements because of the recognition that exclusive dealing arrangements, unlike tying arrangements, may have procompetitive effects and may be motivated by other than anticompetitive desires on the part of the seller."[82]

Thus, courts and the FTC "have made at least some analysis of the competitive effects of the exclusive dealing arrangement."[83] The paired cases, *Standard Stations* and *Tampa Electric,* were described as in tension as to the weight to be accorded the simple foreclosure of a share of the market (6.7 percent in *Standard Stations*). The lower courts were said to apply *Tampa Electric* and allowed significant foreclosure to be justified "if the peculiar circumstances of a market suggest no probability of a lessening of competition."[84] The FTC, with the blessing of the courts, had taken to applying *Standard Stations* under FTC Act, section 5,[85] finding violations based solely upon " 'proof that the user of the exclusive dealing contract controls a "substantial" share of the market.' "[86]

Nine years later, the book had expanded its treatment by a page and added to the list of private cases that had followed *Tampa Electric.*[87] In addition, it reviewed the FTC's lengthy adoption and application of the rule of reason approach in *Beltone Electronics Corp.,*[88] and it highlighted one factor that courts had considered in evaluating exclusive dealing arrangements—the length of the contracts: "[E]xclusive dealing contracts for one year or less have generally been upheld while others having a longer duration sometimes have been found invalid for a variety of reasons, including their length."[89]

By 1997, treatment had expanded to almost 11 pages. Length of contract was the first factor discussed after degree of foreclosure: "Agreements with short terms and providing short notice for termination will usually be upheld. Longer periods of exclusivity may be upheld under the rule of reason where industry circumstances render longer terms desirable."[90]

> Other factors relevant to a rule of reason analysis include the level in the distribution chain (wholesaler or retailer) upon which the restraint is imposed, the presence of alternative distribution channels enabling competition to reach the market, ease of entry, whether consumers are likely to engage in extensive shopping before purchasing the product, the extent to which competitors also employ exclusive dealing arrangements, the relationship between the parties to the exclusive dealing arrangement, the extent to which competition is

actually injured, and the justification for and procompetitive effects of the arrangement.[91]

The commonality among the cited cases was that defendants almost always won, particularly in the then-more recent cases. The problem can be illuminated by consideration of some specific factors: length of contract, completeness of exclusion, and share of market.

A. Length of Contract

Recall the 1984 *Antitrust Law Development*'s declaration that contracts of a year or less "have generally been upheld." That language was almost instantly picked up by Judge Posner in *Roland Machinery Co. v. Dresser Industries, Inc.,*[92] which declared that "[e]xclusive-dealing contracts terminable in less than a year are presumptively lawful under section 3."[93] *Roland Machinery,* in turn, was followed by several different courts.[94] For instance, relying in part on *Roland Machinery,* the Ninth Circuit in *Omega Environmental v. Gilbarco, Inc.*[95] pointed to the relatively short duration of contracts as support for its decision to overturn a plaintiff jury verdict: "Because *all* of Gilbarco's distributors are available within one year, and *most* (90 percent according to the plaintiffs) are available on 60 days notice, a competing manufacturer need only offer a better product or a better deal to acquire their services."[96] As Judge Boudin wrote for the court in *U.S. Healthcare, Inc. v. Healthsource, Inc.,*[97] "an exclusivity clause terminable on 30 days' notice would be close to a *de minimis* constraint (*Tampa* involved a 20-year contract, and one year is sometimes taken as the trigger for close scrutiny)."[98] Indeed, the leading antitrust treatise suggests "presumptively that periods of less than one year be approved."[99]

B. Total Exclusion?

Several courts have pointed to the existence of alternative routes to market to justify the walling off of one. Thus, in *Omega Environmental,* the court rejected a jury's condemnation of exclusive dealing with 500 distributors where (according to the court), "[c]ompetitors are free to sell directly, to develop alternative distributors, or to compete for the services of the existing distributors."[100] The leading treatise has declared that "[e]ven a high foreclosure percentage creates no injury to competition if no one is being excluded in fact by the challenged arrangement."[101] Similar language was used by the *Jefferson Parish* concurrence, which would require proof that a firm was "frozen out of a market."[102] In finding no section 1 exclusive dealing violation, the district court in *Microsoft* held "that liability under §1 must hinge upon whether Netscape was actually shut out of the Web browser market, or at least whether it was forced to reduce output below a subsistence level."[103] Similarly, the district court in *Dentsply* held that "because direct distribution is viable, non-Dentsply dealers are available, and Dentsply dealers may be converted at any time, the DOJ has failed to prove that Dentsply's actions have been or could be successful in preventing 'new or potential competitors from gaining a foothold in the market....' "[104]

C. Share of Market

Although some courts were once worried by foreclosure over 20 percent,[105] the *Jefferson Parish* concurrence's rather casual describing of a hospital with a 30 percent market share as "small"[106] and its inclusion in an exclusive arrangement untroubling quickly shifted the goal posts. Courts now demand proof of higher shares.[107]

Comment

Developments in exclusive dealing law bore considerable resemblance to what happened in the law of nonprice distributional restraints. Bork and others created a general sense that the practices were benign if not beneficial; the law catalogued a series of routes for defendants to exit litigation happily but no manageable way for a plaintiff to win; and all of this was described by the comforting invocation of the "rule of reason." Now that we know that exclusive dealing *can* harm competition, it is no longer enough to invoke the "rule of reason" (or the "Full Monty," as I have referred to it[108]) and compile lists of ways that defendants can win. One has to identify ways for deserving plaintiffs to win.

The important opinions in *United States v. Microsoft Corp.*[109] and *United States v. Dentsply International, Inc.*[110] offer reason for optimism.

III. *Microsoft* and *Dentsply*

It is hard to overstate the importance to exclusive dealing law of the appellate opinions in *Microsoft* and *Dentsply*. Several points are worth noting.

First, from *Microsoft*:

Section 2 vs. section 1. In *Microsoft,* the district court applied a "total exclusion" test and found the government's proof of a section 1 violation wanting[111]—but went on to find a violation of section 2. On appeal, Microsoft argued that the standards for liability under section 1 and section 2 are the same, so it must follow that there is no section 2 liability. The court of appeals disagreed. A monopolist's use of exclusive contracts can give rise to liability where a nonmonopolist's would not.[112]

Total exclusion? Since the Government did not appeal its section 1 defeat, the district court's "total exclusion" test discussed above was not before the appellate court. Nonetheless, the court signaled its disapproval: "The District Court appears to have based its holding with respect to §1 upon a 'total exclusion test' rather than the 40% standard drawn from the case law. Even assuming the holding is correct, however, we nonetheless reject Microsoft's contention."[113] The message to astute readers, of course, is that we should *not* assume that a total exclusion test is appropriate. In *Microsoft,* for instance, it should have been sufficient that "Microsoft had substantially excluded Netscape from 'the most efficient channels for Navigator to achieve browser usage share,' and had relegated it to more costly and less effective methods (such as mass mailing its browser on a disk or offering it for download over the internet)."[114]

Shifting of the burden. The court held that the Government had "establishe[d] a *prima facie* case...by demonstrating anticompetitive effect"[115] such that a burden shifted, and Microsoft was required to justify its exclusive contracts. That government demonstration, however, did not include proof of increased prices or reduced output, such as one might think was necessary to prove anticompetitive effect. Instead, the court found the effect directly in the existence of exclusive contracts with "fourteen of the top fifteen access providers in North America, [which] account for a large majority of all Internet access subscriptions in this part of the world."[116]

Subjective evidence. As part of its examination of competitive effect, the court of appeals considered subjective evidence. In particular, it quoted from Finding of Fact 143, which starts: "Decision-makers at Microsoft worried that simply developing its own attractive browser product, pricing it at zero, and promoting it vigorously would not divert enough browser usage from Navigator to neutralize it as a platform."[117]

Justification. The court of appeals made clear that a defendant's desire to succeed is no justification for otherwise problematic exclusive dealing: "Microsoft's only explanation for its exclusive dealing is that it wants to keep developers focused upon its APIs–which is to say, it wants to preserve its power in the operating system market. That is not an unlawful end, but neither is it a procompetitive justification...."[118]

Points of note from *Dentsply*:

Short-duration not complete defense. Dentsply featured the shortest of exclusive contracts as a legal matter: the product was sold in individual transactions "and essentially the arrangement is 'at-will.'"[119] But Dentsply had long had 75–80 percent of the market and its exclusivity clause forced distributors to surrender all of that business if they wanted to add a rival brand. The court looked not to the legalities but instead to the practical realities: "the economic elements involved—the large share of the market held by Dentsply and its conduct excluding competing manufacturers—realistically make the arrangements here as effective as those in written contracts."[120] And, "in spite of the legal ease with which the relationship can be terminated, the dealers have a strong economic incentive to continue carrying Dentsply's teeth. Dealer Criterion 6 [the exclusivity clause] is not edentulous."[121]

Total exclusion? As noted above, the *Dentsply* district court had ruled against the government because it found that there were "viable" alternative means of distribution. This was an error: "The mere existence of other avenues of distribution is insufficient without an assessment of their overall significance to the market."[122]

Subjective evidence. The *Dentsply* court, too, peeked at subjective evidence. It quoted a Dentsply executive on Dentsply's deliberately adding an (exclusive) dealer in order to hamper a competitor.[123] And it quoted another former manager on Dentsply's game plan: "'You...don't want to give the distributors an opportunity to sell a competitive product. And you don't want to give your end user, the customer...a choice. He has to buy Dentsply teeth. That's the only thing that's available.... That's your objective.'"[124]

IV. Going Forward

The above review suggests to this observer several points to be considered as exclusive dealing law evolves away from the place to which Robert Bork, and his Chicago School colleagues, tried to relegate it.

1. *Remember that short-term or cancelable contracts can be anticompetitive.* This is an important lesson from *Dentsply.* Most of the declarations about presuming legality of short-term contracts had been phrased as presumptions, of course. The problem is that in the rule of reason environment, something said to be a presumption that a defendant should win is often invoked to grant summary judgment or judgment as a matter of law. It is easy to remember the presumption and forget the exceptions.[125] Happily, *Antitrust Law Developments,* which contributed to the problem in its second edition, does a better job of recognizing the limits of any such presumption in its sixth.[126]

2. *Do not require total exclusion.* This is a lesson from both *Microsoft* and *Dentsply,* although at least one court has misread the appellate opinions on this point.[127]

3. *A monopolist can be held to a higher standard.* This is another lesson from *Microsoft* and *Dentsply.* The converse is trickier. *Standard Stations* honored the words and intent of Clayton Act, section 3. Subsequent cases largely blended Sherman Act, section 1 and Clayton Act, section 3 analysis. By abandoning its section 1 cause of action in *Microsoft* and *Dentsply,* the Government has suggested that exclusive dealing never should be illegal when engaged in by a nonmonopolist.[128] Whether this is troubling turns, in significant part, on how difficult it is to prove monopoly power. It would be unfortunate, for instance, to limit exclusive dealing law to firms with 80 percent of a well-defined market with high entry barriers. (There is a separate question whether a system of laws should simply abandon rather clear statutory language in favor of an outcome perceived to be superior.)

4. *Do consider peeking at subjective intent evidence.* There was no need to consider subjective intent under *Standard Stations* because the Court employed a simple rule under which plaintiffs could prevail. If meritorious

cases can be identified, practically, without resort to intent evidence, fine. But if finding liability calls for a more searching inquiry, there may well be times when good evidence of what important business officials were thinking can shed light on otherwise confusing actions.[129] Even as sophisticated a court as *Microsoft* still considered what was motivating the defendant.

5. *Occasionally scrutinize justifications.* The classic justification for exclusive dealing is that provided in *Beltone Electronics,* where the FTC upheld exclusive dealing by a firm with a declining 16 percent share of the vigorously competitive market for hearing aids.[130] A critical part of Beltone's business model was national and cooperative advertising designed to persuade potential customers to visit dealers and be tested for hearing loss (and, where appropriate, counseled to try a hearing aid in spite of the social stigma associated therewith). If dealers were free to switch those Beltone-induced potential customers to other brands, there was substantial risk—supported by theory and empirical evidence—that the efficacy of lead-generating advertising would be destroyed. In contrast, in *Dentsply* the defendant's argument that exclusive dealing was needed to prevent "free-riding" was unpersuasive.[131] In part this was because grandfathered nonexclusive outlets acted inconsistently with the theory (by not switching customers away from Dentsply) and because some of Dentsply's promotions were purely brand-specific and thus unlikely to be affected by the presence or absence of exclusive dealing. There may be times when it is easy to reach a conclusion that clearly identifies procompetitive or anticompetitive "justifications."

6. *Do not require proof that prices have risen.* Some courts have suggested that competitive harm will result in prices increasing, so (they reason) if prices do not increase competition has not been harmed. The problem with this, recognized long ago in *Standard Stations,* is that it is terribly hard to compare reality to a hypothetical alternative. A dominant firm may be much more interested in buying a few more years of dominance than in increasing its prices.

7. *The general legal standard matters.* Were U.S. antitrust to adopt a single test for monopolization (such as "no economic sense" or "equally efficient competitor"[132]), and apply that to all exclusive dealing, there could be unfortunate consequences for exclusive dealing law.[133] Happily we do not appear to be heading in that direction.[134]

8. *Assigning burdens of proof.* Joe Farrell has argued vigorously that with exclusive dealing, whichever side has the burden of proof will lose. It is simply too difficult to measure—really to prove actual anticompetitive effect, or really to prove procompetitive justifications.[135] If this is true—and it may well be—it serves as a reminder of the importance of getting the presumptions right. It is not a new point. To the contrary, *Standard Stations* was quite forceful on the impossibility of litigating competitive effect and on the risk that requiring detailed proof was equivalent to adopting per se legality. The *Standard Stations* solution soon fell out of favor. Under the

influence of Bork's teaching about exclusive dealing, we wandered to the edge of per se legality. Now we are coming back to the center, still needing to get this right.

9. *Empirical research.* There is a lot of speculating about the effects of exclusive dealing but not nearly enough empirical research. If we are not to adopt absolute rules of near-automatic legality or illegality, we need all the help we can get about how the world really works.

Notes

1. Robert H. Bork, The Antitrust Paradox: A Policy at War with Itself, 278 (1978).

2. *Brooke Group Ltd* v. *Brown & Williamson Tobacco Corp.*, 509 US 209 (1993).

3. *Id.*

4. *Id.* The theory of predatory pricing underpinning the *Brooke Group* standard and the standard itself have been criticized by post-Chicago economists who have formulated additional—and sometimes more complex—theories of predatory pricing that have market impacts closer to RRC conduct. *See, e.g.,* Jonathan B. Baker, *Predatory Pricing After Brooke Group: An Economic Perspective,* 62 Antitrust L.J. 585, 590 (1994); Patrick Bolton et al., *Predatory Pricing: Strategic Theory and Legal Policy,* 88 Geo. L.J. 2239, 2241 (2000); Aaron Edlin, *Stopping Above-Cost Predatory Pricing,* 111 Yale L.J. 941 (2002). However, this article will focus on the conventional predatory pricing theory and how that paradigm differs from the RRC paradigm.

5. *Brooke Group,* 509 U.S. at 222–24.

6. Steven Salop & David Scheffman, *Raising Rivals' Costs,* 73 Am. Econ. Rev. 267 (May 1983); Thomas G. Krattenmaker & Steven C. Salop, *Anticompetitive Exclusion: Raising Rivals' Costs to Achieve Power over Price,* 96 Yale L.J. 209 (1986) (hereinafter, Krattenmaker-Salop, *Anticompetitive Exclusion*). The term "RRC" is preferable to the term "non-price predation" for several reasons. First, the conduct often does involve prices, in particular, input prices. Second, the term "predation" has become associated with causing victims to exit from the market, and RRC strategies often involve merely disadvantaging competitors without causing them to exit from the market. Third, courts might mechanically interpret the word "predation" as legally implying the appropriateness of the current legal tests for predatory pricing. *See Covad Communications v Bell Atlantic,* 398 F.3d 666, 676 (D.C. Cir. 2005) (applying a sacrifice standard in an RRC context).

7. *Id.* Output reductions may occur in the short run and the long run, and could involve output reductions flowing from reduced innovation.

8. Pushing up the market price of an input by increased purchasing would raise the costs of an unintegrated rival by more than it would raise the price to the integrated firm that carries out the overbuying. For example, suppose the dominant firm is more integrated or has a technology that uses relatively less of the input. Oliver E. Williamson, *Wage Rates as a Barrier to Entry: The Pennington Case in Perspective,* 82 Q.J. Econ. 85 (1968); *see also*

Steven C. Salop, *Anticompetitive Overbuying by Power Buyers,* 72 ANTITRUST L.J. 669 (2005); Susan A. Creighton et al., *Cheap Exclusion,* 72 ANTITRUST L.J. 975 (2005).

9. The immediate consumer benefit from the low "predatory" prices may or may not be trumped by higher prices during a subsequent recoupment period. Concern with this tradeoff is endemic to all discussions of predatory pricing. Kenneth G. Elzinga & David E. Mills, *Testing for Predation: Is Recoupment Feasible?,* 34 ANTITRUST BULL. 869 (1989).

10. Not all RRC conduct is naked, of course. Some exclusionary conduct leads to cost-savings, product improvements, or elimination of free riding. The existence of such benefits to the excluding firm does not necessarily mean that consumers gain an overall ("net") benefit from the conduct.

11. For a debate on these issues, see the recent symposium in the Antitrust Law Journal. Steven C. Salop, *Exclusionary Conduct, Effect on Consumers, and Flawed Profit-Sacrifice Standard,* 73 ANTITRUST L.J. 311(2006) (hereinafter, Salop, *Flawed Profit-Sacrifice Standard;* A. Douglas Melamed, *Exclusive Dealing Agreements and Other Exclusionary Conduct—Are There Unifying Principles?,* 73 ANTITRUST L.J. 375 (2006); Gregory J. Werden, *Identifying Exclusionary Conduct Under Section 2: The "No Economic Sense" Test,* 73 ANTITRUST L.J. 413 (2006); Mark S. Popofsky, *Defining Exclusionary Conduct: Section 2, the Rule of Reason, and the Unifying Principle Underlying Antitrust Rules,* 73 ANTITRUST L.J. 435 (2006)

12. Aaron Director & Edward H. Levi, *Law and the Future: Trade Regulation,* 51 Nw. U. L. REV. 281 (1956); *Standard Fashion Co. v. Magrane-Houston Co.,* 258 U.S. 346 (1922).

13. Deadweight loss is the efficiency loss from the exercise of monopoly power, as opposed to the wealth transfer from consumers to the monopolist's shareholders. For example, *see* Andrew Gavil et al., ANTITRUST LAW IN PERSPECTIVE: CASES, CONCEPTS AND PROBLEMS IN COMPETITION POLICY 27 (2002). The rent-seeking argument was first analyzed by Gordon Tullock, *The Welfare Costs of Tariffs, Monopolies and Theft,* 5 W. ECON J. 224 (1967); *see also* Richard Posner, *The Social Cost of Monopoly and Regulation,* 83 J. POL. ECON. 807 (1975).

14. *See* Robert Bork, THE ANTITRUST PARADOX 156 (1978).

15. This same leverage theory and the single-monopoly-profit critique also can be applied to other vertical restraints such as tying and exclusive dealing that are said to lead to de facto vertical integration "by contract."

16. *See, e.g.,* Ward Bowman, *Tying Arrangements and the Leverage Problem,* 67 YALE L.J. 19 (1957).

17. Bork, *supra* note 14 at 229.

18. This analysis is easy to illustrate with a numerical example. Suppose that the upstream monopolist is selling an input to buyers who then compete in a perfectly competitive downstream (output) market. Suppose that the downstream firms have constant marginal costs equal to $10, plus the cost of the input that they buy from the monopolist. Suppose that the monopolist's input is used in "fixed proportions" with other inputs; that is, suppose that every unit of output produced by the downstream sellers requires a constant number (say, one) of units of the input sold by the monopolist (e.g., every automobile requires one battery, and four tires).

Suppose that the monopolist's own marginal cost equals $40. And suppose that in light of these costs the downstream monopoly price equals $100. If the monopolist were to vertically integrate into the downstream product and refuse to deal with any of the other firms, what price would it charge for its output? In this case, it would capture the entire market. If it did, it obviously would sell the product at the monopoly price of $100. If it did, this vertically integrated monopolist would earn profits of $50 per unit (i.e., $100 - 40 - 10). This is the monopoly profit level, of course.

It is straightforward to demonstrate the single-monopoly-profit point. Suppose the input monopolist is not vertically integrated. Suppose instead that it is just content with its upstream monopoly. What price should it charge for the input? The answer is that it should charge a price of $90. This is straightforward to explain. Suppose that the monopolist priced the input at $40, in that case the downstream firms' marginal costs would equal $50 (i.e., $40 + $10). Because the downstream firms are perfectly competitive, the competitive downstream price will equal their aggregate marginal cost. (At any higher price, the firms would compete until the price was driven down; at any lower price, the firms would lose money and exit from the market.) Thus, if the monopolist charges $40 for the input, the downstream equilibrium price will be $50.

Of course, the upstream monopolist would be foolish to set an input price equal to its marginal cost of $40. To do so would eliminate its profits. Instead, suppose it charged an input price equal to $90. If so, the downstream firms' marginal costs would rise to $100 (i.e., $90 + $10.) As a result, they would be led to charge a price equal to $100. This price is, of course, the monopoly price. Although the downstream firms are competitive, they charge the monopoly output price because the input monopolist drove up their costs artificially. This $90 is the profit-maximizing price for the upstream monopolist. Why? It will earn profits of $50 per unit (i.e., $90 - $40), exactly the same monopoly profit rate as if it were vertically integrated. And the downstream price of $100 is the same as it would have been if the monopolist were vertically integrated.

This same argument can be applied to tying. Suppose that a firm has a durable monopoly in the tying product A but there is the potential for competition in the tied product B. Suppose that the monopoly price for the bundle of the tying and tied product is $100. Suppose that the tying monopolist's constant per unit costs of making product A equals $10 and its constant per unit costs of making product B equals $50. Suppose that competitors' costs of making B also are $40. In this situation, the tying monopolist would earn the same profits by selling product A on an unbundled basis at a price of $90 as it would by selling the two products on a bundled basis at a price of $100. In short, the upstream monopolist gains nothing by vertically integrating or tying. It can achieve the same level of monopoly profits simply by maximizing its profits as an input monopolist.

19. Tying and vertical integration also can be used to facilitate price discrimination. Economic analysis suggests that price discrimination may be either procompetitive, anticompetitive or competitively neutral. This conclusion depends on the way in which the price discrimination affects the market as well as the economic welfare standard underlying

the antitrust standard. This is a complex issue that goes beyond the scope of this survey.

20. Michael D. Whinston, *Tying, Foreclosure and Exclusion*, 80 AM. ECON. REV. 837 (1990); Dennis W. Carlton & Michael Waldman, *The Strategic Use of Tying to Preserve and Create Market Power in Evolving Industries*, 32 RAND J. 194 (2002); Frank Mathewson & Ralph Winter, *The Economics of Tying in the Microsoft Case*, (Appendix A of AOLTW Submission to the DOJ on the Microsoft PFJ (January 28, 2002).

21. Or, if that market were somewhat larger, perhaps it would be an oligopoly in which the firms could tacitly coordinate.

22. *See* U.S. Department of Justice, *Vertical Restraints Guidelines* (1985) (hereinafter *VRGs*).

23. Applying the numerical example above, suppose the regulated price of the tying product is equal to $40, the monopolist's costs. The monopolist could evade this regulation by setting the price of its tied product at $60 and requiring consumers to purchase the two products together.

24. *VRGs, supra* note 22.

25. *NYNEX Corp. v. Discon, Inc.*, 525 U.S. 128 (1998); *Verizon Communs. Inc. v. Law Offices of Curtis V. Trinko, LLP*, 540 U.S. 398.

26. Bork, *supra* note 14 at 232.

27. *See, e.g.*, Krattenmaker-Salop, *Anticompetitive Exclusion, supra* note 6; Eric Rasmussen et al., *Naked Exclusion*, 81 AM. ECON. REV. 1137 (1991); Michael H. Riordan & Steven C. Salop, *Evaluating Vertical Mergers: A Post-Chicago Approach*, 63 ANTITRUST L.J. 513 (1995).

28. *JTC Petroleum Co. v. Piasa Motor Fuels, Inc.*, 190 F.3d 775 (7th Cir. 1999) (Posner, C. J.). *See also* Elizabeth Granitz & Benjamin Klein, *Monopolization by 'Raising Rivals' Costs': The Standard Oil Case*, 39 J. LAW & ECON. 1 (1996).

29. This type of foreclosure analysis would be analogous to the analysis of tying above, where the tying creates a monopoly over consumers who purchase only the tied product.

30. *See, e.g.*, *Omega Envtl. Inc. v. Gilbarco Inc.*, 123 F.3d 1157 (9th Cir. 1997); *Paddock Publications, Inc. v. Chicago Tribune Co.*, 103 F.3d 42 (7th Cir. 1996); *U.S. Healthcare Inc. v. Healthsource, Inc.*, 986 F.2d 589 (1st Cir. 1993). In contrast, in their classical article, the founders of the Chicago School recognized the potential anticompetitive nature of exclusive dealing in their analysis of the *Standard Fashions* case. Aaron Director & Edward H. Levi, *Law and the Future: Trade Regulation*, 51 NW. U. L. REV. 281 (1956); *Standard Fashion Co. v. Magrane-Houston Co.*, 258 U.S. 346 (1922).

31. These are referred to as "exclusionary rights" by Krattenmaker-Salop, *Anticompetitive Exclusion, supra* note 6.

32. By "staggered" expiration dates, I mean that the contracts do not all expire at the same time. This increases the coordination problem and entry costs facing the new entrant. If all the contracts expire at the same time, the entrant might be able to coordinate its entry with the start-up dates of its own contracts. Of course, getting enough users to switch at the same time is itself a difficult coordination problem. Thus, staggering is not necessary for there to be a competitive problem.

33. For further details, *see* Salop, *Flawed Profit-Sacrifice Standard, supra* note 11.

34. Richard A. Posner, Antitrust Law: An Economic Perspective 194–95 (2d ed. 2001). Posner would also require the plaintiff to prove that the defendant has monopoly power. The defendant could rebut by showing that the conduct is efficient. For other commentaries on this standard, *see* Ken Heyer, *A World of Uncertainty: Economics and the Globalization of Antitrust,* 72 Antitrust L.J. 375, 419 n. 64 (2005) (quoting Joseph Farrell, "Comments at Antitrust Division Conference on the Developments in the Law and Economics of Exclusionary Pricing Practices" (Mar. 18, 2004)); Andrew I. Gavil, *Dominant Firm Distribution: Striking a Better Balance,* 72 Antitrust L.J. 3 (2004); John Vickers, *Abuse of Market Power,* 115 Econ. J. F244 (2005).

35. That is, the firms' costs are both $70. If the entrant wins the bid, its profits would be $70 less its winning bid. If the monopolist wins the bid, its profits would be $200 less its winning bid. Thus, if the monopolist wins the bidding at $71, its profits would be $129.

36. Assume for simplicity of the example that the firm has no sunk capital or fixed costs, and its variable costs are constant for all output levels.

37. Salop, *Flawed Profit-Sacrifice Standard, supra* note 11. For example, in discussing this standard in the context of a fraudulent patent claim, Hovenkamp states that it would be "unreasonably lenient and even perverse. It exonerates the defendant in precisely those circumstances when the conduct is most likely to be unreasonably exclusionary." Herbert Hovenkamp, *Exclusion and the Sherman Act,* 72 U. Chi. L. Rev. 147, 154 (2005).

38. In the context of section 1 allegations that the exclusionary conduct involved vertical or horizontal contracts or combinations, market power would be the relevant standard.

39. *Aspen Skiing Co. v. Aspen Highlands Skiing Corp.,* 472 U.S. 585, n. 31 (1985) ("[b]y disturbing optimal distribution patterns one rival can impose costs upon another").

40. *United States. v. Microsoft Corp.,* 253 F. 3d 34,64 (D.C. Cir. 2001) (barred rivals from "cost-efficient" means of distribution).

41. Robert H. Bork, The Antitrust Paradox 309 (1978).

42. *Id.* at 309.

43. *Id.* at 306 (discussing *Standard Fashions*).

44. *See, e.g.,* Joseph Farrell, *Deconstructing Chicago on Exclusive Dealing,* 50 Antitrust Bull. 465 (2005) (citing the literature); Jonathan M. Jacobson & Scott A. Sher, *"No Economic Sense" Makes No Sense for Exclusive Dealing,* 73 Antitrust L.J. 779 (2006); Louis Kaplow & Carl Shapiro, *Antitrust,* Harvard John M. Olin Discussion Paper No. 575 (Jan. 2007) (same); Ilya R. Segal & Michael D. Whinston, *Naked Exclusion: Comment,* 90 Am. Econ. Rev. 296 (2000).

45. *See* Mancur Olson, The Logic of Collective Action (1965).

46. *See* Warren S. Grimes, *The Sherman Act's Unintended Bias Against Lilliputians: Small Players' Collective Action as a Counter to Relational Market Power,* 69 Antitrust L.J. 195 (2001).

47. 253 F.3d 34 (D.C. Cir. 2001).

48. 399 F.3d 181 (3d Cir. 2005).

49. 337 U.S. 293 (1944) (Frankfurter, J.).

50. *Standard Fashion Co. v. Magrane-Houston Co.,* 258 U.S. 346 (1922) (Day, J., for a unanimous Court). In *Standard Fashion* the Court struck down an exclusive contract between the leading sewing patterns company, which had exclusive contracts with 40 percent of retail outlets, and a single Boston store. Without much analysis the Court affirmed the lower court's decision, but, in the process, indicated that Clayton Act Section 3, 15 U.S.C. § 14, should be read with caution:

> Section 3 condemns sales or agreements where the effect of such sale or contract of sale "may" be to substantially lessen competition or tend to create monopoly. It thus deals with consequences to follow the making of the restrictive covenant limiting the right of the purchaser to deal in the goods of the seller only. But we do not think that the purpose in using the word "may" was to prohibit the mere possibility of the consequences described. It was intended to prevent such agreements as would under the circumstances disclosed probably lessen competition, or create an actual tendency to monopoly. That it was not intended to reach every remote lessening of competition is shown in the requirement that such lessening must be substantial.

51. *See, e.g.,* ANTITRUST LAW DEVELOPMENTS 44–45 (1975) (hereinafter "ANTITRUST LAW DEVELOPMENTS (1975)") ("The Supreme Court's approach in *Tampa Electric* has subsequently been applied by the lower courts in a number of cases...").

52. Only 1.6 percent of service stations were what was known as "'split-pump' stations," selling gasoline from more than one supplier (337 U.S. at 295).

53. 337 U.S. at 296. (These contracts were "terminable 'at the end of the first 6 months of any contract year, or at the end of any such year, by giving to the other at least 30 days prior thereto written notice...'").

54. 15 U.S.C. § 14:

> It shall be unlawful for any person engaged in commerce, in the course of such commerce, to lease or make a sale or contract for sale of goods, wares, merchandise, machinery, supplies or other commodities, whether patented or unpatented, for use, consumption or resale within the United States or any Territory thereof or the District of Columbia or any insular possession or other place under the jurisdiction of the United States, or fix a price charged therefor, or discount from, or rebate upon, such price, on the condition, agreement or understanding that the lessee or purchaser thereof shall not use or deal in the goods, wares, merchandise, machinery, supplies or other commodities of a competitor or competitors of the lessor or seller, where the effect of such lease, sale, or contract for sale or such condition, agreement or understanding may be to substantially lessen competition or tend to create a monopoly in any line of commerce.

55. 78 F. Supp. at 863; *see also id.* at 859 ("...when we consider any other restrictions [besides price-fixing], their legality must be determined *by*

the nature of the contract in relation to the line of commerce which it may effect"). (Emphasis in original.)

56. *Id.* at 872.

57. 337 U.S. at 321 (Jackson, J., dissenting).

58. *Id.* at 322.

59. *Id.* at 322–23. Justice Jackson wrote that the trial court "did not allow the defendant affirmatively to show that such [harmful] effects do not flow from this arrangement. *Id.* at 322. Justice Frankfurter for the Court was more explicit (if puzzling) on this score, writing that the district court "excluded as immaterial testimony bearing on 'the economic merits or demerits of the present system as contrasted with a system which prevailed prior to its establishment and which would prevail if the court declared the present arrangement [invalid].'" 337 U.S. at 298. The puzzle is that no such words appear in the district court's opinion. To the contrary, the district court wrote as follows: "Over the Government's objection, I allowed many comparative statistics, of which the foregoing are examples, to go into the record. This was consistent with the view that in resolving the issues of this case, the potential or actual effect of the agreements is important in determining unreasonableness of restraint under the Sherman Act and substantiality of restraint or tendency to create monopoly under the Clayton Act." 78 F. Supp. at 872. The puzzle is not of great moment, however, for district court continued as follows: "But while the comparative figures bear on the question, they are not determinate." *Id.* And it then found illegality based solely on the market foreclosed and the volume of controlled business.

60. 337 U.S. at 306–07 (citations and footnotes omitted).

61. *Id.* at 308.

62. *Id.* at 308.

63. *See* William E. Kovacic, *The Intellectual DNA of Modern U.S. Competition Law for Dominant Firm Conduct: The Chicago/Harvard Double Helix,* 2007 COLUM. BUS. L. REV. 1.

64. 337 U.S. at 310 n.13 ("The dual system of enforcement provided for by the Clayton Act must have contemplated standards of proof capable of administration by the courts as well as by the Federal Trade Commission....Our interpretation of the Act, therefore, should recognize that an appraisal of economic data which might be practicable if only the latter were faced with the task may be quite otherwise for judges unequipped for it either by experience or by the availability of skilled assistance.").

65. Justice Douglas penned a passionate dissent on just this ground, blasting the Court for setting out "a formula which under our decisions promises to wipe out large segments of independent filling-station operators." He argued that "[t]he requirements contract which is displaced is relatively innocuous as compared with the virulent growth of monopoly power which the Court encourages." He foresaw a pattern of vertical integration through which "[t]he small, independent business man will be supplanted by clerks," with the result being a "tragic loss to the nation." 337 U.S. at 320–21 (Douglas, J., dissenting).

66. 337 U.S. at 310–11.

67. *Id.* at 310 (footnote omitted).

68. *Id.* at 311.

69. *Id.* at 313.
70. *Id.* at 311.
71. *Id.* at 298.
72. 365 U.S. 320 (1961).
73. *Id.* at 329.
74. *E.g.,* 2 ANTITRUST LAW DEVELOPMENTS (1984) 97.
75. 365 U.S. at 333.
76. 466 U.S. 2 (1984). Between *Tampa Electric* and *Jefferson Parish,* the Court issued its frequently mischaracterized opinion in *Lorain Journal Co. v. United States,* 342 U.S. 143 (1951) (Burton, J.). In *Lorain Journal,* the Court affirmed a trial court's condemnation of a monopoly newspaper's informing of its advertisers that if they chose to patronize an upstart competitor (a radio station), they could not advertise in the *Journal.* 92 F. Supp. 794, 796 (N.D. Ohio 1950). The newspaper's action "strengthened the Journal's monopoly" in local advertising and threatened to eliminate the radio station (342 U.S. at 150). The Court held "that a single newspaper, already enjoying a substantial monopoly in its area, violates the 'attempt to monopolize' clause of § 2 when it uses its monopoly to destroy threatened competition." *Id.* at 154.
77. 466 U.S. at 45.
78. *Id.* at 45–46.
79. *Id.* at 7.
80. ANTITRUST LAW DEVELOPMENTS (2007) 217.
81. For the history of this publication, *see* Stephen Calkins, *The Organized Bar and Antitrust: Change, Continuity and Influence,* 14 LOY. CONSUMER L. REV. 393, 404–06 (2002).
82. ANTITRUST LAW DEVELOPMENTS (1975), *supra* note 51, at 43–44 (citing *Standard Oil Co. v. United States,* 337 U.S. 293, 306–07 (1949); *Tampa Elec. Co. v. Nashville Coal Co.,* 365 U.S. 320, 329 (1961)).
83. *Id.* at 44.
84. *Id.*
85. 15 U.S.C. § 45.
86. ANTITRUST LAW DEVELOPMENTS (1975), *supra* note 51, at 46 (quoting *L.G. Balfour Co. v. FTC,* 442 F.2d 1, 20 (7th Cir. 1971)); *see also Brown Shoe Co. v. FTC,* 384 U.S. 316 (1966). The FTC Act's prohibition of "unfair methods of competition" is most frequently interpreted as coterminous with the antitrust laws, although occasionally it is applied more expansively. *See, e.g., Rambus, Inc.,* 2006 FTC LEXIS 102 (2007) (Leibowitz, Comm'r, concurring) (reviewing Act's history and jurisprudence and arguing for more aggressive use).
87. ANTITRUST LAW DEVELOPMENTS (1984), *supra* note 74, 96 n.680. Full disclosure requires me to note that I was a member of the editorial board of this volume.
88. 100 F.T.C. 68 (1982).
89. ANTITRUST LAW DEVELOPMENTS (1984), *supra* note 74, at 98 (citing cases). As the source of the blessing of one-year contracts, the authors cited a consent decree, *FTC v. Motion Picture Advertising Co.,* 344 U.S. 392 (1953), in which the Commission prohibited decrees longer than a year; *United States v. Pfizer,* 246 F. Supp. 464 (E.D.N.Y. 1965) (which upheld

one-year contracts albeit for failure to define a market); and *United States v. American Can Co.,* 87 F. Supp. 18, 29 (N.D. Cal. 1949), which condemned five-year contracts but upheld a one-year one. They included a "cf." cite to *Standard Stations,* which held one-year contracts "invalid in the context including other restraints."

90. ABA Antitrust Section, Antitrust Law Developments (1997) 223–234 (citing cases).

91. *Id.* at 224–25 (1997) (citing cases).

92. 749 F.2d 380 (7th Cir. 1984)

93. *Id.* at 395. The court also cited Lawrence Anthony Sullivan, Antitrust 484–86 (1977), but a little unfairly, since Sullivan had called for a presumption of *illegality* for contracts longer than a year, but a full analysis for contracts of a year or less. The court's "cf." cite to Howard Marvel, *Exclusive Dealing,* 25 J. L. & Econ. 1, 6 (1982), was appropriate, since Marvel cautiously argued that exclusive contracts of "short duration" do not "seem suited as a device to limit competition."

94. *See, e.g., Concord Boat Corp. v. Brunswick Corp.,* 207 F.3d 1039, 1059 (8th Cir. 2000) (citing *Roland Machinery* for the proposition that contracts terminable in less than a year are presumptively lawful); *Bepko, Inc. v. Allied-Signal, Inc.,* 106 F. Supp. 2d 814, 829 ("exclusive contracts terminable after thirty (30) days to one (1) year do not have substantial anticompetitive effects") (citing, *e.g., Roland Machinery*).

95. 127 F.3d 1127 (9th Cir. 1997).

96. *Id.* at 1164.

97. 986 F.2d 589 (1st Cir. 1993).

98. *Id.* at 596.

99. XI Herbert Hovenkamp, Antitrust Law ¶ 1821d3 (2d ed. 2005).

100. *Omega Environmental, Inc. v. Gilbarco, Inc.,* 127 F.3d 1157, 1163 (9th Cir. 1997).

101. Hovenkamp, *supra* note 99, at ¶1821d2.

102. 466 U.S. at 44 (O'Connor, J., concurring) ("Exclusive dealing is an unreasonable restraint on trade only when a significant fraction of buyers or sellers are frozen out of a market by the exclusive deal.") (Citing *Standard Stations.*)

103. *United States v. Microsoft Corp.,* 87 F. Supp. 2d 30, 53 (D.D.C. 2000), *vacated,* 253 F.3d 34 (D.C. Cir. 2001).

104. *United States v. Dentsply Int'l, Inc.,* 277 F. Supp. 2d 387, 453 (D. Del. 2003) (quoting *LePage's Inc. v. 3M,* 324 F.3d 141, 159 (3d Cir. 2003) (en banc)), *rev'd,* 399 F.3d 181 (3d Cir. 2005).

105. *See Twin City Sportservice v. Charles O. Finley & Co.,* 676 F.2d 1291 (9th Cir. 1982) (24 percent); *Luria Bros. v. FTC,* 389 F.2d 847 (3d Cir. 1968) (21 to 34 percent).

106. 466 U.S. at 46 (O'Connor, J., concurring) ("A firm of four anesthesiologists represents only a very small fraction of the total number of anesthesiologists whose services are available for hire by other hospitals....").

107. *See* Antitrust Law Developments (2007), *supra* note 80, at 217 n.1267 (reviewing cases); *see also JBDL Corp. v. Wyeth-Ayerst Laboratories, Inc.,* 2005 U.S. Dist. LEXIS 11676 (S.D. Ohio 2005) (quoting with approval the *Microsoft* district court's requiring, for a Section 1

violation, of " 'exclu[sion]...altogether from access to roughly forty percent of the...market' "), *aff'd on other grounds,* 485 F.3d 880 (6th Cir. 2007).

108. Stephen Calkins, *California Dental Association: Not the Quick Look But Not the Full Monty,* 67 ANTITRUST L.J. 495 (2000).

109. 253 F.3d 34 (D.C. Cir. 2001).

110. 399 F.3d 181 (3d Cir. 2005).

111. *United States v. Microsoft Corp.,* 87 F. Supp. 2d 30, 51 (D.D.C. 2000) (not enough to "preempt[] the most efficient channels" of distribution) ("Where courts have found that the agreements in question failed to foreclose absolutely outlets that together accounted for a substantial percentage of the total distribution of the relevant products, they have consistently declined to assign liability. This Court has previously observed that the case law suggests that, unless the evidence demonstrates that Microsoft excluded Netscape altogether from access to roughly forty percent of the browser market, the Court should decline to find such agreements in violation of § 1.") (Citations omitted.)

112. 253 F.3d at 70. While so ruling, the court of appeals referenced a relatively high threshold for finding Section 1 liability: "[W]e agree with plaintiffs that a monopolist's use of exclusive contracts, in certain circumstances, may give rise to a § 2 violation even though the contracts foreclose less than the roughly 40% or 50% share usually required in order to establish a § 1 violation."

113. *Id.* at 70.

114. *Id.* at 70 (citations omitted).

115. *Id.* at 57.

116. *Id.* at 71 (quoting findings of fact).

117. *United States v. Microsoft Corp.,* 84 F. Supp. 2d 9, 46 (D.D.C. 1999), *quoted in part,* 253 F.3d at 71 ("By ensuring that the 'majority' of all IAP subscribers are offered IE either as the default browser or as the only browser, Microsoft's deals with the IAPs clearly have a significant effect in preserving its monopoly; they help keep usage of Navigator below the critical level necessary for Navigator or any other rival to pose a real threat to Microsoft's monopoly.") (Citing Finding of Fact 143.)

118. 253 F.3d at 70.

119. 399 F.3d at 193.

120. *Id.* at 193.

121. *Id.* at 194 & n.2 (noting that it found the "short duration" cases "distinguishable").

122. *Id.* at 196.

123. *Id.* at 195 ("Moreover, the record demonstrates that Dentsply added Darby as a dealer 'to block Vita from a key competitive distribution point.' According to a Dentsply executive, the 'key issue' was 'Vita's potential distribution system.' He explained that Vita was 'having a tough time getting teeth out to customers. One of their key weaknesses is their distribution system.' ").

124. *Id.* at 189–90.

125. *Cf., e.g.,* Hovenkamp, *supra* note 99, at ¶ 1821d3 ("We suggest presumptively that periods of less than one year be approved, particularly where switching appears to face no substantial impediments, and even

more particularly where dealers in the same distribution system and operating under the same contract provisions can be observed to be switching. We say 'presumptively,' however, because while short contract duration suggests cycling availability of buyers for upstream rivals, it does not guarantee such availability."). *See also* Richard Posner, ANTITRUST LAW 229 (2d ed. 2001) ("The only exception, but an important one, is where there are such large economies of scale in distribution, or (what amounts to the same thing) efficiencies in distributing a variety of products at the same outlet, that a distributor forced to choose between handling only the goods of his present supplier and only the goods of other suppliers—the choice forced upon him by the supplier's insistence on an exclusive-dealing contract— will choose the former.") (Citation omitted.)

126. ANTITRUST LAW DEVELOPMENTS (S2007), *supra* note 80, at 219–20 ("Agreements with short terms and providing short notice for termination have often been upheld on the premise that the competitive effects of short term or easily terminable foreclosure are likely to be minimal, although some recent cases have held that provisions allowing termination on short notice will not prevent a determination of illegality.") (Citations omitted.)

127. *See J.B.D.L. Corp. v. Wyeth-Ayerst Laboratories, Inc.,* 2005 U.S. Dist. LEXIS 11676 (S.D. Ohio 2005) (quoting with approval the *Microsoft* and *Dentsply* district courts' "total exclusion" language while ignoring the court of appeals opinions except to note that the Government did not appeal the section 1 rulings—even though the *Microsoft* appellate court clearly suggested that its views were not limited to section 2, and the *Dentsply* appellate court disapproved of the language quoted by *J.B.D.L.*), *aff'd on other grounds,* 485 F.3d 880 (6th Cir. 2007).

128. *Accord* Posner, *supra* note 125, at 265.

129. For a spirited defense of evidence of subjective intent, see Marina Lao, *Reclaiming a Role for Intent Evidence in Monopolization Analysis,* 54 AM. U. L. REV. 151 (2004).

130. 100 F.T.C. 68, 209–18 (1982) (Clanton, Comm'r).

131. *United States v. Dentsply Int'l, Inc.,* 277 F. Supp. 2d 387, 442–48 (D. Del. 2003); *see also Dentsply,* 399 F.3d at 196–97 (relying on district court's discussion).

132. The leading single-standard candidates are reviewed at ANTITRUST MODERNIZATION COMMISSION REPORT AND RECOMMENDATIONS 91–93 (2007). The "no economic sense" test holds that " 'conduct is not exclusionary or predatory unless it would make no economic sense for the defendant but for its tendency to eliminate or lessen competition.' " Gregory J. Werden, *The Antitrust Enterprise: Principle and Execution: The "No Economic Sense" Test for Exclusionary Conduct,* 31 IOWA J. CORP. L. 293, 293 (2006) (quoting Brief for the United States and the Federal Trade Commission as Amici Curiae Supporting Petitioner at 15, *Verizon Commc'ns, Inc. v. Law Offices of Curtis V. Trinko, LLP,* 540 U.S. 398 (2004) (No. 02–682) (test limited to duty-to-assist-a-rival cases)); *see also* Gregory J. Werden, *Identifying Exclusionary Conduct Under Section 2: The "No Economic Sense" Test,* 73 ANTITRUST L.J. 413 (2006). The "equally efficient competitor" test would require a plaintiff to prove "that the challenged practice is likely in the circumstances

to exclude from the defendant's market an equally or more efficient competitor." POSNER, *supra* note 125, at 194–95.

133. *See, e.g.,* Jacobson & Sher, *supra* note 44.

134. *See, e.g.,* ANTITRUST MODERNIZATION COMMISSION REPORT, *supra* note 132, at 93 ("Thus far, no consensus exists that any one test can suffice to assess all types of conduct that may be challenged under Section 2.")

135. Transcript, United States Federal Trade Commission and United States Department of Justice, Sherman Act Section 2 Joint Hearing: Understanding Single-Firm Behavior: Exclusive Dealing Session (Nov. 15, 2006), at 145 (remarks of Joseph Farrell) ("watch out when you are imposing burdens of proof"), *available at* http://www.usdoj.gov/atr/public/hearings/single_firm/docs/222438.htm.

5

Has the Free Rider Explanation for Vertical Arrangements Been Unrealistically Expanded?

Introduction

Because the effect of minimum resale price-fixing is essentially to establish a horizontal cartel among retailers, supervised by the manufacturer, and all subsequent studies had showed that the result of minimum resale price maintenance was that consumers would pay more, the Supreme Court decided in 1911 in *Dr. Miles Medical Co.* v. *John D. Park & Sons,*[1] that minimum resale price maintenance was illegal *per se*—i.e., without regard to the seller's market power, purpose, or effect. In 1960, Lester Telser, a charter member of the Chicago School approach to antitrust, offered an original explanation of why manufacturers would require their dealers not to sell below a manufacturer set minimum price.

Telser's contribution was to introduce the idea that manufacturers ensure increases in retail prices to guarantee high margins for retailers in order to induce the retailers to provide services—advertising, sales person explanations, credit, repair, and even in-store ambiance. If all retailers were free to sell at any price they chose, the high-end stores would lose business to discounters who do not provide services and eventually would drive the services out of the marketplace. Judges Bork and Posner soon joined the Telser camp; indeed, Posner concluded not just that the *per se* rule was a mistake but because of free rider problems minimum resale price maintenance should be *per se* legal.[2]

Warren Grimes and Marina Lao accept that "free rider" problems occasionally occur. They point out, however, that the free rider justification for vertical restraints has become practically a knee-jerk response by conservatives to challenges to the legality of all vertical distribution arrangements, often in circumstances where the evidence suggests that services were irrelevant to sale of the product, and that if they were relevant they could have been separately contracted for between the manufacturer and the dealer. In any event there is no factual analysis (only the usual economic theory) to indicate that free riding is a frequent as opposed to rare problem in distribution.

Grimes calls free riding a pretext. He offers a detailed analysis of fact and law in *Business Electronics* v. *Sharp Electronics,*[3] a Supreme Court decision, in which Justice Scalia ignored record facts and a jury finding to justify a cutoff of a discounting dealer. Although there was virtually no evidence of free riding by the discounter, Scalia rated the defense as "holy writ," not as a concept to be measured against the evidence. Lao concludes that even if there is a little more to the concept, the right approach is the same one that the present Supreme Court has accorded to horizontal price-fixing—i.e., a "quick look" to see if free riding problems are a serious matter and only if found to be significant would the seller and retailers be accorded a full rule of reason. Other dealers without the slightest basis for claiming a services justification would be left in the *per se* category.

The *Sylvania* Free Rider Justification for Downstream-Power Vertical Restraints: Truth or Invitation for Pretext?

Warren S. Grimes

After three decades, *Continental T.V., Inc. v. GTE Sylvania, Inc.*[4] is a well-entrenched paradigm for analyzing vertical restraints. *Sylvania* received 30th anniversary reaffirmation and expanded reach in *Leegin Creative Leather Products, Inc. v. PSKS, Inc.*,[5] where a divided Court reversed a century-old precedent and completed the process of eliminating per se treatment of vertical restraints.[6]

Justice Powell wrote the *Sylvania* opinion to overrule a vertical restraints decision decided just ten years earlier (*United States v. Arnold Schwinn & Co.*[7]). Overruling a Supreme Court precedent within a decade is an unusual event and one that may have prompted the Court to overreach in justifying its holding. The language that Justice Powell employed has prompted strong criticism,[8] even while the holding itself remains firmly entrenched.

This chapter focuses on a particular justification offered for the *Sylvania* rule: that vertical restraints are a legitimate response to free riding retail firms—dealers that do not provide the manufacturer's desired panoply of retail services. It is widely accepted that the free rider concept derives from conservative economic analysis. This paper will explain that analysis but then go on to show that the concept is flawed in many respects, often criticized, and at a minimum deserving of a less doctrinaire approach.

Some dealers do free ride on others' retail promotion services. When suppliers want to encourage substantial dealer investment in the supplier's product line, free riding can be a strong concern. However, manufacturers that impose vertical restraints frequently do so in industries and in circumstances in which free riding is not a significant concern. Moreover, contractual provisions are a superior tool for dealing with a dealer's free riding. Contrary to constructive economic analysis, there is no sound basis for invoking free riding as an across-the-board justification for vertical restraints.

A number of more specific conclusions about free riding are warranted. Upstream-power vertical restraints such as tie-ins and vertical maximum price-fixing are imposed by power-wielding upstream sellers and are not motivated by concerns with free riding on dealer services, nor do the restraints themselves prevent free riding on such presale services.

With respect to downstream-power vertical restraints such as exclusive dealer territories or vertical minimum price-fixing, manufacturers impose these restraints to create incentives for downstream dealers to carry and promote a manufacturer's brand. These restraints fall into two general categories: (1) restraints that restrict distribution of the manufacturer's brand, such as exclusive dealer territories or dealer location clauses; and (2) restraints that are consistent with wide-open distribution of the dealer's brand, such as vertical minimum price-fixing or minimum advertised prices. Restraints that restrict distribution of the manufacturer's brand may limit dealer free riding because they restrict intrabrand competition among dealers. Such restraints may be warranted when they are ancillary to procompetitive investment by the dealer in carrying and promoting the manufacturer's line.

However, restraints compatible with wide-open distribution, such as vertical minimum price-fixing, are ill-suited to prevent free riding on presale services among the multiple types of retailers likely to carry the manufacturer's brand. Such restraints are not particularly effective in promoting vertically integrating investment by the dealer, have a potentially more far-reaching negative impact on intrabrand and interbrand retail competition, and are more likely to be associated with dealer pressure to end retail price competition.

I. When Does Free Riding Undermine Efficiency and Competition Goals?

In a broad sense, free riding, or taking advantage of another's efforts, is ubiquitous. Whether in commercial, artistic, or athletic endeavors, progress can be measured in the copying of novel, efficient, or attractive ideas. Competition itself assumes the ability of entrepreneurs, subject to intellectual property limitations, to copy and imitate innovative and efficient products, production techniques, services, and distribution methods.

Intellectual property law, unfair competition law, and antitrust law have all had a hand in limiting copying in the interest of maintaining incentives for innovation and for operation of an efficiency enhancing enterprise. In *International News Service v. Associated Press,* the Supreme Court offered a biblical phrase, albeit surely an indiscriminately broad one, that captures the spirit of legal norms that prevent free riding: a divided Supreme Court condemned an actor for attempting "to reap where it has not sown."[9]

The sweeping language of *International News* is suggestive of more recent developments in which property rights have become the starting point for arguments that power-wielding firms should be granted the broadest possible freedom to exploit intellectual property rights or a dominant position in the market. For example, it has been argued that price discrimination implemented through tying practices involving a patented product is a legitimate way to increase the incentive and reward for innovation,[10] or that even dominant firms possess an absolute right to refuse to license a patented product.[11] Following in this vein, Scalia wrote in *Verizon Communications, Inc. v. Trinko* that the "possession of monopoly power, and the charging of monopoly prices, is not only not unlawful; it is an important element of the free market system" because these monopoly prices attract "business acumen" and induce "risk taking that produces innovation and economic growth."[12] This formulation appears to leave little room for the emulation and copying that has been an even greater generator of progress and its dissemination to the general public.

Free riding is a concept that has been narrowly or generously interpreted in many antitrust cases. Free riding in the narrower sense—taking advantage of ongoing marketing efforts of a rival—becomes a substantial issue in joint ventures and collaborations. In *United States v. Topco Associates, Inc.,*[13] independent grocery retailers affiliated to provide more efficient buying and selling under the Topco name. The Court held that restrictions on the territorial reach of a member's stores were a per se violation of section 1 of the Sherman Act. Without territorial protections, Topco's viability might be threatened by free riding members that exploited the advertising and marketing efforts of a competing member. After the Supreme Court's decision, the Justice Department, apparently recognizing the validity of the free rider issue, settled the case on terms that allowed Topco to create primary territories to address the free riding issue.[14]

A holding more sympathetic to a joint venture's need to address free riding came in *Rothery Storage and Van Co. v. Atlas Van Lines.*[15] Atlas was a vertically integrated enterprise made up of a nationwide common carrier of household goods and its independent local agents. The plaintiffs, local agents that were a part of the Atlas network, had been terminated after using the Atlas name and equipment for local moving business, the profits of which flowed exclusively to the local agent. Judge Bork held that the termination of the free riding local agents did not constitute an unlawful boycott:

> To the degree that a carrier agent uses Atlas' reputation, equipment, facilities, and services in conducting business for its own profit, the

agent enjoys a free ride at Atlas' expense. The problem is that the van line's incentive to spend for reputation, equipment, facilities, and services declines as it receives less of the benefit from them. That produces a deterioration of the system's efficiency because the things consumers desire are not provided in the amounts they are willing to pay for. In the extreme case, the system as a whole could collapse.[16]

The distinction between ancillary and naked restraints, initially proposed by Judge Taft[17] and embraced by Bork, works well in determining when restrictions that limit free riding are compatible with competition. *Rothery* suggests that antitrust can and does make room for prohibitions on free riding when those restrictions are ancillary to an efficient, vertically integrated operation.

The limits of this tolerance are suggested by two other court of appeals decisions. In *General Leaseways, Inc. v. National Truck Leasing Assoc.*,[18] 130 small, truck-rental companies reciprocally provided repair service to other members' vehicles in order to compete with rivals that had nationwide service facilities. Following *Topco,* Judge Posner applied the *per se* rule to an agreement among the members not to enter others' territories.

In *Polygram Holding, Inc. v. FTC,*[19] two firms that had jointly agreed to produce a recording of a concert by three famous tenors offered the prevention of free riding as a justification for a moratorium on promotion of two prior recordings by the same artists (each joint venture participant had produced one such recording). The firms argued that their incentive to engage in the joint venture would be undercut without the moratorium because each firm might try to free ride on the publicity surrounding the issuance of the new recording, causing some customers to purchase one of the older recordings instead of the joint venture's recording. Judge Ginsburg agreed with the FTC that the free rider argument did not justify a limit on competition involving non-joint venture products. If accepted, the principle that the restraint would make the joint venture's product more profitable might allow joint venture participants to agree to cease competition on a broad range of products produced by the rivals.[20]

The joint venture cases, although involving an element of horizontal integration, also involve vertical elements (sometimes vertical integration) as well. Collectively, these cases demonstrate a principled application of the ancillary restraints test. *Rothery* deemed lawful a restraint that prevented a member's use of the joint venture's resources for non-joint venture business (and potentially in competition with the joint venture); the restraint was ancillary to, and necessary to sustain, an efficient joint venture. The remaining three cases lack the direct nexus between the restraint and the survival of the joint venture. *Polygram* held unlawful a restraint on competition in products that were not a part of the joint venture. *Topco* and *General Leaseways* suggest that a flat prohibition on competition between members of the joint venture that may extend beyond the joint venture's products or services is per se unlawful, but these decisions do not necessarily preclude lesser measures necessary to discourage free riding (and maintain the viability of the joint venture), including primary territories or location clauses.

As described in parts III and IV, the ancillary restraints test can usefully be applied to classic, downstream-power vertical restraints.

II. Telser's Explanation of Why Manufacturers Impose Vertical Restraints

Writing in 1960, Lester Telser offered an original assessment of why a manufacturer would impose a vertical restraint such as resale price maintenance.[21] Telser theorized that manufacturers use vertical restraints to guarantee the retailer a high margin that pays for a variety of "services" along with the manufactured product. These services include advertising, promotion, delivery, credit, and repair. Telser conceded that some of these services, including credit or postsale repair, could be the subject of separate charges. But presale advertising and promotion might give rise to the classic free rider problem:

> Sales are diverted from the retailers who do provide the special services at the higher price to the retailers who do not provide the special services and offer to sell the product at the lower price. . . . A customer, because of the special services provided by one retailer, is persuaded to buy the product. But he purchases the product from another paying the latter a lower price. In this way the retailers who do not provide the special services get a free ride at the expense of those who have convinced consumers to buy the product.[22]

The result, according to Telser, would be that some full-service dealers, in order to compete with the free rider, would cease providing the full services that the manufacturer desires.

Robert Bork provided a corollary to the Telser model, arguing that vertical restraints were efficient as long as sales (measured by dollar volume) were higher.[23] In answer to arguments that output (measured by items sold) might go down, Bork said,

> The error consists in failing to count the efforts of the reseller, purchased through resale price maintenance, as an economic output. The consumer is no longer offered merely a physical product but a composite product, part of which is the same physical product and part of which consists of the information, display, services, conveniences, etc., that the reseller now provides. . . . Stores charge for decor in the price of the clothing, restaurants charge for atmosphere and service in the price of the food, gasoline stations charge for rest rooms, window washing, and air pumps in the price of the gasoline. It would be completely wrong to say that these additions are not part of the product. . . . [24]

Richard Posner, some years after arguing the *Schwinn* case for the United States, joined Bork in urging that a manufacturer's interest was consistent with the consumer interest and that vertical restraints are imposed because they are efficient. Posner agreed with Bork that efficiency was demonstrated when output (measured by dollars) increased.[25]

Although there were dissenting voices,[26] the view that manufacturers would only impose efficient vertical restraints found favor in Justice Powell's opinion for the Court in *Sylvania*. The Court said that "[v]ertical restrictions promote interbrand competition by allowing the manufacturer to achieve certain efficiencies in the distribution of his products."[27] The Court went on to suggest that a newly entering manufacturer could use vertical restraints to induce "competent or aggressive retailers" to invest capital and labor in the distribution of the new product.[28] The Court then offered its free riding rationale for the use of vertical restraints:

> Established manufacturers can use [vertical restraints] to induce retailers to engage in promotional activities or to provide service and repair facilities necessary to the efficient marketing of their products. Service and repair are vital for many products, such as automobiles and major household appliances. The availability and quality of such services affect a manufacturer's goodwill and the competitiveness of his product. Because of market imperfections such as the so-called "free-rider" effect, these services might not be provided by retailers in a purely competitive situation, despite the fact that each retailer's benefit would be greater if all provided the services than if none did.[29]

The Court's description of the free rider problem is broad-brush and lacking in the refinement that Telser provided in his landmark article. Unlike Telser, the Court failed to acknowledge that free riding would not be an issue when postsale services were provided by dealers who could charge for those services. The Court also failed to connect its stated free riding concern with any record evidence in *Sylvania* (or in other previously decided cases) that prevention of free riding was the motive for, or the result of, imposition of vertical restraints.

A number of other criticisms of the Telser free riding explanation and the *Sylvania* Court's language were offered. Economists Benjamin Klein and Kevin Murphy, who generally favor relaxed antitrust scrutiny of vertical restraints, pointed out that free riding theory was "fundamentally flawed" because a free riding dealer could use the increased margin generated by resale price maintenance in multiple ways in disregard of the manufacturer's preference. Dealers may simply absorb the higher margin while continuing to sell the product without the presale services that the manufacturer desires.[30] Robert Pitofsky and others pointed out that many simple products that have been subject to resale price maintenance do not require information or demonstration services that might most easily be subject to free riding.[31] Pitofsky stressed that with or without vertical restraints, there is a diverse world of retailers offering consumers a range of retail choices from full service to no frills sales.[32] Areeda and Hovenkamp noted that many services (such as luxurious ambience) are not subject to free riding or are services that are not brand specific (and supported by the retailer's sale of a variety of brands).[33] Robert Steiner pointed out that the most effective way for a manufacturer to obtain presale services from retailers is to contract for them, paying promotion allowances to those retailers who comply and denying allowances to those who do not.[34]

As a close examination of the Supreme Court's opinion in *Business Electronics Corp. v. Sharp Electronics Corp.* reveals,[35] Telser's free riding argument runs up against another marketing truth. Even with respect to complex or high-end products that benefit from presale explanation and demonstration to promote sales, most retailers are the first to grasp this marketing reality. The interests of manufacturers and dealers are likely to be closely aligned on this issue. Discount firms that decline to offer such services may have a price advantage, but they will also lose sales because of their no frills marketing strategy. Some efficient dealers will be able to offer both the presale promotion *and* the discounted prices, and will find this strategy to be profit maximizing.[36]

Recognizing that free riding in the narrow sense cannot justify most vertical restraints, economist Howard Marvel has urged that a broader promotional service rationale nonetheless justifies many vertical restraints.[37] Marvel and McAfferty have also argued that free riding by retailers can undermine the brand-certification role that high-image retailers provide by simply carrying the manufacturer's product. Marvel does not convincingly explain why contractual promotion allowances will not ensure that retailers perform desired presale promotion services. Even the brand-certification role of a high image retailer could be protected by promotion allowances and, where necessary, exclusive dealing or location clauses that are less harmful to competition than resale price maintenance.

III. Reexamining Why Manufacturers Impose Vertical Restraints

The writings of economist Robert Steiner offer rich insights into the nature of vertical restraints.[38] There is a strong empirical component to Steiner's writings—before embarking on his career as an economist, Steiner was an owner/manager of a toy manufacturing firm that employed promotion allowances and various other tools to induce retailers to carry the toys. Steiner's writings support the intuitive premise that vertical restraints are imposed by manufacturers as an incentive for dealers to carry and promote the manufacturer's brand. Typically, it is a relatively weak brand that the retailer would not carry absent the guaranteed higher margin that the vertical restraint provides. This explanation for vertical restraints is more comprehensive than Telser's because it does not depend on the existence of free riding problems, nor does it assume the potential of vertical restraints to solve such problems. Instead, it postulates only that the manufacturer needs the vertical restraint as an inducement for the dealer to carry and promote the product, in whatever way the dealer chooses. For many products, merely stocking and shelving the product may be the extent of the retailer's promotion effort.

An additional insight of Steiner's writings is his recognition of the competition that occurs between manufacturer and dealer. The seller of a strong brand enjoys vertical market power that allows a large factory markup. A manufacturer's vertical market power is a product of a strong consumer demand for a particular product or brand.[39] This vertical power usually exists along with the traditional horizontal market power, but not in every case. When a manufacturer has this vertical power, a consumer will switch stores in order to obtain the strong brand at the desired price.

Vertical market power is measured by a ratio of dealer and producer margins.[40] Typically, as the dealer's margin goes up, the producer's margin goes down, and vice versa. As Steiner concedes, this two-stage vertical market power measure is an oversimplification of real markets that can have more than two levels in the distribution system and multiple players at each level. However, measuring the margins of both producers and dealers offers a much more principled, accurate, and instructive model than the current single-stage analysis that looks only at horizontal market power.[41]

The locus of power in a vertical relationship strongly affects competitive outcomes in the distribution system. In every distribution restraint case, a fundamental inquiry should be, Who holds the power? Is the restraint a product of upstream power? Downstream power? Or is it rather the outcome of relatively equally empowered players who negotiate the restraint because it is mutually advantageous? The answer to these questions can greatly aid the court in identifying the anticompetitive risks, in applying focused and appropriate rules of decision, and in screening out restraints that are unlikely to have anticompetitive impact. The type of anticompetitive risk is directly linked to who is exercising the power in the vertical relationship.

Upstream-power restraints include tie-ins and maximum vertical price-fixing. When the power rests with the upstream supplier, free riding is generally of little concern to the supplier because dealers of all types wish to carry the supplier's brand. The potential anticompetitive effects of these restraints flow from the supplier's ability to force the buyer to purchase unwanted products or pay supracompetitive prices for those products. These restraints do not prevent free riding. Indeed, to the extent that an upstream-power restraint squeezes the dealer's retail margin, these restraints may create additional incentives for free riding on presale promotion services.

To be sure, free riding arguments have been employed to justify upstream-power restraints, but they are not the sort of free riding that Telser and the *Sylvania* Court were addressing. In *Eastman Kodak Co. v. Image Technical Services, Inc.*,[42] the Supreme Court declined to accept Kodak's arguments that tying conduct was justified in order to prevent free riding by independent service providers that serviced Kodak machines. These service providers often got their training with Kodak, taking their expertise and training with them when they started a firm that competed with Kodak. The law grants an employee a certain leeway to carry into a new job the expertise learned in previous jobs.[43]

Downstream-power restraints include exclusive territories, dealer location clauses, and vertical minimum price-fixing. Generally, manufacturers lacking in upstream power may find it advantageous to impose vertical restraints that increase a reluctant dealer's margin. Here, the focus of anticompetitive effects is, assuming no cartel-like behavior at the manufacturer level, on the dealer level. Here are some of the potential anticompetitive effects of downstream power restraints: (1) competition and entry at the dealer level may be undermined—new and efficient dealers may be handicapped because vertical restraints cripple their ability to compete; (2) dealer power may be exercised against smaller dealers that are equally or more efficient; (3) the large retail margins provided by vertical restraints may encourage dealers to exploit consumer information gaps and sell non-superior brands at inflated prices.[44]

Downstream-power vertical restraints do promote brand selling, but this promotion may or may not be on the competitive merits of the favored brand. The *Sylvania* Court's statement that vertical restraints "promote interbrand competition" is simplistic because it fails to recognize that vertical restraints promote niche marketing of a brand that may decrease interbrand competition. Moreover, the *Sylvania* language does not acknowledge that vertical restraints promote on-site dealer promotion that is difficult to monitor or control and that can mislead or deceive consumers. When a vertical restraint ensures a large dealer margin, the economic incentive operates indiscriminately to favor any method by which a dealer can increase sales. During the 1970s and 1980s, the manufacturer of Classic Car Wax claimed great success in using vertical minimum price-fixing to market a brand that a consumer magazine found to be above average (superior shine, but lacking in durability and difficult to apply) but substantially more expensive than other tested brands.[45] The *Sylvania* Court also failed to mention the importance of intrabrand competition in situations where a particular brand is unique to the point that a consumer will not substitute a different brand. This may occur, for example, when a customer seeks a copyrighted book, song, video, or computer program.

A. Downstream-Power Vertical Restraints Compared to Other Promotion Methods

A manufacturer with a weak brand will have to offer dealers some sort of an incentive to carry that brand. To address this problem, a producer could choose among the following options:

- Beat the competition on price (a low-price strategy could allow dealers to carry the product and still sell it at an attractive margin)
- Institute producer-sponsored advertising that will build consumer brand loyalty
- Send producer representatives to retail outlets to perform promotional services
- Provide for a producer buyback of a retailer's unsold inventory, lessening the retailer's risk in carrying the brand
- Use promotional allowances to reward retailers for any of a variety of dealer-performed promotional services, including local advertising, on-site demonstrations, or prominent displays
- Institute a downstream-power distribution restraint such as exclusive dealer territories, dealer location clauses, or resale price maintenance that provides the dealer a high margin for selling the product
- Establish a franchise network of retail outlets
- Purchase retail outlets (vertical integration)

The listed alternatives are not equals. Depending on the circumstances, some will work better than others. If the producer does choose to rely on one or more forms of downstream-power restraints to provide dealer incentives, there are additional choices to make. A central choice is between restraints that substantially restrict distribution, such as exclusive territories or location clauses, or restraints that can be used with more wide-open distribution, such as resale price maintenance or minimum advertised prices.

B. Vertical Restraints That Substantially Restrict Distribution

Restricted distribution can be efficient for a manufacturer selling complex products. The Arnold Schwinn Corporation moved to restricted distribution during the 1950s and credited this move with eliminating substantial administrative and communication costs with unproductive dealers.[46] Restricted distribution also provides favored dealers with enhanced incentives to invest in promoting the manufacturer's line. Because overlap among dealers is curtailed or eliminated by the restrictive distribution, free riding on presale services becomes less of an issue for these dealers. The insight here might be that control of free riding on presale services becomes more of an issue if the manufacturer wants dealers to make a more substantial investment in carrying and promoting the manufacturer's line. But not all restrictive distribution restraints involve a commitment by the dealer to make such an investment. A franchisee with a location clause, on the one hand, generally is required to make this substantial investment. A multibrand dealer, on the other hand, may have relatively little stake in the success of a particular manufacturer's line, even if protected by a location clause.

Restricted distribution downstream-power restraints have generally been treated leniently in post-*Sylvania* litigation. This treatment may be justified when there is a substantial dealer investment in the manufacturer's brand. Under the ancillary restraints test, the territorial restriction can be deemed ancillary to the vertical integration achieved through the dealer's investment. Of course, territorial restraints do provide the dealer a degree of protection from free riding rivals. Borrowing from theorists such as Telser and Bork, one could describe the restraint as necessary to a scheme to protect the dealer from free riding. But this description highlights what is only a secondary benefit of the restraint and could lead to perverse results. All dealers want to be shielded from competition. The strongest case for legality of that restraint occurs if the dealer is making a substantial investment in the manufacturer's line.

C. Vertical Restraints Compatible With Open-Ended Distribution

Vertical restraints that are consistent with wide-open distribution—and here vertical minimum price-fixing is the primary example—offer little protection against free riding. Once there are a substantial number of competing dealers offering the manufacturer's brand, a range of full-service and no-frill service dealers is the norm. Unlike a promotion allowance implemented by contract, vertical minimum price-fixing offers no reliable mechanism for compelling a dealer to provide a desired presale service.[47]

In *Leegin Creative Leather Products,* the Supreme Court concluded that vertical minimum price-fixing "alleviates" the problem of free riding rivals.[48] Under the ancillary restraints test, this use of vertical minimum pricing is not justified because such a restriction is not necessary to the enforcement of the presale service contracts and because the restraint is not ancillary to any efficient economic integration. Vertical minimum price-fixing is also highly threatening to retail competition because it can be used in wide-open distribution systems. If vertical minimum price-fixing is tolerated, it threatens to lock up retail prices on a substantial array of brands and make new entry or penetration by efficient retailers more difficult.

IV. Post-*Sylvania* Case Law on Free Riding: Lessons From the *Sharp* Case

In *Business Electronics v. Sharp Electronics,*[49] the Supreme Court addressed a dealer dispute involving minimal economic integration between manufacturer and dealers. Beginning in 1968, Sharp, a manufacturer of electronic calculators, sold its product through a dealer (Business Electronics) in the Houston area. During this period, electronic calculators were novel and expensive, requiring dealer promotion and demonstration to convince buyers to switch from electro-mechanical calculators. Most buyers of an electronic calculator, which sold for up to $1000, were commercial enterprises.

In 1972, Sharp brought in Hartwell as a second dealer, promising Hartwell that it would become the exclusive dealer in the Houston area. For the next two years, Sharp management declined to terminate Business Electronics, allowing both dealers to compete for Houston-area customers. In 1974, Hartwell, the larger of the two dealers, told Sharp that it would no longer carry the Sharp line if it were subjected to competition from the smaller dealer (Business Electronics). Responding to Hartwell's 30-day ultimatum, Sharp quickly terminated the smaller dealer. Business Electronics sued.

The reason for the termination was disputed. Throughout the litigation, Sharp contended that Business Electronics was terminated because of its inadequate performance and because it was free riding on the promotion services provided by Hartwell. Sharp argued that Business Electronics had eliminated its sales staff and promotion efforts after Hartwell became a dealer. Sharp relied on a Hartwell witness who stated that he was unconcerned about the prices charged by Business Electronics but was concerned when a potential customer "worked" by Hartwell was "snatched" by Business Electronics.[50]

Business Electronics, however, contended that it continued to provide advertising and promotion visits to customers after Hartwell was brought on as a competing dealer and did not substantially reduce its sales personnel until it was terminated as a dealer. Kelton Ehrensberger, the founder of Business Electronics, whom a Hartwell witness described as a "formidable opponent" who was "good at what he did," continued to call on customers personally and make calculator demonstrations.[51] Although both dealers apparently occasionally charged prices below Sharp's suggested retail prices, the Supreme Court accepted evidence in the record that Business Electronics had the lower prices.[52] There was also uncontradicted evidence that Sharp's pretermination protestations with Business Electronics dealt with pricing.[53] Hartwell's claims that Business Electronics was a free rider were also undermined by evidence that Hartwell had aggressively solicited accounts developed by Business Electronics and had attempted to pay a former Business Electronics salesman for access to his former employer's customer lists.[54]

The jury found that Business Electronics was terminated not for free riding but because it was discounting Sharp calculators. Nonetheless, Scalia, writing for the Court, repeatedly referred to *Sylvania* free riding theory as a reason for declining to apply the *per se* rule governing vertical minimum price-fixing. The Court quoted with approval the *Sylvania* Court's language extolling vertical restraints as a tool to counter the "so-called free-rider effect."[55] Scalia goes on at several points to reiterate the free rider theory, in each case arguing deductively from Telser's premises, without any reference to the facts or the jury's findings in Sharp. Here is some of the Court's language:

> [P]rice cutting and some measure of service cutting usually go hand in hand.[56]
>
> [V]ertical nonprice restraints only accomplish the benefits identified in GTE Sylvania because they reduce intrabrand price competition to the point where the dealer's profit margin permits provision of the desired services.[57]
>
> [M]anufacturers are often motivated by a legitimate desire to have dealers provide services, combined with the reality that price cutting is frequently made possible by "free riding" on the services provided by other dealers.[58]

The *Sharp* opinion treats the *Sylvania* free rider defense as holy writ, not as a thesis to be either vindicated or disproven by the evidence. At one point, perhaps as a concession to the jury finding, the Court complains that the Justice Stevens's dissenting opinion improperly ignores the "quite plausible purpose of the restriction to enable Hartwell to provide better services under the sales franchise agreement."[59] Plausible or not, the jury did not agree that free riding was the basis for the termination, and neither the Supreme Court nor the court of appeals directly challenged the jury's finding.

Free rider theory is based on the manufacturer's putative desire to have dealers provide presale promotional services. Yet there was evidence showing that Business Electronics did provide presale promotion services, that Sharp wanted to keep Business Electronics as a retailer, and that Sharp offered no objections to Business Electronics's selling methods. Business Electronics was terminated as a dealer only after the larger Houston retailer, Hartwell, gave Sharp the "them or us" ultimatum.

Sharp demonstrates another deficiency in Telser's free rider analysis. When presale demonstration and promotion are necessary to the sale of a product, that reality will be known to competent dealers as well as the manufacturer. In *Sharp,* the high cost of the new generation of electronic calculators presented a marketing challenge which demanded such presale promotion. The record evidence shows that Business Electronics, through its founder Kevin Ehrensburg, was highly effective in providing this presale promotion.[60] To maximize profits and sales, an efficient dealer would, without prompting from the manufacturer, be pushed to provide the presale promotion. A combination of both presale promotion and discounted prices would be the choice of many efficient dealers seeking to gain competitive advantage.

The Court's reasoning in *Sharp* typifies the worst application of the *Sylvania* free rider paradigm. Claims that Business Electronics was a free

rider were countered by evidence from Business Electronics that it continued to offer demonstrations and presale services, and from no clear
evidence from Sharp that it objected to Business Electronics's presale
promotion. The jury may well have concluded that Hartwell's free rider
argument was pretextual. The language in *Sylvania* invites after-the-fact
rationalization, and the Court's opinion in *Sharp* emphatically restates this
invitation.

Scalia offered one additional defense for the Court's holding that
Business Electronics termination should not be a per se violation. The
Court suggested that "since price cutting and some measure of service cutting usually go hand in hand," a manufacturer that terminated a dealer "for
failure to provide contractually obligated services" might expose itself
to "the highly plausible claim that its real motivation was to terminate a
price cutter."[61] There was, of course, no evidence in *Sharp* that Business
Electronics was contractually bound to perform any presale services. In
any event, as Justice Stevens notes in dissent, the Court's lack of confidence
in the integrity of the judicial process to sort out legitimate from illegitim-
ate terminations is hard to justify.[62] Breach of a contract to provide presale
services would seem to present a strong and convincing case for justifying
termination.

However objectionable the Court's reasoning in *Sharp,* the case presents
a legitimate and difficult classification issue deserving further reflection.
Was the conduct of Sharp simply a step by a manufacturer of an insufficiently strong brand to implement restrictive distribution in the Houston
area? Post-*Sylvania* courts have assessed such restrictive distribution
arrangements generously, and for generally sound reasons. These arrangements are less threatening to efficient multibrand retailers, including
efficient new entrants into the retail market.

But, the conduct of Hartwell can be seen as a blatant exclusionary step
to eliminate a smaller and perhaps equally or more efficient competitor. If
there was a bad actor in this case, it was Hartwell, not the manufacturer
Sharp. Antitrust challenges to this sort of behavior should focus on the
power-wielding retailer, not on the manufacturer. If Hartwell may with
impunity act to eliminate rival retailer competition, the door is open for
other large retailers all over the country to take similar steps involving
multiple brands from many manufacturers.

The Supreme Court's decision in *Leegin* amplifies many of the concerns
expressed here. As in *Business Electronics,* there was no evidence that the
terminated dealer was a free rider on presale services. To the contrary, it
appears PSKS had invested in the Leegin line, had prominently advertised
the line, and received a major share of its profits from the sale of Leegin
products. It seems unlikely that substantial presale services were required
to promote the sale of leather goods and accessories. Yet the majority in
Leegin offered the free rider argument as justification for overturning the
per se rule governing vertical minimum price fixing.[63]

IV. Conclusions

A manufacturer's desire to limit free riding by its dealers cannot provide a justification for either upstream or downstream power vertical restraints.

Downstream-power vertical restraints that restrict distribution, including exclusive dealer territories and dealer location clauses, can be an effective way of limiting free riding dealers. Free riding on dealer presale services is constrained because the limited distribution minimizes the competitive overlap among dealers. The justification for such restraints is not because they end free riding—that can be accomplished with fewer anticompetitive costs by implementing contract-enforced promotion allowances—but because such restraints can promote economically efficient investments by the dealer in the manufacturer's line.

Downstream power restraints such as vertical minimum price-fixing or minimum advertised prices threaten greater harm to competitive retailing and are ineffective in preventing free riding. A manufacturer with wide-open distribution can still limit the adverse effects of free riding dealers by implementing contractually enforced promotion allowances.

The language of *Sylvania,* repeated and reinforced in *Business Electronics* and in *Leegin,* offers defendants an open invitation for pretextual arguments on free riding. All three cases are examples of deductive reasoning from the unsubstantiated theory offered by Telser. Free riding was not argued in *Sylvania,* and not stressed in *Leegin,* because there was little factual basis for it, and squarely rejected by a jury in *Sharp.* The Court's acceptance of the free riding rationale seems squarely at odds with the Sylvania Court's warning that "[r]ealities must dominate the judgment.... The Antitrust Act aims at substance."[64]

The Court should correct the record. Free riding is unlikely to be an issue in most vertical restraint cases. There are efficiencies associated with some downstream-power vertical restraints, in particular, providing incentives for dealer investment in the manufacturer's line, and it is these efficiencies that should be the focus of justification for the restraints.

Free Riding: An Overstated, and Unconvincing, Explanation for Resale Price Maintenance

Marina Lao

Introduction

Lester Telser's free rider theory, developed almost 50 years ago, provided a rational efficiency explanation for vertical restraints under the conditions of his model.[65] Under conservative economic analysis, it became the basis for a comprehensive claim that vertical restraints, including vertical price-fixing (commonly referred to as resale price maintenance or "RPM"), generally increase distribution efficiency, enhance interbrand competition, and hence improve consumer welfare.[66]

This hypothesis was largely responsible for the Supreme Court's decision, in *Continental T.V., Inc. v. GTE Sylvania Inc.,* to overrule an earlier precedent and apply the rule of reason to non-price distribution restraints.[67] And, it was also a principal rationale for the divided Court's recent decision, in *Leegin Creative Leather Products, Inc. v. PSKS, Inc.,*[68] to overrule *Dr. Miles Medical Co. v. John D. Park & Sons Co.*[69] and end *per se* treatment for minimum resale price maintenance as well.

In this essay, I argue that the free rider concept, though theoretically correct and valid in certain circumstances, cannot support the broad claim that minimum RPM is usually only explicable as an efficiency response to free riding.[70] As several commentators have observed, and as even some supporters of minimum RPM acknowledge, the free rider theory has limited application in its original formulation because, quite simply, few goods require tangible services from retailers for effective marketing and few dealers provide them.[71]

Realizing that Telser's classic free rider theory was seldom applicable in the real world, some economic analysts expanded the concept to give it broader relevance. Instead of focusing on tangible, special, point-of-sale dealer services important for effective distribution, as Telser did, the expansive analysis included general intangible services, such as ambiance and other factors that provide a pleasant shopping experience,[72] as well as reputation or "quality certification" free riding.[73] In fact, the defendant and its amici in *Leegin* relied in part on just such a variant of the free rider argument in urging the reversal of the per se illegality rule against minimum RPM.

I argue that the broad versions of the free rider theory are flawed. Even if free riding does occur, it should not be of antitrust significance unless it erodes the sales of full-service dealers to a degree that they lose the incentive to provide the valuable services. After all, free riding exists throughout the economy and the law generally does not ban it.[74] Furthermore, the dealer services at issue must enhance consumer welfare, or its loss would not be detrimental. Closely related to this point, the restraint must, on balance, benefit consumers. A close analysis of the free rider argument will show that these conditions are seldom satisfied, and free riding does not often become an economic problem that needs to be addressed through minimum resale price-fixing.

In overruling *Dr. Miles* without good empirical evidence of (or consensus about) the regularity or harshness of the free rider problem,[75] especially given undisputed evidence of RPM's potential severe anticompetitive effects,[76] the *Leegin* majority apparently assumes that the *per se* rule is inappropriate for any class of conduct for which procompetitive benefits are possible. This approach seems contrary to modern decision theory, which should require focus, not so much on whether a practice has any procompetitive benefit (or anticompetitive harm), but on the frequency and relative magnitude of those benefits and harms and on whether there are less anticompetitive means of achieving the benefits in question.[77]

It will obviously be very difficult to challenge anticompetitive resale price maintenance practices post-*Leegin*. But the full implications of the case will depend largely on how lower courts, going forward, interpret the opinion and apply the rule of reason. If the *Sylvania* standard is adopted, RPM will effectively become de facto *legal,* as full rule of reason cases are notoriously expensive to litigate and virtually impossible for plaintiffs to win. Consumers will be better served if courts, instead, apply the "quick-look" (or abbreviated) rule of reason standard that is now frequently employed in horizontal restraint cases.[78]

Under a quick-look standard, identifying and prohibiting the anticompetitive uses of minimum RPM will be a more realistic task. Its application to RPM would be consistent with *Leegin,* given the majority's expressed vision of the rule of reason as a truly workable rule of reason, and not as a de facto legality rule that the full rule of reason has become, at least in the area of vertical restraints.

This essay will begin with an analysis of *Leegin* in part I. An examination of the free rider theory will follow in part II, which concludes that the free rider explanation for vertical restraints has been greatly overused; the expansive variants of the theory, in particular, are flawed on their own terms. In part III, I argue for a more positive or neutral perspective of free riding as positive externalities. So viewed, free riding should not be considered a problem that must be countered (with RPM) whenever it exists. Under this view, free riding is probably infrequently harmful and therefore minimum RPM seldom provides the competitive benefits proponents of RPM claim for it. In part IV, I briefly discuss the potential anticompetitive effects of minimum RPM. And, in part V, I discuss the policy implications of *Leegin* and argue for a quick-look rule of reason standard for minimum resale price maintenance in the wake of *Leegin*.

I. *PSKS v. Leegin Creative Leather Products*

Leegin, the manufacturer of the "Brighton" line of women's accessories, sells its products nationwide through over 5,000 independent stores and 70 company-owned stores.[79] Several years ago, it announced a retail pricing policy under which it refused to sell to retailers who sold Brighton products below Leegin's suggested prices.[80] It later went further and extracted agreements from the retailers to abide by its minimum retail pricing policy.[81]

Kay's Kloset, a Brighton retailer which had spent substantial amounts of its own money advertising the brand,[82] strayed from the agreement by conducting a sale and was terminated by Leegin.[83] Kay's Kloset sued Leegin alleging violation of section 1 of the Sherman Act and prevailed in the lower courts, based on an application of the *per se* rule established in *Dr. Miles*.[84]

On appeal to the Supreme Court, Leegin did not deny the existence of a minimum RPM,[85] but argued that "modern economic analysis" called for the overruling of *Dr. Miles* and the adoption of a rule of reason standard.[86] Its primary assertions were that its minimum RPM was procompetitive because it might attract more retailers for its products, encourage existing ones to carry more inventory, and provide more service and a pleasant shopping experience for customers.[87] It also contended that discounting undermined the brand's image.[88] The free rider argument was that, absent minimum RPM, retailers would have little incentive to provide these described services.[89]

The free rider theory ultimately played an important role in the majority's decision to overrule *Dr. Miles*.[90] Writing for a 5–4 majority, Justice Kennedy concluded that the *per se* rule should be limited in its application to restraints "that would always or almost always tend to restrict competition and decrease output."[91] Though Kennedy admitted that the "empirical evidence ... is limited,"[92] he cited extensively to economics (and economics-based) literature[93] to show a general economic consensus that minimum RPM can have procompetitive effects.[94] And, he identified two such benefits: the ability of RPM to (1) overcome free rider problems, encourage dealer services, and enhance interbrand competition;[95] and (2) facilitate entry of new firms and new products,[96] which is essentially a variation of the free rider argument.[97]

In his dissent, joined by Justices Souter, Ginsburg, and Stevens, Justice Breyer acknowledged that minimum RPM is sometimes beneficial.[98] But he rejected the notion that *Dr. Miles* should consequently be overruled in the absence of evidence demonstrating how often the benefits occur, and how easy or difficult it is "to separate the beneficial sheep from the antitrust goats."[99]

Breyer emphasized the lack of empirical data showing that free riding is a common occurrence, or has serious effects, and the disagreement among economists on the issue.[100] Clearly skeptical of the idea that free riding is a significant problem, he observed that "[w]e do, after all, live in an economy where firms, despite Dr. Miles' per se rule, still sell complex technical equipment (as well as expensive perfume and alligator billfolds) to consumers."[101] Naturally, if free riding is infrequent or its effects negligible, then the procompetitive uses of minimum RPM discussed in the economic literature would be inconsequential, especially when viewed against the practice's known consumer harms.

With respect to such harms, the majority made a point of describing and acknowledging some of the well-recognized ones: RPM can facilitate cartels at either the producer or retailer level,[102] and it can be used by dominant producers or retailers to hinder innovation and competition.[103] Kennedy refused, however, to attribute any antitrust significance to the undisputed evidence that minimum RPM almost always raises prices to consumers,[104] stating that higher prices could be consistent with either procompetitive or anticompetitive theories.[105] The dissent, in contrast, did attach importance to that evidence,[106] and suggested that uniformly higher prices can provide empirical support for an anticompetitive theory of minimum RPM.[107]

In the final analysis, the majority and the dissent held very different perspectives on the free rider issue. The majority relied heavily on, and deferred to, economic theories that postulated that free rider problems may result in an underprovision of dealer services, and RPM may remedy that problem. While the dissent did not dispute those theories, it noted the absence of good empirical data, made observations of the real world, and questioned whether the problem was more theoretical than practical.

II. The Free Rider Theory

A. The Classic Free Rider Analysis and Its Limited Application

Virtually all economists and antitrust commentators today agree that the now-classic free rider hypothesis set forth by Telser decades ago is theoretically sound within the parameters of that model.[108] The analysis demonstrated that, for some products, effective marketing depends on the willingness of dealers to provide showrooms, demonstrations of the product, or other specialized services. But dealers would be willing to provide these costly services only if they expect to recover the costs that must be incurred, which would be difficult if consumers in large numbers use their services but patronize discounters who offer no such services. By preventing discounting within a brand, minimum RPM can remove the fear of free riding and induce dealers to compete through service, thereby enhancing interbrand competition.[109]

This consensus on the theoretical validity of the free rider analysis was a central rationale for the *Sylvania* decision, and for the majority's overturning of *Dr. Miles* in *Leegin*. Yet, as Breyer pointed out in dissent in *Leegin*, economists disagree on how often free riding actually occurs and how significant its effects, and thus how common it is for RPM to confer benefits, and there is hardly any empirical data on the issue.[110] Even some commentators favorably disposed toward minimum RPM concede that the classic free rider hypothesis, though theoretically valid, has limited applicability in its original formulation.[111] It appears to be valid mostly in the sale of complex or novel products that require consumer education, or in-store demonstration to display their features, quality, and general appeal.

One case to which the classic theory probably applied is *Sylvania*[112] itself, where the manufacturer of a lesser-known television brand imposed territorial restraints on its dealers to induce promotional services.[113] Given the brand's weakness and the nature of the product, successful distribution likely required dealer demonstrations of the quality of the television picture and other features to potential customers. It was reasonable then to fear that, absent territorial limitations, "invading" dealers could attract, with lower prices, buyers who had been sold on the merits of Sylvania televisions through the full-service dealers' efforts. And, if the loss of sales to free riders is substantial, full-service dealers could lose the incentive to continue providing the promotional services that were evidently effective in increasing Sylvania's sales.[114]

Another frequently mentioned example of legitimate free rider concerns involves sophisticated audio and video equipment, where acoustic rooms and dealer demonstrations of the product's complex features are important for generating sales.[115] Additionally, because these products are relatively expensive and infrequently purchased, comparison price shopping is probably worthwhile to consumers.[116] If many buyers purchase from discounters after being educated by full-service dealers, the full-service dealers may eventually cease to provide the needed demonstrations, leading to an overall decrease in sales. In this context, some form of distribution restraint could alleviate a substantial free rider problem and enhance efficiency.[117]

Outside of these types of products, however, the classic free rider theory does not readily explain most distribution restraints. As Robert Pitofsky and others have noted, very few products require dealer demonstrations, consumer education, operational expertise, special showrooms and the like for effective marketing, and few dealers actually provide any such services.[118] Yet, minimum resale price maintenance has been observed in the sale of a wide range of products, including cosmetics, over-the-counter pharmaceuticals, pet food, vitamins, shampoo, men's underwear, small appliances, various toiletries, and jeans,[119] and women's fashion accessories (*Leegin*)—goods for which the classic free rider theory can have no plausible application.

Even for those goods for which special point-of-sale dealer services may be required, and thus free riding could be a problem, it is open to question how significant the problem is. Despite *Dr. Miles*'s long-standing per se prohibitions against minimum RPM, we do have retailers who sell complex technical equipment to consumers,[120] and there is nothing to indicate an underprovision of such goods in our economy.

Many who favor vertical restraints tend to automatically assume that a discounter is a free rider and also reflexively ascribe an efficiency motive to any observed minimum resale price-fixing. Take, for example, *Business Electronics v. Sharp Electronics Corp,*[121] a dealer termination case involving alleged resale price maintenance in the sale of calculators.[122] Although the Court continued to pay lip service to the *per se* rule against RPM (while overturning the jury verdict in favor of the plaintiff),[123] its opinion, written by Scalia, unequivocally embraced Chicago School doctrine, including the theory that minimum RPM is usually an efficiency response to free riding.[124]

Seeming to assume that the hypothetical generalities of the free rider theory applied,[125] Scalia theorized, without reference to any evidence, that "price cutting and some measure of service cutting usually go hand in hand,"[126] and that "a quite plausible purpose of the restriction [was] to enable Hartwell to provide better services...."[127] In essence, Scalia was suggesting that a discounter is necessarily a free rider, when in fact a discounter may simply be an efficient retailer who is passing along some of its cost savings to consumers. Although the free rider explanation did not seem plausible under the facts, the Court did not consider the possibility that the discounter might have been able to charge lower prices because of lower overall costs resulting from its efficiencies, and not because of inferior services and free riding.[128]

This tendency to automatically equate a discounter with a free rider likely stems from an implicit assumption that reasonable producers could not possibly prefer a less-efficient retailer to a more efficient one.[129] Therefore, distribution restraints favoring the higher-priced retailers are explicable only if the discounter is a free rider, who then has to be restrained for the greater good. But there is, in fact, an alternative, rational, and equally likely explanation. The higher-priced traditional dealers may have larger operations and account for more sales than the discounter. In that event, it would be economically sensible for producers to choose the higher-priced, but less efficient, retailers over the more efficient discounters who have less market share.[130] Thus, one cannot automatically conclude, from the producer's accommodation of the high-priced dealer at the expense of the discounter, that the discounter *must* be a free rider.

In *Leegin,* the defendant did not make the usual classic free rider claim, as it probably recognized that no matter how compelling the theory might be under some circumstances, the facts simply could not support such a claim. Kay's Kloset had heavily advertised the Brighton brand at its own expense, and was clearly not free riding on other retailers' promotions. There was no claim that Kay's Kloset provided less service than other dealers or even that it allocated insufficient shelf space to Brighton products. Common experience also informs us that women's handbags and fashion accessories are not information-intensive goods requiring consumer education, dealer demonstration, or other particularized sales expertise—services that lend themselves to free riding.

B. The Expansive Free Rider Theory

Some supporters of minimum RPM have long recognized the limitations of the classic free rider theory but have expanded the theory. Under the expanded model, dealer services include not only the tangible services that Telser had in mind, but also (1) general intangible services, such as pleasant employees, ambiance, and so forth;[131] and (2) reputation free riding, or "certification" free riding.[132]

1. Intangible Services

The gist of the intangible services free rider argument is that many consumers desire a pleasant shopping experience.[133] Prestigious store locations, plush surroundings, and other intangibles, therefore, enhance the product's value to the consumer.[134] Free riding, the argument continues, may cause retailers to underprovide these enhancements.[135] Vertical minimum price-fixing, in ameliorating or eliminating the problem, would hence be efficient.[136]

In its brief to the Supreme Court, Leegin offered this theory, or a variant of it. It said that "attractive presentation and customer service [are] central to the shopping experience,"[137] and that its price floor was designed to encourage dealers to pay "special attention" to prospective Brighton customers and provide "high-quality service."[138] It also noted that the most frequently cited rationale for minimum RPM was "to ensure that dealers provide demand-creating services"[139] that they would otherwise be disinclined to provide because of free riding.[140]

In an amicus brief in support of Leegin, a group of economists likewise suggested that, for women's accessories, free riding may involve dealer services such as "longer store hours, more convenient or prestigious store locations, better-trained and more enthusiastic employees, or favoritism in shelf placement."[141] They argued that free riding concerns may cause retailers to offer less of this type of services than is optimal for society.[142] In eliminating free riding, minimum RPM would encourage the provision of these intangible services and benefit consumers.[143]

This argument, however, is fundamentally flawed. While general amenities can indeed enhance a product's value, at least to some consumers, it is not clear how *free riding* can plausibly occur, much less become a severe problem that must be remedied through distribution restraints. As a practical matter, buyers cannot benefit from a store's pleasant and efficient employees, its convenient hours and locations, its nice ambiance, its fuller inventory, or its generous return policy, for example, while patronizing another store. If these services are invulnerable to free riding, then intrabrand competition *cannot* adversely affect their provision.

The United States seems to recognize this point and, in its amicus brief supporting Leegin, does not make a similar free rider argument. Instead it contends that, even absent free riding, minimum RPM can encourage this sort of service, which could increase interbrand competition.[144] But the logic of this argument is also elusive, though the majority in *Leegin* accepted it.[145]

As long as free riding is not a likely risk, then, in a free market, we would expect dealers to *voluntarily* invest to provide the enhancements truly valued by consumers, without the need for RPM. Prospective buyers who attribute substantial value to a pleasant shopping experience would presumably be willing to pay a higher price for the product in order to enjoy the added value. And, dealers can be expected to compete for sales by providing the enhanced value these consumers desire, as efficiently as possible.

If some dealers choose *not* to offer these intangible services, and provided the services at issue are not vulnerable to free riding, the logical conclusion must be that *some* consumers do *not* value these intangible services, and would prefer to pay lower prices for the unadorned product. If free riding is not an issue, then it is difficult to see how imposing minimum RPM could be beneficial to consumers: it would only prevent some retailers from catering to the class of customers who do not want the services, without benefiting those who do, because those services were not at risk in the first place. The net result would only be less consumer choice with no significant countervailing consumer benefit.

It is also unclear how offering many of these intangible services would "attract customers away from other brands" and increase interbrand competition, as the United States argued in its *Leegin* amicus brief.[146] Most retailers today are multibrand dealers, while the tangible services typically mentioned[147] are not specific to the brand subject to a minimum RPM arrangement. An attractive store, pleasant employees, and other enhancements to the shopping experience are amenities that cannot be limited *only* to those customers interested in the brand protected by RPM but will necessarily be enjoyed by *all* customers patronizing the store. Thus, it is hard to follow the logic of the argument that minimum RPM would foster interbrand competition, even in the absence of free riding, by encouraging the provision of these intangible services.

2. Reputation or Image Free riding: "Certification" or "Signaling" Free Riding

A theoretically more plausible expansive free rider claim that some commentators have put forth involves reputation or image free riding. The basic argument here is that certain retailers invest substantially to develop and maintain reputations for high fashion, quality, or special expertise. They incur costly expenditures on rent for prestigious store locations, the maintenance of an appropriate décor, salaries for bright employees, and so forth. Because of their reputation, these retailers' decision to carry a brand enhances the value of that brand, and also "certifies" (or "signals") to consumers that the chosen products have qualities that appeal to discriminating customers.[148]

The free rider argument is that, if discounters are allowed to offer the same brands at lower prices, consumers would buy from them instead, after benefiting from the prestige retailer's signals on what products are deemed desirable.[149] Deprived of sales diverted to discounters, reputable retailers may lose their incentive to maintain their reputation or carry the product, and consumers would no longer be able to rely on the prestige retailers' signaling, causing harm to all concerned.[150] Minimum RPM, it is argued, prevents free riding, thereby assuring sufficient profits for the prestige retailers to maintain their image and continue serving their certification or signaling function. Leegin presented a version of this argument, by asserting that its minimum RPM policy was procompetitive because it protected its brand image.[151] Its amici likewise asserted that the policy protected prestige retailers from reputation free riding.[152]

This expanded free rider argument, though theoretically legitimate, seems weak. Reputation free riding is indeed plausible in that consumers may covet brand *X* jeans, for example, because Bloomingdales carries it; and, in the absence of minimum RPM, they may search for and purchase it from a discounter. However, from an economic and antitrust perspective, such free riding is not harmful to social welfare unless it is so pervasive that it interferes with the availability of the service or product. Whether that happens often with respect to reputation free riding cannot be easily answered empirically. There is certainly no demonstration that it does.

For reputation free riding to be pervasive, most image conscious customers who take their cues from Bloomingdales, for example, would have to be willing to spend time reviewing Bloomingdales's selections to learn what is in style and then turn to no-frills stores to scout for and buy those items on discount. But how realistic is that assumption? Consumers who value their time and/or the shopping experience, as many do, are unlikely to free ride in this fashion. Those purchasing gifts are also unlikely to free ride because, rightly or wrongly, having the reputable store's label on the gift, or its packaging, or its gift receipt, is often important, and purchase of the same item from a discounter would not be an acceptable alternative. As long as enough customers benefiting from Bloomingdales's signals purchase from Bloomingdales to allow it to recoup its investment in developing its reputation, the fact that *some* free riding surely occurs is unimportant.[153]

Even assuming that image free riding is substantial for select products, it still should not matter unless it adversely affects the prestige retailers' willingness to continue to provide the service or product. While there is no empirical evidence pointing in either direction, reputation free riding seems unlikely to have this drastic effect. First, higher-priced prestige stores typically have a head start over other stores in the sale of the fashionable or quality product in question.[154] After Bloomingdales has selected a product to carry based on its assessment of the product's stylishness or quality, for example, it will necessarily take some time for the "certification" to circulate among consumers, and for other dealers to act on it. During the inevitable time lag, Bloomingdales will be able to charge premium prices without fear of losing sales to discounters. By the time any substantial reputation free riding might occur for a given product, the prestige retailer may well have already recouped its image building investment.

Second, costs incurred in reputation development are usually not specific to a brand but are similar to general fixed costs for the retailer.[155] Free riding in connection with a few select brands is unlikely to so diminish the incentives of the reputable retailer handling many brands that it would give up investing in its reputation.[156] Stated differently, unless severe free riding on reputation occurs over a wide range of products, it is doubtful that Bloomingdales would be discouraged from maintaining its image and carrying on its certification role in the retail market. From an economic perspective, then, reputation free riding should rarely warrant antitrust accommodation. There is certainly no evidence of an underprovision of luxury goods or of upscale stores in our economy. Nor is there indication of a trend, among elite stores, toward failure or compelled conversion to no-frills formats.

Furthermore, implicit in the free rider justification for distribution restraints (though rarely noted) is the premise that the services sought to be protected benefit consumer welfare; otherwise, they would not be worth protection. That premise is generally valid where the classic free rider theory is applicable. For example, skilled dealer demonstration effectively showed consumers the personal computer's utility and ease of use when it was first introduced in the early 1980s, which allowed it to quickly and successfully penetrate the market, becoming the product that most of us cannot now do without.[157]

However, once we move beyond information-intensive services, particularly for complex electronic products for which the classic free rider theory has most applicability, not all "services" unambiguously benefit consumers. Bloomingdale's decision to carry brand X jeans, for example, no doubt enhances the image of the brand in the eyes of consumers and allows the producer to charge higher prices; and RPM would serve to maintain that enhanced image. While that "service" is certainly profitable to both the producer and Bloomingdales, the consumer benefit is not as readily apparent.

Similarly, Bloomingdale's "certification" of brand X jeans is informative or valuable to consumers in the sense that it reveals what discriminating customers are likely to purchase. Consumers may also know that they would be recognized as having the characteristics of such customers if they, too, purchase the chosen brand. Again, it is open to question whether this "service" is so beneficial to consumer welfare that we should seek to protect it from free rider effects through minimum RPM.

I recognize that, in administering antitrust law, we usually do not make judgments about the subjective value of consumer choices but must take the choices as we find them. But the legal issue here is not whether antitrust law should be in the business of regulating strategies aimed at persuading consumers to pay high prices for the perception of enhanced value that may or may not be objectively based; I agree that is not the role of antitrust law. Rather, the issue is whether the producer should be permitted to eliminate price competition among its dealers on the grounds that preventing such competition enhances the brand's image and informs consumers on the image status of products. My contention is that it should not. The benefits of reputation free riding seem insufficiently important to justify restricting a major dimension of competition—price—especially in light of the known anticompetitive effects of minimum RPM.

B. Facilitating Market Entry

Probably the most persuasive argument that has been presented in favor of relaxing the *per se* rule against minimum RPM is that the practice can facilitate new market entry.[158] Producers contemplating entry into a market with a new product (or into a new region with an existing product) usually need the assistance of dealers. But it would be difficult to attract dealers willing to make the necessary investments unless they have some assurance that their investments would be recoverable.

Without minimum RPM, dealers may not have that assurance because later-appointed dealers, who have lower costs because they did not invest in the early market development efforts, would be able to undercut the pioneer dealers' prices and increase sales, while benefiting from the pioneer dealers' earlier efforts.[159] The pioneer dealers would then be forced to reduce their prices, making it difficult for them to recover their costs in helping launch the product. To the extent that minimum RPM may help manufacturers recruit dealers for new products, it could be efficient, and a strict *per se* rule may be inappropriate in this situation.

III. Perspectives On Free Riding: When Does It Warrant Legal Accommodation?

Though the above discussion argues that the free rider explanation for minimum RPM is greatly exaggerated and overused, free riding surely does occur, which raises the question of when it should warrant legal action or accommodation. Unfortunately, the term "free rider" has acquired pejorative connotations that conjure up images of slackers who are unjustly enriched from the efforts of others.[160] This is especially true in intellectual property law, where the concept of free riding is narrowly focused on whether the alleged infringer has received a benefit from an invention without paying for it, leading to an obsession with efforts to eliminate all free riding.[161]

The distaste for free riding found in IP law has spilled over to antitrust law. Some commentators now approach the concept of free riding in antitrust from an almost property-right perspective, viewing minimum RPM as giving producers or dealers a legal right to fully capture the value of their promotional or retailing investments and to prevent any dealer from reaping where it has not sown.[162] Under this view, a discounter selling an identical item as Bloomingdales at a lower price would probably be seen as an undesirable free rider, simply because Bloomingdale's reputation enhanced the desirability of the item, on which the discounter was able to capitalize without compensating Bloomingdales.

This perspective is unnecessarily negative and undesirable. In reality, free riding is not an unmitigated evil that must be rooted out wherever it may be found. Instead, it can be viewed more favorably as the positive externalities of one actor's activities spilling over to benefit another. As Breyer mentioned in dissent in *Leegin,* free riding is ubiquitous in our economy.[163] Its effects can be beneficial on balance; and the law generally tolerates it.[164] For example, as homeowners, many of us plant beautiful gardens that can be enjoyed by our neighbors, and yet no one assumes that we have a right to demand compensation from them.[165] Or a popular department store such as Macy's may increase traffic (and sales) to lesser-known businesses located nearby, but the law does not "protect" Macy's against the smaller businesses' benefiting from its positive externalities.

Free competition is widely accepted as the norm in our economy. It logically follows that any deviation from it should be tolerated *only* when and to the extent necessary to correct for market imperfections that make free competition unworkable. The current expansion of intellectual property rights notwithstanding, even IP protection has traditionally been based on similar principles. Patent and copyright laws provide rights limited in time and scope to authors and inventors whose work meets certain requirements, for the purpose of creating incentives to innovate.[166]

From an economic perspective, then, free riding should be considered a social harm warranting legal accommodation only when it is so substantial that it undermines the actor's incentives to produce the beneficial activities.[167] In the case of patent and copyright laws, Congress essentially determined that free riding presents such a strong risk of discouraging innovation that it passed legislation effectively prohibiting free riding for a limited period of time.[168] Outside of the intellectual property law context, though, the law makes no such assumptions and does not automatically treat free riding as a detriment that must be remedied wherever it exists. Society, for example, does not presume that we will be discouraged from planting our flower gardens unless the law allows us to fully internalize the benefits of our labor.[169] Or that Macy's will lack adequate incentives to advertise or generate good will if potential customers attracted to the area by Macy's are allowed to drift off to patronize neighboring stores without compensation being paid to Macy's.

Applying the same logic in the context of vertical relationships, we should not be so quick to accept the argument that minimum RPM is socially beneficial because it remedies free riding. Because price is an important aspect of competition,[170] and our economy normally favors competition, any restraints on such competition should be considered beneficial only if a severe free rider problem exists, the restraint actually provides an efficient cure, and there are no less restrictive alternatives available. This suggests that at least a few conditions must be present.

First, at a minimum, a free riding problem must be identifiable. This means the services at issue must be desired by consumers, actually provided by dealers, and important in effective marketing. The services must also be susceptible to free riding. Second, the free rider effects must be strong enough to substantially diminish the full-service dealers' profits and their incentives to continue providing the service before they should have any antitrust significance. Third, the service sought to be encouraged through distribution restraints, logically, should be beneficial to consumers, and the restraint must benefit rather than harm consumers and the economy; otherwise, the distribution restraint would not enhance consumer welfare.

The analysis of the free rider theory in the previous section shows that these conditions are not often satisfied. There is certainly no empirical evidence to support an argument that free riding is a serious problem. Even the majority in *Leegin* could only say that the "limited" empirical evidence "does not suggest efficient uses of the agreements are infrequent or hypothetical."[171] In the absence of good empirical evidence, there is reason to be skeptical of the assumption that free riding generally presents a severe economic problem that must be addressed through minimum RPM.

As Breyer perceptively noted in *Leegin*: "[O]ne can easily *imagine* a dealer who refuses to provide important presale services...lest customers [free ride]....But does it happen often?"[172] He suggested that it does not, observing that we obviously have stores selling complex equipment and prestige goods in our economy.[173]

The real question that *Leegin* raised was this: in view of the consensus among economists that free rider concerns *may* sometimes be legitimate and minimum RPM *may* sometimes be procompetitive, should a *per se* rule apply? The majority believed that it should not, while the dissent disagreed. In my view, the dissent has the better of the debate. The procompetitive case that is made for minimum RPM is largely theoretical, with at most some weak supporting empirical evidence. In contrast, the anticompetitive effects of RPM are real, significant, and sometimes well-documented.[174] Under modern decision theory, whether or not minimum RPM can lead to positive welfare effects in some cases should not be dispositive in fashioning an appropriate antitrust rule. It is more important to determine the frequency and magnitude of the benefits relative to the harms, and the availability of other less anticompetitive and equally effective alternatives.

IV. Potential Anticompetitive Effects and Less Restrictive Alternatives

A. Facilitating Manufacturer or Dealer Cartel, or Excluding Competitors

Even those who approve of minimum RPM generally concede its most commonly recognized potential anticompetitive effects. In *Leegin,* the majority acknowledged that the practice can be used anticompetitively to facilitate a cartel or otherwise stabilize prices at either the producer or dealer level.[175] It also agreed that, even without concerted action, RPM can be anticompetitive if it results from pressure from a dominant dealer, or is imposed by one or more powerful producers acting alone.[176]

Minimum RPM can facilitate a manufacturers' price-fixing agreement (explicit or implicit) by removing the participants' incentive to "cheat." In a "normal" market, each producer in a cartel is tempted to secretly grant price concessions to retailers because retailers would likely react by reducing the product's resale prices, thereby leading to higher sales. But if retail prices cannot be reduced because of minimum RPM, this temptation would be eliminated because a producer knows that, unless it also reduces its RPM price, any price concessions granted to retailers would not lead to additional sales. And, because retail prices are transparent, any attempt by a producer to couple a clandestine wholesale price cut with reduced RPM would easily be detected by its coconspirators. Knowing that, a producer is less likely to destabilize a manufacturer cartel by cheating.[177]

Minimum RPM can also be used to facilitate a dealer cartel.[178] Ward Bowman, a distinguished economist, noted in a seminal article that producers are often pressured by dealer groups to help enforce their price-fixing agreements, under the guise of resale price maintenance.[179] Historical examples show that dealer-initiated RPM is not merely a theoretical concern but a real one.[180] Indeed, there is ample evidence demonstrating that the resale price maintenance in *Dr. Miles* was "imposed" by the manufacturer at the behest of a group of retail drug stores to implement their horizontal price-fixing agreement.[181] While the majority in *Leegin* acknowledged these harmful uses of RPM, it believed that they could be condemned under the rule of reason.[182]

Leegin also recognized that resale price maintenance can be anticompetitive, even without concerted action, if it is implemented under pressure from one or more powerful dealers acting alone, usually to forestall innovation or competition from a more efficient or innovative dealer.[183] Since there is strong empirical evidence that the retailing market has become much more concentrated since 1975,[184] the risks of this type of anticompetitive RPM will only increase in the future.

An RPM imposed by a powerful producer acting alone can also be anticompetitive, since such a producer can use RPM to guarantee generous margins to retailers to induce them not to carry the products of smaller, but innovative, up-and-coming rivals.[185] This concern is not purely theoretical as existing data show that at least some subsets of some producer markets have become more concentrated in the past three decades.[186]

B. Raising Prices

There is virtually no dispute that RPM almost always leads to higher consumer prices.[187] For a period of 45 years, Congress permitted states to override *Dr. Miles* by passing "fair trade" laws legalizing RPM agreements.[188] Because some states chose to experiment with "fair trade" laws while others did not,[189] and studies were consequently conducted, we have reliable empirical data comparing prices of similar items in states where RPM was legal and in states where it was not.[190] The data is unambiguous: consumer prices were between 19 percent and 27 percent higher in "fair trade" states than in "free trade" states.[191] More recently, in an RPM case brought by the FTC against major music companies that was subsequently settled, the FTC estimated that the defendants' pricing restraints cost purchasers of music CDs in excess of $480 million.[192]

The majority and the dissent differed in their approach to this clear evidence of higher prices. For the dissent, the fact that minimum RPM almost inevitably produces higher prices is at least suspect,[193] whereas the majority attaches no antitrust significance to it.[194] Higher prices may reflect more services to consumers, which could be procompetitive because they could enhance demand for the good.

It is true that the data showing uniformly higher prices under RPM does not empirically answer the question of whether consumers received enhanced value worth the increase in price.[195] Consequently, the fact that consumers almost always pay higher prices under minimum resale price maintenance cannot *prove* that resale price maintenance is, by definition, anticompetitive. However, given that price is the "central nervous system of the economy,"[196] and the basic antitrust assumption is that consumers should have a choice in price/quality tradeoffs, the consistently and substantially higher prices that result from private restrictions on price competition is at least suggestive of anticompetitive effect. It is hard to see, for example, what sort of "enhanced value" consumers could possibly have received in return for higher prices paid across the board for music CDs as a result of vertical price restraints.

C. Adverse Effects of Restricting Intrabrand Price Competition

Intrabrand price competition has more value, and its suppression has more harm, than proponents of RPM generally attribute to it. Permitting price competition within brands, especially popular brands, encourages new or existing multibrand dealers to develop innovative and cost-effective ways of performing normal retailing functions, or to offer different (but not inferior) services.[197] But if price competition for most products is prohibited, there would be little incentive for such innovation. Minimum RPM does not permit efficient retailers to pass along their efficiencies to customers by reducing prices. If Costco cannot hope to increase sales of popular brands (by reducing prices), it would have had less reason to conceive of an innovative sales format that relies on volume sales at narrow margins in large warehouse settings that has proven very successful.[198] And, our retail economy would be the poorer for it.

Chicago School economists tend to dismiss the importance of intrabrand competition, which minimum RPM clearly restricts, and their views have greatly influenced the law of vertical restraints. *Sylvania* and *Leegin,* for example, both endorsed the Chicago view that interbrand competition is "the primary concern of antitrust law."[199] Other cases have similarly declared that protecting intrabrand competition "is not a concern of the antitrust laws."[200] There are, however, dissenting voices stressing that competition at *all* levels of distribution is, in fact, beneficial to consumer welfare.[201]

Economist Robert Steiner, in particular, contends strongly in his writings that vigorous intrabrand competition actually stimulates and enhances interbrand competition, rather than diminishes it.[202] He explains that intense intrabrand competition on a popular brand tends to minimize retail markups of that brand which, in turn, often results in lower retail prices on competing brands that the multibrand retailer also sells.[203]

Intrabrand competition is, in fact, vital when one or more brands within a market enjoy substantial product differentiation.[204] Strong brand name acceptance insulates a brand from interbrand competition to a certain degree. Limiting *intra*brand competition in these circumstances is particularly detrimental because the *Leegin* and *Sylvania* Chicago School presumption that interbrand competition will constrain the "exploitation of intrabrand market power"[205] would be invalid.

D. Less Restrictive Alternatives

In view of these potential anticompetitive effects, even if RPM does remedy a free rider problem, there should be some consideration of whether less anticompetitive, equally effective, and no more costly, means could be used to achieve the same results. In some instances, a producer could grant promotional allowances to dealers to provide the desired services. Or, it could separately contract for the services with dealers, or perform the services itself, such as engaging in national advertising. Where it is feasible, the producer could have dealers charge consumers separately for the services. Professor Warren Grimes and others have already written extensively on the issue,[206] and I will not belabor the point here, except to note that the Court in *Leegin* does not seem to have taken this factor into consideration.

V. Policy Implications

A. The Full-Fledged Rule of Reason

Were it not for the inconvenient realities of antitrust litigation, the application of a rule of reason standard for minimum RPM would hardly seem radical. After all, if there is general consensus in the economic literature that free riding does exist and, hence, minimum RPM may have procompetitive effects, having a standard that looks at all factors relating to a restraint to determine if it is, on balance, anticompetitive or procompetitive seems eminently sensible.

The problem with a full rule of reason standard, however, is that it often operates as a de facto *legality* rule, particularly in vertical restraint cases after *Sylvania*. Full-fledged rule of reason cases are exceedingly expensive and difficult to litigate.[207] Plaintiffs must employ economic experts to define the relevant market, calculate market shares, measure elasticity of demand or supply, examine and calibrate barriers to entry and the like, in addition to proving the existence of the restraint. Litigation often becomes a dueling match between competing experts with contradictory economic theories on these issues.

One commentator has portrayed rule of reason cases as presenting "a defendant's paradise."[208] Another has quite aptly described the test as "a euphemism for endless economic inquiry resulting in a defense verdict."[209] Judge Douglas Ginsburg of the D.C. Circuit Court of Appeals, a former assistant attorney general who headed the Antitrust Division under the Reagan Administration, once characterized the *Sylvania* rule of reason legal standard as one of *de facto* legality.[210]

Given the realities of its application, if the *Sylvania* rule of reason test is adopted for minimum RPM post-*Leegin,* the adverse impact on consumer welfare could be significant. Under this formidable standard, most private plaintiffs (who are usually terminated discounters) would likely be deterred from challenging any resale price maintenance arrangement, even ones that are highly suspect. Though federal antitrust enforcers could continue to litigate these cases, their resources are obviously limited. The knowledge that resale price maintenance will probably face few legal challenges, post-*Leegin,* may embolden some producers and dealers to enter into more vertical pricing agreements that are anticompetitive.[211]

A rule of reason standard may also lead to more dealer-driven resale price maintenance arrangements, by weakening the hand of reluctant producers under pressure from powerful dealers to adopt the practice. Before *Leegin,* unwilling producers could at least resist with an argument that what was demanded of them was per se illegal. A full rule of reason standard, especially with its defendant-friendly results in real world application, would take away the force of that argument and make it more difficult for a weak producer to stand firm against powerful dealers, either acting alone or in concert.

B. A Quick-Look Proposal

While *Leegin* has obviously made it very difficult to challenge minimum resale price maintenance in the future, the general prediction that the practice will effectively become per se lawful going forward need not become a reality. In establishing a rule of reason as the legal test for minimum RPM, the majority in *Leegin* took pains to admonish courts to recognize, and prohibit, the anticompetitive uses of RPM.[212] It listed a few factors that could be considered, including the number of producers within the market engaged in RPM,[213] and the source of the restraints.[214] And it further suggested that courts could "devise rules over time for offering proof, or even presumptions where justified" to ensure that the rule of reason is effectively implemented.[215] The majority, then, clearly did not envision a de facto *legality* rule, as the rule of reason for vertical non-price restraints has become after *Sylvania.*

In light of these instructions from the Court, it would be consistent with *Leegin* to apply, in minimum RPM cases, the "quick-look" rule of reason test that is now employed in many horizontal restraint cases, rather than the full rule of reason.[216] Under a quick-look, if only one or two nondominant producers among many in the relevant market voluntarily imposed minimum resale price maintenance, then the behavior most likely would have little anticompetitive effect and should be analyzed under the full rule of reason. Or, if a quick-look evaluation shows that the producer was a new entrant to the market, and there is therefore a likely free rider explanation for resale price maintenance, a full rule of reason test could also be triggered.

But, if a quick-look reveals no credible free rider problem, and the involved producer is not a new entrant to the market seeking to attract dealer investment, then neither a formal market analysis nor empirical proof of anticompetitive effect should be required. This would alleviate the need for plaintiffs to engage in the expensive and time-consuming process of putting forth economic experts to duel with the defendant's experts to try to define the market, and establish and apply abstract and technical models to the ill-defined markets, in an effort to show anticompetitive effect.

It would also dispense with the need for plaintiffs to prove *actual* anticompetitive effect, e.g., demonstrate that minimum RPM was adopted to facilitate a horizontal cartel. This would reduce the risk that resale price maintenance with horizontal effects, which are usually severely anticompetitive, would escape unpunished because of problems of proof. Where an RPM is used to facilitate a horizontal agreement, the agreement is often tacit and thus difficult to prove. Moreover, having to prove the source of an RPM could also be extraordinarily challenging.[217] Under a quick-look rule of reason, so long as the plaintiff shows a vertical agreement to fix higher prices, and no apparent procompetitive reason for the agreement, a prima facie case would be established.

This approach would be very similar to that taken by the Seventh Circuit Court of Appeals in *Toys "R" Us, Inc. v. F.T.C.*[218] and *General Leaseways Inc. v. National Truck Leasing Association,*[219] two (non-RPM) cases in which the courts entertained but quickly dismissed the defendants' free rider justification under what appeared to be a quick-look rule of reason review. In neither case did the court require formal market analysis or elaborate proof of anticompetitive effect.

In *Toys "R" Us* (TRU), the FTC charged TRU with inducing a manufacturer group boycott of TRU's competitors by declining to sell them the same toys that were sold to TRU.[220] While TRU did not directly challenge the appropriateness of the *per se* rule to group boycotts, it did so indirectly by making arguments relevant in rule of reason cases: it raised a free rider justification for its role in the group boycott, and an assertion that the FTC had failed to prove TRU's market power and, hence, the anticompetitive effect of its actions.[221]

Instead of simply dismissing these challenges as irrelevant to a per se case, Judge Diane Wood considered but rejected them. With respect to the free rider issue, she observed that, while TRU did perform various services for the toy manufacturers—advertising, warehousing, and keeping good inventory year round—whereas its competitors did not, it received separate compensation from the manufacturers for those services.[222] Thus,

Wood concluded, "there was little or no opportunity to 'free' ride on anything here." Because the *manufacturer* was paying for TRU's services, the services were "not susceptible to free riding."[223]

With respect to the argument that the FTC failed to make its case as it had not proven the defendant's market power, Woods held that "no . . . elaborate market analysis was necessary."[224] It was enough for the FTC to have shown that the TRU-orchestrated boycott caused the manufacturers to reduce output to TRU's competitors, and "that reduction in output protected TRU from having to lower its prices to meet the [warehouse] clubs' price levels."[225]

Similarly, in *General Leaseways,* after carefully analyzing the defendant's free rider claim under a quick-look rule of reason, Judge Richard Posner rejected the argument as implausible[226] and found the horizontal market division illegal per se. The core mission of the defendant, an association of local truck-leasing companies, was to coordinate a reciprocal service arrangement among members binding them to provide emergency repair service for other members' customers whose leased trucks broke down in their vicinity; the service provider was paid by the member whose customer received service.[227] The association, however, also imposed location and other restrictions on its members, effectively prohibiting them from competing against each other.[228] In response to an antitrust challenge alleging that the restrictions were unlawful, the association asserted a free rider defense, arguing that the restrictions were designed to prevent members from free riding on other member's efforts to promote the association trademark and on their repair service.[229]

In a detailed analysis, Posner concluded that the free rider explanation was implausible for several reasons.[230] Because members paid the service provider for emergency work performed for their customers, there could be no free riding of services.[231] Moreover, although members with more locations (and therefore more trucks on the road) would potentially need more service, they would also potentially *provide* more service out of their multiple locations.[232] Thus, a member with an additional location cannot be said to be a free rider. Finally, Posner noted that association members made minimal efforts to advertise the association trademark[233] and, therefore, no claim of free riding with respect to others' promotional efforts could be made.

After finding the free rider justification without merit, Posner proceeded to analyze whether the defendant had sufficient market power to cause anticompetitive effect. Though the plaintiff had not presented a formal market analysis, Posner found that the evidence it did present—higher prices in local markets with fewer competing firms—was sufficient to find substantial anticompetitive potential.[234] This finding, Posner concluded, was sufficient under the rule of reason because the defendant's free rider justification was unpersuasive.[235]

Toys "R" Us and *General Leaseways* show a very sensible approach that could be used in RPM rule of reason cases post-*Leegin,* instead of a full-fledged rule of reason test. Courts could first see if there is a credible procompetitive justification for the resale price maintenance. Specifically, is there an apparent substantial free rider problem that is being addressed by the vertical price-fixing? Is the producer a new entrant to the market, introducing a new product, or expanding into a new regional market?

If no valid free riding claim or procompetitive justification is apparent, then the existence of a private restraint limiting intrabrand price competition (RPM) should be sufficiently suspect to warrant condemnation. The plaintiff would not be required to undertake a lengthy, expensive, economic market analysis. Even assuming that *Leegin* might be interpreted to require weightier proof of anticompetitive effect, a formal market power analysis is not necessarily required, as proof of market power is merely a proxy for demonstrating anticompetitive effect.[236] Instead, the plaintiff should be permitted to meet its burden by showing, for example, that the resale price maintenance has resulted in higher profit margins for the brand with no noticeable added value to the product.

Conclusion

The free rider explanation for vertical restraints has become overbroad and overused since *Sylvania*. While one can easily *imagine* dire consequences from free riding, the reality is that there is no apparent underprovision of complex electronic goods, or luxury, highly fashionable, or quality branded goods in our economy. This suggests that free riding, which surely does take place sometimes, does not usually cause much consumer or economic harm. Despite the negative connotations of the term, free riding, ubiquitous in our economy, is not necessarily harmful to consumer welfare and does not have to be eliminated wherever it occurs. Consequently, in the absence of good empirical data, there is insufficient basis to assume that minimum RPM usually confers substantial benefits to consumers.

The Supreme Court, nonetheless, has spoken. Minimum vertical price-fixing will, hereafter, no longer be prohibited per se but will be analyzed under the rule of reason. Given the real anticompetitive dangers associated with minimum RPM, however, it would be a mistake to apply the full rule of reason, which usually operates as a de facto *legality* rule in real world antitrust litigation. Instead, the quick-look rule of reason that is often used in horizontal restraint cases can be applied, which would make it easier for courts to identify and prohibit the anticompetitive uses of minimum RPM. This standard would also be consistent with *Leegin*'s vision of the rule of reason as a legal standard that will actually separate the "bad" RPM from the "good."

Notes

1. 220 U.S. 373 (1911).

2. Richard A. Posner, *The Next Step in the Antitrust Treatment of Restricted Distribution: per se Legality,* 48 U. CHI. L. REV. 6 (1980).

3. 485 U.S. 717 (1988).

4. 433 U.S. 36 (1977).

5. 127 S.Ct. 2705 (2007).

6. Tying, an upstream-power vertical restraint, is subject to a modified *per se* rule, but that rule, because of its requirements that a plaintiff demonstrate market power or forcing in the tying product and an economic basis for treating the tying and tied products as separate products, has been equated with a "structured rule of reason." Lawrence A. Sullivan & Warren S. Grimes, THE LAW OF ANTITRUST: AN INTEGRATED HANDBOOK, at 419 (2d ed. 2006) (describing the rule governing tie-ins as a "modified per se rule" or "structured rule of reason").

7. 388 U.S. 365 (1967).

8. One of the first and most insightful critics of *Sylvania* is the economist Robert Steiner, *Sylvania EconomicsBA Critique,* 60 ANTITRUST L.J. 41 (1991).

9. 248 U.S. 215, 239–240 (1918). The phrase is taken from the New Testament's Book of Matthew, 25:26 ("You wicked and lazy servant, you knew that I reap where I have not sown, and gather where I have not scattered seed.")

10. Benjamin Klein & John Shepard Wiley Jr., *Competitive Price Discrimination as an Antitrust Justification for Intellectual Property Refusals to Deal,* 70 Antitrust L.J. 599, 617 (2003) (" . . . price discrimination is a tool that allows intellectual property holders to collect more of the economic value of their property. This added return increases the rewards to innovation and thereby prompts more innovation.").

11. Speech of Deputy Assistant Attorney General Masoudi, Intellectual Property and Competition: Four Principles for Encouraging Innovation (April 12, 2006), available at http://www.usdoj.gov/atr/public/speeches/215645.pdf.

12. 540 U.S. 398, 407 (2004).

13. 405 U.S. 596 (1972).

14. *United States v. Topco Assoc.,* 1983 CCH Trade Cas. ¶74,391 (E.D. Ill. 1972) (allowing Topco to establish primary territories and require compensation for promotion expenditures when a member sells in another member's primary territory).

15. 792 F.2d 210 (D.C. Cir. 1986), cert. denied, 479 U.S. 1033 (1987).

16. 792 F.2d. at 221.

17. *United States v. Addyston Pipe & Steel Co.,* 85 F. 271 (6th Cir. 1898) (Taft, J.), *modified* and *aff'd,* 175 211 (1899).

18. 744 F. 2d 588 (7th Cir. 1984).

19. 416 F.3d 29 (D.C. Cir. 2005). For a similar result on analogous facts, *see Yamaha Motor Co. v. FTC,* 657 F.2d 971 (8th Cir. 1981) (restraints on competition in products not subject to the joint venture deemed unlawful).

20. *Polygram*, 416 F.3d at 37–38.

21. Lester G. Telser, *Why Should Manufacturers Want Fair Trade?* 3 J. L. & Econ. 86 (1960).

22. *Id.* at 91.

23. Robert H. Bork, The Antitrust Paradox 291–98 (1978).

24. *Id.* at 296.

25. Richard A. Posner, *Antitrust Policy and the Supreme Court: An Analysis of the Restricted Distribution, Horizontal Merger and Potential Competition Decisions,* 75 Colum. L. Rev. 282, 283–88 (1975).

26. *See* William S. Comanor, *Vertical Territorial and Customer Restrictions: White Motor and Its Aftermath,* 81 Harv. L. Rev. 1419 (1968).

27. *Sylvania*, 433 U.S. at 54–55.

28. *Id.* at 54.

29. *Id.*

30. Benjamin Klein & Kevin Murphy, *Vertical Restraints as Contract Enforcement Mechanisms,* 31 J. L. & Econ. 265, 266 (1988) ("...retailers may merely take the additional money created by the vertical restraint and continue to free ride").

31. Robert Pitofsky, *In Defense of Discounters: The No-Frills Case for a Per Se Rule Against Vertical Price Fixing,* 71 Geo L.J. 1487, 1493 (1983). (If presale service "is only marginally relevant to the product's success, the manufacturer should be indifferent as to whether it is provided."); F. M. Scherer & David Ross, Industrial Market Structure and Economic Performance 552 (3d ed. 1990) ("relatively few products qualify...under Telser's free-rider theory").

32. *Id.*

33. Philip E. Areeda & Herbert Hovenkamp, Antitrust Law, ¶1601e, at 13 (2d ed. 2004).

34. Robert L. Steiner, *Manufacturers' Promotional Allowances, Free riders and Vertical Restraints,* 36 Antitrust Bull. 383 (1991).

35. 485 U.S. 717 (1988). See the discussion of *Sharp* in part IV, *infra*.

36. Pitofsky, *supra* note 31, at 1493 (recognizing that dealers will recognize when a presale service is essential and provide it or "be driven out of business").

37. Howard Marvel, *The Resale Price Maintenance Controversy: Beyond Conventional Wisdom,* 63 Antitrust L.J. 59, 62–73 (1994).

38. Among Steiner's contributions to the literature are Robert L. Steiner, *Sylvania Economics B A Critique,* 60 Antitrust L.J. 41, 59 (1991); Robert L. Steiner, *Manufacturers' Promotional Allowances, Free-Riders and Vertical Restraints,* 30 Antitrust L. Bull. 383 (1991).

39. Robert L. Steiner, *The Evolution and Applications of Dual-Stage Thinking,* 49 Antitrust Bull. 877, 890–92 (2004).

40. *Id.*

41. As Steiner also acknowledges, there are industry structures in which the margins of retailers and manufacturers are positively related—in which total market power in the category may be very low to the benefit of consumers or very high to their detriment. For example, Steiner has written about a case in which collusion between a manufacturer of a strong brand and its retailers resulted in high margins for both the

manufacturer and the retailers. Robert L. Steiner, *Exclusive Dealing + Resale Price Maintenance: A Powerful Anticompetitive Combination,* 33 Sw. U. L. Rev. 447 (2004).

42. 504 U.S. 451 (1992).

43. Another argument related to free riding has been voiced in tying cases involving a patented tying product. Klein and Wiley have argued that tying in this context provides a fuller reward for IP rights and can, in this way, enhance innovation. *See* note 10, *supra.* Their argument has been challenged. Lawrence A. Sullivan & Warren S. Grimes, The Law of Antitrust, An Integrated Handbook 431–438 (2d ed. 2006). The argument is, in any event, not related to the Telser free riding argument that is central to the *Sylvania* holding.

44. For a discussion of these potential anticompetitive effects, *see id.* at 341–349.

45. Warren S. Grimes, *Spiff, Polish and Consumer Demand Quality, Vertical Price Fixing Revisited,* 80 Cal. L. Rev. 815, 832–834 (1992).

46. Warren S. Grimes, *From* Schwinn *to* Sylvania *to Where? Historical Roots of Modern Vertical Restraints Policy, in* Antitrust Stories 145, 147–48 (Eleanor M. Fox & Daniel A. Crane, eds. 2007).

47. Bork argues that rival dealers will complain about a free riding dealer, creating a ready enforcement mechanism. Bork, *supra* note 23, at 291. But these complaints are likely to be driven by intolerance of a discounting rival, regardless of whether the rival is a free rider.

48. 127 S. Ct. at 2715–16.

49. 485 U.S. 717 (1988).

50. *Business Electronics Corp.,* Brief for Respondent Sharp, 1987 WL 881326, at 7 (Hartwell "did not want to see customers that he had discovered and educated snatched away").

51. *Business Electronics Corp.,* Reply Brief for Petitioner Business Electronics, 1988 WL 1031912, at 4.

52. 485 U.S. at 721 ("petitioner's retail prices were often below respondent's suggested retail prices and generally below Hartwell's retail prices").

53. *Business Electronics,* Reply brief for Petitioner Business Electronics, 1988 WL 1031912, at 6.

54. *Id.* at 4.

55. 485 U.S. at 724–25, quoting *Sylvania,* 433 U.S. at 55.

56. 485 U.S. at 727–28.

57. *Id.* at 728.

58. *Id.* at 731.

59. *Id.* at 729.

60. If Business Electronics was providing discount prices along with its presale demonstrations, the question may arise why Sharp added a new Houston dealer in 1972 and terminated Business Electronics in 1974. Hartwell was a larger dealer with a higher volume of sales. Despite this, Sharp did not want to terminate Business Electronics, perhaps in recognition of that dealer's effectiveness. The termination occurred only after Hartwell issued its ultimatum.

61. *Sharp,* 485 U.S. at 727–28.

62. *Id.* at 751–52 (Stevens, J., dissenting) ("...the majority exhibits little confidence in the judicial process as a means of ascertaining the truth").

63. *Leegin,* 127 S. Ct. at 2711 (PSKS "promoted Brighton" [the Leegin brand], "ran Brighton advertisements," and earned "40 to 50 percent of its profits" from Brighton sales). For a more detailed analysis of the relevance of free riding to *Leegin, see* Marina Lao, *Free riding: An Overstated, and Unconvincing, Explanation for Resale Price Maintenance, infra.*

64. 433 U.S. at 46–47, citing with approval Justice Hughes in *Appalachian Coals, Inc. v. United States,* 288 U.S. 344, 360, 377 (1933).

65. Lester G. Telser, *Why Should Manufacturers Want Fair-Trade?,* 3 J. L. & ECON. 86 (1960). Telser's theory is drawn from, and built upon, earlier work by Ward Bowman and B. S. Yamey. *See* Ward Bowman, *The Prerequisites and Effects of Resale Price Maintenance,* 22 U. CHI. L. REV. 825 (1955); B. S. Yamey, THE ECONOMICS OF RESALE PRICE MAINTENANCE 3–27 (1954).

66. *See* Robert Bork, *The Rule of Reason and the Per Se Concept: Price Fixing and Market Division* (pt. 2), 75 YALE L.J. 373 (1966). Bork argued that vertical restraints *must* be procompetitive because a producer would only impose them if they would lead to increased sales and profits. At the same time, consumers would increase their purchases only if the value of the added services exceeds their incremental costs. Thus, it follows that vertical restraints must be efficiency-enhancing. *Id.* at 397–405.

67. 433 U.S. 36, 54–55 (1977) (overruling *United States v. Arnold Schwinn & Co.,* 388 U.S. 365 (1967)).

68. 127 S.Ct. 2705 (2007).

69. 220 U.S. 373 (1911).

70. For literature stressing the benefits of distribution restraints and favoring virtual legality for them, *see* Bork, *supra* note 66; Richard Posner, *The Next Step in the Antitrust Treatment of Restricted Distribution: Per Se Legality,* 4 U. CHI. L. REV. 6 (1980); Frank Easterbrook, *Vertical Arrangements and the Rule of Reason,* 53 ANTITRUST L.J. 135 (1984); Howard P. Marvel and Stephen McCafferty, *Resale Price Maintenance and Quality Certification,* 15 RAND J. ECON. 346 (1984); Howard Marvel, *The Resale Price Maintenance Controversy: Beyond the Conventional Wisdom,* 63 ANTITRUST L.J. 59 (1994); Benjamin Klein & Kevin M. Murphy, *Vertical Restraints as Contract Enforcement Mechanisms,* 31 J. L. & ECON. 265 (1988). Frank Mathewson & Ralph Winter, *The Law and Economics of Resale Price Maintenance,* 13 REV. INDUS. ORG. 57, 67 (1998). For dissenting voices, *see, e.g.,* William S. Comanor, *Vertical Price Fixing and Market Restrictions and the New Antitrust Policy,* 85 HARV. L. REV. 983, 990–98 (1985); Peter C. Carstensen, *The Competitive Dynamics of Distribution Restraints: The Efficiency Hypothesis Versus the Rent-Seeking Strategic Alternatives,* 69 ANTITRUST L.J. 569 (2001); Warren S. Grimes, *Brand Marketing, Intrabrand Competition, and the Multibrand Retailer: The Antitrust Law of Vertical Restraints,* 64 ANTITRUST L.J. 83 (1995); Robert F. Pitofsky, *In Defense of Discounters: The No-Frills Case for a Per Se Rule Against Vertical Price Fixing,* 71 GEO. L.J. 1487 (1983); Robert L. Steiner, *How Manufacturers Deal with the Price-Cutting Retailer: When Are Vertical Restraints Efficient?,* 65 ANTITRUST L.J. 407 (1997).

71. *See, e.g.,* 8 Phillip Areeda & Herbert Hovenkamp, ANTITRUST LAW ¶1601e, at 13; Robert Pitofsky, *Why Dr. Miles Was Right,* 8 REGULATION 27, at

29 (1984); S. Orstein, *Resale Price Maintenance and Cartels,* 30 ANTITRUST BULL. 401, 428 (1985); F. M. Scherer & David Ross, INDUSTRIAL MARKET STRUCTURE AND ECONOMIC PERFORMANCE 552 (3d ed. 1990); F. M. Scherer, *The Economics of Vertical Restraints,* 52 ANTITRUST L.J. 687 (1983); Kevin Arquit, *Resale Price Maintenance: Consumers' Friend or Foe?,* 60 ANTITRUST L.J. 447, 452 (1991). Commentators favorably disposed to resale price maintenance who, nonetheless, agree with this observation include Benjamin Klein and Howard Marvel. *See, e.g.,* Benjamin Klein, *Distribution Restraints Operate by Creating Dealer Profits: Explaining the Use of Maximum Resale Price Maintenance in State Oil v. Khan,* 7 SUP. CT. ECON. 1, 7–8 (1999); Howard Marvel, *supra* note 70.

72. *See, e.g.,* Brief of Amici Curiae Economists In Support of Petitioner on Petition for a Writ of Certiorari at 6–7, *Leegin Creative Leather Products, Inc. v. PSKS, Inc.,* No. 06–480, 127 S.Ct. 2705 (2007) (hereinafter Brief of Amici Economists).

73. *See, e.g.,* Marvel & McCafferty, *supra* note 70; Marvel, *supra* note 70, at 65–67; Thomas R. Overstreet, Jr., *Resale Price Maintenance: Economic Theories and Empirical Evidence* 56–62 (Bureau of Econ., Fed. Trade Comm'n 1983).

74. *See Leegin,* 127 S.Ct. at 2729 (Breyer, J., dissenting); *see also* Brett M. Frischmann & Mark A. Lemley, *Spillovers,* 107 Colum. L. Rev. 257 (2007) (arguing, in the intellectual property context, that "spillovers" are commonplace and good for society in many instances).

75. *See Leegin,* 127 S.Ct. at 2729–30 (Breyer, J., dissenting) (discussing at length the lack of empirical data and economic consensus on how often free riding actually takes place, and voicing skepticism that it is a serious problem).

76. *See id.,* at 2717 (acknowledging that "[h]istorical examples (of anticompetitive uses of RPM) suggest this (anticompetitive) possibility is a legitimate concern," and that "the potential anticompetitive consequences of vertical price restraints must not be ignored or underestimated.").

77. *See generally* C. Frederick Becker, III & Steven C. Salop, *Decision Theory and Antitrust Rules,* 67 ANTITRUST L.J. 41 (1999); *see also* Arndt Christiansen & Wolfgang Kerber, *Competition Policy With Optimally Differentiated Rules Instead of "Per Se Rules vs. Rule of Reason,"* 2 J. COMP. L. & ECON. 215, 238 (2006) (discussing the "error cost approach" and stating that merely showing resale price maintenance can have "positive welfare effects" in some cases is insufficient to discard the per se rule against minimum RPM).

78. *See, e.g.,* Brief of the American Antitrust Institute As Amicus Curiae in Support of Respondent at 28–30, *Leegin Creative Leather Products, Inc. v. PSKS, Inc.,* No. 06–480, 127 S.Ct. 2705 (2006) (hereinafter Brief of Amicus AAI) (urging retention of *Dr. Miles,* but recommending a rebuttable presumption of legality test in its place should the Court decide to abandon the per se rule); Robert Pitofsky, *Are Retailers Who Offer Discounts Really "Knaves"?: The Coming Challenge to the Dr. Miles Rule,* ANTITRUST, Spring 2007 (same).

79. *Leegin,* 127 S.Ct. at 2710.

80. *Id.* at 2711.

81. *Id.*

82. *Id.; see also PSKS Inc. v. Leegin Creative Leather Products Inc.,* 171 F. App'x 464, 465 (2006).

83. *Leegin,* 127 S.Ct. at 2711.

84. *Id.* at 2712.

85. *Id.*

86. Brief for Petitioner On Writ of Certiorari at 1, *Leegin Creative Leather Products, Inc. v. PSKS, Inc.,* No. 06–480, 127 S.Ct. 2705 (2006) (hereinafter Brief for Petitioner). The Petitioner's position was supported by the U.S. Department of Justice and the Federal Trade Commission, which filed a joint brief as amicus curiae in support of the Petitioner. Brief for the United States As Amicus Curiae Supporting Petitioner On Writ of Certiorari, *Leegin Creative Leather Products, Inc. v. PSKS, Inc.,* No. 06–480, 127 S.Ct. 2705 (2006) (hereinafter Brief of U.S. As Amicus).

87. *Brief for Petitioner, supra* note 86, at 3–4, 20–21, and 22–24.

88. *Id.* at 3–4.

89. *Id.* at 15–16, 19–20.

90. In deciding to overrule *Dr. Miles,* the majority also rejected the stare decisis argument and the argument that a *per se* rule was needed for administrative convenience. 127 S.Ct. at 2720–25. In fact, with respect to the stare decisis argument, the majority reasoned that the Court "has continued to temper, limit, or overrule once strict prohibitions on vertical restraints" for years since *Dr. Miles,* and suggested that maintaining the *per se* rule in *Leegin* would be inconsistent with the principles of those post-*Dr. Miles* cases. *See id.* at 2721–22.

91. *Id.* at 2713 (citing *Business Electronics Corp. v. Sharp Electronics Corp.,* 485 U.S. 717, 723 (1988)). The majority also stated that a *per se* rule is appropriate "only if courts can predict with confidence that [the type of restraint at issue] would be invalidated in all or almost all instances under the rule of reason." *Id.* (Internal citation omitted.)

92. *Id.* at 2717.

93. *See, e.g.,* Mathewson & Winter, *supra* note 70, at 74–75; Klein & Murphy, *supra* note 70, at 295; Raymond D. Deneckere, Howard P. Marvel, & James Peck, *Demand Uncertainty, Inventories, and Resale Price Maintenance,* 111 Q. J. Econ. 885, 911 (1996); Marvel & McCaffery, *supra* note 70, at 347–49; Brief of Amici Economists, *supra* note 72, at 6–7 ("In the theoretical literature, it is essentially undisputed that minimum [resale price maintenance] can have procompetitive effects and that under a variety of market conditions it is unlikely to have anticompetitive effects"); Brief of the U.S. as Amicus, *supra* note 86 at 9 ("[T]here is a widespread consensus that permitting a manufacturer to control the price at which at which goods are sold may promote *inter*brand competition and consumer welfare in a variety of ways.").

94. *See Leegin,* 127 S.Ct. at 2710 ("Respected economic analysts, furthermore, conclude that vertical price restraints can have procompetitive effects."); *id.* at 2714 (stating that "economics literature is replete with procompetitive justifications for a manufacturer's use of resale price maintenance" and citing sources); *id.* at 2715 ("Even those more skeptical of resale price maintenance acknowledge that it can have procompetitive effects.").

95. *Leegin,* 127 S.Ct. at 2715–16; *accord Sylvania,* 433 U.S. at 55.

96. *Leegin,* 127 S.Ct. at 2716; *accord Sylvania,* 433 U.S. at 55.

97. *See infra* [part IIC].

98. *Leegin,* 127 S.Ct. at 2729 (Breyer, J., dissenting).

99. *Id.*

100. *Id.* ("I find no economic consensus on this point. There is a consensus in the literature that 'free riding' takes place. But 'free riding' often takes place in the economy without any legal effort to stop it."); *id.* at 2730 (citing an amicus brief in *Leegin* that notes "skepticism in the economic literature about how often [free riding] actually occurs") (internal citation omitted).

101. *Id.* at 2730.

102. *See id.* at 2716–17; *see also* Richard Posner, ANTITRUST LAW 172 (2d ed. 2001); Overstreet, *supra* note 73, at 13–23; Marvel & McCafferty, *supra* note 70, at 373 (providing a historical example of resale price maintenance being used to facilitate a horizontal cartel of retail drug stores).

103. *See Leegin,* 127 S.Ct. at 2717; *Toys "R" Us, Inc. v. FTC,* 221 F.3d 928, 937–38 (7th Cir. 2000); Overstreet, *supra* note 73, at 31; 8 Areeda & Hovenkamp, *supra* note 71, at 47; Marvel, *supra* note 70, at 366–68.

104. For studies, analyses, and literature indicating that resale price maintenance almost always raises prices, *see, e.g.,* Overstreet, *supra* note 73, at 160 (noting that "price surveys indicate that [minimum RPM] in most cases increased the prices of products sold"); 8 Areeda & Hovenkamp, *supra* note 71, ¶1604b, at 40 ("The evidence is persuasive on this point."); Brief for William S. Comanor and Federic M. Scherer as Amici Curiae at 4, *Leegin Creative Leather Products, Inc. v. PSKS, Inc.,* 127 S.Ct. 2705 (2007) (hereinafter Brief of Amici Comanor and Scherer) ("It is uniformly acknowledged that [minimum RPM] and other vertical restraints lead to higher consumer prices."); Hearings on H.R. 2384 before the Subcommittee on Monopolies and Commercial Law of the House Committee on the Judiciary, 94th Cong., 1st Sess., 122 (1975) (statement of Keith I. Clearwaters, Deputy Assistant Attorney General, Antitrust Division); Hearings on S.408, Subcommittee on Antitrust and Monopoly of the Senate Judiciary Committee, 94th Cong., 1st Sess., 174 (1975); Robert L. Steiner, *Sylvania Economics—A Critique,* 60 ANTITRUST L.J. 41, 56 (1991); Willard F. Mueller, *The Sealy Restraints: Restrictions on Free riding or Output?,* 1989 Wis. L. Rev. 1255, 1293–96. Even commentators who view vertical restraints as generally procompetitive implicitly concede that RPM tends to raise consumer prices. *See, e.g.,* Easterbrook, *supra* note 70, at 156 ("the manufacturer can't get the dealer to do more without increasing the dealer's margin."); *but see* Marvel, *supra* note 70, at 69–71 (contending that RPM does not necessarily raise consumer prices because the wider dealer margin may be offset by lower wholesale prices).

105. *Leegin,* 127 S.Ct. at 2718–19.

106. *Id.* at 2727–28 (Breyer, J., dissenting) ("Resale price maintenance agreements, rather like horizontal price agreements, can diminish or eliminate price competition among dealers of a single brand or [if practiced generally by manufacturers] among multibrand dealers.").

107. *Id.* at 2727–28 (noting uniform acknowledgement by economists and other commentators that resale price maintenance leads to higher

consumer prices, and citing studies showing that prices were 19 percent to 27 percent higher under resale price maintenance).

108. Even scholars most skeptical of the free rider explanation generally agree that the hypothesis is valid in limited circumstances. *See, e.g.,* Robert Pitofsky, *Why Dr. Miles Was Right, supra* note 71, at 29; *see also* Arquit, *supra* note 71, at 452; Orstein, *supra* note 71, at 428.

109. *See generally* Telser, *supra* note 65; Posner, ANTITRUST LAW, *supra* note 102, at 172–73; Robert Bork, THE ANTITRUST PARADOX 290–91 (1978).

110. *See, e.g.,* Brief for Amici Comanor & Scherer, *supra* note 104, at 6 ("There is skepticism in the economic literature about how often [free riding] occurs."). *See* Scherer & Ross, *supra* note 71, at 551–55 (noting "relatively few products qualify... under Telser's free rider theory" and explaining the "severe limitations" of the free rider justification for resale price maintenance).

111. *See supra* note 71.

112. *Continental T.V., Inc. v. GTE Sylvania, Inc.,* 433 U.S. 36 (1977) (departing from an earlier *per se* rule that had applied to all vertical restraints, and applying the rule of reason to vertical non-price restraints).

113. *See id.* at 38. Before adopting the challenged vertical territorial restraint, Sylvania had 1–2 percent of the national television sales, while RCA, the leader, had between 60–70 percent. *Id.*

114. *See id.* (noting that Sylvania's share of the national television sales market rose from 1–2 percent to 5 percent after the new distribution policy, with territorial restrictions, was adopted).

115. *See* Pitofsky, *Are Retailers Who Offer Discounts Really "Knaves"?, supra* note 78.

116. *See* Klein, *supra* note 71, at 6–7 (noting that classic free riding most often involves "costly consumer durable goods, such as consumer electronics goods" because "it is often cost effective for consumers making large purchases to expend the time and effort to first shop a full service dealer before buying the product at a low service discount dealer").

117. *See Sylvania,* 433 U.S. at 55.

118. *See* Pitofsky, *Why Dr. Miles Was Right, supra* note 71, at 29–30.

119. *Id.* at 29; *see also* E. Corey, *Fair Trade Pricing: A Reappraisal,* 30 HARV. BUS. REV. 42 (Sept.-Oct. 1952) at 47 (noting that minimum resale prices had been set for cosmetics, perfumes, over-the-counter drugs, tobacco products and accessories, simple photographic supplies, drugstore watches and clocks, and small appliances, none of which require dealer services); Sharon Oster, *The FTC v. Levi Strauss: An Analysis of the Economic Issues, in* IMPACT EVALUATIONS OF FEDERAL TRADE COMMISSION VERTICAL RESTRAINTS CASES 47 (Robert N. Lafferty et al., eds. 1984) (discussing RPM for Levi's jeans).

120. *See Leegin,* 127 S.Ct. 2705, 2730 (2007) (Breyer, J., dissenting).

121. 485 U.S. 717 (1988).

122. For a detailed and insightful discussion of this case, *see* Warren S. Grimes, *The Sylvania Free rider Justification for Downstream-Power Vertical Restraints: Truth or Invitation for Pretext?, supra.*

123. The Court held that for the *Dr. Miles per se* rule to apply, in addition to showing an agreement between Sharp and Hartwell to terminate Business Electronics because of its price-cutting, Business Electronics

must also show "a further agreement on the price or price levels to be charged by the remaining dealer." *Business Electronics,* 485 U.S. at 726.

124. *See id.* at 725–31. The majority opinion also reiterated the Chicago view that protecting intrabrand competition is unimportant, on the theory that interbrand competition would sufficiently constrain a producer's anti-competitive tendencies. *See id.* at 725.

125. *See id.* at 725, 727–28, 729.

126. *Id.* at 727–28.

127. *Id.* at 729.

128. The opinion is devoid of any discussion of what services, if any, each dealer provided in the sale of the Sharp calculators, and seems to just assume that the general free rider hypothesis applied.

129. *See Continental T.V., Inc. v. GTE Sylvania, Inc.,* 433 U.S. 36, 56, 56 n.24 (1977) (noting that "manufacturers have an economic interest in maintaining as much intrabrand competition as is consistent with the efficient distribution of their products").

130. *See* Steiner, *How Manufacturers Deal with the Price-Cutting Retailer, supra* note 70, at 407, 416–17.

131. *Leegin,* Brief for Amici Economists, *supra* note 72, at 5–7.

132. *See,* Marvel, *supra* note 70, at 65–67; Marvel & McCafferty, *supra* note 70, at 347–49; Overstreet, *supra* note 73, at 56–62; Ronald N. Lafferty et al., *Impact Evaluations of Federal Trade Commission Vertical Restraints Cases* 34–35 (FTC 1984); *Leegin,* Brief of Amici Economists, *supra* note 72, at 7–8; *Leegin,* Brief of U.S. As Amicus, *supra* note 86, at 14.

133. *Leegin,* Brief of Amici Economists, *supra* note 72, at 6 ("A fashion item...may benefit from longer store hours, more convenient or prestigious store locations, better-trained and more enthusiastic employees, or favoritism in shelf placement," but free riding may cause retailers to offer less of these things than "would be best for manufacturers and consumers.")

134. *Id.* ("From an economics perspective, all of these services can enhance the quality (real or perceived) of the product because they demonstrably have value to consumers.")

135. *Id.* at 7 ("Free riding creates externalities that lead each retailer—and thus retailers collectively—to spend less on service than is optimal.").

136. *Id.* at 5–8.

137. *Leegin,* Brief for Petitioner, *supra* note 86, at 3.

138. *Id.* at 3–4.

139. *Id.* at 19–20 ("The most frequently cited rationale for resale price maintenance is that a manufacturer might impose a price floor to ensure that dealers provide demand-creating services. In the absence of resale price restraints, free rider problems may diminish retailers' incentives to provide these services, harming the manufacturer and dampening interbrand competition.") (Internal citations omitted.)

140. *Id.*

141. *Leegin,* Brief of Amici Economists, *supra* note 72, at 6.

142. *Id.*

143. *Id.* at 5–8.

144. *Leegin,* Brief of U.S. as Amicus, *supra* 86, at 15.

145. *Leegin,* 127 S.Ct. at 2716.

146. *Leegin,* Brief of U.S. as Amicus, *supra* note 86, at 15.

147. *See, e.g., id.* (mentioning "the attractiveness and location of retail stores and the speed and efficiency with which retailers complete customer transaction" as the intangible services that could be used to promote inter-brand competition).

148. *See supra* note 132; *see also* Victor P. Goldberg, *The Free rider Problem, Imperfect Pricing, and the Economics of Retailing Services,* 79 Nw. U. L. Rev. 736, 744–46 (1984) (arguing that producers can use minimum resale prices to purchase a prestige dealer's "endorsement" of its product).

149. *See, e.g., Leegin,* 127 S.Ct. at 2715–16 ("[C]onsumers might decide to buy the product because they see it in a retail establishment that has a reputation for selling high-quality merchandise.").

150. *See id.* at 2716.

151. *See supra* note 87–89 and accompanying text.

152. *Leegin,* Brief of U.S. as Amicus, *supra* note 86, at 14; Brief of Amici Economists, *supra* note 72, at 7–8.

153. *See Leegin,* 127 S.Ct. at 2729–30 (Breyer, J., dissenting) (emphasizing the importance of asking, not merely whether free riding occurs and whether RPM confers any benefits in overcoming its effects, but how *often* it occurs and whether its effects are severe enough to discourage the provision of the dealer services).

154. *See* Scherer, *supra* note 71, at 695.

155. *See* 8 Areeda & Hovenkamp, *supra* note 71, at 162.

156. *See id.*

157. Some commentators persuasively argue that even these types of services for complex or novel products do not benefit *all* consumers: they may be superfluous for inframarginal consumers—those who do not need or desire the additional services but, because of distribution restraints, do not have the choice of trading those services for lower prices. *See* Comanor, *supra* note 70, at 990–1000; Scherer & Ross, *supra* note 71, at 547–48.

158. *See Leegin,* 127 S.Ct. at 2716.

159. *See* 8 Areeda & Hovenkamp, *supra* note 71, ¶¶1617a, 1631b, at 193–96, 308.

160. *See* Mark A. Lemley, *Property, Intellectual Property, and Free riding,* 83 Tex. L. Rev. 1031, 1068 (2005) (discussing and criticizing the tendency in intellectual property law to view free riding in this light).

161. *See id.* ("The concept of free riding focuses on the economic effects on the alleged free rider—whether the accused infringer obtained a benefit from the use of the invention, and if so whether it paid for that benefit.")

162. *See, e.g.,* Alan J. Meese, *Property Rights and Intrabrand Restraints,* 89 Cornell L. Rev. 553 (2004); Marvel, *supra* note 70, at 62: "RPM can be used to create for dealers property rights in their promotional investments on behalf of the manufacturer's product."

163. *Leegin,* 127 S.Ct. at 2729 (Breyer, J., dissenting) ("But 'free riding' often takes place in the economy without any legal effort to stop it. Many visitors to California take free rides on the Pacific Coast Highway. We all benefit freely from ideas, such as that of creating the first supermarket. Dealers often take a 'free ride' on investments that others have made in building a product's name and reputation.").

164. *See id.; see also* 8 Areeda & Hovenkamp, *supra* note 71, at 152–53; Wendy J. Gordon, *On Owning Information: Intellectual Property and the Restitutionary Impulse,* 78 Va. L. Rev. 149, 167 (1992) ("A culture could not exist if all free riding were prohibited within it.").

165. 8 Areeda & Hovenkamp, *supra* note 71, at 153.

166. *See* Marina Lao, *Unilateral Refusals to Sell or License Intellectual Property and the Antitrust Duty to Deal,* 9 Cornell J. Law & Pub. Pol'y 193, 213–14 (1999) (arguing that IP laws "are intended to encourage innovation by correcting the "public good" problem of intellectual property" and that "[o]ptimally, intellectual property rights should be allowed only to the extent that societal benefits exceed the costs of protection.").

167. *See Leegin,* 127 S.Ct. at 2729 (Breyer, J., dissenting) (asserting that the appropriate question to ask is not whether free riding takes place, but "how often the 'free riding' problem is serious enough significantly to deter dealer investment."); Lemley, *supra* note 160, at 1050 (arguing, in the IP context, that "[i]nternalization of positive externalities is not necessary at all unless efficient use of the property requires a significant investment that cannot be recouped another way.").

168. 35 U.S.C. §§ 101, 154 (conferring on a patentee an exclusive right to use or otherwise exploit its patent and to exclude others from the field claimed by the invention for a limited time); 17 U.S.C. § 106 (granting copyright owners an exclusive right to reproduce and otherwise exploit their copyright works for a specified period of time).

169. *See* 8 Areeda & Hovenkamp, *supra* note 71, at 153.

170. *See, e.g., United States v. Socony-Vacuum Oil Co.,* 310 U.S. 150, 226 n. 59 (1940) ("Price is the 'central nervous system of the economy.' ").

171. *Leegin,* 127 S.Ct. at 2717.

172. *Id.* at 2730 (Breyer, J., dissenting).

173. *Id.*

174. *See id.* at 2729 ("I have already described studies and analyses that suggest (though they cannot prove) that resale price maintenance can cause harms with some regularity—and certainly when dealers are the driving force. But what about benefits? How often, for example, will the benefits to which the Court points occur in practice? I can find no economic consensus on this point.").

175. *Id.* at 2716–17.

176. *Id.* at 2717.

177. *See* Pitofsky, *In Defense of Discounters, supra* note 70, at 1490–91.

178. *Leegin,* 127 S.Ct. at 2717. Though the majority also cites two empirical studies that seem to suggest that minimum RPM is seldom adopted to facilitate producer or dealer cartels, *Id.* (internal citations omitted), the dissent responds by demonstrating fundamental flaws with both studies. *Id.* at 2732. For example, one study analyzed litigated RPM cases from 1975 to 1982 and concluded that they mostly did not involve dealer or producer cartel, based upon the absence of horizontal collusion allegations in the complaints. *See* Ippolito, *Resale Price Maintenance: Empirical Evidence from Litigation,* 34 J. L. & Econ. 263, 281–82, 292 (1991). Breyer observed that horizontal collusion is often tacit and suggested that, when RPM is already per se illegal, plaintiffs have no reason to allege and prove such a

difficult allegation. Thus, the absence of allegations of horizontal collusion in litigated RPM cases is, at best, "mild support for the majority's position." *Leegin,* 127 S.Ct. at 2732 (Breyer, J., dissenting).

179. Bowman, *supra* note 65.

180. *See Leegin,* 127 S.Ct. at 2717. Even strong supporters of vertical restraints concede that. *See* Marvel & McCafferty, *supra* note 70, at 13.

181. *See* Herbert Hovenkamp, THE ANTITRUST ENTERPRISE 186 (2005).

182. *See Leegin,* 127 S.Ct. at 2717 ("To the extent a vertical agreement setting minimum resale prices is entered upon to facilitate either [a producer or dealer] cartel, it, too, would need to be held unlawful under the rule of reason.").

183. *See id.; see also Toys "R" Us Inc. v. FTC,* 221 F.3d 928, 937–38 (7th Cir. 2000); 8 Areeda & Hovenkamp, *supra* note 71, at 47; Overstreet, *supra* note 73, at 31.

184. *See, e.g., Leegin,* 127 S.Ct. at 2733 (Breyer, J., dissenting) (citing numerous studies).

185. Even the majority in *Leegin* acknowledged this. *See Leegin,* 127 S.Ct. at 2717; *see also* Marvel, *supra* note 70, at 366–68.

186. *See Leegin,* 127 S.Ct. at 2733–34 (citing studies showing increased concentration among manufacturers in some markets).

187. *See* note 104 *supra.*

188. Miller-Tyings Act, Pub. L. No. 314, ch. 690, Title III, 50 Stat. 693 (1937), repealed in The Consumer Goods Pricing Act of 1975, Pub. L. No. 94–145, 89 Stat. 801.

189. *See* Hearings on S. 408 before the Subcommittee on Antitrust and Monopoly of the Senate Committee on the Judiciary, 94th Cong., 1st Sess., 173 (1975) (statement of Thomas E. Kauper, Assistant Attorney General, Antitrust Division) (testifying that, at the time of the hearing, minimum resale price maintenance was lawful in 36 states, under the states' "fair trade" laws, and was unlawful in 14 states without such laws).

190. For a summary of this data, see Overstreet, *supra* note 73, at 160 (showing, through price surveys, lower prices in "free trade" jurisdictions).

191. *See Leegin,* 127 S.Ct. at 2727–28 (Breyer, J., dissenting); Hearings on H.R. 2384, Subcommittee on Monopolies and Commercial Law of the House Committee on the Judiciary, 94th Cong., 1st Sess., 122 (1975) (statement of Keith I. Clearwaters, Deputy Assistant Attorney General, Antitrust Division); F. M. Scherer, *Comment on Cooper et al.'s "Vertical Restrictions and Antitrust Policy,"* 1 COMP. POLICY INT'L, Autumn 2005, 65, 72–74 (citing studies showing substantial price decreases after termination of RPM in light bulbs, over-the-counter drugs, jeans, and other items).

192. *See* FTC, *Record Companies Settle FTC Charges of Restraining Competition in CD Music Market,* May 10, 2000.

193. *See Leegin,* 127 S.Ct. at 2727–28, 2729.

194. *See id.* at 2718–19.

195. *See* Overstreet, *supra* note 73, at 106 (price comparison data "do not necessarily tell us anything conclusive about the welfare effects" of resale price maintenance).

196. *United States v. Socony-Vacuum Oil Co.,* 310 U.S. 150, 226 n.59 (1940).

197. *See* Joseph C. Palamountain, Jr., The Politics of Distribution (Greenwood Press ed. 1968) (providing numerous examples of the efficiency benefits of competition between different types of retail formats); Robert L. Steiner, *How Manufacturers Deal with the Price-Cutting Retailer, supra* note 70, at 419–24, 439–40 (discussing the evolution of new retailing formats, e.g., department stores; chain stores, mail order houses, and supermarkets; using many examples to illustrate the efficiencies and different service package that each new format introduced; and arguing that RPM tends to retard growth of innovative and more efficient retailing forms).

198. *See* Brief for Consumer Federation of America as Amicus Curiae at 5, *Leegin Creative Leather Products, Inc. v. PSKS, Inc.,* No. 06–480 (2006) (stating that large discounters would not exist without *Dr. Miles,* and warning that minimum RPM, "by stabilizing price levels and preventing low-price competition, erects a potentially insurmountable barrier to entry for such low-price innovators"); *see also* Lawrence A. Sullivan & Warren S. Grimes, The Law of Antitrust: An Integrated Handbook § 6.3a2, at 335 (2d ed. 2006) (stating that intrabrand competition preserves "entry opportunities for new retailers and new retailing approaches").

199. *Sylvania,* 433 U.S. at 52 n.19 (1977). *Accord Leegin,* 127 S.Ct. at 2718 ("the antitrust laws are designed primarily to protect interbrand competition, from which lower prices can later result"); *State Oil Co. v. Khan,* 522 U.S. 3, 15 (1997); *Business Elecs. Corp. v. Sharp Elecs. Corp.,* 485 U.S. 717, 724, 726 (1988). *See also* Brief of U.S. as Amicus, *supra* note 86, at 9 ("permitting a manufacturer to control the price at which its goods are sold may promote *inter*brand competition and consumer welfare in a variety of ways."). For an extensive critique of the assumptions underlying this conclusion, *see* Steiner, *Sylvania Economics, supra* note 104, at 42–45.

200. *Exxon Corp. v. Superior Ct. of Santa Clara Cty.,* 60 Cal. Rptr. 2d 195, 200 (Cal. Ct. App. 1997). *See also Crane & Shovel Sales Corp. v. Bucyrus-Erie Co.,* 854 F.2d 802, 807 (6th Cir. 1988) (claimant must allege anticompetitive effect on interbrand competition to survive a Rule 12(b)(6) motion to dismiss).

201. *See generally* Grimes, *Brand Marketing, supra* note 70; Steiner, *Sylvania Economics, supra* note 104, at 59; Robert L. Steiner, *Manufacturers' Promotional Allowances, Free riders and Vertical Restraints,* 36 Antitrust Bull. 383 (1991); William S. Comanor, *The Two Economics of Vertical Restraints,* 21 Sw. U. L. Rev. 1265 (1992).

202. *See, e.g.,* Steiner, *How Manufacturers Deal with the Price-Cutting Retailer, supra* note 70, at 440–42.

203. *Id.* at 441 (citing case studies involving Levi's jeans); Robert L. Steiner, *Jeans: Vertical Restraints and Efficiency, in* Industry Studies 182 (Larry L. Duetsch ed., 1993).

204. *See* Grimes, *Brand Marketing, supra* note 70, at 93–96.

205. Sylvania, 433 U.S. at 52 n.19.

206. *See, e.g.,* Grimes, *Brand Marketing, supra* note 70, at 100–02; Steiner, *Manufacturers' Promotional Allowances, supra* note 201.

207. *See* Pitofsky, *In Defense of Discounters, supra* note 70; Hovenkamp, The Antitrust Enterprise, *supra* note 181, at 105 (making the generally

recognized observation that litigating a rule of reason case is "one of the most costly procedures in antitrust practice").

208. Stephen Calkins, *California Dental Association: Not A Quick Look But Not the Full Monty,* 67 ANTITRUST L.J. 495, 521 (1999)

209. Maxwell M. Blecher, *Schwinn—An Example of Genuine Commitment to Antitrust Law,* 44 ANTITRUST L.J. 550, 553 (1975).

210. Douglas H. Ginsburg, *Vertical Restraints: De Facto Legality Under the Rule of Reason,* 60 ANTITRUST L.J. 67 (1991).

211. *See Leegin,* 127 S.Ct. at 2731 (Breyer, J., dissenting) ("And since enforcement resources are limited, that loss may tempt some producers or dealers to enter into agreements that are, on balance, anticompetitive.").

212. *Id.* at 2719–20 ("If the rule of reason were to apply to vertical price restraints, courts would have to be diligent in eliminating their anticompetitive uses from the market.").

213. *Id.* at 2719 ("Resale price maintenance should be subject to more careful scrutiny, by contrast, if many competing manufacturers adopt the practice.") *See also* Scherer & Ross, *supra* note XX, at 558.

214. *Leegin,* 127 S.Ct. at 2719 ("If there is evidence retailers were the impetus for a vertical price restraint, there is a greater likelihood that the restraint facilitates a dealer cartel or supports a dominant, inefficient retailer."). *See also* Brief for Amici Comanor & Scherer, *supra* note XX, at 7–8.

215. *Leegin,* 127 S.Ct. at 2720.

216. *See, e.g., Broadcast Music, Inc. v. Columbia Broadcasting System, Inc.,* 441 U.S. 1 (1979); *National Soc'y of Professional Engineers v. United States,* 435 U.S. 679 (1978); *NCAA v. Bd. of Regents of the Univ. of Oklahoma,* 468 U.S. 85 (1984); *see also* Marina Lao, *Comment: The Rule of Reason And Horizontal Restraints Involving Professionals,* 68 ANTITRUST L.J. 499, 502–07 (2000) (discussing the quick-look application in these three cases).

217. *See e.g., Leegin,* 127 S.Ct. at 2730 (Breyer, J., dissenting) (explaining the difficulty in identifying the "moving force" behind an RPM agreement when, for example, several small producers set price floors because "several large multibrand retailers all sell resale-price-maintained products" and the small producers fear that, unless they do likewise, "the large retailers will favor (say, by allocating better shelf-space) the goods of other producers who practice resale price maintenance.").

218. 221 F.3d 928 (7th Cir. 2000)

219. 744 F.2d 588 (7th Cir. 1984).

220. *Toys "R" Us,* 221 F.3d at 930, 931–32.

221. *Id.* at 933, 937–38.

222. *Id.* at 933, 938.

223. *Id.* at 938.

224. *Id.* at 937.

225. *Id.*

226. *See General Leaseways,* 744 F.2d at 592–93.

227. *Id.* at 589.

228. *Id.* at 590.

229. *Id.* at 592.

230. *Id.* at 593 ("[The defendant] has not yet made a plausible free-rider argument.").

231. *Id.* at 592.

232. *Id.*

233. *Id.* at 592–93.

234. *Id.* at 596.

235. *Id.* at 597.

236. *See FTC v. Indiana Federation of Dentists,* 476 U.S. 447, 460–61 (1986) (finding that demonstration of actual anticompetitive effects obviates the need to prove market power).

6

Reinvigorating Merger Enforcement That Has Declined as a Result of Conservative Economic Analysis

Introduction

In many respects, the decline of antitrust enforcement against mergers between direct rivals ("horizontal mergers") is the most pronounced and unfortunate effect of the influence of Chicago School economics. Jonathan Baker and Carl Shapiro take on the underlying issues, demonstrate the extraordinarily low level of government merger enforcement in recent years, and conclude with a brilliant and innovative roadmap describing how merger enforcement *should* be done.

The authors trace the arc of over- and underenforcement of antitrust against horizontal mergers in the second half of the twentieth century, and attribute the lax enforcement in recent years to excessive reliance on defenses rooted in theoretical economics, such as alleged ease of entry if the merging parties raise prices and asserted claims of efficiencies. These defenses are mostly traced to conservative economic analysis, often implemented by conservative judges with pronounced noninterventionist attitudes toward private sector transactions.

To bolster their conclusion that recent enforcement has been inadequate, Baker and Shapiro compare statistics on recent levels of enforcement with prior periods and find that recent levels—particularly at the Antitrust Division of the Department of Justice—are the lowest in many decades. They also report on a survey of experienced antitrust practitioners who responded overwhelmingly that the current enforcement authorities accept defenses that would have been rejected in earlier periods and advise that it is easier to persuade the enforcement authorities to clear mergers in recent years than at any time in the last quarter century.

In a concluding section, the authors offer an innovative roadmap show-ing how horizontal merger analysis should be conducted and how to avoid the excesses and rigidities of extreme theoretical economic analysis that has come to characterize recent antitrust enforcement.

Reinvigorating Horizontal Merger Enforcement

Jonathan B. Baker and Carl Shapiro

The past 40 years have witnessed a remarkable transformation in horizontal merger enforcement in the United States. With no change in the underlying statute, the Clayton Act, the weight given to market concentration by the federal courts and by the federal antitrust agencies has declined dramatically. Instead, increasing weight has been given to three arguments often made by merging firms in their defense: entry, expansion, and efficiencies. We document this shift and provide examples where courts have approved highly concentrating mergers based on limited evidence of entry and expansion. We show—using merger enforcement data and a survey we conducted of merger practitioners—that the decline in antitrust enforcement is ongoing, especially at the current Justice Department. We then argue in favor of reinvigorating horizontal merger enforcement by partially restoring the structural presumption and by requiring strong evidence to overcome the government's prima facie case. We propose several routes by which the government can establish its prima facie case, distinguishing between cases involving coordinated versus unilateral anticompetitive effects.

Introduction

For half a century, horizontal merger law in the United States has been framed around a concern with market concentration. The strength of that concern has steadily eroded over the past 30 years, however, as industrial organization economists have assembled evidence and refined their theories of market structure and competition. As in many other areas of the law, the intellectual assault of the Chicago School of law and economics has been highly influential on the evolution of horizontal merger law.[1]

Chicago-oriented antitrust commentators recommended raising the level of market concentration above which horizontal mergers would be presumed to raise competition concerns. They also embraced a more flexible economic analysis. The latter approach gives merger proponents the ability to rebut a presumption of harm to competition based on concentration with evidence about other aspects of the market or the transaction, including ease of entry of new competitors, the likelihood of output expansion by nonmerging firms, or efficiencies flowing from mergers.

These analytical initiatives found an attentive audience in the enforcement agencies and courts, and they led to significant improvements in antitrust merger review. But some courts and enforcers have taken flexibility too far, allowing mergers to proceed based upon dubious economic arguments about concentration, entry, expansion, and efficiencies.

I. Trends in Horizontal Merger Analysis

During the 1960s, the Supreme Court interpreted the Clayton Act §7—the antimerger statute, which had been amended in 1950—to require a presumption of harm to competition from merger based on market concentration. An "intense congressional concern with the trend toward concentration" in the U.S. economy warranted "dispensing, in certain cases, with elaborate proof of market structure, market behavior, or probable competitive effects," according to the Court.[2] Accordingly, the Supreme Court held in 1962, in *Philadelphia National Bank,* that "a merger which produces a firm controlling an undue percentage share of the relevant market, and results in a significant increase in the concentration of firms in that market is so inherently likely to lessen competition substantially that it must be enjoined in the absence of evidence clearly showing that the merger is not likely to have such anticompetitive effects."[3] The Court explained that application of this rule—now often termed the "structural presumption"—"lightens the burden of proving illegality only with respect to mergers whose size makes them inherently suspect."[4] It added that the test is "fully consistent with economic theory," as it is "common ground among most economists" that competition is likely greatest where there are many sellers, none of which has any significant market share.[5] In the Court's view, this basic economic proposition "was undoubtedly a premise of congressional reasoning about the antimerger statute."[6]

The practical result of establishing a strong structural presumption for horizontal merger analysis during the 1960s was to prohibit virtually all mergers among rivals. The poster child for structural era excess in merger enforcement, according to commentators associated with the Chicago School, was the 1966 Supreme Court decision in the *Von's Grocery* merger case.[7] In that case, the Court stopped the merger of two grocery chains serving Los Angeles that together accounted for only 7.5 percent of retail sales. At that time no other firm served more than 8 percent of the market and even after a wave of grocery store consolidations, more than 3500 single grocery stores remained in the area. We very much doubt that a similar merger would draw any enforcement interest today.

One problem was the low level of market concentration at which the structural presumption kicked in. Prohibiting mergers among small firms "obviously cuts far too deeply into the efficiencies of integration," according to Chicago School commentator Robert Bork.[8] Another problem was the inability, in practice, of the merging firms in *Von's Grocery* to rebut the structural presumption with evidence of what Bork termed "an intensely competitive market,"[9] or with proof that what another commentator associated with the Chicago School, Richard Posner, described as "the ease and rapidity of entry," would deter or counteract the possibility of higher industry prices.[10] As applied in *Von's Grocery* and other decisions of that era, the structural presumption was virtually conclusive, leading to Justice Potter Stewart's famous observation in his dissent in *Von's Grocery* that the one common thread in merger cases at that time was that "the Government always wins."[11] As a result of *Von's Grocery,* Bork claimed, horizontal mergers had "all but disappeared from the economy."[12]

These criticisms of *Von's* had bite because they were rooted in changing economic thinking. During the 1960s, the "structure-conduct performance" (SCP) approach was the dominant paradigm in industrial organization economics.[13] This approach was based on the idea that industries with market power could be identified through simple, easily observed indicia, particularly by reference to market concentration (at least in industries protected by entry barriers). For several reasons, however, economists largely gave up on this simple paradigm. Empirically, the broad cross-sectional evidence linking market concentration to prices, margins, profits, and hence performance was seriously challenged.[14] Theoretically, it was recognized that tacit collusion was not inevitable even in oligopolistic markets.[15] Conceptually, there was a growing recognition that firms with high market shares could be very profitable either because they exercised market power or because they had achieved low costs or other efficiencies.[16]

The courts responded to the Chicago School criticisms of *Von's Grocery* and other structural era merger decisions by undermining the structural presumption. An opening to do so had been created by the 1974 decision in *General Dynamics,* where the Supreme Court allowed the merging firms to rebut the structural presumption by showing that concentration had been measured incorrectly.[17] The acquired firm's market share based on historical sales was found to mislead as to its future competitive significance.

When shares were measured in appropriate units (production capacity based on coal reserves rather than past sales), they showed that the firm's future ability to compete was "severely limited," and that showing "fully substantiated" the lower court's conclusion that its acquisition by a rival would not substantially lessen competition.[18]

At the time, *General Dynamics* was not thought to have signaled a change of course. Writing two years later, Robert Bork described it and some roughly contemporaneous Supreme Court bank merger decisions as cases that "stress the particular aspects of each situation in ways that do not reform existing doctrine" rather than enunciating "rules of general applicability that would undo the damage done by the earlier cases."[19] But *General Dynamics* nevertheless created a basis for lower courts to reform merger law by reading that decision to permit a wide-ranging analysis of whether market shares accurately reflected the merging firms' ability to compete.

The 1982 Merger Guidelines, promulgated by Assistant Attorney General William Baxter, showed the courts how to proceed.[20] The 1982 Guidelines took the view that market concentration was highly influential but not outcome-determinative in evaluating horizontal mergers. They indicated that the Justice Department, in exercising its prosecutorial discretion, would allow the inference of harm to competition from merger to be rebutted by a number of factors, including a showing that entry was easy or that features of the market would make it difficult for firms to collude tacitly even after the merger.[21] Taking advantage of this flexibility allowed the Justice Department during the later Reagan years to adopt a much more lenient policy with respect to horizontal mergers than was indicated at that time based on the case law.

At the same time, the lower courts, under the influence of Chicago School criticisms of structural era merger policy, seized the opportunity offered by *General Dynamics* and identified by the 1982 Guidelines. During the mid-1980s, for example, two courts and the Federal Trade Commission held that the structural presumption could be trumped by proof of ease of entry.[22] By 1990, the D.C. Circuit, in *Baker Hughes,* an influential decision authored by future Justice Clarence Thomas and joined by another future Justice, Ruth Ginsburg, declared that the "Supreme Court has adopted a totality-of-the-circumstances approach…, weighing a variety of factors to determine the effects of particular transactions on competition."[23] The structural presumption had eroded to the point where "[e]vidence of market concentration simply provides a convenient starting point for a broader inquiry into future competitiveness."[24] Accordingly, "[t]he Herfindahl-Hirschman Index cannot guarantee litigation victories."[25]

As a result of this trend, the emphasis in merger enforcement has shifted over three decades from proving market concentration to telling a convincing story of how the merger will actually lead to a reduction in competition. Put simply, market definition and market shares have become far less important relative to proof of competitive effects.

The 1992 Horizontal Merger Guidelines, promulgated in the wake of *Baker Hughes,* set forth two classes of competitive effects theories, coordinated and unilateral, and outlined the factors that the federal enforcement agencies would look to in order to determine whether they applied.[26] But market concentration remains important in competitive effects analysis, and properly so. All else equal, greater market concentration makes both coordinated and unilateral effects more likely, and empirical studies show that in comparisons involving the same industry, higher concentration is associated with higher prices.[27] Accordingly, the federal enforcement agencies continue to rely on market concentration in analyzing the competitive effects of merger, and concentration remains an important predictor of agency action, even in recent years.[28]

We believe that the 1992 Horizontal Merger Guidelines, now 15 years old, offer a good general framework in which to analyze horizontal mergers, especially for cases in which the theory of harm is based on coordinated effects. Satisfaction with the current overall framework for analysis is reflected in the conclusion of the Antitrust Modernization Commission, which stated,

> The Commission does not recommend legislative change to the Sherman Act or to Section 7 of the Clayton Act. There is a general consensus that, while there may be disagreement about specific enforcement decisions, the basic legal standards that govern the conduct of firms under those laws are sound.[29]

By its nature, however, the modern approach, which involves many judgment calls and a great deal of balancing of the evidence, gives a great deal of discretion to decision makers at the agencies. Likewise, a "totality of the circumstances" approach gives a great deal of discretion to the courts. Predispositions and burdens of proof are very important in applying this framework.

Concerns about the effectiveness of merger enforcement using an economically sophisticated, fact-specific inquiry are far from new. Nearly half a century ago, Derek Bok, writing about the interpretation of section 7 of the Clayton Act, foresaw the problem:

> Economic theory has provided us with much of what little sophistication we now possess in identifying and measuring market power and in comprehending the interdependence, and its significance, of large, powerful firms. The aims and applications of section 7 are rooted in these concepts, and it would be arrogant to suppose that we could muddle through without further assistance. But neither can we succumb to the economists who bid us enter the jungle of "all relevant factors," telling us very little of the flora and fauna that abound in its depths, but promising rather vaguely that they will do their best to lead us safely to our destination.... This problem cannot be solved, nor can the economist-critic be placated, by embracing more and more of the niceties of economic theory into our antitrust

proceedings. Unless we can be certain of the capacity of our legal system to absorb new doctrine, our attempts to introduce it will only be more ludicrous in failure and more costly in execution.[30]

Below, we consider explicitly the limits on our ability to predict the specific effects of individual horizontal mergers and the implications for establishing burdens of proof and burdens of persuasion. Unlike Bok, we do not question the utility of a fact-intensive approach based on economic principles. Rather, we explore whether such an approach, now firmly established at the agencies and in the courts, has been properly implemented in ways that reflect current economic theory and empirical evidence.

II. Some Courts and Agency Leaders Have Gone Too Far

Many of the changes in merger enforcement law and policy over the past 30 years, going back to *General Dynamics,* have been significant improvements. They have reflected new economic learning and corrected for certain structural era excesses. Generally speaking, the shift from a more formulaic approach based on market definition and market shares to an approach that places less weight on market structure, pays closer attention to possible expansion by smaller suppliers and entry by new ones, and exhibits less hostility to merger efficiencies, has been a big step toward more effective merger control policy. Like most economists, we support the modern approach, with its more nuanced, fact-intensive economic inquiry focusing on mechanisms of competitive effects. We are concerned, however, that the pendulum has now swung too far in the direction of nonintervention.[31]

A. Judicial Decisions With Dubious Economic Reasoning

The modern trend in horizontal merger law toward a lessened significance for concentration does not mean that firms can merge with their rivals without antitrust scrutiny. The modern approach simply substitutes a more wide-ranging factual analysis of likely competitive effects for a strong presumption based on market concentration. But some courts, perhaps overly impressed by Chicago School criticisms of structural era excess, have in reaction overshot the mark in the other direction.

One leading example is the 1990 appellate decision in *Syufy,* upholding a district court decision declining to enjoin a merger to monopoly in the Las Vegas movie theater market on grounds of ease of entry.[32] The holding of the case is unremarkable given its procedural posture. But the reasoning and rhetoric of Judge Alex Kozinski's opinion shows what mischief can arise when a court, having discarded the discipline of the structural presumption, chooses to indulge its noninterventionist prejudices rather than engage in serious economic inquiry and careful antitrust analysis.

The case arose when the Justice Department challenged three acquisitions by a movie theater owner named Syufy.[33] The acquisitions collectively gave Syufy control of virtually all the theaters in Las Vegas. Syufy's only remaining competitor was Roberts, a small exhibitor of mostly second-run films. Justice did not allege that the merger had led to higher ticket or popcorn prices for moviegoers; instead it charged that Syufy had exercised *monopsony* power over distributors of first-run films, exploiting its position as the only major exhibitor in Las Vegas to pay distributors less than they would have received in a competitive market. The main defense, accepted by the trial court and the court of appeals, was that competition was not and could not have been harmed because entry into movie exhibition in Las Vegas was easy.[34]

The Ninth Circuit accepted the lower court's view that entry was easy and that competition was not harmed, primarily because Roberts had expanded a year after Syufy had acquired its last major rival.[35] With a single contested example of fringe firm expansion in hand,[36] the court did not investigate the ability and incentive of other firms to enter by following Roberts's model. Instead, the court disclaimed any need to conduct such an analysis. It dismissed without serious consideration an argument that any serious economist would treat as a legitimate possibility[37]: the government's assertion that entry at a scale large enough to achieve low costs would turn out to be unprofitable because it would depress market prices.[38] The *Syufy* panel rested its entry analysis on consideration of whether new firms *could* enter the market, without recognizing that it is necessary also to evaluate whether those firms likely *would* do so.[39]

In explaining this decision, Judge Kozinski openly displayed a deep skepticism about the value of enforcing the antitrust statutes.[40] The opinion emphasizes the way government enforcement can create "a real danger of stifling competition and creativity in the marketplace," and argues that in a free enterprise system, merger decisions "should be made by market actors responding to market forces, not by government bureaucrats pursuing their notions of how the market should operate."[41] Judge Kozinski does not appear to consider the possibility that antitrust law in general, and merger enforcement in particular, could benefit society by deterring or remedying business conduct that lessens competition and creates market power.[42]

Another example of judicial overreaction to criticism of 1960s merger policy can be found in the recent district court decision declining to enjoin Oracle's acquisition of PeopleSoft.[43] The case involved a merger between two leading producers of enterprise resource planning software, which is used by large and complex enterprises to integrate firm-wide data.

The Justice Department viewed the merger as threatening adverse unilateral competitive effects, resulting from the loss of competition between two differentiated product producers.[44] As an economic matter, unilateral effects do not turn on market definition. The economic analysis is the same regardless of whether the case is framed as a merger generating high concentration within a narrow market or as the loss of direct competition between the merging firms within a broader market where concentration is lower.[45] The Justice Department chose the former route, alleging that the merger harmed competition within a product market of high function financial management systems and human relations management software. Justice contended that three firms dominated this category of business software—the merging firms and SAP—and that Oracle and PeopleSoft were the leading choices for many customers. The merging firms claimed that the market was broader, and that in consequence several more firms should be recognized as rivals, including Lawson, AMS, and Microsoft. The court concluded that Justice had failed to prove the product market it alleged and hence declined to enjoin the merger.

The *Oracle* case raised three issues related to proof of unilateral effects: the evidentiary value of customer views, the legal standard, and the role of merger simulation. Judge Vaughn Walker, the author of the *Oracle* opinion, claimed in his opinion to accept unilateral effects, but in discussing these issues, the court's opinion betrays a deep hostility to unilateral effects that interferes with careful antitrust analysis.

In support of its position, the Justice Department introduced evidence about customer views. Customer views surely are an important source of information about buyer substitution, the economic force at issue in the analysis of unilateral effects (regardless of whether that analysis is framed legally as a market definition issue or a competitive effects question).[46] Indeed, and not surprisingly, customer complaints in general raise the likelihood of agency merger enforcement substantially.[47]

But Judge Walker was skeptical of the customer testimony in the case. He properly noted that customer evidence must be tested for its probative value.[48] In doing so, Judge Walker recognized that the customer witnesses proffered by the Justice Department were "extremely sophisticated buyers" with "decades of experience."[49] He nevertheless refused to credit the customer testimony because the witnesses did not perform extensive new analyses for the case.[50] Judge Walker accepted that customer views are relevant to the analysis of buyer substitution, but he made clear that he would not trust those views unless they came in a form rarely found in practice in the business world.[51] If the standard employed in *Oracle* were adopted, customer views would rarely be usable in practice to prove unilateral competitive effects.

Judge Walker's position as to the appropriate legal standard for evaluating unilateral effects claims similarly reflects hostility to unilateral effects. The *Oracle* decision inappropriately requires the government to prove that the merger would lead to a monopoly or near-monopoly in a narrow market,[52] while simultaneously expressing skepticism about narrow markets as arbitrary or unprincipled submarkets.[53] Unfortunately, Judge Walker failed to understand the basic economics underlying unilateral effects. "In a unilateral effects case," Judge Walker writes, "a plaintiff is attempting to prove that the merging parties could unilaterally increase prices. Accordingly, a plaintiff must demonstrate that the merging parties would enjoy a post-merger monopoly or dominant position, at least in a 'localized competition' space."[54] This statement is incorrect and constitutes a clear error in economic reasoning. It is not true even in the commonly used horizontal differentiation model that Judge Walker appears to have in mind: unilateral effects will arise so long as some customers of one of the merging firms consider its merger partner's product as their second choice, even if more of the firm's customers consider a third firm's products to be their second choice. Moreover, large anticompetitive effects can easily arise in the logit model of demand, which lacks any notion of location or proximity between the competing firms.[55] Accordingly, when Judge Walker holds that "[t]o prevail on a differentiated products unilateral effects claim, a plaintiff must prove a relevant market in which the merging parties would have essentially a monopoly or dominant position,"[56] he incorrectly applies the modern economic understanding of unilateral competitive effects. Again Judge Walker creates a method of analysis that throws up unreasonable barriers to proving unilateral competitive effects.

Judge Walker also considers a third method of proving unilateral effects: merger simulation.[57] While the court endorses the method in theory,[58] on reviewing the simulation study of the Justice Department's economic expert, the court dismissed the application of this method in practice as based on unreliable data.[59] In our experience, the real-world data on prices, costs, and output available for use in simulation studies are invariably imperfect, especially when products are sold in markets with differentiated products where each supplier offers a complex array of products, where products are sold in bundles at negotiated prices, and where the products are changing over time due to technological progress—all conditions present in the *Oracle* case. One wonders whether real-world data could ever be good enough for this court.

The *Oracle* decision is deeply troubling because it suggests that three important enforcement agency tools for proving unilateral competitive effects of merger among sellers of differentiated products—customer complaints, demonstration of significant direct competition between the merging firms within the context of a market that includes other rivals, and merger simulation—may not be accepted in practice. Furthermore, the *Oracle* decision could effectively nullify the structural presumption in many cases, by making it difficult for plaintiffs to define any relevant market other than an extremely broad one in which market shares are low.

To the extent that other courts adopt Judge Walker's hostile approach toward proving unilateral effects, the ability of the agencies to rely on the theory of unilateral effects, which is well established in economics, and which has been used effectively in the past by the agencies to attack a large class of anticompetitive mergers, will be severely undermined.[60] By attempting to create a safe harbor for mergers in which unilateral effects are alleged unless market concentration rises to near monopoly levels, the *Oracle* court overshot the mark. As we shall see immediately below, there is, unfortunately, some evidence that the *Oracle* decision has indeed caused the Justice Department to scale back its merger enforcement efforts.

B. The Decline of Agency Merger Enforcement

In January 2007, the *Wall Street Journal* reported that "[t]he federal government has nearly stepped out of the antitrust enforcement business, leaving companies to mate as they wish."[61] Accordingly, "the message is clear for deals with antitrust issues: It's now or never."[62] Similarly, in March 2007, the *New York Times* declared that two merging firms proposing a controversial deal "have reason to be optimistic" about Justice Department approval "because the Bush administration has been more permissive on antitrust issues than any administration in modern times."[63]

Prior to the current administration, the low point for modern merger enforcement was set by the Antitrust Division during the second term of the Reagan Administration.[64] The rate of merger challenges then was unusually low; as will be demonstrated below, senior officials frequently overruled staff recommendations to challenge acquisitions,[65] and those few mergers that were challenged were typically mergers to very high levels of concentration.[66] A task force established by the American Bar Association Section of Antitrust Law, writing in 1990, highlighted the "public perception that the [Antitrust] Division may be pursuing an enforcement policy more lenient than the 1984 [Merger] Guidelines dictate" during Reagan's second term,[67] and cautioned that "[a]ny significant departure from the standards of the 1984 Merger Guidelines would be unwise."[68]

The nonenforcement approach to mergers of the Reagan II Antitrust Division is evident in the statistical record on merger enforcement. The key statistic is agency enforcement actions as a fraction of Hart-Scott-Rodino filings.[69] Commissioner Thomas Leary used this measure to argue that merger policy has been characterized more by continuity over time than wild swings.[70] Based on agency data on enforcement actions and HSR filings, Leary constructed the following table.[71]

Table 6.1.   Merger Enforcement

	Challenges as a Percentage of Adjusted HSR Filings				
	1982–85	1986–89	1990–93	1994–97	1998–2000
	Reagan I	Reagan II	Bush	Clinton I	Clinton II
FTC	1.0	0.7	1.5	1.1	0.7
DOJ	0.8	0.4	0.8	0.9	1.1
Total	1.8	1.1	2.3	2.0	1.8

Leary assigned years to presidential terms with a one year lag (for example, President Reagan's second term began in 1986, but the figures for that year are assigned to his first term), because the data refer to fiscal years (which begin three months before the calendar year) and because it often takes time for a new administration to staff senior agency positions.[72] Enforcement actions in the data include court cases, consent settlements, and transactions abandoned or restructured prior to filing a complaint as a result of an announced challenge. Multiyear averages smooth year-to-year variation in the data. (Please see the appendix for the survey instrument.)

These figures can be interpreted as reflecting merger enforcement activity at the agencies, with two very important caveats.[73] First, merger enforcement rates may be affected by unobservable changes in the composition of HSR filings. For example, suppose in a given year that a greater-than-normal fraction of filed deals are not horizontal, perhaps because they involve management buyouts or acquisitions made by passive investors.[74] Since such deals are far less likely to raise antitrust issues than deals in which one company is acquiring another, the reported merger enforcement percentage could well decline in that year, even if there had been no change in the underlying enforcement policy.[75]

Second, and even more important, the mix of deals presented to the agencies, in terms of the severity of antitrust issues they raise, is endogenous. Firms learn about changing agency enforcement patterns from their antitrust advisors, who are members of an industry with a strong financial incentive to track enforcement trends. To the extent that advice is informed and heeded, we would expect to see a similar fraction of challenged deals every year, mainly comprised of "judgment calls" close to the line, regardless of where the line is drawn.[76] It is unlikely that this type of adjustment is instantaneous—it may take time for lawyers to infer changes in agency views from enforcement decisions and official rhetoric, and perhaps longer for clients to be convinced. To the extent this dynamic is important, and we suspect it is, it means that the interpretation of the statistics should focus on the deviation of the merger enforcement rate from the average (which was 0.9 percent for the agency enforcement figures in the table). That is, an unusually low figure should be interpreted as indicating an unanticipated recent decrease in merger enforcement, and an unusually high figure should be interpreted as indicating an unanticipated recent increase in merger enforcement.[77] More generally, changes over time in the enforcement rate are more informative regarding agency policies than are the absolute levels of the enforcement rate.

With this interpretation, the figures in Commissioner Leary's merger enforcement table can be explained in a plausible way. Most notably, the strikingly low merger enforcement rate of 0.4 percent during the second term of the Reagan Administration suggests that the Antitrust Division under Assistant Attorneys General Ginsburg and Rule surprised the antitrust bar with their lack of interest in challenging mergers.[78] These data are consistent with the view that the Antitrust Division during that period was unusually permissive toward horizontal mergers.

To analyze merger enforcement trends in the twenty-first century, we updated Commissioner Leary's statistics.[79] The main data challenge was to account for the changes in Hart-Scott-Rodino reporting rules that took effect in February 2001, which dramatically reduced the number of mergers filed in the HSR statistics.[80] We determined that filings after the change were 40 percent of what they would have been had the reporting rules stayed the same,[81] and adjusted the recent merger enforcement statistics accordingly,[82] in order to derive comparable merger enforcement statistics for the four year period 2002–2005, which corresponds to the first term of the George W. Bush Administration.[83] We also derived preliminary estimates of merger enforcement statistics for the second term of the George W. Bush Administration. These estimates are preliminary because they include data for only two years of the four year period (2006 and 2007), and because the data for 2007 is for 11 months of the fiscal year, not the full year.[84]

During the first term of the George W. Bush Administration, the rate of merger challenges for DOJ and the total for both agencies were below the average of those reported by Commissioner Leary, while the FTC figure was close to the average. The DOJ number was identical to the merger enforcement rate observed during the second term of the Reagan Administration, which was the lowest in modern history. According to the preliminary estimates for the second term, the merger enforcement rate at DOJ remained at the same low level observed during the previous four years. Because the FTC rate simultaneously declined to a below-average figure, the total federal merger enforcement rate for the second term dropped below the lowest level previously recorded.[85]

We interpret these figures as indicating that merger enforcement during the current administration has been surprisingly low, particularly at the Antitrust Division, even after accounting for any expectations that a new Republican administration might resolve close cases more in favor of permitting mergers than would the Democratic administration that preceded it.[86] Had the two federal enforcement agencies challenged mergers during

Table 6.2.   Merger Enforcement

| | Challenges as a Percentage of Adjusted HSR Filings | |
	2002–05 George W. Bush I	2006–07 George W. Bush II[p]
FTC	0.8	0.6
DOJ	0.4	0.4
Total	1.2	1.0

p = preliminary estimates

2006 and 2007 at the rate the FTC did during the first term of the current administration (which was slightly below the historical average), the agencies would have challenged 24 more mergers each year (15 more at the Antitrust Division and nine more at the FTC).[87] While we do not know which particular mergers would have been challenged had merger enforcement been closer to the average rate, and thus had merger enforcement been consistent with the antitrust community's expectations, this computation offers a conservative estimate of the number.

We confirmed our interpretation that merger enforcement became much more lenient during the current administration by surveying 20 experienced antitrust practitioners. We administered our survey during March 2007, when the agencies were headed by Assistant Attorney General Thomas Barnett and FTC Chairman Deborah Majoras. We attempted to contact the 24 attorneys listed as the leading antitrust lawyers in the District of Columbia in an annual survey.[88] We were able to interview 20 of these 24 individuals, for an 83 percent response rate. Eight of our twenty respondents had worked at one time at the Antitrust Division, and nine had worked at the Federal Trade Commission, so 85 percent of our respondents had prior agency experience. Our survey instrument is included as an appendix.

Our survey respondents consistently told us that in reviewing horizontal mergers, both the Antitrust Division and the FTC are "more receptive to arguments made by the merging firms" today than ten years ago.[89] On a 5-point scale, with 5 corresponding to "significantly more receptive,"[90] the average score for the DOJ was 4.8 and the average score for the FTC was 4.6.[91] Similarly, our respondents consistently reported that the "likelihood of successful agency review for the merging firms" for a given horizontal merger is sharply higher now than it would have been ten years ago. On a 5-point scale, with 5 corresponding to "significantly more favorable," the average score was 4.9.[92] By asking about a given horizontal merger, this question was designed to correct for any possible shift in the mix of deals presented to the agencies. Our survey respondents report changes in merger enforcement occurring at all stages of the merger review process: fewer second requests, a greater likelihood that an investigation will be closed rather than lead to an enforcement action, and a willingness to accept weaker remedies in those cases where enforcement actions are taken. We believe that our survey provides compelling evidence that there has been a sharp shift over the past ten years toward a more lax horizontal merger enforcement policy.

This shift appears to have been much more pronounced at the Justice Department than at the Federal Trade Commission. We asked our survey respondents whether they saw a significant substantive difference today between merger enforcement at the DOJ and the FTC. On a 5-point scale, where 5 corresponds to the DOJ being significantly tougher, the mean score was 1.9, indicating that the DOJ is generally seen as more lax. Our respondents unanimously believed that their clients' interests would be better served by DOJ than FTC review; this preference resulted from a combination of procedural and substantive considerations. The preference of merging parties for DOJ review based on a more lax approach is especially pronounced at the current time. The DOJ is seen as increasingly pulling back from merger enforcement. One of our survey respondents said, "*Oracle* has been a major factor in DOJ decisions not to bring a case." Another respondent stated, "DOJ is just going through the motions." In contrast, as noted above, our respondents see a slight increase in FTC merger enforcement over the past five years.[93]

The perception that the Justice Department has adopted a very lax merger enforcement policy was unquestionably fueled by the March 2006 decision of Assistant Attorney General Barnett not to take any enforcement action when Whirlpool sought to acquire Maytag.[94] For a number of reasons, this merger was especially revealing regarding the current Justice Department's merger enforcement policy and especially influential in shaping the advice given by antitrust lawyers to their clients:

- The merger was highly visible, in large part because it involved two U.S. companies with storied brand names that are well known by many consumers.
- The merger involved a traditional manufacturing industry, namely residential clothes washers and dryers. As a result, the contrast between the lack of enforcement in this case and historical merger enforcement in manufacturing industries was especially pronounced. A similar outcome in, say, a software merger would not have been as influential.
- The merger involved a dramatic increase in concentration in the markets for both residential washing machines and dryers. According to publicly available data for 2004, Whirlpool's share of unit shipments of residential washing machines in the U.S. was 51 percent and Maytag's share was 20 percent. (GE was third with 17 percent and Electrolux was fourth with 9 percent of shipments; other firms supplied 3 percent of the market.) The corresponding figures for dryers were 56 percent for Whirlpool and 20 percent for Maytag.[95] (GE was third with 13 percent and Electrolux was fourth with 9 percent of shipments; other firms supplied 1 percent of this market.) Using these figures, the merger would raise the HHI in each of these markets by about 2000, from around 3400 to around 5400, and leave Whirlpool with a market share of more than 70 percent.
- In explaining its decision not to take any enforcement action, the Justice Department embraced three arguments often made by merging firms: (1) the ability of two recent entrants into the U.S. market (LG and Samsung) to expand significantly their imports into the U.S.; (2) the presence of large buyers in the wholesale markets for washing machines and dryers (Sears, Lowe's, The Home Depot, and Best Buy); and (3) cost savings from the merger would "reduce the likelihood" of harm to competition.[96]

The lack of enforcement action in this case puts into sharp relief the decline in the practical significance of the structural presumption. Given the very large combined market shares of Whirlpool and Maytag, 50 percent plus 20 percent, if the structural presumption had been given much weight at all, it would presumably have been very hard to overcome with these numbers. Yet the Justice Department's closing statement gives short shrift to at least three important points which could have supported an enforcement action.

First, the statement does not explain why the recent entry by LG and Samsung was sufficient to solve any competitive problems caused by the merger. In a mature market in which brand names are important and market shares have generally been stable, why does the presence of a new entrant into the market that has grown to, say, 5 percent of the market over two or three years imply that there is no competitive harm when the leading firm, with 50 percent of the market, acquires the number two firm, with 20 percent of the market? In the case at hand, would LG, Samsung, or other foreign firms or fringe domestic products have the production capacity and brand reputation needed to convince large distributors like Best Buy to carry them? If so, would their products be attractive to those consumers who now see Whirlpool and Maytag as their first and second choices?

Second, the statement does not address the extent of direct competition between Whirlpool and Maytag or the extent to which the merger raised a unilateral effects problem (absent entry, repositioning, or efficiencies). Following the standard approach to unilateral effects, as discussed in the 1992 Merger Guidelines, one would naturally hypothesize that a post-merger unilateral price increase would be profitable for Whirlpool, with the magnitude of the price increase depending on the price-cost margins on washers and dryers and on the diversion ratio between Whirlpool and Maytag models. Unless Whirlpool and Maytag are positioned in very different places in the market, standard models of the pricing of differentiated products would tend to predict large unilateral effects given their large shares, especially for Maytag models, with the precise amounts depending upon the gross margins on washers and dryers. In fact, since the inroads made by LG and Samsung largely involved higher-end, front-loading washing machines, Whirlpool and Maytag may be closer competitors in the lower-end, top-loading segment than would be reflected in their overall market shares. Moreover, the statement does not acknowledge that unilateral competitive effects can be significant even if rivals have excess production capacity, since these effects are based on brand names and product differentiation, not on capacity constraints.

Third, the statement does not explain the basis for concluding that the efficiencies asserted by the merging parties were merger-specific and sufficient in magnitude to offset the elimination of Maytag as an independent competitor in the markets for washers and dryers. The press has reported widely that Maytag was a high-cost producer and that Whirlpool was a more efficient manufacturer than Maytag. Normally, absent merger, the lower-cost firm would compete to gain share from the higher-cost firm, to the benefit of consumers. Such competitive pressure often also causes the higher-cost firm to become more efficient, again to the benefit of consumers. Plus, rivalry from the higher-cost firm with a substantial (if slowly declining) market share typically puts important competitive pressure on the lower-cost firm, inducing it to trim its costs and improve its products. The Justice Department does not explain why consumers will be better off if the lower-cost firm, here Whirlpool, is allowed to acquire the higher-cost firm, here Maytag, thereby short-circuiting this normal competitive process. We note in this respect that in July 2006 Whirlpool announced price increases of 6 percent to 12 percent for the second half of 2006. Among other factors behind the price increase, Whirlpool cited the drag on its earnings caused by the Maytag acquisition.[97]

We are deeply concerned that the Whirlpool case is indicative of an overly lax approach to merger enforcement at the current Justice Department. While we can understand that the Justice Department might want to wait for strong facts before bringing its next unilateral effects case after *Oracle,* in order to take on the problematic legal conclusions of that district court, the Justice Department never raised this litigation issue as a reason not to challenge Whirlpool's acquisition of Maytag. One experienced practitioner in our survey cited Whirlpool/Maytag as a "close deal" in today's merger environment that "would have had a hard time" getting through the Justice Department ten years ago. We are confident that the Whirlpool/Maytag deal would have been challenged by Assistant Attorney General Klein ten years ago.[98]

We find it instructive to compare the Whirlpool case with the drug wholesaling mergers successfully challenged by the Federal Trade Commission nearly a decade ago.[99] Those mergers led to high concentration, but they were close cases in part because of a few examples of expansion by small drug wholesalers. The FTC refused to credit easy entry based on a limited number of examples of fringe expansion without further analysis, and after that analysis concluded that entry would not solve the competitive problem in the case. In court, the FTC argued that fringe expansion would be insufficient to counteract or deter harm to competition from the transaction. Judge Stanley Sporkin agreed, holding that "[t]he record developed at trial is not strong enough for this Court to conclude that the Defendants' claim of entry and expansion is sufficient to rebut the Government's *prima facie* case."[100] The core issue dividing the drug wholesaling cases from Whirlpool/Maytag is how much weight to place on one or a few instances of entry leading to a small market share, in the context of a proposed merger that will cause a large increase in market concentration. In contrast to the approach taken by the FTC and the court in the drug wholesaling case, the Justice Department, in its review of the Whirlpool/Maytag merger, like Judge Kozinski in *Syufy,* appears to have been willing to accept entry and expansion arguments in highly concentrating mergers, despite the fact that the entrants had only been able to achieve a relatively small market share.

The merger enforcement data, our survey of experienced practitioners, the fallout from the *Oracle* case, and the treatment of the Whirlpool/Maytag deal combine to paint a picture of overly lenient horizontal merger enforcement, especially at the current Antitrust Division.[101] The FTC and the DOJ must pay close attention to the ongoing decline in the structural presumption in the courts. Nonetheless, one of our survey respondents expressed a worry that the agencies have grown "a little gun-shy after *Oracle*." Another stated that he/she was giving the following advice to clients: "If you want to do a dicey deal, get it done before the [2008] election." This view was echoed by a number other respondents.

III. Economic Arguments Merging Firms Love to Make

In a world where the structural presumption carries little weight, evaluating the merger enforcement record is inherently difficult and controversial, precisely because each case is fact intensive. The difficulty of assessing the enforcement record is much greater because so much of the relevant evidence typically remains confidential (except in those rare cases that are litigated). We therefore would not presume to offer opinions on the many transactions that are reviewed by the agencies about which there is precious little by way of facts or agency reasoning in the public record.[102] Instead, we bolster the evidence provided above by discussing several arguments that are commonly made by merging parties and which appear to be accepted more readily by the agencies, especially the Justice Department, than in years past. Our discussion here starts from the proposition that the agencies typically no longer consider it sufficient to show that a proposed merger will lead to a significant increase in concentration in a properly defined relevant market. Rather, the agencies typically seek to establish a particular *mechanism* of anticompetitive effects. Likewise, the courts place far less weight on structural presumptions than they did in the past.

Merging parties routinely put forward several substantive claims that, if routinely and uncritically accepted by the agencies and the courts, would collectively remove virtually all mergers from antitrust review. We structure our analysis around three substantive claims where we detect over-reaching.[103]

- Effective competition generally requires only three, or even two, rivals.
- The prospect of entry typically deters or counteracts anticompetitive effects of mergers.
- Mergers often spur competition and benefit consumers by enabling efficiencies.

We now address these arguments in turn.

A. What Has Become of the Structural Presumption?

The noninterventionist approach to merger control policy relies heavily on the proposition that little can be learned in general about the extent of rivalry, and industrial performance, from market concentration. A strong version of this proposition states that effective competition typically requires only three, or even two, strong suppliers. In contrast, a more balanced approach begins with the proposition that market structure matters, in the following specific sense: in the absence of entry and merger efficiencies, a merger that leads to a substantial increase in market concentration will tend to raise price, harm consumers, and reduce economic efficiency.[104] Put differently, a merger is not simply an event that calls attention to a market structure with a certain number of firms postmerger; it is also the method by which that postmerger market structure is created. In analyzing the competitive effects of a proposed transaction, we do not simply have fewer firms; we also have a merger, a specific form of business conduct with the potential to harm competition, and must think about both the merger and the resulting market structure in evaluating the transaction.

Our survey results confirm that the strength of the structural presumption in agency enforcement policy has significantly declined over the past decade. Our survey respondents reported that the agencies are much more receptive now than ten years ago to the argument that "market concentration is not a good basis for predicting competitive effects." On a 5-point scale, with 5 corresponding to "much more receptive," the average score from our 20 respondents was 4.6.

As a practical matter, the key question regarding market structure for merger control policy is whether much weight should be given to the structural presumption. The clear lesson from oligopoly theory is that market concentration matters, in the specific sense noted above.[105] By the nature of game theory, there are special cases where concentration does not matter, but these examples are not robust. Yet there is a danger that these special cases will have greater impact than is warranted.

To illustrate, consider how a merger affects the equilibrium price in an oligopoly in which the firms offer differentiated products and set prices independently. There is a general result in such models that mergers will raise prices unless they trigger new entry or product repositioning by existing competitors or generate merger-specific efficiencies.[106] In one special case, however, a merger will have no impact on price, so long as at least two firms remain after the merger: the case in which the firms sell homogeneous products, have identical costs, and set prices in a one-shot (Bertrand) game. In this special case, prices are equal to marginal cost so long as at least two firms remain after the merger. In virtually all mergers, this special case can easily be shown not to apply; usually, one can directly observe that prices are not close to marginal cost, typically because the firms sell differentiated products or brand names are important, and real-world price-cost margins must be large enough to allow recovery of various fixed costs such as R&D costs. Likewise, in a bidding market, mergers typically cause price to rise, unless one of the merging firms is generally known to be an ineffective competitor, in the sense that it has no real chance of being the first or second choice of any buyer. Yet this does not stop merging firms, and noninterventionists, from arguing that "two is enough."[107] Plus, additional dangers arise under a theory of coordinated effects when a maverick is acquired by one of its rivals.[108] We are not suggesting a return to a mechanical, concentration-based approach to merger policy. We are simply suggesting that large increases in market concentration should be given real weight in merger analysis and that any contrary presumption that "two is enough" (or even three) is unsupported by economic theory.

The assertion that only mergers to monopoly or near-monopoly should concern antitrust enforcers can be seen at least as early as 1978 in Robert Bork's highly influential book *The Antitrust Paradox*.[109] This view corresponds roughly to a policy of allowing most or all mergers short of merger to monopoly; notice the similarity between this approach and that of Judge Walker in *Oracle*. While there are no doubt some markets with only two major firms in which those firms compete vigorously against each other (possible examples that come to mind are Boeing vs. Airbus in commercial aircraft and Intel vs. AMD in microprocessors), there is simply no theoretical or empirical basis for a *presumption* that horizontal mergers are innocuous (or beneficial) so long as they are not to monopoly.

An even more striking example of overreaching in denying an effect for market concentration can be found in a recent article by Tom Campbell. Campbell contends that "[p]roducers of a good should be allowed to merge whenever there is only one purchaser of the good, or when the large majority of purchases are in favor of the merger of producers."[110] Campbell argues in favor of permitting even mergers to monopoly based on the assertion that bilateral bargaining leads to efficient outcomes because the quantity sold under bilateral bargaining is always equal to the amount that would be sold under perfect competition.[111] Campell's theory is inconsistent with the modern economic understanding that bargaining with asymmetric information typically leads to inefficient outcomes.[112] His paper illustrates the danger of basing sweeping policy recommendations on a simple and special theoretical model that is not robust and lacks empirical support.

B. Evaluating Entry and Expansion Arguments

We noted earlier that entry and expansion arguments were accepted in *Syufy* and in the Whirlpool/Maytag merger investigation based on limited examples, while such arguments were not accepted in the drug wholesaling merger litigation.

Our survey results confirm that the agencies are more willing to accept entry arguments now than they were ten years ago. Our survey respondents reported that the agencies are more receptive now than ten years ago to the argument that "entry will counteract or deter any competitive problem." On a 5-point scale, with 5 corresponding to "much more receptive," the average score from our 20 respondents was 3.9.

Again, there is a simple economic model in which the prospect of entry does indeed counteract or deter any competitive problem. That is the model in which there is a perfectly elastic supply from entrants at the current market price. This is a variant of the standard model of perfect competition, in which many small firms are just as efficient as the merging firms, even if the latter are far larger. That model might apply to some markets for homogeneous products, but it is extremely special and certainly not an appropriate basis for a general presumption in merger policy.

A variant of this special case arises when considering how to treat foreign production capacity in analyzing mergers in U.S. markets when there are some imports. In such cases, it is a clear economic error to assume that the entire foreign capacity would be devoted to the U.S. market if prices were to rise a small amount.[113] Rather, the effects of the merger depend upon the elasticity of supply of imports at prices at and above the premerger price. To the extent that foreign capacity is being used profitably to supply customers elsewhere in the world, it will typically become increasingly costly for the importing firm to divert that capacity to the U.S. market. Furthermore, any coherent analysis must be consistent with the premerger level of imports being optimal for the foreign firms. Simply stating that foreign firms have sufficient capacity to discipline a price increase by the merging firms (or by a broader group of domestic suppliers) is an incomplete and misleading story.

There is one other model in which potential entry is a very potent force and mergers between incumbents have no anticompetitive effects: the model of contestable markets, in which entry does not involve any sunk costs. This model has the advantage of applying to industries in which there are significant scale economies. However, the model generally is not suitable or reliable for merger analysis.[114] To begin with, in the model of contestable markets there is no strategic difference between an incumbent (however large) and a potential entrant, so it is not clear why a merger would ever be profitable. More importantly, this model does not allow for any unique firm-specific assets such as brand names or reputation, or other unique capabilities, such as those associated with patents and trade secrets. Nor does the model place any limit on the rate of internal growth by an entrant; entry can occur instantly at efficient scale, however large. Once one understands the many strong and unrealistic assumptions behind the model of contestable markets, it becomes clear that the model is rarely applicable to real-world mergers.

In practice, merging parties like to point to specific instances of entry in order to suggest that entry is easy. Frequently, there will indeed be at least one or two examples of past entry. But evidence of past entry is inherently double-edged, consistent both with low entry barriers in the past (which permitted it) or past exercise of market power (which induced it). Truly successful entry, in which the entrant has achieved (or predictably will soon achieve) a sizeable market share and places substantial competitive pressure on incumbents, should certainly be the basis for careful entry analysis, focusing on whether other firms would likely also have success following a similar plan, and whether such entry would likely counteract or deter any postmerger exercise of market power. But the mere presence of *some* examples of entry, in which the entrants have not (yet) exited the market, should not form a basis for embracing the view that entry will solve any competitive problems caused by the merger, especially when the shares of the merging firms are large and those of the entrants are small.[115]

Several important issues regularly arise when evaluating entry arguments. Many of these considerations were relevant in the Whirlpool/ Maytag case. As a general proposition, we doubt that these arguments are receiving sufficient weight today in merger policy:

- Taking as given the presence of a "poster-child" recent entrant, the elimination of competition caused by the merger may still be significant. The particular entrant's competitive role may reasonably be assessed based on its current market share, adjusted as necessary to reflect likely changes in that share in the near future.
- The fact that one firm has been able to enter does not necessarily imply that others will find it profitable to do so. Regardless of past entry, future entry may not be profitable, especially if the demand is stagnant or declining. Furthermore, if the entrant enjoyed an advantage based on certain firm-specific assets that made entry attractive, one should study whether other potential entrants also possess comparable assets, or other assets that are valuable for entry.[116]
- Entry may be easier in some segments of the market than others. In markets with differentiated products, the fact that entry has proven possible in one segment, such as the low-price segment, does not imply that entry would be profitable in another segment. For example, brand name and reputation may be more important, and take longer to build, or technical requirements may be greater, in the high-price, high-performance segment of the market. Or transportation costs may be more important at the low end of the market. If both of the merging firms operate in a segment of the market where entry has not been demonstrated, entry is less likely to solve competitive problems.[117]
- Entry generally takes time, and competition can be harmed while entrants gain enough scale, scope, and credibility to replace the lost competition from merger, for example by competing as effectively as did the weaker of the two merging parties.[118]

C. Evaluating Efficiency Claims

In 1997, a new section on merger efficiencies was added to the Horizontal Merger Guidelines.[119] This was a positive development, since a proper analysis of competitive effects should surely account for merger efficiencies above and beyond the presumed efficiencies implicit in the "safe harbors" that have long been a feature of the Guidelines. In fact, one of the advantages of the unilateral effects theory is that it allows for the integration of efficiencies into the competitive effects analysis, comparing quantitatively the incentive to raise price due to lessened competition and the incentive to lower price based on reductions in variable costs.[120] We believe that the revised merger guidelines provide a sound framework within which claims of merger efficiencies can be evaluated. We highlight two aspects of that framework that we consider especially important: the requirements that efficiencies be (1) merger-specific and (2) verified before they can be counted to offset any to anticompetitive effects of the merger. If the standards used to meet these requirements are lowered, some phantom efficiencies will be credited, leading to overly lax enforcement.

Our survey results confirm that the agencies are more willing to accept efficiency arguments now than they were ten years ago. Our survey respondents reported that the agencies are more receptive now than ten years ago to the argument that "the procompetitive benefits of efficiencies from merger outweigh the threat of harm to competition." On a 5-point scale, with 5 corresponding to "much more receptive," the average score from our 20 respondents was 4.3. While our respondents identified a clear trend, a number also believe that there remains a great deal of skepticism at both agencies about efficiency arguments mounted by the merging parties.

There is considerable evidence, moreover, that acquiring firms are systematically overoptimistic about the efficiencies they can achieve through acquisition.[121] Evidence from the finance, managerial, and economics literatures shows that many mergers do not work out well, either in terms of shareholder value or organizationally. This evidence supports the view that many mergers are motivated by managerial hubris, perhaps exacerbated by distorted managerial compensation schemes, and that managers often underestimate integration problems. This evidence certainly does not support the view that merger-specific efficiencies are common or that claims of efficiencies made by merging parties should generally be credited. Some mergers are undoubtedly motivated by the pursuit of genuine efficiencies and go on to generate them. But we caution that arguments by merging firms that efficiencies will enhance their ability and incentive to compete, resulting in lower prices, higher quality or new products, should not be accepted based solely on their plausibility, but only after careful analysis.[122]

IV. Structuring Merger Analysis in a Post-Chicago World

The challenge facing those who seek effective and principled merger enforcement policy is to develop a set of analytical steps that charts a moderate course: relying on measures of market share but not excessively, and not accepting the three "E" arguments of entry, expansion, and efficiency without first testing them rigorously using real-world evidence. We believe that such a moderate course must include the use of suitably crafted presumptions that have real bite in the sense that strong evidence is required to overcome them.

Presumptions and burdens of proof are critical when analyzing horizontal mergers. Most merger review is prospective, requiring predictions about how a proposed merger will affect competition.[123] These predictions are inherently difficult to make and subject to a considerable uncertainty—such is the nature of complex social and economic systems. Therefore, in many if not most cases, neither the government nor the merging parties will be able to offer ironclad proof of a theory of how the proposed merger will affect competition. Unless the government has some simple and sensible way of establishing a presumption of harm to competition, consistent with sound economic analysis, which the merging parties must then overcome to persuade a court to permit the transaction, few proposed mergers will be subject to effective challenge. While some may welcome that result, we do not believe such a lax approach to merger enforcement is consistent with sound antitrust policy. Our survey respondents generally agree with us that the decline in merger enforcement over the past decade has been detrimental to effective competition policy. We asked respondents whether the changes in agency enforcement policy over the past ten years have "improved competition policy" or "been detrimental to effective competition policy." On a 5-point scale, with 5 corresponding to "significantly improved competition policy," the average response in our survey to this question was 2.2, distinctly less than the neutral figure of 3.0.[124]

Moreover, presumptions, like other bright-line rules, have many advantages in merger analysis from a decision-theoretic perspective. They give guidance to firms seeking to stay within the law, and they give guidance to lower courts on how to apply the law when reviewing proposed deals. They also help make merger law more easily administrable. That is, they reduce the transaction costs of antitrust enforcement and adjudication, by structuring and simplifying the analysis used by the courts to determine whether firms have acted within the law. Their primary disadvantage is that they can generate more errors in determining whether business conduct is harmful than would occur with a less structured and potentially more wide-ranging inquiry. To minimize this disadvantage, it is essential that presumptions employed in merger review have a sound economic grounding. They must be based on observable features of market structure that economic understanding suggests correlate well with harm to competition.[125]

Historically, in analyzing horizontal mergers, the courts have relied on a presumption based on market concentration. We have traced above the dramatic erosion in the structural presumption over time, and the profound effects of that erosion on merger control policy. The time has come to update the structural presumption to reflect advances in economic learning as well as the lessons learned from the record of merger enforcement over the past forty years. We do not seek to discard structural presumptions, or to return to the more mechanical approach from the 1960s. Rather, we seek to reinvigorate horizontal merger enforcement with presumptions that are both practical and based on sound economic analysis.

V. Presumptions and Burden-Shifting in a Post-Chicago World

How should a court, confronted with the obligation to decide whether to enjoin a proposed horizontal merger, make that decision? How should it incorporate modern economic thinking and avoid the erroneous economic reasoning we have criticized, while remaining faithful to the established legal approach to merger review? Our answer is to rely on the familiar legal framework based on presumptions and burden-shifting, but to specify those presumptions in a way that is simultaneously consistent with precedent and more closely attuned to the modern economics of horizontal merger analysis. This section sketches our suggested approach.[126] When we offer specific benchmarks (for HHI levels, number of firms, price increases, and the like), we do so tentatively to make clear the type of showing we think appropriate and as an impetus to further discussion of the specific details.

A. Steps in Merger Analysis in the Courts

Under the well-established legal framework for merger analysis,[127] the government bears the burden of persuasion but, as with all other cases, the burden of production shifts during litigation.[128] The government satisfies its initial burden of production by introducing evidence that concentration in a well-defined market is high and will significantly increase as a consequence of the merger (thus establishing a prima facie case through application of the structural presumption), and by articulating the economic logic by which it believes competition will be harmed, such as coordinated or unilateral effects.[129] This demonstration shifts a burden of production to the merging firms to explain why the inference of likely competitive harm from the change in market concentration is unlikely in fact to be realized. If the merging firms satisfy their burden of production, the burden of production shifts back to the government, which may discredit the defendants' showing or provide additional evidence of anticompetitive effect. The burden of persuasion remains on the government at all times.

Within this framework, the structural presumption identifies the minimum quantum of evidence the government must present in order to satisfy its burden of production, and hence shift a burden of production to the merging firms. Understood this way, the structural presumption specifies elements sufficient to prove an offense (a merger that violates the Clayton Act). But this observation does not fully capture the significance of the structural presumption in merger analysis because it does not explain how the identical presumption could be virtually irrebuttable during the 1960s while readily rebutted today. Indeed, in practical effect, the presumption has varied in strength along with the confidence of economists in the strength of the relationship between concentration and competition—from a showing that once created a virtual *per se* prohibition against horizontal mergers to simply a factual predicate that triggers a wide-ranging analysis of the proposed transaction.

In this subsection, we outline the factual showing we think should be sufficient to create a presumption that a proposed horizontal merger creates adverse coordinated or unilateral competitive effects, given the modern economic understanding of the effects of mergers on competition. We intend this stage of the analysis to fill the dual role the structural presumption played in the past: to identify factual showings that would satisfy the government's initial burden and to give a court confidence that if the specified elements are ultimately established, harm to competition would indeed likely result. Under our recommended approach, rebuttal is certainly possible, but requires that the merging parties present strong evidence, consistent with premerger market conditions and economic theory, showing that the anticompetitive effects alleged by the government are not in fact likely to result from the merger.[130]

We also intend the presumptions we set forth to be consistent with the established legal framework for merger analysis. This raises a fundamental issue with respect to unilateral competitive effects. The structural presumption, based on market concentration, was developed by the Supreme Court in a context in which coordinated effects were at issue. However, market concentration can be a poor predictor of harm to competition when the theory of competitive harm involves unilateral competitive effects among sellers of differentiated products. One reason is the difficulty of drawing lines to define markets when products are differentiated and clear gaps in the chain of substitutes do not exist. In addition, oligopoly theory tells us that the merging firms' market shares will tend to overstate the unilateral effects of the merger if the firms' products are relatively distant within the relevant market. Likewise, the merging firms' market shares will tend to understate the unilateral effects of the merger if the firms' products are especially close within the relevant market. Predicted unilateral effects depend upon the degree of demand substitution between products sold by the merging firms, not market shares.[131]

For all of these reasons, in cases involving unilateral effects among sellers of differentiated products, it is important to allow the government also to establish its prima facie case with evidence that the degree of buyer substitution between the products offered by the merging parties, as measured by diversion ratios or cross-price elasticities of demand, is substantial. This approach appropriately emphasizes an aspect of market structure that is more closely related in modern economic theory to unilateral effects than is overall market concentration. This approach also will protect against faulty outcomes, as in *Oracle,* where there was strong evidence of direct competition between the merging parties but the government lost due to the difficulty of defining the relevant market absent clear gaps in the chain of substitutes.

We believe that our recommended approach is consistent with modern antitrust analysis. Since the 1960s, the Supreme Court has come to recognize in other areas of antitrust that direct evidence of harm to competition can obviate the need for inferring that harm from market concentration.[132] Indeed, direct evidence regarding competition, such as evidence of buyer responses to past price movements or the costs of consumer switching, can be more probative than indirect evidence in the form of market shares. To the extent we employ markers other than market concentration for identifying adverse competitive effects, therefore, we think that doing so is consistent with the contemporary judicial understanding of the role played by market structure and other economic evidence in demonstrating market power and anticompetitive effects.

We also discuss the type of showing we think the merging parties should be required to make to satisfy their burden of production if they seek to rebut the government's case by proving that entry or expansion will counteract or deter the competitive harm alleged by the government or by showing that efficiencies from merger will undermine the government's prediction of adverse competitive effects.[133] We recognize that in the litigation context, the government will typically offer as part of its affirmative case evidence that entry would not solve the competitive problem, and that it has the option to do so as well with respect to efficiencies.[134] If the government has done so, defendants would typically need to offer more to satisfy their burden of production. Our purpose in specifying what would count as a minimal showing for defendants with respect to entry, expansion, and efficiencies under the assumption that the government has offered no affirmative evidence on these issues is simply to discourage courts from relying on entry, expansion, and efficiency evidence that we believe to be insufficient even in the best of circumstances for the merging firms.

B. Coordinated Competitive Effects

The modern economic understanding of coordinated competitive effects focuses on whether coordination makes sense for each market participant.[135]

In order for firms in a market to coordinate successfully, they must find a way to make the coordinated price more attractive than price-cutting for each. To do so they must reach consensus over the coordinated equilibrium they will seek to achieve—selecting prices and allocating output or market shares among the sellers—and they must deter deviation from that consensus by making it unprofitable for each participant to expand output and reduce price below what would be required by the coordinated consensus.[136] Although some influential Chicago-oriented commentators have been persuaded that these cartel problems are virtually insurmountable,[137] modern economists generally accept that coordination can and does occur.[138] Moreover, coordination may well be imperfect and incomplete.[139] Under such circumstances, we would expect that some firms would be nearly indifferent between coordination and cheating, while others strongly prefer the coordinated outcome. In antitrust parlance, a firm that is nearly indifferent between coordination and cheating, and in consequence constrains coordination from becoming more effective, is termed a "maverick."[140]

Within this framework, horizontal mergers affect the likelihood and effectiveness of coordination by altering the constraints imposed by maverick producers. If an acquisition involves a maverick, the merged firm would likely pose less of a constraint on coordination than before, leading to higher prices.[141] An acquisition involving a non-maverick may have a variety of effects on competition. For example, it could have no effect if it leaves the maverick's incentives unchanged; it may benefit competition by creating a new industry maverick through efficiencies; or it may harm competition, if it leads to exclusion of the maverick.[142]

This perspective on coordinated effects suggests two different approaches to establishing a presumption of harm to competition through coordinated effects.[143] Both approaches begin by defining the relevant market, along the lines described in the Merger Guidelines and by showing that the firms participating in that market could reasonably expect to solve the "cartel problems" of reaching consensus on terms of coordination and deterring deviation from those terms. Beginning with market definition dovetails nicely with theories of coordinated effects, since it involves identifying a group of firms, including the merging parties, that would find it profitable to engage in coordination.[144]

The first approach then identifies the maverick firm constraining coordination,[145] and evaluates the effects of the merger on the coordination incentives of the various sellers in the relevant market. Mavericks can be identified based on past conduct that constrained more effective coordination, based on the results of natural experiments that would be expected to lead a maverick to alter its price but would not affect the pricing of non-maverick firms, or by inference from features of market structure that tend to suggest that a firm would prefer a lower coordinated price than would its rivals.[146]

The second approach proceeds by identifying changes in the structure of the relevant market that raise the odds that a merger would reduce the constraint that the maverick poses for coordination. This approach is feasible even if a specific maverick firm cannot reliably be identified. In implementing the second approach, the focus will usually be on the reduction in the number of significant sellers participating in the market and on changes in the extent to which the market participants differ, i.e., on asymmetries among sellers in the relevant market. The reduction in the number of sellers raises the odds that a merger involves a maverick—the type of merger most likely to enhance seller coordination—and those odds generally grow the most when the number of significant sellers is few.[147] If a merger narrows asymmetries among sellers—as by reducing the differences among sellers in product attributes or seller costs—it most likely reduces the odds that a maverick firm would prefer a substantially lower coordinated price than its rivals, and thus tends to lead to higher prices by making coordination more effective.[148]

These two approaches suggest what the government should be expected to prove in order to create a presumption that a horizontal merger makes coordination more likely or more effective. Under either approach, the government must begin by defining the relevant antitrust market and by showing that the market is conducive to coordination, i.e., that the firms could reasonably expect, after a merger, to reach consensus on the terms of coordination and deter deviation from those terms. The latter is a familiar inquiry in antitrust analysis.[149] Then the government must explain why it is plausible that the merger will make a difference, relying on either of the above two approaches.

Under the first route for establishing a presumption that the merger matters, the government would identify the likely maverick and explain how the merger would change the maverick seller's incentives so as to make coordination more likely or more effective. Proof that the acquisition involves a likely maverick should be sufficient basis to presume harm to competition, for example.[150]

Under the second route, the government would show that the odds are high that a maverick firm (not specifically identified) would prefer a higher coordinated price postmerger, thus making coordination more likely or successful. To do so, the government would look to the number of significant firms[151] and to the effect of the merger on the differences among sellers. We could imagine several ways of making the necessary demonstration. One involves simply a reduction in the number of significant firms. For example, if the merger reduces the number of significant firms from, say, four to three, three to two, or two to one,[152] that change in market structure alone may be enough to create a presumption that the merger would make coordination more likely or more effective.[153] Alternatively, if it is difficult to be confident which individual sellers are significant, a presumption based solely on market concentration could be applied, illustratively if the postmerger Herfindahl-Hirschman Index (HHI) exceeds 2800.[154] In addition, if there are more than four significant sellers premerger, or if the postmerger HHI is less than 2800, a court could still presume that the merger makes coordination more likely or more effective if the government also shows that the merger has made sellers more similar, as by reducing asymmetries in costs or product attributes. Then a (weaker) presumption of harm to competition might reasonably be invoked for a merger that reduces the number of significant sellers to five, six, or seven, for example, or raises the postmerger HHI to roughly equivalent levels.[155]

Consistent with the legal framework, these presumptions would be rebuttable. Some forms of rebuttal might go to whether the presumption was properly invoked.[156] Other forms of rebuttal might show that the merger will not in fact alter the prospects for industry coordination, for example because the firms have no incentive to raise prices above the level likely to obtain absent the merger,[157] or because the maverick would have no less incentive to constrain coordination after the merger than before.[158] Or the merging firms might seek to rebut the presumption of harm to competition on the ground that entry or expansion would likely undermine or counteract any competitive effect of coordination, or that efficiencies from merger would make the deal procompetitive on balance.

When entry is offered as a rebuttal argument, our primary concern in this paper is to discourage courts from presuming that entry is easy based on one example, as some courts have improperly done in the past. This error can be avoided through careful application of the standards of the Horizontal Merger Guidelines, which require that committed entry be timely, likely, and sufficient.[159] When efficiencies are offered as a rebuttal argument to a presumption about coordinated effects, it is important to note that efficiencies would not affect the coordinated price—would not be passed through to buyers—unless they lead the maverick to prefer a lower price or the merger creates a new maverick with the ability and incentive to compete more aggressively than before.[160] That is, the analysis of efficiencies must go beyond ensuring that they are merger-specific and can be verified—the primary criteria of the Horizontal Merger Guidelines for efficiencies to be cognizable—and explain how the efficiencies would lead to lower prices given the way the market participants are thought to behave.

We do not claim to have provided an exhaustive list of methods the merging firms might employ to rebut the presumption of coordinated effects. Nor have we attempted to sketch the kinds of evidence the government, on which the burden of persuasion rests, might offer in response to those rebuttal efforts. It should nevertheless be clear that there are many routes that defendants could employ to rebut the presumption. The fact that there are many types of rebuttal arguments, however, does not mean that the presumption of coordinated effects afforded to the government is weak. A court should not lightly discard the inference that competition will be harmed that follows from a demonstration by the government of the factual predicates for invoking the presumption of coordinated effects set forth above. In particular, to prevail, rebuttal arguments based on entry, expansion, and efficiencies must be based on strong evidence that is consistent with economic theory and premerger industry conditions.

C. Unilateral Competitive Effects

Since the 1992 Horizontal Merger Guidelines were introduced, theories of unilateral effects have been pursued frequently by both agencies. Even though our survey respondents reported a marked decline in interest at the agencies in unilateral effects cases over the past decade, they still reported seeing unilateral effects cases somewhat more frequently today than coordinated effects cases (with the mix varying greatly by industry).

The economic theory of unilateral effects theories follows directly from non-cooperative theories of oligopoly, including the Cournot and Bertrand theories of oligopoly, which go back to the nineteenth century.[161] Over the past 25 years, substantial progress has been made in refining these theories and applying them to merger analysis, and in developing tools for this purpose, including sophisticated econometric methods of estimating demand and methods for simulating the effects of mergers using calibrated structural models. The economic theory of unilateral effects is now very well understood, and we will not repeat that theory here.[162]

In practice, unilateral effects cases typically arise in markets where the suppliers sell differentiated products, very often without binding capacity constraints, at least in the medium to long term. Our treatment here focuses on that central case.[163]

In cases involving unilateral effects among sellers of differentiated products, the link between the market definition exercise and the theory of competitive effects tends to be much less direct than in cases involving coordinated effects. In coordinated effects cases, the market definition exercise identifies a set of firms that collectively have an incentive to coordinate their prices, this being the mechanism of harm to competition. In unilateral effects cases, the mechanism of harm does not directly involve any nonmerging firms. Instead, the theory is based on postmerger changes in the incentives of the merging parties. Predicted unilateral effects depend primarily upon the cross-elasticity of demand between products sold by the merging firms, and on the price-cost margins associated with their products, but not directly on the market shares of the merging firms. Furthermore, defining the relevant market may require that a bright line be drawn between products that are "in" or "out" of the market, when there is in fact no clear gap in the chain of substitutes.

Our proposal for establishing presumptions in unilateral effects cases takes account of these inherent economic features of markets with differentiated products. The government can establish its prima facie case in either of two ways. Both routes require the government to show that the merger will give the merged firm an incentive to raise the price of one or more of its products significantly, taking as given the prices charged by nonmerging firms. The incentive of the merged firm (A+B) to raise the price of a Product A sold by Firm A will typically depend most strongly on two variables: (1) the diversion ratio between Product A and Product B sold by Firm B, which is defined as the fraction of the lost sales for Product A that will be captured by Product B, and (2) the gross margin for Product B.[164] Both routes focus on demand-side factors only; we specify the elements that create a presumption based on the empirical generalization that within product-differentiated industries, an enquiry which looks only at demand substitution to identify market power, ignoring supply-side factors like cost differences and production capacities, is in general likely to be largely right.[165]

The first, and more traditional route, is for the government to define the relevant market, following the methods in the merger guidelines, to show that the merger will substantially increase concentration in that market, and to articulate the mechanism by which the merger will cause a price increase.[166] This mechanism will typically follow from the basic logic of unilateral competitive effects, with reference to the size of the premerger price-cost margins on the overlap products sold by the merging firms.[167] This route is consistent with a "default" assumption that the diversion ratios between the products sold by the merging firms are proportional to their market shares, as in the logit model of demand.

The second route is more direct and does not rely on defining the relevant market and measuring market shares. Following this route, the government must establish that the diversion ratio between the merging firms' products and the gross margins on those products are large enough to give the merged firm an incentive to raise the price of one or more of those products significantly (e.g., 5 percent, or some other appropriate figure).[168] Many types of evidence as to buyer substitution between the products sold by the merging firms, and thus as to the relevant diversion ratios, may potentially be used by the government at this stage.[169] Diversion ratios (or demand cross-elasticities) would summarize this information in a quantitative way, even if the most probative evidence about the magnitude of buyer substitution were qualitative rather than quantitative. We envision the government offering a straightforward calculation based on diversion ratios and price-cost margins, along with some sensitivity analysis, although the government also could obtain the benefit of the presumption by presenting a more detailed simulation model.

If the government establishes its prima facie case, the burden shifts to the merging parties. The first group of rebuttal arguments directly undermines the propositions put forward by the government. If the government has taken the first route, the merging parties could show that the market has not been defined properly, that the government measured market shares incorrectly, or that the market shares mislead as to the likelihood of unilateral effects (as by presenting evidence of diversion ratios and price-cost margins). If the government has taken the second route, the merging firms could show that the merged entity will not in fact have an incentive to raise the prices of any of its products significantly. They could make this showing by proving that the diversion ratio between the merging firms' products is lower than claimed by the government or that the margin on the product to which sales are diverted is lower than claimed by the government.

If the government's case withstands any such attacks, then the merging parties can also rebut by showing that other firms with similar products can and will reposition their products in response to the postmerger price increase asserted by the government and that such repositioning will deter or counteract any anticompetitive effects of the merger. Lastly, the merging firms can turn to the conventional three E rebuttal points: entry, expansion, and efficiencies. These arguments would be treated in the same manner as we described above in our discussion of coordinated effects.[170]

Conclusion

Prospective horizontal merger enforcement is essential for protecting competition in a dynamic economy. It is simply impractical to protect competition by adopting a policy of waiting for mergers to display adverse effects on competition and then seeking to undo the acquisitions that prove to be anticompetitive. Unfortunately, prospective horizontal merger enforcement has fallen into decline, as a result of an unhappy combination of a more flexible economic approach, which we endorse, with the too-ready acceptance by some courts and enforcers of unproven noninterventionist economic arguments about concentration, entry and efficiencies.

To reinvigorate horizontal merger enforcement, we propose that enforcement agencies and courts rely more seriously on presumptions that allow the government to establish a prima facie case, which the merging parties can only rebut with strong evidence. Relying more on presumptions would confer the advantages of clearer rules, thus reducing the transaction costs of enforcement and providing guidance to firms and courts. By basing the presumptions on the modern economic understanding of the competitive effects of mergers, moreover, merger review can become more accurate. We have proposed an analytical framework using presumptions that avoid systematically deterring beneficial mergers or permitting harmful ones.

We certainly do not propose a return to the horizontal merger control policies and precedents of the 1960s. The presumptions we have described here would not be irrebuttable, though they would be influential. They would be based on aspects of market structure, but not solely on market concentration, and in some cases, not on market concentration at all. We have sketched here in general terms the types of presumptions we envision,

recognizing that further refinement is required to put our ideas into operation. We hope that our proposals will stimulate discussion about how
best to reinvigorate merger enforcement, while leaving the details of an
improved merger control framework to that discussion and future work.

*Jonathan Baker and Carl Shapiro are grateful to John Briggs, Marian
Bruno, Dennis Carlton, Joseph Farrell, Andy Gavil, Ken Heyer, Tom Leary,
Rick Liebeskind, Jamie Mikkelsen, Jodi Newman, Steve Salop, and Louis
Silvia, and to Kirkpatrick Conference participants.*

Notes

1. For a broader perspective on the evolution of U.S. antitrust policy
during these years, *see* William E. Kovacic & Carl Shapiro, *Antitrust Policy:
A Century of Economic and Legal Thinking,* 14 J. Econ. Per. 43 (2000).

2. *United States v. Philadelphia National Bank,* 374 U.S. 321, 363 (1963).

3. *Id.*

4. *Id.*

5. *Id.*

6. *Id.*

7. *United States v. Von's Grocery Co.,* 384 U.S. 270 (1966). Robert Bork
termed *Von's Grocery* "the best example of Clayton 7's disorientation."
Robert H. Bork, The Antitrust Paradox: A Policy at War with Itself 217
(1978).

8. Bork, *supra* note 8 at 217. Here Bork was specifically criticizing a com-
panion case to *Von's Grocery,* decided during the same Supreme Court term:
United States v. Pabst Brewing Co., 384 U.S. 546 (1966). In *Pabst,* the Court
prevented a merger between two brewing firms that together accounted for
24 percent of beer sales in Wisconsin, 11 percent of sales in a three-state
area of the upper Midwest, and less than 5percent of sales nationally. "In
accord with our prior cases," the Court held that the Clayton Act was violated "in each and all of these three areas." *Id.* at 552. Bork framed the problem with the Court decisions as where to draw the line. "As the law moves
down the spectrum from the 100 percent merger," he wrote, "the problem of
the trade-off between restriction of output and efficiency rapidly becomes
severe." Bork, *supra* note 8 at 219 (1978). Accordingly, he argued that "mergers up to 60 or 70 percent of the market should be permitted," *id.* at 221, thus
proposing a standard far more easily satisfied by merging firms than that
promulgated by the 1960s merger cases he was criticizing.

9. *Pabst,* 384 U.S. at 552.

10. Richard Posner, Antitrust Law: An Economic Perspective 106 (1976).

11. *United States v. Von's Grocery Co.,* 384 U.S. 270, 301 (1966) (Stewart, J.,
dissenting).

12. Bork, *supra* note 8 at 217.

13. Joe S. Bain, Barriers to New Competition (1956).

14. *See* Michael Salinger, *The Concentration-Margins Relationship
Reconsidered,* 1990 Brookings Papers on Economic Activity: Microeconomics 287, for a relatively recent discussion of this literature.

15. George Stigler, *A Theory of Oligopoly*, 55 J. POL. ECON. 44 (1964).

16. Harold Demsetz, *Industry Structure, Market Rivalry and Public Policy*, 16 J. L. & ECON. 1 (1973). For further discussion of the problems economists faced when seeking to evaluate the structure-conduct-performance paradigm empirically, *see* Jonathan B. Baker & Timothy F. Bresnahan, *Economic Evidence in Antitrust: Defining Markets and Measuring Market Power, in* Paolo Buccirossi, ed., HANDBOOK OF ANTITRUST ECONOMICS, (2007) (forthcoming).

17. *United States v. General Dynamics Corp.*, 415 U.S. 486 (1974).

18. *Id.* at 504.

19. Bork, *supra* note 8 at 218.

20. U.S. Department of Justice, Merger Guidelines (1982) available at http://www.usdoj.gov/atr/hmerger/11248.htm. Baxter was a highly respected Chicago-oriented law professor before he headed the Antitrust Division.

21. The 1982 Merger Guidelines did not recognize an efficiencies defense, however, except in "extraordinary cases," mainly because of difficulties of proof. Here the Guidelines followed the lead of Richard Posner and Robert Bork, both of whom recommended accounting for efficiencies by limiting merger challenges to transactions in markets with high concentration rather than by allowing an efficiencies defense. Posner, *supra* note 11 at 112; Bork, *supra* note 8 at 124–29. Since that time, the Guidelines have become more receptive to allowing properly documented efficiencies from a transaction to count in its favor. Most of the shift was recent. The 1984 Guidelines revisions took a small step toward recognizing an efficiencies defense, and the 1997 revisions to what had become the Horizontal Merger Guidelines of both enforcement agencies went farther. U.S. Department of Justice and Federal Trade Commission, Horizontal Merger Guidelines (1992, revised 1997) available at http://www.usdoj.gov/atr/public/guidelines/hmg.htm.

22. *United States v. Waste Management, Inc.*, 743 F.2d 976 (2d Cir. 1984); *United States v. Calmar, Inc.*, 612 F.Supp. 1298 (D.N.J. 1985); *Echlin Mfg. Co.*, 105 F.T.C. 479 (1985).

23. *United States v. Baker Hughes, Inc.*, 908 F. 2d 981, 984 (1990). David Sentelle also served on the three-judge panel.

24. *Id.* The structural presumption did not disappear, however. The court acknowledged that "[t]he more compelling the prima facie case [based on market concentration], the more evidence the defendant must present to rebut it successfully. *Cf. Federal Trade Commission v. H.J. Heinz Co.*, 246 F.3d 708 (2001) (merging firms did not successfully rebut the presumption of harm to competition in a merger to duopoly with evidence that the efficiencies from merger would allow the merged firm to compete more effectively against the dominant firm in the market).

25. *Baker Hughes*, 908 F. 2d at 992 (1990).

26. U.S. Department of Justice and Federal Trade Commission, Horizontal Merger Guidelines (1992, revised 1997), available at http://www.usdoj.gov/atr/public/guidelines/hmg.htm. These Guidelines were revised again in 1997 to set forth an analysis of efficiencies.

27. *See generally*, Jonathan B, Baker & Steven C. Salop, *Should Concentration be Dropped from the Merger Guidelines?*, ABA Antitrust Section Task Force Report, 339–54 PERSPECTIVES ON FUNDAMENTAL ANTITRUST THEORY, July 2001.

28. Federal Trade Commission, Horizontal Merger Investigation Data, 1996–2005 available at http://www.ftc.gov/os/2007/01/P035603horizmerge rinvestigationdata1996–2005.pdf.

29. Antitrust Modernization Commission, Report and Recommendations (April 2007), available at http://www.amc.gov/report_recommendation/ toc.htm. The AMC did make a number of recommendations for procedural reforms relating to merger enforcement.

30. Derek Bok, *Section 7 of the Clayton Act and the Merging of Law and Economics,* 74 HARV.L. REV. 226, 227–28 (1960) (footnotes omitted).

31. The "pendulum swings" metaphor for antitrust enforcement was criticized by senior FTC officials at the start of the George W. Bush Administration. They instead defended a narrative of continuity between enforcers in the administrations of both parties since around 1980, both in general and with respect to mergers in particular. William E. Kovacic, *The Modern Evolution of U.S. Competition Policy Enforcement Norms,* 71 ANTITRUST L.J. 377 (2004); Thomas B. Leary, *The Essential Stability of Merger Policy in the United States,* 70 ANTITRUST L.J. 105 (2002). We agree that there has been continuity in some enforcement norms, particularly the prohibitions on naked horizontal price-fixing and market division. But other antitrust areas, particularly those involving exclusionary conduct, have been and remain contested ground as to which perspectives have varied. We see horizontal merger enforcement as an in-between case, characterized by substantial agreement over time on fundamental economic principles, but also subject to variation in enforcement approaches, which has been particularly evident in the minimalist enforcement policy of the Antitrust Division during the second term of the Reagan administration and during the George W. Bush Administration. For this reason, we have not avoided use of the pendulum metaphor in discussing merger policy.

32. *United States v Syufy Enters.,* 903 F.2d 659 (9th Cir. 1990). The government attacked Syufy's acquisitions under the Clayton Act, and alleged both monopolization and attempted monopolization under the Sherman Act. *Id.* at 662 n.3. For additional discussion of the case and its significance for entry analysis in merger review, *see* Jonathan B. Baker, *The Problem with* Baker Hughes *and* Syufy: *On the Role of Entry in Merger Analysis,* 65 ANTITRUST L.J. 353 (1997).

33. The case was tried four years after the last acquisition, so some of the evidence was retrospective.

34. The court also dismissed the government's evidence that after obtaining a virtual monopoly Syufy had lowered the fees it paid to movie distributors (exercising monopsony power), on the view that the government had not controlled for other factors affecting those payments, and based on the absence of distributor complaints. *Syufy,* 903 F.2d at 669, 671 n.19.

35. Roberts opened three multiplexes, none as luxurious as Syufy's. *Id.* at 665, 669 n. 15, 672. Syufy's share of the box office from first-run films

in Las Vegas declined from 93 percent after its last merger to 75 percent three years later, *id.* at 666, when Roberts sold its theaters to a large national chain. *Id.* at 665. The court also suggested that movie distributors were large players that could protect themselves, even from a monopoly exhibitor. *Id.* at 670, 672.

36. In the government's view, the evidence instead showed that Roberts's entry was not successful (its facilities were inferior, its share was small, and none of its theaters made money), and that other informed potential entrants had reasonably concluded that entry would not be profitable. Brief for the United States at 39–41, *United States v. Syufy Enters.*, 903 F.2d 659 (9th Cir. No. 89–1575) (Apr. 21, 1989), 1989 WL 1129298.

37. This possibility forms the basis for the entry "likelihood" analysis in the 1992 Horizontal Merger Guidelines issued by the two federal antitrust enforcement agencies two years after the *Syufy* opinion.

38. The court saw no need to evaluate this claim because it did not understand it. In the court's view, the government was advancing "a shopworn argument we had thought long abandoned: that efficient, aggressive competition is itself a structural barrier to entry." *Syufy,* 903 F.2d at 667. The court went on to say that absent a claim that entry would be prevented by some sort of structural barrier—as might be created, for example, by "government regulation," "onerous front-end investments," dependency "on a scarce commodity" controlled by the incumbent, or "distribution arrangements designed to lock out potential competitors"—it saw no reason to analyze the issue further. *Id. See* Baker, *supra* note 33 at 370: "The government's argument was about the scale necessary for an entrant to do business efficiently and whether committed entry at that scale would be profitable; the court instead heard, and rejected, an argument about whether the incumbent was performing efficiently."

39. *Syufy,* 903 F.2d at 667 n. 13: "We cannot and should not speculate as to the details of a potential competitor's performance; we need only determine whether there were barriers to the entry of new faces into the market."

40. That skepticism may have contributed to the court's failure to take seriously the economic arguments raised by the government.

41. *Id.* at 673.

42. *See also,* Stephen Calkins & Frederick Warren-Boulton, "The State of Antitrust in 1990," Paper Presented at Cato Institute Conference, *A Century of Antitrust: The Lessons, The Challenges,* Washington, D.C. (Apr. 1990) ("the opinion exudes antipathy for merger enforcement"); William E. Kovacic, *Reagan's Judicial Appointees and Antitrust in the 1990s,* 60 FORDHAM L. REV. 49, 112 (1991) (the opinion "dispatched the government's case in a torrent of ridicule" and "depicted[ed] the Justice Department's decision to prosecute as virtually irrational").

43. *United States v. Oracle Corp.,* 331 F.Supp.2d 1098 (N.D. Calif. 2004).

44. *See generally,* Carl Shapiro, *Mergers with Differentiated Products,* 10 ANTITRUST 23 (1996); Louis Kaplow & Carl Shapiro, *Antitrust, in* HANDBOOK OF LAW AND ECONOMICS, A. Mitchell Polinsky & Steven Shavell, eds., (Elsevier, forthcoming, 2007) (Working Paper at 65–70), available at http://faculty.haas.berkeley.edu/shapiro/antitrust2007.pdf. This theory

is well-established among antitrust economists, described in the 1992 Horizontal Merger Guidelines, and routinely employed at the federal antitrust enforcement agencies. *See* Jonathan B. Baker, *Why Did the Antitrust Agencies Embrace Unilateral Effects?*, 12 Geo. Mason. U. L. Rev. 31 (2003).

45. *See* Kaplow & Shapiro, *supra* note 45 at 92. The market definition alternatives for framing litigation over unilateral effects of merger are evaluated in Jonathan B. Baker, *Stepping Out in an Old Brown Shoe: In Qualified Praise of Submarkets,* 68 Antitrust L.J. 203 (2000). For a recent proposal to dispense with market definition in mergers with unilateral effects, see Joseph Farrell & Carl Shapiro, "Mergers with Unilateral Effects: A Simpler and More Accurate Alternative to Market Definition," available at http://faculty.haas.berkeley.edu/shapiro/simpler.pdf.

46. *See* Jonathan B. Baker, *Market Definition: An Analytical Overview,* 74 Antitrust L. J. 129, 139–41 (2007) (describing sources of evidence on buyer substitution).

47. Federal Trade Commission, Horizontal Merger Investigation Data, 1996–2005, available at http://www.ftc.gov/os/2007/01/P035603horizme rgerinvestigationdata1996–2005.pdf (Tables 4.6 & 8.1) (in raw data, about half of mergers reducing the number of firms from 4 to 3 in industries other than groceries, oil, chemicals, and pharmaceuticals are challenged absent customer complaints, and in all markets 100 percent of 4 to 3 mergers are challenged if the agency has received strong customer complaints); Malcolm B. Coate & Shawn W. Ulrick, "Transparency at the Federal Trade Commission: The Horizontal Merger Review Process 1996–2003," available at http://www.ftc.gov/os/2005/02/0502economicissues.pdf (Table 6) (for a 4 to 3 merger with an HHI of 2000 and a delta of 400, the probability of challenge is 8 percent with no customer complaints and rises to 62 percent with complaints).

48. "[U]nsubstantiated customer apprehensions do not substitute for hard evidence." *Oracle,* 331 F.Supp.2d at 1131. It is appropriate for a court to inquire, for example, whether surveyed customers are representative, whether the witnesses are well situated to judge the response of their firm to changing prices, just what are the customer's commercial interests in the proposed merger, and whether the witnesses articulate sensible rationales for their views.

49. *Id.*

50. Judge Walker explained that the witnesses did not present "cost/benefit analyses of the type that surely they employ and would employ" in making software purchasing decisions. *Id.*

51. That is, firms rarely in practice undertake cost/benefit analyses of purchasing decisions that assume a hypothetical merger among suppliers.

52. *Id.* at 1117–18, 1123. This statement of the law misunderstands the economics of unilateral competitive effects among sellers of differentiated products and, if followed by other courts, would create an unfortunate gap in merger law. As the discussion of unilateral effects in the 1992 Horizontal Merger Guidelines makes clear, competition can be harmed through this route within a broad market in which the merged firm has a market share well below monopoly levels.

53. *Id.* at 1119–21.

54. *Id.* at 1118.

55. In the logit model, though not in general in unilateral effects models, anticompetitive effects depend upon market shares. *See, e.g.,* Gregory Werden & Luke Froeb, *Unilateral Competitive Effects of Horizontal Mergers, in* Paolo Buccirossi, ed., HANDBOOK OF ANTITRUST ECONOMICS (2007) (forthcoming). Judge Walker's rejection of the unilateral effects theory in *Oracle* can also be questioned on the facts. For any given diversion ratios (or demand cross-elasticities) between the products of the merging firms, unilateral anticompetitive effects are greatest when premerger price-cost margins are large, as they were for the products at issue in the *Oracle* case.

56. *United States v. Oracle Corp.,* 331 F.Supp.2d 1098, 1123 (N.D. Calif. 2004).

57. Merger simulations integrate information on buyer substitution, rival conduct, and firm costs in a mathematical model, in order to infer the price increase from merger. These methods are useful for clarifying issues, identifying where more evidence is needed, and putting measures of buyer substitution into a useful metric. They do not necessarily require market definition. For a brief discussion with references to the sizeable economic literature on this topic, *see* Kaplow & Shapiro, *supra* note 45 at 99–100.

58. *Oracle,* 331 F.Supp.2d at 1122.

59. *Id.* at 1170.

60. *Accord* Amanda J. Parkison Hassid, *An Oracle Without Foresight? Plaintiffs' Arduous Burdens Under* U.S. v. Oracle, 58 HASTINGS L.J. 891 (2007).

61. WALL ST. J., Jan. 16, 2007, at C1.

62. *Id.*

63. Stephen Labaton, *Sirius Chief Talks of Ways to Get XM Deal Approved,* N.Y. TIMES, March 1, 2007.

64. In 1986 the Reagan Administration seemed to signal a change of course toward merger enforcement minimalism by proposing that Congress replace the incipiency language and lessening of competition test for merger under the Clayton Act with a requirement that the courts consider "all economic factors" and only enjoin a transaction when it found "a significant probability" that the merger "will substantially increase the ability to exercise market power." 50 ANTITRUST & TRADE REG. REP. (BNA) 347 (Special Supp. Feb. 20, 1986).

65. *See* Robert Pitofsky, *Antitrust in the Decade Ahead: Some Predictions About Merger Enforcement,* 57 ANTITRUST L.J. 65, 71 (1988): "The Senate Judiciary Committee recently identified ten mergers for which the relevant Antitrust Division Section Chief recommended that a challenge be filed, only to see that recommendation overruled by the front office. Post-merger HHIs were available in two of those cases; they were 3025 and 5128."

66. In 1987 John DeQ. Briggs surveyed Justice Department consent decrees in merger cases, and observed that "the level of concentration is *very* high in most of them; one wonders how they got off the ground at all." John DeQ. Briggs, *An Overview of Current Law and Policy Relating to Mergers and Acquisitions,* 56 ANTITRUST L.J. 657, 721 (1987) (citing twelve cases). *Accord* Robert Pitofsky, *Antitrust in the Decade Ahead: Some Predictions About Merger Enforcement,* 57 ANTITRUST L.J. 65 (1988): "As to

horizontal mergers, virtually all cases have involved extremely large mergers in highly concentrated markets."

67. *Report of the American Bar Association Section of Antitrust Law Task Force on the Antitrust Division of the U.S. Department of Justice,* 58 ANTITRUST L.J. 747, 761 (1990).

68. *Id.* at 760. The report also noted that "in the face of a large increase in merger activity, the total amount of resources devoted to merger enforcement has actually declined." *Id.* at 755. More generally, the report highlighted the perception that the Division "is more concerned with its non-enforcement agenda—the studied avoidance of 'bad' cases that might hurt consumers coupled with support for legislative modifications that would limit the antitrust laws" than with its enforcement program, outside of its vigorous attacks on price-fixing. *Id.* at 748–49.

69. We do not examine the ratio of merger challenges to second requests because that statistic is double-edged: an increase in the rate could result either from stronger enforcement or from greater efficiency in targeting problematic transactions in the initial merger review.

70. Leary, *supra* note 31.

71. *Id.* at 139 (Table 2).

72. Leary ended his data collection with fiscal year 2000, so the Clinton II record is assessed with only three years data.

73. Leary, *supra* note 31, discusses other interpretive issues at 121–26. We also followed Leary by using in the denominator the number of transactions in which the agencies were authorized to issue a second request rather than the number filed; the adjusted figure is slightly lower than those filed to account for mistaken filings, secondary filings and filings in which a party files to cross multiple notification thresholds in the same year.

74. The number of reported transactions spiked during the late 1990s, raising the possibility that different kinds of transactions arose during that merger wave relative to other years. (The late 1980s were considered a merger wave at the time, but the increase in filings then is small in comparison to what was observed a decade later.) Anecdotal evidence, moreover, suggests that management buyouts were common during the late 1980s, and financial investments by private equity buyers and hedge funds have become common in recent years.

75. Similarly, it is possible that in some years, merger filings are concentrated in industries where transactions are typically reviewed by the Antitrust Division while in other years they are concentrated in industries where transactions are typically reviewed by the FTC. If so, the observed enforcement rate at individual agencies could change without a difference in either agency's enforcement policy, although the total enforcement rate would not necessarily change. We have not attempted to account for this possibility.

76. This idea arises generally in any analysis based on data about disputes that reach certain procedural stages. For an important and early contribution, see George Priest & Benjamin Klein, *The Selection of Disputes for Litigation,* 13 J. L. STUD. 1 (1984).

77. It is possible in theory that changes in the observed enforcement rate instead reflect changes in the loss functions of firms contemplating merger.

If CEOs become more risk averse, for example, they would be expected to negotiate fewer mergers that generate antitrust enforcement actions. However, we think this theoretical possibility is unlikely to explain the observed variation in the merger enforcement rate.

78. Similarly, the strikingly high merger enforcement rate, 1.5 percent during the George H. W. Bush Administration (1990–1993), suggests that the FTC under Chairman Steiger surprised the antitrust community with its willingness to challenge deals. This interpretation is consistent with anecdotal information about the perception of antitrust practitioners at the time that the line had been moved toward merger challenges even more than they had expected. Under this interpretation, moreover, the decline in the enforcement rate that followed during the Clinton Administration does not mean that the FTC under Chairman Pitofsky was less enforcement-minded than it was under his predecessor; it simply means that the Pitofsky Commission did not surprise the antitrust bar with its approach to merger review. Similarly, the decline from Clinton I to Clinton II in the FTC's merger enforcement rate likely means that practitioners were surprised that the FTC stayed on an even keel after its high-profile successful challenge to the Staples/Office Depot merger, rather than ratcheting up its review standards. Baker worked at the FTC and Shapiro worked at the DOJ during the Clinton administration.

79. The raw data on adjusted HSR filings and number of enforcement actions for the two agencies came from Antitrust Division, Workload Statistics, FY 1997–2006, available at http://www.usdoj.gov/atr/public/workstats.htm, and Annual Report to Congress, Fiscal Year 2005, Appendix A, available at http://www.ftc.gov/reports/hsr05/P98931twentyeighthannualhsrreport.pdf.

80. Premerger Notification, 66 Fed. Reg. 8680 (Feb. 1, 2001).

81. To determine the magnitude of this adjustment, we collected quarterly time series on the number and value of mergers from *Mergers & Acquisitions* magazine (which in turn collects the data from the SDC database). We related HSR filings to both the number and value of transactions because HSR filings are fewer and on average likely larger than those in the comparison data as a consequence of the size of parties and size of transactions screens in the HSR reporting rules. Using quarterly data from 1990:1 through 2005:3, we regressed the log of HSR filings on the log of the number of transactions, the value of transactions, an indicator variable reflecting the change in reporting rules set to one beginning in 2001:2 (assigning it the value of 2/3 in 2001:1), dummy variables for three of the four quarters of the year, and a constant. The point estimate of the decline in filings was 60.3 percent using data on "completed" mergers and 59.6 percent using data on "proposed" mergers. These regression results are available from the authors upon request.

82. Two adjustments were required. The first reflected the fact that the denominator was too low (by a factor of 2.5), because the number of reported HSR filings would have been much greater had the previous premerger notification rules continued to apply. The second reflected the fact that the numerator was too low, because some of the mergers that would have been reported had the rules not changed would have led to

enforcement actions that did not actually occur. (These are transactions that the agencies would have noticed, investigated, and identified as anticompetitive had they been reported, but did not investigate or challenge after the change in rules.) To adjust the numerator, we observed that the bulk of the mergers screened out by the change in rules were less than $50 million (in size of transaction), and that in 2000, the last fiscal year before the rule changed, the agencies issued 22 second requests in reviewing the 2247 transactions in that category, a rate of 0.98 percent. Federal Trade Commission and Department of Justice, Annual Report to Congress, Fiscal Year 2000 (Table 2). (The three year average for the fraction of second requests issued on transactions less that $50 million—all the data available—was 0.97 percent, virtually identical to the figure we employed.) We also observed that during the eleven years from 1990 through 2000, enforcement actions at both agencies together averaged 61.6 percent of total second requests (614 out of 997). *See* Leary, *supra* note 32, at 137. Hence every 1000 transactions not filed that previously would have been filed would have yielded approximately 6 additional enforcement actions for the two agencies taken together. In adjusting the numerator, we allocated the total additional enforcement actions in proportion to the observed enforcement rate during the 2002–05 period, i.e., one-third to DOJ and two-thirds to the FTC.

83. In the raw data for 2002 to 2005, not corrected to account for the change in HSR reporting rules, the FTC enforcement rate was 1.5 percent of adjusted HSR filings, and the DOJ enforcement rate was 0.75 percent of adjusted HSR filings. Had each agency instead reported an enforcement rate of 1.8 percent of adjusted HSR filings under current reporting rules, the rate for each would have been equivalent to the 0.9 percent average rate for agency enforcement under the pre-2001 HSR reporting rules.

84. The raw data on enforcement actions and HSR filings for 2006 are found in the DOJ workload statistics and the FTC's annual report on the HSR program. The preliminary data for 2007 are taken from congressional testimony by the heads of the two agencies, available at http://judiciary. house.gov/media/pdfs/Barnett070925.pdf (DOJ) and http://www.ftc.gov/os/testimony/P040101antitrust_laws.pdf (FTC). Although the FTC testimony does not say so explicitly, our understanding is that the number of HSR filings it reports is the number of transactions in which the agencies were authorized to issue a second request. Due to small numbers problems, we place greater weight on averages taken over a number of years than on data from a single year.

85. During the current administration, both agencies have also, and commendably, sought to become more efficient in merger review, by reducing the compliance burden on merging firms and by targeting second requests to deals that turn out to raise competitive issues. Thomas O. Barnett, "Merger Review: A Quest for Efficiency" (Jan. 25, 2007), available at http://www.usdoj.gov/atr/public/speeches/221173.htm; Deborah Platt Majoras, "Reforms to the Merger Review Process," (Feb. 16, 2006), available at http://www.ftc.gov/os/2006/02/mergerreviewprocess.pdf. But an emphasis on efficiency in targeting can be taken too far, leading the agencies not to investigate mergers that merit a hard look.

86. *Cf.* Deborah L. Feinstein, *Recent Trends in U.S. Merger Enforcement: Down But Not Out,* 21 ANTITRUST 74, 80 (2007): "The data suggest that [the current heads of the Antitrust Division and FTC] may have been less aggressive than their predecessors—and may have more difficulty persuading judges of the merits of the cases they do bring." We considered the possibility that the current agency merger enforcement figures could be low without reflecting a change in enforcement policy because they now include a greater proportion of nonhorizontal mergers involving private equity and hedge fund buyers that do not tend to raise competition issues. Based on the following calculation, we are skeptical of this alternative interpretation. Between 2002 and 2005, DOJ brought enforcement actions in 38 cases. For those 38 enforcement actions to represent 1.8 percent of filings, the rate that now corresponds to the pre-2001 average, the number of filings would need to be 2111. During those years 5097 transactions were actually filed (after removing a small number as noted in footnote 72), implying, implausibly, that nearly 60 percent of all filings during those years (2986) would need to have been non-horizontal private equity or hedge fund deals that would not have occurred in previous time periods. *Cf.* Mark Hulbert, *Shareholders Benefit When Managers Have a Serious Stake,* N.Y. Times, May 13, 2007 at Business Section p.5 (chart indicates that private equity accounted for approximately 10 percent of merger and acquisition activity from 2002 through 2005). We also considered the possibility that the enforcement rate declined over time with no change in agency enforcement policy because the agencies have become more transparent, allowing the antitrust bar to improve its ability to predict enforcement agency decisions and do a better job of discouraging firms from proposing transactions that would generate enforcement actions. We are skeptical of this interpretation of the low enforcement rate at the Antitrust Division because the enforcement rate did not decline at the FTC, which has made similar efforts to become more transparent.

87. These estimates were based on the observed merger enforcement rates, without converting the observed enforcement statistics to pre-2001 units. Without that conversion, the merger enforcement rate was 1.5 percent at the FTC and 0.75 percent at the DOJ during the first term of the George W. Bush Administration, and 1.0 percent at the FTC and 0.7 percent at DOJ during the second term. The average merger challenge rate during the period studied by Commissioner Leary (0.9 percent in pre-2001 units) corresponds to a 1.8 percent rate in these units, and the low merger enforcement rate during the second term of the Reagan Administration (0.4 percent in pre-2001 units) corresponds roughly to a 0.75 percent rate in these units.

88. 2006 Chambers USA, The Client's Guide at 426 ("leading individuals" in antitrust in the District of Columbia, groups 1 through 3).

89. In 1997 the Antitrust Division was headed by Assistant Attorney General Joel Klein and the FTC was headed by Chairman Robert Pitofsky.

90. Our respondents gave narrative answers, which we coded on a 5-point scale to facilitate analysis.

91. *See* questions #1b and #2b in the survey instrument. Some survey respondents indicated that the FTC has grown tougher in its review of oil industry mergers over the past decade. With respect to the FTC, the views of our survey respondents differed from the conclusion of two FTC economists,

who found that Commission review standards did not vary between the Clinton and George W. Bush administrations based on a study of internal agency memoranda. Coate & Ulrick, *supra* note 48. When the comparison was over five years—from early in the George W. Bush Administration (AAG James and FTC Chairman Muris) to today, the survey answers differed by agency. See questions #1a and #2a. Our respondents viewed DOJ as more receptive now to merging party arguments than five years ago; the mean score for this question was 3.9. In contrast, the FTC was seen as about the same, with a mean score of 2.8. Although "more receptive" to merging firm arguments is not necessarily a synonym for more lenient enforcement, it is evident to us from the narrative comments our respondents gave and their responses to other survey questions that this is how our respondents understood the question.

92. *See* question #9b in the survey instrument. When the comparison was over five years, a much smaller shift in favor of the merging firms was reported. The mean score to this question (#9a) was 3.5.

93. During 2007, the FTC also exhibited a commendable willingness to litigate merger challenges—even taking on the high profile merger of Whole Foods and Wild Oats on a unilateral effects theory, notwithstanding *Oracle. Federal Trade Commission v. Whole Foods Market, Inc.,*—F. Supp. 2d—, 2007 WL 2377000 (D.D.C. 2007). The analytical steps followed in the district court's decision declining to enjoin the transaction are questioned in Farrell and Shapiro, *supra* note 46.

94. One of us (Shapiro) was retained by the Justice Department as part of its investigation of the Whirlpool/Maytag merger. The views expressed here are ours alone and do not rely on any confidential information.

95. These data are from *Appliance,* September 1, 2005, "Share-of-Market Picture for 2004." For additional data and analysis, see Diana Moss, "Antitrust Analysis of Whirlpool's Proposed Acquisition of Maytag," American Antitrust Institute, January 2006, available at http://www.antitrustinstitute.org/archives/files/477.pdf. For an analysis of the transaction by an attorney who represented Maytag, *see* Brian Byrne, *Whirlpool/Maytag: What Does it Mean for Your Deal?,* 7 THE THRESHOLD 3 (2006/2007).

96. DOJ Closing Statement March 29, 2006, at http://www.usdoj.gov/atr/public/press_releases/2006/215326.pdf. Further discussion of the DOJ's analysis of this case is provided by Elizabeth Armington, Eric Emch, & Ken Heyer, *The Year in Review: Economics at the Antitrust Division, 2005–06,* 29 REV. IND. ORG. 305 (2006). This article is one of a useful annual series describing the economic analysis conducted at the DOJ and the FTC.

97. Ilan Brat, *Whirlpool Plans to Increase Prices, as Profits Fall 5.2 %,* WALL ST. J., July 26, 2006. Another reason given for the planned price increase was rising raw materials costs. Materials cost increases of $150 million were noted for 2006, but these correspond to less than 1 percent of Whirlpool's revenues, which were in the neighborhood of $18 billion for 2006.

98. For this reason, the Whirlpool/Maytag merger would be a good candidate for a retrospective analysis in a few years.

99. *Federal Trade Commission v. Cardinal Health, Inc.,* 12 F.Supp.2d 34 (D.D.C. 1998). One of us (Shapiro) was the expert economic witness for the FTC; the other (Baker) was Director of the FTC's Bureau of Economics.

100. *Id.* at 58.

101. We do not mean to suggest that during the current administra-tion, the Antitrust Division has avoided all merger challenges or adopted cookie-cutter merger reviews designed to avoid serious analysis. We credit the Antirust Division with, for example, litigating the unilateral effects case against *Oracle;* challenging the electricity generation merger between Exelon and PSEG during 2006 (Competitive Impact Statement available at http://www.usdoj.gov/atr/cases/exelon.htm), which the firms later abandoned; and employing an innovative coordinated effects analy-sis in *United States v. Premdor Inc.,* 66 Fed. Reg. 45,326 (Aug. 28, 2001) (Competitive Impact Statement), available at http://www.usdoj.gov/atr/cases/f9000/9017.pdf. We also do not fault DOJ for choosing not to appeal its loss in *Oracle.* Even if an appellate court corrected the error in eco-nomic reasoning in the legal rule applied by Judge Walker, the outcome of the case, permitting the merger, may well not have changed given the facts found by the district court (which appeals courts are usually quite reluctant to second guess).

102. Agency merger enforcement could in principle be evaluated by undertaking a large-scale retrospective analysis, examining whether the agencies made good decisions either based on the information available to them at the time the decision was made or based on how the indus-try performed years later. In specifying such a study, it would be desir-able to study both the mergers that the agencies investigated, whether the transactions were challenged or not, and the mergers that the agencies did not investigate. This kind of retrospective analysis is difficult for enforcement agency insiders to conduct, however, and even more diffi-cult for outsiders like us. Outsiders do not have access to the information that the merging firms, rivals and customers provided to the agency at the time the enforcement decision was made. *Cf.* Coate & Ulrick, *supra* note 48 (concluding that FTC review standards did not vary between the Clinton and George W. Bush administrations, based on a review of internal mem-oranda). Nor is it easy to analyze the effects of a consummated merger retrospectively. To attribute a price increase to merger, for example, it is necessary to rule out other explanations, including quality improvements, shifts in demand to favor higher-priced products among those sold in the market, outward shifts in demand along an upward-sloping marginal cost curve, and increases in marginal cost. Marginal cost in particular can be difficult to measure, because it can depend on more than input prices and scale economies, but also on changes in the opportunity cost of diverting output from another market and the magnitude of economic depreciation. Furthermore, declining prices might be observed even after anti-com-petitive mergers, if technological change drives down costs. For all of these reasons, merger retrospectives are in practice typically conducted one case at a time, do not always succeed in providing a clear assessment of merger effects, and are best conducted by the FTC, which can employ compulsory process for this purpose. Given these problems, we are unable to point to specific mergers that the Antitrust Division should have chal-lenged during the first term of the current administration beyond rais-ing questions about the Whirlpool/Maytag transaction, even though it is

likely that there were some, and perhaps many such deals. For a survey of merger retrospectives, *see* Kaplow & Shapiro, *supra* note 45, at 76–78.

103. These are not the only arguments made by merging firms to which the agencies may have become overly receptive. The "big buyer" argument, which was accepted by the Justice Department in the Whirlpool case and Judge Kozinski in *Syufy,* is another.

104. This is a different proposition from the much broader cross-sectional question of whether more concentrated markets are performing poorly in some overall sense. An important and correct part of the Chicago critique was that market concentration may be the desirable by-product of economies of scale and the growth of more efficient firms. Here we are making a statement about the likely effects of highly concentrating mergers in the absence of convincing evidence about ease of entry or merger-specific efficiencies, not about concentration that arises due to internal growth.

105. *See* Kaplow & Shapiro, *supra* note 45, and Carl Shapiro, *Theories of Oligopoly Behavior, in* Richard Schmalensee & Robert Willig, eds., HANDBOOK OF INDUSTRIAL ORGANIZATION (1989) for surveys that address the relationship between market concentration and market performance in oligopoly theory.

106. *See* Raymond Deneckere & Carl Davidson, *Incentives to Form Coalitions with Bertrand Competition,* 16 RAND J. ECON. 473 (1985).

107. *See* Paul Klemperer, Bidding Markets (June 2005), available at http://ssrn.com/abstract=776524 (criticizing the view, attributed to unnamed antitrust consultants, that market power is impossible in bidding markets).

108. We discuss below the role of mavericks in coordinated effects cases.

109. According to Bork, "[o]ligopolistic structures probably do not lead to significant restrictions of output." Bork, *supra* note 8 at 196. On this basis, he concludes that "most mergers involving fewer than all significant rivals in the market would rarely increase the slope of the firm's demand curve enough to pose a serious problem. The effect would usually be outweighed by cost savings." *Id.* at 221.

110. Tom Campbell, BILATERAL MONOPOLY IN MERGERS, (University of California at Berkeley, 2006).

111. Campbell contends that "[o]utput is at the competitive level when a monopolist sells to a monopsonist," *id.* at 2, and argues that "[t]his truth compels that mergers to monopoly be viewed as socially desirable when the purchaser is a monopsony." *Id.* at 12. Campbell testified similarly on behalf of Oracle in the *Oracle* case.

112. A large theoretical literature examines the inefficiencies that arise in bilateral bargaining situations, beginning with Roger Myerson & Mark Satterthwaite, *Efficient Mechanisms for Bilateral Trading,* 29 J. ECON. THEORY 265 (1983). Myerson and Satterthwaite establish the general impossibility of achieving efficiency in voluntary bilateral bargaining with private information. While two-part tariffs and other contractual forms can reduce the inefficiency associated with supplier market power, it is easy to find empirical examples where suppliers with market power charge prices well above marginal cost (thus causing some inefficiency) in situations

where those suppliers engage in bilateral bargaining with their customers. Microsoft's dealings with its computer manufacturer customers such as Dell or Hewlett-Packard are but one obvious example. Campbell's approach also departs sharply from the traditional focus of merger control policy on consumer welfare.

113. William Landes and Richard Posner make this error in the context of geographic market definition in their influential article on market power. William M. Landes & Richard A. Posner, *Market Power in Antitrust Cases,* 94 HARV. L. REV. 937, 963 (1981). For other criticism of Landes and Posner's argument, *see* Timothy J. Brennan, *Mistaken Elasticities and Misleading Rules,* 95 HARV. L. REV. 1849 (1982); Louis Kaplow, *The Accuracy of Traditional Market Power Analysis and a Direct Adjustment Alternative,* 95 HARV. L. REV. 1817, 1835–43 (1992).

114. The 1992 Horizontal Merger Guidelines call this "uncommitted entry," i.e., entry that occurs quickly and does not require the entrant to incur significant costs that would be lost in the event of subsequent exit, and include the production capacities of such firms when measuring market shares. We believe that the Guidelines set forth an appropriate way of treating uncommitted entry, and we agree with the Guidelines and courts that if there were unlimited uncommitted entry, no merger would harm competition. Our claim here is simply that rapid uncommitted entry on a large scale rarely if ever arises in the oligopoly markets where mergers are given close scrutiny, and in consequence it is inappropriate to presume that such markets are contestable. For a survey of the empirical evidence demonstrating that the airline industry is not contestable, contrary to what the authors of the theory originally conjectured, *see* Jonathan B. Baker, *Mavericks, Mergers, and Exclusion: Proving Coordinated Effects Under the Antitrust Laws,* 77 N.Y.U. L. REV. 135, 170–71 (2002).

115. This inappropriate reasoning was arguably adopted by the appellate court in *Syufy. See* Baker, *supra* note 33.

116. *Cf.* U.S. Department of Justice and Federal Trade Commission, Horizontal Merger Guidelines § 3.1 (1992, revised 1997) (evaluating entry by analyzing specific entry alternatives); *id.* at § 3.4 (analyzing sufficiency of entry).

117. The Merger Guidelines make a similar point: "[W]here the competitive effect of concern is not uniform across the relevant market, in order for entry to be sufficient, the character and scope of entrants' products must be responsive to the localized sales opportunities that include the output reduction associated with the competitive effect of concern. For example, where the concern is unilateral price elevation, as a result of a merger between producers of differentiated products, entry, in order to be sufficient, must involve a product so close to the products of the merging firms that the merged firm will be unable to internalize enough of the sales loss due to the price rise, rendering the price increase unprofitable." U.S. Department of Justice and Federal Trade Commission, Horizontal Merger Guidelines § 3.4 (1992, revised 1997).

118. It is possible to imagine situations in which the entrant must compete more (or less) effectively than the weaker merging firm in order to

counteract or deter adverse competitive effects of merger, but comparing the entrant to the weaker of the merging firms can be useful in structuring the timeliness and sufficiency analysis.

119. U.S. Department of Justice and Federal Trade Commission, Horizontal Merger Guidelines § 4 (1992, revised 1997).

120. A very useful and important result along these lines can be found in Gregory Werden, *A Robust Test for Consumer Welfare Enhancing Mergers Among Differentiated Products,* 44 J. INDUS. ECON. 409 (1996). Joseph Farrell & Carl Shapiro, *Horizontal Mergers: An Equilibrium Analysis,* 80 AMER. ECON. REVIEW, 107 (1990) provide a general analysis for the case of Cournot oligopoly.

121. This evidence is reviewed in Kaplow & Shapiro, *supra* note 45.

122. For an example of a case where one of us (Baker) testified that the exacting standards of the Merger Guidelines were met, *see* Jonathan B. Baker, *Efficiencies and High Concentration: Heinz Proposes to Acquire Beech-Nut* (2001), in John E. Kwoka, Jr. & Lawrence J. White, eds., THE ANTITRUST REVOLUTION 150 (4th ed. 2004).

123. Given the inherent uncertainty of predicting the effects of proposed mergers, decision theory might seem to suggest an alternative approach in which most merger challenges would be deferred until after the mergers have been consummated and their effects can be discerned. Unfortunately, this approach is not attractive because of the uncertainty it would create surrounding consummated mergers. For this reason alone, we very much doubt that the business community would welcome a shift in this direction. Relying largely on *ex post* merger review would present other serious problems as well: competition could well be harmed on an interim basis, the conduct of the merged entity would be influenced by the prospect of subsequent review, the competitive effects of merger can be difficult to isolate after years of intervening market developments, divestiture often is much more costly after the merging firms' assets have been scrambled, and subsequent divestiture may be ineffective in restoring competition. Sound public policy unavoidably requires that the primary review of proposed mergers take place before they are consummated.

124. Whether respondents believed the changes have improved competition policy or been detrimental to competition policy, they reported the same shift over the past decade toward less merger enforcement. For this reason, we are confident that our survey results regarding the decline of merger enforcement over time are not biased by partisan considerations.

125. They must also be difficult to manipulate by firms seeking to disguise a harmful merger in order to avoid triggering the presumption.

126. For clarity, we talk exclusively about mergers between competing sellers. A similar analysis would apply when buyers merge and thus gain additional buying power over certain suppliers, i.e., when monopsony power is the issue rather than monopoly power. Throughout, we assume that the merger analysis is prospective. For simplicity, and following the literature, we talk about the comparison between "premerger" and "postmerger" competition. The term "premerger" as used here should be understood to mean "but-for" the merger. To the extent that the market is changing in ways that can reasonably be foreseen at the time the merger is

being reviewed, conditions "but-for" the merger will differ from the actual, pre-merger conditions. For simplicity, we also refer to the plaintiff as the "government," which is typically but not always the case.

127. *United States v. Baker Hughes, Inc.,* 908 F.2d 981 (D.C. Cir. 1990); *Fed. Trade Comm'n v. H.J. Heinz Co.,* 246 F.3d 708 (D.C. Cir. 2001).

128. To satisfy a burden of production, a party must provide enough evidence to avoid summary judgment or judgment as a matter of law in favor of the other side.

129. Although the government's initial burden is satisfied by proof of market shares in the structural era Supreme Court precedents, lower courts and the 1992 Horizontal Merger Guidelines today routinely and sensibly expect the government to articulate an economic theory by which the merger would harm competition (such as unilateral or coordinated effects). Doing so is not formally part of the government's initial burden of production, but it arguably has become so as a practical matter.

130. It is difficult to articulate the deference that should be accorded to the presumption in a way that could be reduced to a jury instruction. One possibility would be for courts to insist on "clear and convincing" evidence for rebuttal, appealing to an evidentiary standard that is higher than a preponderance of the evidence. We have instead said that rebuttal evidence needs to be "strong" in order to convey our sense that the elements we specify for invoking a presumption give good reason to think that harm to competition will indeed result, while leaving for later discussion the question of how the resulting deference should best be incorporated into a legal standard.

131. As a default, one might be prepared to assume that diversion ratios are proportional to market shares (as they are in the logit model of demand). 1992 Horizontal Merger Guidelines § 2.211. However, additional information is commonly available, supporting an adjustment to this default assumption.

132. *Federal Trade Comm'n v. Indiana Federation of Dentists,* 476 U.S. 447 (1986); *Nat'l Collegiate Athletic Ass'n v. Board of Regents,* 468 U.S. 85 (1984).

133. These possibilities do not exhaust the ways that the defendants could mount a rebuttal. For example, the defendants could also offer evidence that undermines the probative value of the government's showing of unilateral or coordinated effects. We assume throughout that efficiencies would be analyzed as a defense—that is, that efficiencies are offered to defeat the government's proof of higher prices or other competitive harm rather than as an affirmative defense that would excuse higher prices.

134. In current practice, the government may instead addresses efficiencies in cross-examination and in rebuttal. But a litigating party always has the option of exceeding its burden of production if it chooses to do so.

135. George J. Stigler, *A Theory of Oligopoly,* 72 J. POL. ECON. 44 (1964).

136. On the economics of oligopolistic coordination, see generally Kaplow & Shapiro, *supra* note 45.

137. *E.g.,* Bork, *supra* note 8 at 175.

138. The active criminal antitrust docket shows that firms, even large and sophisticated ones, do find ways to fix prices; empirical research has

identified coordinated conduct in some concentrated industries; and economic models of repeated oligopoly interaction show that higher-than-competitive coordinated pricing is often plausible even absent an express agreement on price.

139. Coordinating firms may not achieve an outcome that maximizes their joint profits for a number of reasons, including the following four. First, they may not be able to punish cheating as strongly as would be necessary. In addition, they may not be able to allocate joint profits in a manner satisfactory to all because they may be unable to make side payments. Third, they may need to reduce the coordinated price below the joint profit maximizing level or engage in occasional price wars in order to deter cheating in an environment of uncertainty. Fourth, they may have difficulty identifying the joint profit maximizing outcome when coordinating over multiple products or markets without communicating.

140. *See* 1992 Horizontal Merger Guidelines § 2.12 ("In some circumstances, coordinated interaction can be effectively prevented or limited by maverick firms—firms that have a greater economic incentive to deviate from the terms of coordination than do most of their rivals (e.g., firms that are unusually disruptive and competitive influences in the market.)." *See generally,* Baker, *supra* note 115.

141. Baker, *supra* note 118 at 177–79. It is also possible, though much less likely, that a merger involving a maverick would enhance the maverick's incentives to keep prices low by generating large efficiencies in a setting where the merged firm has a strong incentive to pass cost savings through to buyers. *Id.* at 179.

142. *Id.* at 186–88. In addition, the merger of non-mavericks could lead the industry maverick to act less competitively than before, as by increasing the likely punishment were the maverick to cheat, or lead the industry maverick to act more competitively than before, for example if buyer responses to the merger reduce the maverick's demand and make that demand more elastic. *Id.* at 186–87. These latter possibilities raise obvious difficulties of proof.

143. *See generally,* Baker, *supra* note 115; Andrew R. Dick, *Coordinated Interaction: Pre-Merger Constraints and Post-Merger Effects,* 12 Geo. Mason. L. Rev. 65 (2003).

144. *See generally,* Baker, *supra* note 47.

145. If the market premerger is not conducive to coordination, and firms are competing, there may be multiple mavericks that prevent coordination. In the settings we are most concerned with, where it is more plausible that firms could reach consensus on the terms of coordination and deter deviation and firms are coordinating imperfectly premerger, it is possible to imagine multiple mavericks but that is unlikely unless the maverick firms are nearly identical.

146. Baker, *supra* note 115 at 173–77.

147. *Id.* at 198–99; *see* Dick, *supra* note 144 at 70–72.

148. *See* Dick, *supra* note 144 at 72–76. A merger might also narrow asymmetries by increasing the extent of multimarket contact among the firms. *See* B. Douglas Bernheim & Michael D. Whinston, *Multimarket Contact and Collusive Behavior,* 21 Rand J. Econ. 1 (1990); William N.

Evans & Ioannis N. Kessides, *Living By the "Golden Rule": Multimarket Contact in the U.S. Airline Industry,* 109 Q. J. Econ.341 (1994); *but cf.* David Genesove & Wallace P. Mullin, *Rules, Communication, and Collusion: Narrative Evidence from the Sugar Institute Case,* 91 Am. Econ. Rev. 379, 391–93 (2001) (colluding sugar refiners chose not to exploit multimarket contact to enhance punishment of cheaters).

149. For example, transparency of pricing combined with small, frequent transactions is thought to facilitate coordination by making it easier for firms to reach consensus and detect and police cheating. *See generally, e.g.,* 1992 Horizontal Merger Guidelines §§ 2.11, 2.12; Andrew I. Gavil, William E. Kovacic, & Jonathan B. Baker, Antitrust Law in Perspective: Cases, Concepts and Problems in Competition Policy 223–28 (2002). A history of collusion in the industry under study also provides evidence that coordination could occur, notwithstanding structural factors that might tend to suggest otherwise.

150. That is, the acquisition of a maverick can be expected to alter the maverick's incentives, and so make coordination more likely or more effective. *Cf.* Horizontal Merger Guidelines § 2.12 ("Consequently, acquisition of a maverick firm is one way in which a merger may make coordinated interaction more likely, more successful, or more complete.").

151. A significant firm with respect to a coordinated effects theory is one that could not be ignored by a cartel. (Coordinating firms might be able to ignore small firms unable to expand substantially, for example, because those sellers could not practically undermine coordinated pricing.) If a cartel could ignore, say, one of two firms but not both, only one would count as significant for purposes of determining the number of significant sellers. In analyzing their own past enforcement policy, the Federal Trade Commission notes that significant competitors usually have at least a 10 percent market share. Federal Trade Commission, Horizontal Merger Investigation Data, 1996–2005 at 5 n. 16, available at http://www.ftc.gov/os/2007/01/P035603horizmergerinvestigationdata1996–2005.pdf. This figure could be adjusted in any particular case based on information about the ability and incentive of small firms to expand their sales in the relevant market.

152. If the merger reduces the number of significant sellers from two to one, it may be more apt to describe the harm to competition as arising from the creation of a monopoly rather than by making postmerger coordination more likely or more effective.

153. A four-to-three merger is a natural break point for creating a presumption of harm to competition from coordinated effects based solely on the number of firms. If it is likely that a maverick firm constrains more effective coordination but the maverick's identity is unknown, a merger combining at random two of the n significant firms participating in the market has a $2/n$ chance of involving a maverick. (Mergers involving a maverick in a market conducive to coordination are highly likely to harm competition.) Moreover, if the acquisition of a maverick can enhance the ability of firms to coordinate, the odds that a proposed merger would involve a maverick firm are likely greater than if merger partners were chosen at random. Accordingly, it is more likely than not that a merger

reducing the number of significant firms to three or less in a market conducive to coordination would harm competition by reducing the constraint posed by the maverick.

154. The logic underlying this illustrative HHI break point for a presumption is related to the idea that a presumption based solely on the number of firms might be invoked for a merger reducing the number of significant firms to three or fewer. An HHI of 3333 has a "numbers equivalent" of three firms, because a market with three identically-sized firms (market shares of 33.3 percent) would produce an HHI of 3333. This is a conservative estimate of the HHI in a three-firm market, though. If the market shares of the three sellers are not identical, as is almost invariably the case, the HHI would be higher. In offering 2800 as a possible break point, we assume that the market is served by three significant firms that are identical and one just not-significant (proxied as a market share just under 10 percent), generating market shares of 30 percent, 30 percent, 30 percent, and nearly 10 percent, for an HHI of nearly 2800. (Had we instead assumed two firms just insignificant based on market share, the HHI would have been about 2333.) The difference between the HHI calculated this way and the numbers equivalent shrinks as the number of firms grows toward ten, so we simply use the numbers equivalent in reporting approximate HHI levels when we discuss market structures with more than three significant firms. A presumption triggered by a post-merger HHI of 2800 is less restrictive than the presumption applied by the Supreme Court during the 1960s. In all but one of the government's Supreme Court merger victories between 1963 and 1970, including *Philadelphia National Bank, Pabst,* and *Von's Grocery,* the postmerger HHI was less than 2800. Donald I Baker & William Blumenthal, *The 1982 Guidelines and Pre-Existing Law,* 71 CALIF. L. REV. 311, 334 (1983).

155. An HHI of 1667 has a numbers equivalent of six firms, for example. The more convincing the demonstration that the firms could reasonably expect, after a merger, to reach consensus on the terms of coordination and deter deviation from those terms, the more comfortable a court could be in presuming coordinated effects based on postmerger market structure when the HHI is below 2800. Accordingly, we could imagine a court invoking a presumption of coordinated effects when a merger makes sellers more similar in a market with, say, ten firms postmerger (HHI greater than 1000) if the market has a strong history of collusion and there was no good reason to think that the features of the market that had permitted successful collusion in the past had markedly changed.

156. For example, the merging firms might seek to show that the government did not properly define the market, that shares were not calculated in appropriate units, that some firms were improperly deemed insignificant, or that the market has features not noted by the government suggesting that it is not conducive to coordination, and argue that these differences should affect whether the presumption was appropriately invoked.

157. For example, the merging firms might show that industry participants have little incentive to raise price above the price that would likely obtain without merger given the effect of higher prices on their costs (loss of scale economies), the effect of higher prices on the profits they receive from

the sale of future products (if the firms are investing in market share), or the effect of higher prices in the market on profits to the same firms from selling complementary products (including sales of other products in "two-sided" markets).

158. For example, the merging firms might seek to show that the maverick is not the firm the government claims and that the true maverick would not constrain coordination less than before; to show that the maverick would have no less incentive or a greater incentive to constrain coordination than before; or, when the government bases its presumption on market concentration rather than on identifying a maverick, to demonstrate that there is a maverick and it would not constrain coordination less post-merger than before.

159. For a recent discussion of entry analysis under the merger guidelines, *see* Jonathan B. Baker, *Responding to Developments in Economics and the Courts: Entry in the Merger Guidelines,* 71 ANTITRUST L.J. 189 (2003).

160. Under an aggregate welfare standard, however, efficiencies would count in favor of the transaction even if they did not directly benefit buyers.

161. Under the Cournot theory, firms compete by choosing output levels. Under the Bertrand theory, firms compete by choosing prices. *See* Shapiro, *supra* note 106 for an extensive discussion of these and other theories of oligopoly.

162. For an extensive treatment, *see* Werden & Froeb, *supra* note 55. *See also* Marc Ivaldi, Bruno Jullien, Patrick Rey, Paul Seabright, & Jean Tirole, "The Economics of Unilateral Effects," Interim Report for DG Competition, European Commission, IDEI, Toulouse, 2003. Kaplow & Shapiro, *supra* note 45, review and discuss this literature.

163. Unilateral effects also arise in other settings, including the following three. First, in bidding markets and auctions, the merging firms compete by bidding for the business of one or more customers, or participate in an auction to supply services to one or more customers. This includes the case of price discrimination markets, where the suppliers compete to serve one customer or a group of similarly situated customers. Competition in *Oracle* was of this nature. The analysis of unilateral effects in bidding and auction markets is similar in spirit to the main case of differentiated product pricing competition. Second, in markets with relatively homogeneous goods, firms may compete by choosing quantities, either production levels or capacities. Market shares are highly relevant in these settings, where the Cournot model of oligopoly is applicable. *See* Farrell & Shapiro, *supra* note 121. Third, in a market with a dominant firm and competitive fringe, a merger may reduce fringe competition (or, in the limit, create a monopolist).

164. For a very simple version of the unilateral effects arithmetic, *see* Shapiro, *supra* note 45. *See also* Jonathan B. Baker, *Unilateral Competitive Effects Theories in Merger Analysis,* 11 ANTITRUST 21, 23 (1997). For a recent articulation of the logic of unilateral effects combined with a policy proposal to dispense with market definition in cases involving unilateral effects, see Farrell and Shapiro, *supra* note 46. For much more elaborate and sophisticated calculations, *see* Werden & Froeb, *supra* note 56. In a bidding or auction setting, the comparable logic depends upon the likelihood that

the merging firms will be the first and second choices for the buyer or buyers involved.

165. Baker & Bresnahan, *supra* note 17 (working paper at 26–7). Baker and Bresnahan explain that a "key challenge for both antitrust analysis and empirical industrial organization economics going forward, not recognized in antitrust to the extent it is understood in economics, is to exploit similarities among related industries to focus an inquiry involving the industry and firms under study" and they identify and defend the empirical generalization we employ here.

166. We would not insist that the merged firm have a dominant or near-dominant market share (contrary to what the court required in *Oracle*). Because we would not require proof of any particular price increase when following this route (simply the showing of a mechanism by which prices would rise), we would permit the merging firms to take advantage of the general Guidelines safe harbor for an HHI less than 1000. We also note that the specific unilateral-effects safe harbor in § 2.211 of the Horizontal Merger Guidelines, requiring that a merged firm have a market share of at least 35 percent, applies only when the unilateral effects mechanism is demonstrated through market shares. We question whether the 35 percent figure is justified in light of the increased understanding of unilateral effects over the past fifteen years, though, and suggest that the enforcement agencies consider varying it on a sliding scale depending on price-cost margins or dispensing with it altogether.

167. The magnitude of likely unilateral effects is stronger, the larger are these margins. If the margins are very small for all of the overlap products, the government may fail to meet its initial burden.

168. We are not proposing any particular quantitative benchmark for calibrating a price increase based on diversion ratios and price-cost margins. For illustrative purposes a "significant" price increase here might be defined as 5 percent. This figure might be thought to be low, given that the government would prove this predicate for invoking a presumption without consideration of repositioning, entry or efficiencies, all of which would generally tend to reduce the actual magnitude of the price rise from merger. On the other hand, this figure might be thought to be high, given that in principle a merger could violate the Clayton Act if it would lead to any harm to competition, including a price increase smaller than 5 percent in an appropriate case, and that in a large industry, substantial consumer harm could flow from a merger leading to, say, a 3 percent price increase. We specify 5 percent here to illustrate our approach. Farrell and Shapiro, *supra* note 46, propose an approach for evaluating unilateral effects without market definition. They emphasize that there will be an initial tendency for price to rise if the diversion ratio times the gross margin exceeds the reduction in marginal cost resulting from the merger. They thus propose a threshold for the product of the diversion ratio time the gross margin based on the level of cost savings that will be credited to the merger by default. Werden, *supra, note 121* calculates the cost savings necessary to offset the anti-unilateral competitive effects in terms of gross margins and diversion ratios.

169. Categories of evidence include buyer surveys, demand elasticity studies, information about buyer switching costs, and inference from

company documents and monitoring of competitors. *See* Baker, *supra* note 47 at 139–41 (discussing sources of evidence of buyer substitution in the context of market definition).

170. We emphasize that in the unilateral-effects context (as in the coordinated-effects context discussed previously), claims that there is an elastic supply of entrants at a price at or just above the pre-merger price are more easily made than proven. Michael Katz & Carl Shapiro, *Critical Loss: Let's Tell the Whole Story,* 17 ANTITRUST 49 (2003), explain how one can test for consistency between premerger evidence and claims of postmerger price responses in the context of defining relevant markets. This analysis is directly relevant for consistency checks in unilateral effects cases. In general, claims of conveniently placed kinks in the supply curve of nonmerging firms should be greeted with considerable skepticism.

Appendix

Merger Enforcement Survey

March 2007

1. Comparing Antitrust Division now (Barnett) vs. 5 (James) or 10 (Klein) years ago
   1a. Compared with five years ago, do you believe that the Antitrust Division, in reviewing horizontal mergers, is more receptive to arguments made by the merging firms, less receptive or about the same?
   1b. Would your answer change if the comparison were between DOJ merger enforcement today and merger enforcement ten years ago? If so, how?
2. Comparing FTC now (Majoras) vs. 5 (Muris) or 10 (Pitofsky) years ago
   2a. Compared with five years ago, do you believe that the FTC, in reviewing horizontal mergers, is more receptive to arguments made by the merging firms, less receptive or about the same?
   2b. Would your answer change if the comparison were between FTC merger enforcement today and merger enforcement ten years ago? If so, how?
3. Identifying where in the process enforcement has changed Note: Only for those who answered "more receptive" or "less receptive" to 1 or 2 or both.
   At what stage or stages of the merger review process do you notice that change?
   3a. In the likelihood that the agency [or agencies] will terminate an investigation rather than issue a second request in a given case.

3b. In the likelihood that it [they] will close an investigation after a second request has been issued rather than seek remedies?

3c. In the breadth and strength of the fix that the agency [or agencies] requires to avoid or settle litigation?

4. Comparing DOJ with FTC

4a. Do you see a significant *substantive* difference today between merger enforcement at the DOJ and at the FTC? If so, what is the nature of the difference?

4b. When you are hired to work on a deal and it is not clear whether the deal will be reviewed by the DOJ or the FTC, do you more often believe your client's interests will be served by DOJ review, FTC review, or is there no difference? If so, why?

5. Receptivity of the agencies to various arguments. Note: respondent may need to distinguish between DOJ and FTC

I am now going to describe three arguments that merging firms sometimes make. With respect to each, please tell me whether you believe that the agencies are more receptive, equally receptive, or less receptive to the argument today as compared with ten years ago:

5a. "Market concentration is not a good basis for predicting competitive effects."

5b. "Entry will counteract or deter any competitive problem."

5c. "The procompetitive benefits of efficiencies from merger outweigh the threat of harm to competition."

6. Competitive Effects Theories

Note: respondents may wish to distinguish between DOJ and FTC

6a. In your horizontal merger practice today, do you find that the agencies more often raise concerns based on a unilateral effects theory of competitive effects, a coordinated effects theory, or are the two theories raised with equal frequency?

7. Unilateral Effects

7a. Are the agencies more interested, equally interested, or less interested in unilateral competitive effects theories today than five years ago?

7b. Would your answer change if you went back ten years?

8. Coordinated Effects

8a. Are the agencies more interested, equally interested, or less interested in coordinated competitive effects theories today than five years ago?

8b. Would your answer change if you went back ten years?

9. Assessment of prospects

9a. For a given horizontal merger, would your assessment of the likelihood of successful agency review for the merging firms be different now than it would have been five years ago? If so, how?

9b. Would your answer change if you went back ten years?

10. For better or for worse?
    10a. Have the changes in agency enforcement policy that you
         have described generally improved competition policy or
         have they been detrimental to effective competition policy?
11. Looking back longer
    11a. What have been the major changes in the agency review of
         horizontal mergers over the past twenty years?
12. Prior Agency Affiliations
    12a. Have you ever worked at the FTC or Antitrust Division? If so,
         what was your highest position and in what years did you
         serve in that capacity?
13. Open Ended Final Question
    13a. Is there anything else you would like to say about horizontal
         merger enforcement at the federal antitrust agencies?

Index